Formulating Policy in Postsecondary Education

FORMULATING POLICY IN POSTSECONDARY EDUCATION

The Search for Alternatives

Edited by
JOHN F. HUGHES *and* OLIVE MILLS

AMERICAN COUNCIL ON EDUCATION   •   *Washington, D.C.*

© 1975 by American Council on Education
One Dupont Circle, Washington, D.C. 20036

Library of Congress Cataloging in Publication Data

American Council on Education.
  Formulating policy in postsecondary education.

  Papers presented at the 57th annual meeting of the
American Council on Education, held at San Diego in the
fall of 1974.
    1. Universities and colleges—United States—Adminis-
tration—Congresses.   2. Universities and colleges—
United States—Finance—Congresses.   3. Education,
Higher—United States—Congresses   I. Hughes, John F.
II. Mills, Olive.   III. Title.
LB2341.A576   1975   658'.91'37873   75-20253
ISBN 0-8268-1293-7

Contributors

David Alexander, President, Pomona College

Franklin G. Bouwsma, Vice-President for Instructional Resources, Miami-Dade Community College

Albert H. Bowker, Chancellor, University of California, Berkeley

Ernest L. Boyer, Chancellor, State University of New York

Margaret E. Chisholm, Dean, College of Library and Information Services, University of Maryland

John E. Corbally, Jr., President, University of Illinois

K. Patricia Cross, Senior Research Psychologist, Educational Testing Service

Richard M. Cyert, President, Carnegie-Mellon University

Estelle A. Fishbein, Special Assistant Attorney General for the University of Maryland

John Folger, Executive Director, Tennessee Higher Education Commission

Richard A. Fulton, Executive Director and General Counsel, Association of Independent Colleges and Schools

Joseph W. Garbarino, Professor of Business Administration, University of California, Berkeley

Winfred L. Godwin, President, Southern Regional Education Board

Peggy Heim, Associate Director, National Center for Higher Education Management Systems

Warren G. Hill, Project Director, Inservice Education Program, Education Commission of the States

Harold L. Hodgkinson, Project Director, Center for Research and Development in Higher Education, University of California, Berkeley

Elliot Jaqow, President, Hiram College

Hans H. Jenny, Vice-President for Finance and Business, College of Wooster

Edward J. Kormondy, Vice-President and Provost, Evergreen State College

Juanita M. Kreps, Vice-President and *James B. Duke* Professor of Economics, Duke University

Richard W. Lyman, President, Stanford University

Jacquelyn Mattfeld, Dean of the Faculty and Academic Affairs, Brown University

G. Theodore Mitau, Chancellor, Minnesota State College System

Donald J. Nolan, Director, New York Regents External Degree Program, University of the State of New York

James G. O'Hara, Chairman, Special Subcommittee on Education, Committee on Education and Labor, U.S. House of Representatives

Harold Orlans, Senior Research Associate, National Academy of Public Administration Foundation

John D. Phillips, Associate Commissioner for Student Assistance, U.S. Office of Education

John W. Porter, Superintendent of Public Instruction, State of Michigan

Sister Joel Read, President, Alverno College

Lois D. Rice, Vice-President, College Entrance Examination Board

Elliot L. Richardson, former Secretary of Health, Education, and Welfare

G. M. Sawyer, President, Texas Southern University

*Ann Scott,** Associate Executive Director, American Association for Higher Education

Helen Thomas, White House Reporter, United Press International

William Van Alstyne, Perkins Professor of Law, Duke University; President, American Association of University Professors

George B. Weathersby, Associate Professor, Harvard Graduate School of Education

* Deceased.

Contents

v   Contributors

xi   Foreword, *Roger W. Heyns*

xiii   Preface

Part One: Strategies for Improving Higher Education Management

FACULTY-MANAGEMENT RELATIONS

3   Administration of Equal Employment Opportunity Laws
on Campus
Estelle A. Fishbein

11   Faculty Unions, Senates, and Institutional Administrations
Joseph W. Garbarino

17   Financial Exigency: Avoidance of Litigation and Friction
William Van Alstyne

CREATIVE MANAGEMENT

30   Reconciling Contradictions: The Task of Creative Management
Ernest L. Boyer

39   Factoring the Concept of Creative Management
G. M. Sawyer

49   Management as a Political Process: Overt versus Covert
Ann Scott

PLANNING FOR THE STEADY STATE

58   Higher Education in a Low-Growth, High-Inflation Economy
Juanita M. Kreps

67   Management Talents Required for the Steady State
Elmer Jagow

77   Managing the Faculty Resource in the Steady State
Albert H. Bowker

Part Two: Alternatives for Financing Higher Education

INSTITUTIONAL FINANCE POLICIES

87 Current Issues in Fund Raising
David Alexander

97 Financing Private Higher Education: Assessment and Suggestions
Peggy Heim

108 Higher Education Finance: Health and Distress
Hans H. Jenny

PUBLIC AND PRIVATE TUITION

118 A Quid pro Quo Approach to Tuition
John E. Corbally, Jr.

123 The Market Approach to Higher Education
Richard M. Cyert

133 Needed: A National Cost Adjustment Factor for Higher Education
G. Theodore Mitau

STUDENT AID

140 Don't Forget the "Student" in Student Assistance
John D. Phillips

149 Federal Student Assistance: Title IV Revisited
Lois D. Rice

169 Grants for Students Based on Their Own Income
George B. Weathersby

180 Differentiated Aid Programs for Today's Emancipated Students
Richard A. Fulton

Part Three: Strategies for Improving Programs in Higher Education

191   The Elusive Goal of Educational Equality
K. Patricia Cross

NONTRADITIONAL PROGRAMS

202   The Evergreen State College: An Alternative
Edward J. Kormondy

206   Articulation of Vocational and Career-Oriented Programs
at the Postsecondary Level
John W. Porter

214   A Degree by Any Other Name . . . The Alverno Program
Sister Joel Read

STATEWIDE PLANNING

227   Three Questions about Statewide Planning
John K. Folger

236   Regional Dimensions of Planning and Coordination
Winfred L. Godwin

246   To Keep from Being King
Warren G. Hill

CREDENTIALING OF EXPERIENCE

253   Alternative Functions and Structures in Credentialing
Harold L. Hodgkinson

260   Toward an Examining University: The New York Regents
External Degree
Donald J. Nolan

272   The Fatuity of Credentialing Everyone and Everything
Harold Orlans

INSTRUCTIONAL DELIVERY SYSTEMS

284   Instructional Delivery Systems and Open Learning
Franklin G. Bouwsma

294   The Media Paradox
Margaret E. Chisholm

302   The Perceptive Eye
Jacquelyn Mattfeld

Part Four: Addressing Policy Issues in Education

311   Public Policy for a Pluralistic System of Higher Education
      Elliot L. Richardson

316   A Congressman's Views on Student Assistance and on Civil Rights
      Obligations
      James G. O'Hara

323   The Search for Alternatives
      Richard W. Lyman

332   Reporting from the White House
      Helen Thomas

Foreword

POSTSECONDARY EDUCATION in the last quarter of the twentieth century will be influenced by recent shifts in public policy as well as by major changes in national and world social forces. Both federal and state policies have moved steadily toward emphasizing student access to and choice within the educational system while deemphasizing expansion and support of that system through direct institutional funding. Concurrently, a demographic shift has seen the college student body modified from the traditional 18–22 cohort to an older group of students who seek reentry to education. Government economists predict a decline in the employment prospects for college-educated persons in the 1980s, and already graduating classes are feeling the pinch of a tight labor market. Institutions have been subjected to shock waves of problems induced by inflation and rising operating costs, by declining revenues and enrollments, and by internal conflicts over personnel policies and employment equities.

In order to provide institutional leaders and public policy makers with a forum for the discussion of policy options with respect to these and other issues, the American Council on Education dedicated its fifty-seventh Annual Meeting to "the search for alternatives." The program was based on the assumption that national, state, and institutional policies and decisions must be formulated with careful consideration to the forces at work in our society. The nation must not be diverted from the central goal of providing high-quality educational programs that offer equal participation to all citizens. Education leaders have a continuing obligation to examine systematically the alternatives available to them in formulating policies that will promote quality education along with social equality.

The Annual Meeting discussions focused on such issues as faculty-management relationships, institutional finance and management, tuitions, student aid, and nontraditional programs and the credentialing of experience. These discussions, supported by position papers contributed by the panel members and coupled with five major addresses, provide the substance for this book. The American Council on Education takes pleasure in making this volume available for further study by scholars and for immediate use by administrators in the continuing process of policy formulation and decision making.

Meeting plans and programs were directed by John F. Hughes and coordinated by Donna C. Phillips. The Council is indebted to the contributors to this volume as well as to the staff members who helped prepare for and carry out the eventful fifty-seventh Annual Meeting of the American Council.

ROGER W. HEYNS, *President*
American Council on Education

Preface

THE SAN DIEGO setting for the 1974 Annual Meeting of the American Council on Education provided an exhilarating blending of mountains, sun, and sea. The surroundings, however, failed to draw attention from the severity of the problems and issues that had brought the leadership of American higher education to this scene. The sessions themselves offered a lesson in direct confrontation of issues and explorations of solutions. Although the problems of student access and choice and of program quality and performance do not yield to easy answers, institutional leaders were reminded anew that a comparison of ideas and solutions is a necessary process in finding best answers to problem situations. Institutional leaders were also being reminded that politicians, administrators, students, and faculty are seeking an increased role in the process of social policy making in education.

Principal speakers at the meeting included former Cabinet officer Elliot L. Richardson, Congressman James G. O'Hara, Richard W. Lyman, K. Patricia Cross, and Helen Thomas. Their addresses brought a sense of balance to the discussions, reminding participants of the role of public policy and social purpose in setting education goals and policies. The generous mix of institutional leaders, faculty members, state and federal administrators, and foundation staff stimulated discussions that were thoughtful and provocative. The Council trusts that the volume produced as a result of the contributors' efforts will further the usefulness of the meeting.

As director of the Annual Meeting, Mr. Hughes takes this opportunity to express indebtedness to Donna Phillips for the expertness and persistence of her efforts to conduct a successful meeting. Laura Kent and Nancy Suniewick edited a number of the papers as presented at the meeting. Finally it is a welcome obligation to acknowledge to the authors presented in this volume appreciation owed for their efforts to contribute constructively to the process of, and the substance for, making appropriate policy decisions for postsecondary education.

J. F. H.

O. M.

Part One

STRATEGIES FOR IMPROVING HIGHER EDUCATION MANAGEMENT

Administration of Equal Employment Opportunity Laws on Campus

ESTELLE A. FISHBEIN

THE PASSAGE of equal employment opportunity laws has enormously increased the exposure of educational institutions, their officers, administrators, and faculty members to legal liability for their actions and decisions. The laws in this area are so numerous and the statutes, executive orders of the President, and agency regulations are so broadly stated that the college administrator feels compelled to seek legal counsel with greater frequency than ever before. As a result, legal counsel of educational institutions are becoming involved in the institutional decision-making process to an unprecedented extent.

During the past decade colleges and universities have been confronted with a variety of new legal problems to which university counsel have been expected to find solutions. Although college presidents have borne the primary burden of handling campus violence and disruption and the resulting student disciplinary problems, it was the college attorney who was called upon to guide administrators through the thicket of constitutional doctrine and emerging principles of college law. No sooner had the institutional attorney mastered the art of the preliminary injunction and temporary restraining order than a new and urgent problem demanded his attention. Faculty members, suddenly faced with a diminishing market for scholarly talents and increasingly conscious of their constitutional rights, particularly those rights grounded in the First Amendment, began to contest tenure decisions in the courts. As soon as university counsel and their adversaries had hammered out in the judicial arena the basic legal principles governing the relationship between faculty and university administration—and that is not to imply that all questions in that area of the law

3

have been definitively settled—the latest wave of new legal problems began to appear.

Today, wherever university and college legal counsel gather, the talk is mainly concerned with the new legal problems associated with the administration of equal employment opportunity laws on campus. Although some of these laws and regulations have been on the statute books for years, their full effect on institutions of higher education and on the institution's decision-makers has only begun to be realized in the past two years.

The Laws and Their Enforcement on Campuses

There are several federal laws and regulations that have an impact on equal employment opportunity on the campuses of public and private colleges. By way of example, Executive Order 11246, issued by President Lyndon B. Johnson in 1965, decreed that contractors doing business with the federal government must agree not to discriminate in employment against any employee because of race, color, religion, or national origin. That decree was amended on October 13, 1968, by Executive Order 11375 to prohibit discrimination because of sex. Colleges and universities that are the recipients of government contracts in excess of $10,000 are subject to the provisions of the executive orders. Title VII of the Civil Rights Act of 1964, as amended by the Equal Employment Opportunity Act of 1972, which bans discrimination in employment on the same grounds as the executive orders, now covers all educational institutions with fifteen or more employees, whether or not they are the recipients of federal monies. The Equal Pay Act of 1963, as amended by the Higher Education Act of 1972, forbids all institutions of higher education to discriminate on the basis of sex in setting salaries in all programs or activities receiving federal assistance. Title IX of the Education Amendments of 1972 (Higher Education Act) bans sex discrimination in all institutions receiving federal assistance by means of grants, loans, or contracts. The Age Discrimination in Employment Act bars bias against persons between forty and sixty-five years of age. Moreover, discrimination on the basis of race or color can also be a violation of the Civil Rights Acts of 1866 and 1870.

In addition to the federal equal employment statutes, executive orders, and regulations, most states have enacted legislation to prohibit discrimination in employment for reasons of race, religion, national origin, sex, and age. Moreover, many local governments and municipalities have similar ordinances.

As a result of these similar statutes and regulations, compliance is enforced by numerous federal, state, and local agencies as well as by the federal and state courts. Thus, not only does the individual alleging discrimination on one of the prohibited grounds have a multiplicity of remedies to choose from, but also that person has recourse to a host of governmental agencies, some having concurrent and overlapping jurisdiction over the matter. If a complaint of discrimination concerns an institution of higher education, it may be filed with and investigated by the Division of Higher Education in the Office for Civil Rights of the U.S. Department of Health, Education, and Welfare, which has been designated by the Office of Federal Contract Compliance of the Department of Labor as the compliance agency responsible for the enforcement of the executive orders for all contracts with educational institutions. A complaint under title VII of the Civil Rights Act may be filed with the United States Equal Employment Opportunity Commission. Complaints under the Equal Pay Act come within the jurisdiction of the Wage and Hour Division of the Employment Standards Administration of the Department of Labor. However, there is nothing to prevent an individual from filing complaints with several agencies. Therefore, any one complaint can generate investigations by more than one federal agency as well as by state and local agencies, either simultaneously or consecutively because of overlapping jurisdictions. Indeed, many institutions report having to defend against a single complaint under such circumstances. When the activities of the several federal agencies are added to those of state and local antidiscrimination agencies, it becomes apparent that the laws relating to equal employment represent the greatest opportunity in the history of this nation for the presence of government to be felt on campus.

REVERSE DISCRIMINATION AND OTHER EFFECTS

The effects of that governmental presence on campus and the present methods of enforcement of the equal employment opportunity laws are both numerous and significant. It appears that all of the involved government agencies employ a method of enforcement of the equal employment opportunity laws which can be described succinctly as "the numbers game." In surveying the employment picture at a university, the government investigator always rivets attention on numbers. He will want to know how many minorities and women are employed this year as against how many were employed last year; but he probably will not inquire into such matters as whether the institution is in a period of growth or retrenchment, whether certain priorities have been established at the institution which affect the need for particular faculty, or whether the manner in which the university views its educational mission in any way affects its ability at this time to attract minority and women faculty. These government agencies measure progress solely with reference to numbers. There is, after all, no government agency which is charged with measuring progress toward excellence. Colleges and universities are not given points for having achieved distinction, but only for achieving what is unilaterally determined by the enforcement agency to be the "proper" numerical ratio between the races and sexes. As a result, campus administrators are wont to worry over even statistically insignificant numbers. I have seen that a decrease of even one in the number of minority faculty members employed in a certain segment of the faculty can cause great consternation. My wonder at this consternation turned to admiration for the perspicacity displayed by administrators when that statistically insignificant decrease subsequently was cited by government investigators as evidence of lack of good faith in pursuing affirmative action.

The legal hazards to an institution flowing from a failure to adhere to a policy of nondiscrimination are at once obvious and subtle. They include the possibility of loss of federal contracts and grants and of being named as a defendant in litigation. Curiously, however, the legal risks are not diminished as the institution undertakes an aggressive effort to add women and minorities to its staff. For example, it cannot be ignored that the incredible pressures radiating from Washington have led colleges and universities to practice reverse discrimination in many forms. The small pool of qualified minorities and women in particular disciplines has led to a fierce competition for their services. In bidding frantically against each other, institutions may offer a salary and even an academic rank vastly disproportionate to credentials, all to appease the government investigators.

The trouble is that reverse discrimination can lead to legal problems as severe as ordinary kinds of prohibited discrimination. Claims of reverse discrimination are being made with increasing frequency by members of majority classes as they come to realize that the legal remedies employed by minorities and women are equally available to white males. It is, however, much harder for a university counsel to defend his client against a charge of reverse discrimination because the facts are usually so blatant. An attorney, after all, must do the best he can with the facts presented to him. He may be called upon to defend his client against a charge of reverse discrimination based on a $5,000 differential between the salary offered a new black faculty member and a comparably qualified new white male faculty member. The university lawyer seeks an explanation and is told: "It's worth it to us to be able to show a black faculty member in the department." Clearly it is the minority status, not the individual's merit, which inspired the terms of the offer. Then, too, there is the correspondence between department chairmen and job applicants who are told outright that the department is looking for a woman or member of a minority to fill a vacancy. As yet the United States Supreme Court has not advised us by its decisions whether such purposeful reverse discrimination is permissible under the Constitution. Until the Supreme Court decides this issue, university administrators must continue to act at their peril.

All the legal and administrative troubles engendered by an act of reverse discrimination are not readily apparent. Blatantly favored treatment of a woman or a minority member with respect to salary or rank is practically guaranteed to impair morale of other department members and to produce hostility toward the newcomer on the part of colleagues, even those who have worn the badge of civil libertarianism for many years. The newcomer often may detect a chill in the air and, consequently, when a request is denied for any reason—be it for a particular schedule, use of facilities, or committee assignment—he or she may perceive race or sex discrimination to be the cause of the decision and, as the result of that perception, may initiate a charge with the Equal Employment Opportunity Commission and/or other agencies.

BIAS IN ENFORCEMENT

Perhaps the most frustrating assignment that can befall a university attorney today is to shepherd his client through an HEW, EEOC, or Department of Labor investigation of a discrimination complaint. The first skirmish can be expected to revolve around the right of members of administration and faculty to have their counsel present during interviews conducted by the investigator. The federal agency is likely to attempt to discourage or even prohibit the institution's counsel from attending the investigatory interviews. Notwithstanding that denial of the request to have counsel present constitutes a violation of the civil rights of the person who expresses such a wish, there are important practical reasons to resist attempts by government agencies to restrict or deny the right to counsel. In their present mode of organization, EEOC and HEW simultaneously act in the roles of prosecutor and judge. The history of administrative agencies demonstrates that the agency which does not separate prosecutorial and judicial functions may justifiably be charged with an abuse of its powers.

Moreover, the agencies charged with the administration of the antidiscrimination laws are not neutral fact-gatherers. EEOC, for example, is frank to admit that it considers itself an advocate of the complainant. HEW and the equal pay investigators are not as forthright as EEOC in admitting partiality, but their actions almost invariably demonstrate that perspective. Experience then indicates that these investigators cannot be expected to ask the questions which might solicit information favorable to the institution. University counsel, if present, can ask those questions of the person being interviewed and can elicit information to build a record favorable to the institution and to the persons whose decisions are challenged. Moreover, counsel will be alert to attempts to delve into matters or documents not relevant to the matter under inquiry and can raise proper legal objections to such demands.

No discussion of the role of university attorney in the administration of equal employment laws can be complete without reference to the problem of agency bias. University counsel, like their counterparts in other areas of practice, want the opportunity to defend their clients before an impartial judge. The impartiality of the trier of facts is so basic to our concept of justice that we are likely to take it for granted. It comes as a rude shock, therefore, to be confronted with the openly prejudiced government investigator who apparently has formed conclusions before commencing any adequate investigation. Indeed, such an investigator bears the indicia of prejudice, a word quite appropriate in this instance since it is derived from the Latin *praejudicium,* a judgment reached before knowledge or examination of the facts.

University counsel frequently complain that government investigators arrive on campus armed with little or no knowledge of the academic world, with a self-serving version of the facts furnished by the complainant, and with unswerving faith in the credibility of the complainant and the duplicity of the university's officers and employees. Their bias is reflected in their arrogant demeanor during interviews with administrators, in discourtesies highly inappropriate coming, as they do, from civil servants, in the sweeping demand for voluminous information to be supplied on extremely insufficient notice and in utter disregard of the time and financial burdens placed on the responding university.

Agency bias is a fact of life today that university counsel have learned or are fast learning to expect. It takes vigorous and tireless counsel to counter successfully the effects of such bias, and it is one more reason why counsel must be involved early in an investigation.

To the university attorney engaged in defending a college or university against a charge of discrimination, the problems of agency bias are magnified when the government investigator is unqualified—as he almost always is—to delve into academic affairs and make a reasoned judgment on the facts presented to him. He lacks the vocabulary of academe, lacks an appreciation of the indicia of scholarship, and approaches problems of hiring and promotion in a simplistic fashion devoted to quantitative rather than qualitative measurement. He often tends to treat educational institutions as he would a manufacturer of plumbing supplies. Typically, he ignores the realities that the mission of a university is unique in the organizations of our society and that monetary profit is not the raison d'être of the institution.

Effects on Traditional Values

University counsel also have had the opportunity to observe that the equal employment laws and resulting litigation are having an intimidating effect on college administrators and on faculty members who participate in hiring, promotion, and tenure decisions. This situation is particularly apparent in state universities where faculty members are state employees acting under color of state law, and thus, in their individual capacities, are subject to suit for monetary damages in cases alleging discrimination. However, academicians in both private and public institutions are becoming reluctant to give candid written evaluations of applicants for positions or of colleagues who are candidates for promotion for fear their comments will not be held confidential. Documents relating to qualifications of other faculty members are considered relevant evidence in government investigations into allegations of employment discrimination. This material is held confidential only for the initial stages of the enforcement process. For example, once a suit is filed under title VII, EEOC will permit either party to inspect its files of materials obtained in the course of investigation. Thus letters of recommendation and evaluation, which had been written in expectation of confidentiality, and minutes reflecting committee deliberations will be available to the suing faculty member and may be spread on the public record even though they relate to other persons.

There is reason to anticipate that in any litigation based on an allegation of employment discrimination such material would be subpoenaed and made part of the court record in the case. Undoubtedly the disclosure of comments on the merits, talents, and deficiencies of colleagues in a discipline is certain to increase departmental tensions and to heighten latent antipathies. It is no wonder that once exposed to an equal employment dispute, academicians thereafter become reluctant to commit to writing their true opinions of colleagues and are cautious to share adverse oral comments that might find their way into memoranda.

ADVOCATES FOR ACADEME

Obviously, then, the extension of the equal employment opportunity laws to campuses has wrought many changes quite distinct from an increase in the numbers of women and of minority faculty and staff members. University counsel, together with other observers of the academic scene, have profound concerns over the effect on institutional autonomy of the governmental presence on campus. They are concerned foremost that academic decisions must now be justified to nonacademicians. They are concerned with the diversion of vast amounts of university resources away from the academic mission of the institution in order to meet the cumulative demands of equal employment enforcement agencies. They are concerned with the long-term effects of faculty intimidation. They are concerned with a most serious loss of confidentiality of university records.

There are those who are not convinced that higher education must pay this price in order to achieve greater representation of women and minorities on campuses. There is no logical reason why the purpose and spirit of antidiscrimination laws cannot coexist with institutional autonomy and the traditional values of academic life. What is needed to solve this dilemma is a greater role for the academic world in shaping the patterns of government enforcement activities. In this way, whatever is good and useful in preserving academic freedom and academic excellence will not be discarded with outmoded attitudes and practices which for too long denied classes of our citizenry significant access to scholarly careers.

It cannot be overemphasized that legal counsel must, from sheer necessity, be invited early to participate in matters pertaining to equal employment opportunity. The early involvement of counsel is required because— to put it bluntly—the stakes are too high to warrant any but the most serious approach to each government investigation of a complaint. The risk of termination of funds and the vulnerability to suit not only of institutions, but also of their administrators and even their faculty members in their individual capacities, require legal guidance. The equal employment opportunity laws now represent the most troublesome area of faculty-management relations. Although there are those who decry the increasing visibility of university counsel in academic affairs, it is the inevitable result of increased government regulation.

Finally, it must be remembered that the purpose of the equal employment opportunity laws is, of course, to eliminate discrimination on the basis of race, religion, national origin, sex, and age from the employment process. The laws were intended to be salutary in opening employment opportunities to persons who had been unjustly deprived of an opportunity to compete in the labor market by accidents of birth and for other reasons wholly irrelevant to ability. There have been instances in our history, however, where laws intended to have a salutary effect have created unforeseen problems because the modes of their administration were inappropriate and unwieldy, or even because the otherwise constitutional statutes were being applied by the misdirected bureaucracy in an illegal fashion. If the equal employment laws are to serve as instruments of justice, which they must, then they must be administered in a just fashion. If we permit otherwise, we will merely have substituted one form of injustice for another and, in the process, we will have surrendered much of this country's academic independence to the government bureaucracy.

Faculty Unions, Senates, and Institutional Administrations

JOSEPH W. GARBARINO

IN ITS FINAL REPORT, the Carnegie Commission on Higher Education predicted that "The 1970s may belong to faculty activism as the 1960s did to student activism. . . ." The commission identified four sources of potential initiatives in higher education and concluded that "those originating with faculties, and particularly collective bargaining, may be the more dominant ones in the near future."[1]

This paper is adapted from Joseph W. Garbarino, "Faculty Bargaining and Institutional Change," sponsored by the Carnegie Commission on Higher Education and the Ford Foundation (New York: McGraw-Hill, in preparation).
1. *Priorities for Action: Final Report of the Carnegie Commission on Higher Education* (New York: McGraw-Hill, 1973), p. 56.

By mid-1974 the commission's conclusion could be supported by citing that faculties in more than three hundred institutions had chosen exclusive bargaining agents. Possibly, more significant is the finding that two-thirds of all faculty members responding to the most recent American Council on Education survey of faculty opinion agreed that collective bargaining by faculty had a place in colleges and universities.[2] Faculty activism may be evidenced in ways other than through collective bargaining, but the activist's chosen vehicle in the present context is likely to be the faculty union. Here I shall try to analyze the implications for institutional management of the experience with faculty unionism, focusing on union-senate relations and the resulting indirect effects for administrations.

Three models of union-senate relationships may be designated: cooperation, competition, and cooptation.

THE COOPERATIVE MODEL

Surprising as it may seem, in terms of numbers of bargaining situations, the opinion of most observers (including the author) seems to be that the most common relationship between unions and senates has been one of cooperation or, at a minimum, coexistence. However, the most important qualifications to this conclusion may, unfortunately, turn out to be critical.

To date, cooperation has been the dominant style at single-campus and main-branch institutions where administrative structures are simple and unions are essentially guild unions of regular rank faculty. Senates and unions are least cooperative and most competitive in the bargaining units of large, complex institutional systems with comprehensive unions and these include a majority of all unionized faculty members. This phenomenon results in part from the generally higher degree of conflict that appears to characterize such institutions with respect to large-scale changes in governance structures, an extended administrative hierarchy, and a more heterogeneous set of interest groups. Thus, in such cases, on both employer and faculty sides, institutionwide mechanisms for decision making are likely to be relatively new and unseasoned, although often the relations between local campus senates and the local branches of the union are relatively cooperative.

One factor that has made cooperation work has been a natural division of labor, which is suggested by the results of the 1970 governance survey of the American Association of University Professors.[3] Senates clearly are

2. Alan E. Bayer, *Teaching Faculty in Academe: 1972–73,* ACE Research Reports (Washington: American Council on Education, 1973), p. 30.
3. "Report of the Survey Subcommittee of Committee T," *AAUP Bulletin,* Spring 1971, p. 70.

most active in academic matters, followed by personnel matters and, finally, administrative matters. Unions have concentrated on the last two; little attention is paid to academic affairs in union contracts.

Where guild unions exist, there often is a common membership and an overlapping group of leaders and activist members, and there is likely to be agreement on the agenda of problems and a willingness to accept a division of responsibility. Where a bargaining unit includes faculty senate members and a heterogeneous professional staff, opinions are much more likely to differ on the goals of the organization, their relative urgency, and the methods to be employed in their pursuit. In institutions where such differences exist, whether in guild or comprehensive unions, the relationship will be marked less by cooperation than by competition.

THE COMPETITIVE MODEL

In a competitive relationship, competition between senate and union dominates the elements of cooperation. The organizations compete for representation rights on major issues and for the loyalty and the support of the faculty. The struggle is for control of the decision-making process, for the right to identify the objectives of the faculty, to pursue their achievement, and to gain credit for the result. For a union without compulsory membership or the agency shop, winning support is a life-or-death matter. Not only must the union almost always win an election campaign to gain representation rights, but it must also win repeated votes of confidence expressed by the willingness of a major proportion of the bargaining unit membership to pay monthly dues.

Even when the constituencies of a faculty senate and a guild union are essentially the same, the activist elements in each are self-selected and may be quite different. Senate leadership reflects a certain distribution of political power among subgroups of the faculty. If the support for the union comes from faculty members outside the existing political power structure, then the union will appear to be a means for supplanting the current power holders, and those electing to join and to pay dues to the union will generate a new and competitive leadership. This latter development is much more likely to occur when a comprehensive union faces a faculty senate, since by definition their constituencies are different and there is often a legacy of resentment between some of the nonteaching professionals and the traditional faculty leadership.

Faced with a choice between two different representatives of the "faculty," administrations are likely to show a clear preference for the senate version, thereby bringing a latent competition to the surface.

The usual prescription for avoiding competition is to define separate spheres of influence for the senate and the union either in the relevant bargaining law or by agreement between the administration and the union. The usual prognosis for the success of this effort is unfavorable. In the United States it is generally accepted that the effects on conditions of employment of almost any management action create bargainable issues so that any barrier between bargainable and nonbargainable issues is likely to leak badly.

Where conflict levels are low, union-senate cooperation can work indefinitely in a good many situations. In hard fact, however, cooperation really amounts to a system of voluntarily shared authority on the part of union. Just as a governing board in a time of crisis often revokes the delegation of its authority to a senate, so too unions may decide to exercise their legal right to bargain on issues traditionally handled by the senate. A decision that is important to a politically significant segment of the union's membership—say, on the fate of a department or on the nonretention of a faculty member—cannot be left to a final determination by another body without challenge.

If senate-union cooperation is not viable in a conflict situation, the outcome of the resulting competition may not be the elimination of the senate, but an integration of the two institutions so that they are coextensive.

The Cooptative Model

The simplest description of a cooptative bargaining model is bargained collegiality or collegiality by contract. In some versions of cooptative systems, the senate as a formal organization with separate facilities and its own officers may not even exist on a unionized campus. Conversely, on a campus without a formally recognized exclusive bargaining agent, the senate might dominate administration-faculty-union relationships, including the determination of bargaining policy.

Formulating the analysis in this way poses the question of identifying the essence of the problem: the exact nature of the distinction between senates and unions as faculty representatives. Perhaps the heart of the distinction is the role of "collegiality" in decision making versus the role of bargaining. What I will call the union definition of collegiality means decision making by the appropriate independent faculty body, with the burden of proof for failure to follow the decision placed on the administration and, in most cases, with the right of appeal from the administrative decision to a body outside the administrative structure.

In the administration's eyes collegiality is a more amorphous and more complicated system. It involves decisions by the faculty, although sometimes with some faculty-administrators participating in the deliberations as part of the peer group and sometimes with the administration even influencing the selection of at least some faculty members. The decision reached is to be accorded very serious consideration and is to be accepted unless there are overriding reasons for changing it. The authority to override is based on inherent "management rights" and is not subject to review. This version of collegiality implies that decisions by the faculty will usually be accepted, will be changed only after careful consideration for weighty reasons that, except in personnel cases, will be reported to the faculty.

Looking at "shared" authority in this way suggests that most discussions regarding bargaining and the senate system really concern the effect of bargaining on collegiality as a process of decision making. Unions may have no objections to collegiality if they participate in selecting the "peers" who make the decisions, if the process is free from administration domination, and if a favorable decision is binding or, if reversed, the reversal is subject to objective review.[4] The potential threat to the union position lies in the possibility that the senate's existence as a separate organization will permit the administration to define collegiality in its own terms.

This line of analysis suggests how a cooptative system of faculty representation and participation might work as a negotiated mix of decision-making procedures incorporating both collegiality and collective bargaining: (1) For certain types of decisions (for example, academic organization or administrative appointments), the union may be willing to accept the administration's definition of collegiality. (2) For others (for example, personnel decisions), the union may insist on its definition of collegiality. (3) Another set of decisions (for example, salaries) would be the subject of direct bargaining. Senate machinery might be retained for the administration version of collegiality, including independent faculty committees or joint faculty-administration committees whose faculty representatives are selected by and responsible to the union and whose recommendations are accepted in all but unusual circumstances. Under the union version of collegiality, decisions would be made by faculty committees with the union having the right to independent review of an administrative reversal

4. A provocative statement that collegiality and peer evaluation may leave something to be desired from the standpoint of some faculty members appears in Donald H. Wollett, "Historical Development of Faculty Collective Bargaining and Current Extent," *Proceedings, First Annual Conference, April 1973,* National Center for the Study of Collective Bargaining in Higher Education (New York: City University of New York, Baruch College, n.d.), especially pp. 29–37.

under certain conditions. Under the last of the three types, decisions would be subject to bargaining and, most important, the structure of the overall system would be subject to the bargaining as well. The form of representation, the division of subject matter, and the extent of review would be themselves negotiable topics.

The Massachusetts State College system contracts resemble this model in that faculty representatives in the governance system are selected by the union. Other contracts provide for the union to name members to various governance bodies as well. In the next several years many unions are virtually certain to achieve some form of compulsory membership or the agency shop, in essence providing them with universal membership. In this way the union will gain legitimacy as the vehicle of faculty participation and enhance its claim to control the entire representation system.

The cooptative model differs from the competitive model in that the primacy of the union is acknowledged and the distribution of subject matters among the various types of procedural mechanisms is negotiated between the parties. This projected status for the union will not, however, mean that the union can bring all issues into bargaining, much less dominate the results. The results of collective bargaining to date do not suggest that administrations which know what they want and are competent in bargaining are being overpowered in negotiations.

In summary, the predictions that senates would be displaced from the decision-making process by unions have proved to be exaggerated or at least premature. The variety of possible relationships between senates and unions was underestimated, and extended periods of cooperative relations appear to be possible, particularly with guild unions. At least one possible outcome is that union and senate functions will be integrated, with the unions as dominant partners but with senate-style collegiality surviving in important areas of academic decision making. If something like this last system is to develop, it is important to realize that it will have to be at administrative initiative. Unions are unlikely to make the self-denying distinction between issues on their own, and senates are not usually in a position to bargain for this division. Developing the pattern and policing its retention will be the administration's responsibility.

When academicians gather to discuss faculty unionism, the air is filled with calls for development of a genteel alternative to the "industrial union model." Alternatives to the industrial model of academic unionism already exist in the various forms of faculty representation currently operating in the 90 percent of the four-year colleges still unorganized. The choice of a faculty union as a bargaining representative with legal status may well mean that the union will replace the existing organizational structure, but an administration that believes in the old-time collegial religion may be able to retain its procedures over substantial areas of academic decision making.

Financial Exigency: Avoidance of Litigation and Friction

WILLIAM VAN ALSTYNE

ALTHOUGH THE EXACT litigative margins and the educational repercussions of affirmative action and collective bargaining in higher education are still uncertain, the basic legal framework in which those questions continue to arise is reasonably well settled. Additionally, there is no paucity of professional writing on those subjects; to the contrary, the very profusion of writing probably makes it difficult to keep abreast.

Neither of these things is true, however, of faculty-administration relations and financial exigency. "The law" respecting tenure, contract, termination, financial exigency, and administrative prerogative is simply not there except so far as one may be able to argue from analogy. In the first few confrontations in the courts, the results and analyses have had little or nothing in common. Reference to two decisions, both within 1974, may make the point quite clear.

In *Lumbert* v. *University of Dubuque* (Law No. 39973, D.C. Iowa, 1st dis., July 15, 1974), it took the judge less than a page and a half to state "the law" according to his view: Assuming that the university had agreed not to terminate a faculty member without cause unless a bona fide, demonstrable financial exigency left it no other recourse, such an agreement was unenforceable because it lacked "consideration," and thus the contract was terminable at will. In short, the promise was legally worthless. Quite apart from this, the court opined, assuming only that the university can indicate a general poor financial trend, then "the determination of where . . . retrenchment should fall is strictly the province of the Defendant *with no right of review in the Court"* (emphasis added). Frankly, I read this case with the same bemusement as might poor Mr. Pickwick. It also makes me wonder how much the judge may have contributed to the local need for collective bargaining which might produce a contract less likely to be treated so lightly in a court of law.

In *Amer. Ass'n of Univ. Professors* v. *Bloomfield College* (Sup. Ct. N.J., Ch. Div. No. C-4241-72, June 26, 1974), the judicial construction of that Faculty Handbook provision (that "termination of continuous appointment because of financial exigency . . . must be demonstrably *bona fide"*) was very different. In an elaborate review the court held: (1) The provision was fully binding and formed "an essential part of the contractual terms. . . ." (2) The burden was on the institution affirmatively to establish each element without which termination could not be justified by this clause. (3) The clause would sustain terminations only on the basis of the circumstance for which it provided excuse and none other; that is, terminations to facilitate new programs or terminations related to redirecting the general mission of the college have nothing to do with (and, correspondingly, cannot be defended by) a clause itself excusing termination solely for financial exigency. (4) Evidence establishing a good faith *belief* of financial distress was not sufficient to meet the full provision that required that the *fact* of financial distress be demonstrable. (5) Evidence of facts demonstrating a general condition of financial decline was insufficient to fulfill the clause, and "exigency" implies the existence of imminent necessity—an immediate relationship—that such terminations were *presently required* by the circumstances. (6) The evidence presented in court by the college did not meet either of these contractual requirements of "good faith" and of exigent need for recourse to termination. (7) Even in circumstances where they might be met, they would at most justify what the provision itself allows, specific terminations, but *not* the general abolition of the college's tenure system.

A third decision, also summer 1974 (*Johnson* v. *Board of Regents,* W.D. Wis. 74-C-142, June 13, 1974), examined the relationship of tenure and termination for alleged financial exigency from the wholly different perspective of constitutional law. Its approach is far different from either of the other two cases, as it necessarily would be given the different (and far more reified) legal framework of the case, and its conclusions likewise differ.

But the point is not to provide a digest of recent cases. It is, rather, simply to emphasize the obvious: the "law" to which one might turn in respect to faculty-administration relations and financial exigency, unlike that of collective bargaining or affirmative action, remains essentially a *terra incognita* (or, more accurately, a *lex tabula rasa*).

I cannot, therefore, write either as a reporter of decisions or as a minion of "the law" or as a beleaguered critic of what the "law" has done. Rather, I think it useful simply to share some ways that the common law may plausibly affect faculty-administration relations in circumstances of financial exigency, and to relate these suggestions to the guidelines recommended by the American Association of University Professors as one helpful way of avoiding the costs, the uncertainties, and the friction of litigation.[1]

VARIETIES OF PROBLEMS: A SERIES OF CASES

In Dr. Furniss's article, the observation is made that the legal rights of faculty in respect of personnel policy may vary, depending on the specific provisions of "state law, existing regulations of the institution, collective bargaining contracts, the Civil Rights Act, and other federal and local employment legislation,"[2] in addition to some implications of constitutional law as well. Some of these items not only obviously vary already, from state to state and from institution to institution, but several are readily alterable by the institution itself (for example, its own regulations) and others are negotiable (for example, collective bargaining contracts).

Exactly because all of this is true, it is therefore obviously impossible to examine a series of cases as though they were cast in concrete, as though our speculative conclusions accurately describe immutable results. But one must start with *some* description to make any sense at all and, having thus made the appropriate disclaimer, it seems to me to be useful to assume reasonably *typical* circumstances, at least in the following two respects: that the institution in question operates under a tenure system[3] and that, according to the rules of the institution, "termination of a con-

---

1. The guidelines—"On Institutional Problems Resulting from Financial Exigency: Some Operating Guidelines," *AAUP Bulletin,* Summer 1974, pp. 266–67—are reprinted at the end of this paper. Additionally, W. Todd Furniss, "Retrenchment, Layoff, and Termination," *Educational Record,* Summer 1974, pp. 159–70, is especially helpful, and see Furniss's recommendations, pp. 169–70.
2. Furniss, "Retrenchment," p. 169.
3. Some may be annoyed that a tenure system is "assumed," insisting that a panel of faculty-administration relations should be considering, instead, whether tenure should be abolished. But there is a massive literature already available on the subject, and this paper is simply not the place to offer still another defense. Moreover, problems of faculty relations are not only typically arising at institutions the vast majority of which do have tenure systems, but an examination of tenure and financial exigency may also contribute some insight into reconcilability of the two.

tinuous appointment because of financial exigency should be demonstrably bona fide."[4] At the same time, according to the rules of the institution, such a termination is not regarded as one "for cause" in the usual sense; that is, it is not a dismissal for unprofessional conduct or neglect of duty to be determined strictly in accordance with full academic due process. Rather, it is assumed that the decisions to terminate members of the faculty are meant to be impersonal and without invidious reflection upon their competence or integrity, but simply a consequence of an alleged lack of means to provide them with work to do.

Unless "tenure" is misconstrued as a legal commitment to pay a certain salary irrespective of the financial condition of the academic firm, it cannot be construed as a guarantee of lifetime employment subject only to one's observance of standards of professional integrity. Thus, we assume (and rightly so) that tenure is subject to judgments required by the financial condition of the institution, but this leaves us with very little idea as to what limitations may police the reasonableness of those judgments. Indeed, the kinds of problems likely to generate controversy traverse the whole range of academic planning, from the decisions of statewide boards down to the most local determination of what faculty members, if any, are to be unemployed. Consider, for instance, each of the following cases, and think about each a little in advance of seeing whether the ensuing discussion is merely redundant of what seemed obvious:

Case 1

A state board of higher education develops plans for the construction and funding of community colleges with course offerings it has reason to anticipate will attract some students otherwise likely to have enrolled at the nearby established state university. The board neglects to advise the university that the university should anticipate a decline in enrollment as a consequence of the board's plan. Enrollment does in fact decline at the university and the board adjusts its budget recommendation for the university downward, to compel the university to reduce its faculty to reflect that decline. Responding to the reduction in its budget, the university administration directs the various academic departments to reduce the faculty in proportion to the new, reduced level of student enrollment in each department. In English, all probationary appointees receive notices of "nonrenewal" and several tenured appointees receive notices of "termination due to bona fide financial exigency."

The adversely affected faculty members subsequently file suit on two theories of law. One is a conventional contract action, and the other, a more experimental "contract-tort" theory. The first admits that the university's contractual

4. Quoted from "Academic Freedom and Tenure: 1940 Statement of Principles and Interpretive Comments," *AAUP Bulletin,* Summer 1974, pp. 269–72.

duty to pay is subject to an express condition subsequent that the duty comes to an end in the event of demonstrable bona fide financial exigency, but maintains that, consistent with general contract theory, the university is also subject to an implied promise not to be an agent in creating that condition—more bluntly, that the financial exigency is not "bona fide" unless it arose from circumstances reasonably beyond the control of the university itself. The alternative theory, complement of the first, is that the state board of higher education was under a duty of reasonable care to alert the university to the foreseeable consequences of the board's own community college plan to enable it sensibly to anticipate the decline in enrollment by adjusting its hiring practices rather than, as actually happened, permitting the university to be misled to the detriment of faculty members subsequently fired.

What result and why?

(*Question:* To what extent may a statewide board expense its own neglect in anticipating the consequences of its own action by shifting the cost of that neglect to those without fault?)

Case 2

The administration of a private university, facing its third successive deficit budget, declares a condition of financial exigency and alerts the various academic departments. The administration specifies the number of academic positions that must be eliminated in each department, leaving to the departments the more particular decisions. Subsequently, faculty members terminated not "for cause," but solely on grounds of "demonstrable bona fide financial exigency," file suit for breach of contract. Being wholly uncertain whether in fact there was a genuine condition of financial exigency, not having access to "the books," and not wishing to finance the cost of retaining outside accountants to review "the books," these faculty members simply deny in their pleading the existence of the exigency.

(*Question:* On whom does the burden of proof rest regarding the issue of financial exigency: on the faculty members who are suing, or on the administration that invoked it as a condition subsequent, the occurrence of which terminates their contractual duties?)

Case 3

In case 2, the manner of determining that there was a "continuing deficit" excluded appreciated market value of stock holdings in the university endowment investment portfolio and other items as well. (Financial embarrassment was determined in a way that Earl Cheit has criticized: universities use their development offices in a similar portrayal of financial conditions in order to stimulate fund-raising campaigns.) As in case 2, terminated faculty members file suit for breach of contract, contesting the "demonstrable bona fides" of the alleged condition of financial exigency.

(*Question:* What is the proper legal standard to be applied in determining *whether* a bona fide condition of financial exigency did in fact exist?)

Case 4

In case 2, it has become clear that conditions beyond the control of the institution have in fact brought it to a state of genuine, severe financial distress: half-empty dormitories are operating at a loss, food services no longer pay for themselves, gate receipts from sports are way below expenses, most courses are undersubscribed, enrollment has declined, and any rise in tuition or fees may simply aggravate the situation. The academic personnel payroll is by far the largest item in the college budget. Accordingly, the trustees approve a one-third reduction in the faculty, and notices of termination are mailed shortly thereafter. Several of the disaffected faculty members nonetheless file suit alleging breach of contract and placing in issue the standard of judgment used by the trustees in meeting the fiscal problem wholly by faculty reductions.

(*Question:* Is the *choice of means* utilized by a college to cope with conditions of financial exigency subject to judicial review and, if it is, what is the appropriate standard of that review—one of "strict necessity," one of "reasonable business judgment," one of "an absence of clearly arbitrary judgment"?)

Case 5

Faced with a clear condition of overstaffing in several departments where enrollment has steadily declined, a worsening deficit budget, and faculty within those departments whose skills are honestly not transferable to other departments, the administration proceeds to issue notices of termination on a "fifo" basis: those first in (first hired) are first out (first fired). The reason for this system is twofold. First, those with the longest service at the institution tend to receive the highest salaries even while teaching proportionately fewer courses; thus, it is believed that the fifo method will yield the greatest financial savings with the smallest curricular reduction. Second, the basic policy having been set, a strict fifo method of determining who shall be terminated avoids the administrative indelicacy and hassle of making invidious comparisons among faculty members to be selected for termination—a comparison that would necessarily involve assessing the relative merits of faculty members and to that extent resemble a dismissal for cause which would require the full panoply of academic due process.

Necessarily, however, the means chosen in this case affect the faculty members in a manner inverse to their tenure; those with tenure are precisely those who are terminated while others on term contracts or on probationary appointments are retained. The terminated faculty members file a class action suit alleging that the trustees' method of financial retrenchment violates one of the implied rights of tenure.

(*Question:* To what extent does tenure carry with it "displacement rights" vis-à-vis the probationary faculty members under conditions of financial exigency?)

Case 6

Rejecting the simplistic rigidity of what the college in case 5 did, and rejecting its opposite rule as well (a "lifo" rule of termination), the college in this case requests the academic departments to make their own determination respecting prospective terminations due to financial exigency, requesting that the departments utilize the following four criteria: (*a*) viability of academic program; (*b*) tenure; (*c*) competence and productivity; (*d*) personal hardship. Eventually, a significant number of faculty members, most of whom were term or probationary appointees and several of whom were tenured, receive notices of termination. Of these, a significant number believe that although the criteria were themselves legal and proper, they were misapplied. Two believe, moreover, that they were in fact terminated for reasons not reflected in the criteria, but rather because they had been personally active in community affairs of which their "colleagues" privately disapproved and because they had attempted to organize a collective bargaining unit within the college. Alleging these things, each seeks within the college some sort of due process, intramural review. The request is refused because the notices of termination clearly specify "financial exigency" as the sole reason for termination.

Each of the two disaffected faculty members then sues in state court, alleging breach of contract insofar as the college gave finality to the terminal notices without opportunity for even informal review.

(*Question:* Is either entitled by law to any degree of intramural review under these circumstances? Is the answer the same whether the affected individual was tenured or untenured? *Second-level question:* Is either entitled to judicial review of their affirmative claims that they were terminated for impermissible reasons?)

DISCUSSION

When an institution of higher learning has satisfied itself from the professional accomplishments of a faculty member whose work and teaching it has been at liberty to review without constraint during his untenured, probationary service, the institution puts an end to his annual (or biennial) contractual uncertainty by approving his tenure. In doing so, the institution registers a formal statement that, by its own standards, the work of the individual has earned him a presumption of competence and excellence. Insofar as his subsequent conduct provides cause to reconsider that judgment, he may of course have to answer to the alleged case in a fair hearing. If sufficient cause is shown, not subject to redress or correction by less drastic means, he may be dismissed in spite of his tenure.

When there is no suggestion that the faculty member warrants dismissal for such cause, but that he must nonetheless be let go because of circumstances beyond the institution's control, I think it is obvious (and merely fair) that the subsequent event which the institution recites as operating to relieve it of its contractual obligation can only be defined as a "condition subsequent" for which the law allocates the burden of proof to the party relying upon it—the institution. Where the means of sustaining the burden are so obviously more within the capacity of the university to demonstrate (than it is within the means of the faculty member to "disprove"), moreover, I believe that courts of law will rely on that fact as well, in allocating the burden of coming forward with the evidence, as well as the burden of persuasion. Insofar as "dismissals for cause" would themselves reflect this allocation of the burden of proof in jeopardizing the career of the tenured faculty, a similar allocation respecting termination from alleged necessity arising from financial exigency is merely consistent. Moreover, a different view would seem both strange and conducive to the use of a claim of financial exigency as an artifice; that is, the law would be placing an incentive before the institution for the disingenuous use of financial exigency claims to avoid its obligation to test a belief that dismissal for cause was warranted, in a fair hearing in which it would have to maintain the burden of proof. For all these reasons, the answer to hypothetical case 2 seems clear to me—and to carry with it an obvious suggestion to academic administration.

Identically, the burden cannot be seen as readily satisfied simply by a casual showing that there was a demonstrable financial crisis according to the way in which the institution's accounts were maintained, i.e., that a court is ousted from any critical review or from entering objections to the manner of that accounting. Dubious internal customs of accountancy which may be useful for promotional purposes (for example, to convince the alumni that they really need to give more, or to make a better case of need for state legislative committees), do not per se sustain the requirement that the alleged exigency be "demonstrably bone fide," and they are assuredly subject to challenge by persons whose careers are in jeopardy. In short, I believe the state court in the Bloomfield College case was correct in respect to the standards it applied, and that this in turn does much to answer hypothetical case 3.

Ordinarily, moreover, when one party undertakes a contractual commitment to another subject only to some condition subsequent, it is understood that good faith is implied in the specific sense that the promisor will not himself act in a manner to create the condition. For example, a farmer, promising to deliver a certain crop of alfalfa by a certain date and for a certain price *unless* it should rain for more than twenty days during the growing season, may not seek to bring about the excusing contingency himself (as by hiring someone to seed the clouds, to produce a twenty-first day of rain). There is some correspondence here to our first hypothetical case, although, of course, the correspondence is far from perfect. Rather, it is in the aggregation of accompanying negligence and poor planning that the outcome becomes more certain. Assuming that the state board of education may very well act responsibly as a matter of public policy in developing additional or alternative educational enterprises in spite of the foreseeable adverse impact they may necessarily produce, at least where the ensuing and foreseeable "financial exigency" could readily have been avoided through an adjustment in prospective appointment policies plus normal rates of turnover and attrition, I should think a court would disapprove any attempt to shift the cost of the board's own negligence to the faculty. In short, the common sense construction of a "demonstrable *bona fide* financial exigency" is one in which there was no institutional lack of reasonable care in respect to its personnel policies.

As to case 4, almost surely an institution's choice of means in coping with financial exigency is subject to judicial review. Where measures not involving the termination of tenured faculty have not first been explored and utilized, it simply cannot be said that the requisite condition subsequent has been proved. One must, rather, be prepared to relate it to the particular action which the condition is said to excuse—terminating the faculty. The existence of financial distress cannot be converted into a gratuitous occasion for termination, but rather must be shown to be causally related to the particular action it is relied upon to excuse. In that respect as well, I do not see that Judge Antell was less than wholly correct in the legal standard he applied in the Bloomfield College case.

Rather, it is here that reference to and use of the AAUP guidelines may be affirmatively helpful to a college or university, and I should want to argue that they are intended to be entirely helpful—rather than to be viewed as an officious attempt to intrude into purely administrative matters. Exactly insofar as the institution has itself involved a representative element of the faculty (for example, an elected budget committee from the faculty senate), insofar as it has drawn into its consideration specific assessments of program viability from each of the departments, and insofar as "early, careful, and meaningful faculty involvement"[5] in weighing the financial dilemmas of the college has been respected, the integrity of this internal process is likely to be of great evidentiary value to the college. Additionally, the conventions of candor and shared responsibility

5. "On Institutional Problems Resulting from Financial Exigency," p. 267.

are, in my view, far better calculated than their opposite qualities to cement a sense of closer identification with the institution itself: that from the faculty's view the institution's problems are also "our" problems, and that the treatment of either as adversaries fulfills its own prophecy, exacerbating a condition by promoting internecine conflict, injurious to both faculty and administration alike.

Similarly, hypothetical case 5 (the "fifo" plan of impersonal human inventory that stands tenure on its head) and case 6 as well provide occasion to speak more sensibly to policies of good reason than to the leverages of law. As a dryly legal matter, I would think that the "fifo" plan would not withstand judicial challenge. As to case 6, moreover, I am reasonably confident that both untenured and tenured faculty members would be entitled to judicial review to attempt to establish that illicit considerations in fact accounted for their own terminations, and that at least members of the tenured faculty would, in respect to any public institution subject to the Fourteenth Amendment of the Constitution, have a fair claim that they were entitled to intramural review of such a claim as well.

But it is the coalescence of sound policy with sound law that one may stay out of the Bleak House of litigation, and so I would conclude this brief essay by looking at these cases in a different way. Neither the "fifo" means nor the "lifo" means per se of coping with a genuine distress unavoidable other than by some reduction of a faculty has any virtue to it save only that of sheer simplicity and utter impersonalism. Forgoing any raises at all may produce sufficient savings—for instance, that against a short-term forecast, an overall good faculty, and a willingness of those in the most hard-hit specialties to adapt their skills to other related disciplines—that neither tenured nor untenured terminations are necessarily required. Assuming that this is not true, however, it is extremely doubtful that the thoughtless woodenness of a "one criterion" personnel policy makes good sense—or good law.

In the view of the AAUP, for instance, although tenure must necessarily be respected as between two persons when the decision is compelled between a nonrenewal of one individual's contract and the dissolution of another's continuing contract (for that is the essential legal difference between the two), there are still extremely hard decisions to be made before that collision in status locks in. The most obvious of these is the viability of a given academic program and the assumption of what it is that tenure relates to. It is not the AAUP position that all untenured faculty throughout a college must be released before any with tenure are terminated, that an instructor in nuclear physics with a sustaining enrollment must be non-renewed so to vacate the position for a professor of French literature automatically to acquire. Yet, neither is it correct to say that there is no porousness within disciplines, for example, that one is "tenured" only so long as financial distress has not deepened to the point where the offering of a course in the "Harbuston Theorems of Econometrics," where no students have elected to take the course for the preceding three years, requires that it be closed out—and the professor of economics given terminal notice. Again, it simply seems to me that the involvement of the faculty itself is an indispensable prerequisite in the affairs of the university, from their participating awareness involving the most long-term financial condition and vicissitudes of the institution to a shared responsibility in the molecular decisions of financial distress and academic personnel. One cannot with assurance declare the viability of given programs, the transposability of skills, the implicit scope of tenure, or the availability of means other than termination of faculty, as necessarily required by declining fiscal fortunes without that participation, and correspondingly neither could one be as confident either about the legal outcome of ensuing challenges.

APPENDIX

[Reprinted from AAUP BULLETIN, Summer 1974]

On Institutional Problems Resulting from Financial Exigency: Some Operating Guidelines

The guidelines which follow reflect Association policy as set forth in the Recommended Institutional Regulations on Academic Freedom and Tenure, The Role of the Faculty in Budgetary and Salary Matters, *and other policy documents. They were formulated by the Association's staff, in consultation with the Joint Committee on Financial Exigency, Committee A on Academic Freedom and Tenure, and Commmittee T on College and University Government. They were first issued in 1971, and reissued in slightly revised form in 1972.*

1. There should be early, careful, and meaningful faculty involvement in decisions relating to the reduction of instructional research programs. In making such decisions, financial considerations should not be allowed to obscure the fact that instruction and research constitute the essential reason for the existence of the university.

2. Given a decision to reduce the overall academic program, it should then become the primary responsibility of the faculty to determine where within the program reductions should be made. Before any such determination becomes final, those whose life's work stands to be adversely affected should have the right to be heard.

3. Among the various considerations, difficult and often competing, that have to be taken into account in deciding upon particular reductions, the retention of a viable academic program should necessarily come first. Particular reductions should follow considered advice from the concerned departments, or other units of academic concentration, on the short-term and long-term viability of reduced programs.

4. As particular reductions are considered, rights under academic tenure should be protected. The service of a tenured professor should not be terminated in favor of retaining someone without tenure who may at a particular moment seem to be more productive. Tenured faculty members should be given every opportunity, in accordance with Regulation 4(c) of the Association's *Recommended Institutional Regulations on Academic Freedom and Tenure,*[1] to readapt within a department or elsewhere within the institution; institutional resources should be made available for assistance in readaptation.

5. In some cases, an arrangement for the early retirement of a tenured faculty member, by investing appropriate additional institutional funds into the individual's retirement income (and ordinarily feasible only when social security benefits begin), may prove to be desirable if the faculty member is himself agreeable to it.

6. In those cases where there is no realistic choice other than to terminate the services of a tenured faculty member, the granting of at least a year of notice should be afforded high financial priority.

7. The granting of adequate notice to nontenured faculty should also be afforded high financial priority. The nonreappointment of nontenured faculty, when dictated by financial exigency, should be a consideration independent of the procedural standard outlined in the *Recommended Institutional Regulations* 4(c), with one exception: when the need to make reductions has demonstrably emerged after the appropriate date by which notice should be given, financial

---

[1] *Recommended Institutional Regulations 4(c):*

Where termination of an appointment with continuous tenure, or of a nontenured appointment before the end of the specified term, is based upon bona fide financial exigency or discontinuance of a program or department of instruction, Regulation 5 [dismissal proceedings] will not apply, but faculty members shall be able to have the issues reviewed by the faculty, or by an appropriate faculty committee (such as the faculty's grievance committee), with ultimate review of all controverted issues by the governing board. In every case of financial exigency or discontinuance of a program or department of instruction, the faculty member concerned will be given notice or severance salary not less than as prescribed in Regulation 8 [at least a year of notice for faculty members on continuing appointment]. Before terminating an appointment because of the abandonment of a program or department of instruction, the institution will make every effort to place affected faculty members in other suitable positions. If an appointment is terminated before the end of the period of appointment, because of financial exigency, or because of the discontinuance of a program of instruction, the released faculty member's place will not be filled by a replacement within a period of two years, unless the released faculty member has been offered reappointment and a reasonable time within which to accept or decline it.

See "1972 Recommended Institutional Regulations on Academic Freedom and Tenure," *AAUP Bulletin,* Winter, 1972, pp. 428-433.

compensation to the degree of lateness of notice should be awarded when re-appointment is not feasible.

8. A change from full-time to part-time service, on grounds of financial exigency, may occasionally be a feature of an acceptable settlement, but in and of itself such a change should not be regarded as an alternative to the protections set forth in the *Recommended Institutional Regulations* 4(c) or as a substitute for adequate notice.

9. When one institution merges with another, the negotiations leading to merger should include every effort to recognize the tenure of all faculty members involved. When a faculty member who has held tenure can be offered only a term appointment following a merger, he should have the alternative of resigning and receiving at least a year of severance salary.

10. When financial exigency is so dire as to warrant cessation of operation, the institution's highest obligation in settling its affairs should be to assist those engaged in the academic process so that, with minimal injury, they can continue their work elsewhere.

Reconciling Contradictions: The Task of Creative Management

ERNEST L. BOYER

"THINGS ARE in the saddle," wrote Emerson, "and ride mankind." In a way, that tells the story of American higher education for the past three decades. First came the GI Bill bringing a huge influx of new students to the campus. Then Sputnik's jolt opened wider the federal cornucopia. Within the social revolution of the sixties, the enrollment of minorities was expanded, black studies were introduced, and such matters as equal access and affirmative action were tackled.

Somehow, almost miraculously, the nation emerged from this inundation of outside forces with a network of colleges which C. P. Snow characterized as "one of the world's greatest glories."[1] More college buildings were constructed during these three decades than during the preceding three hundred years of our history, and the proportion of high school graduates attending college ballooned from 36 percent to 61 percent. Institutional planning at the colleges was preoccupied with problems of expansion—a trend some assumed would never end.

But now the glory days are gone. Higher education now faces a painful reappraisal. The bulging postwar budgets are behind us; the baby boom has fizzled down to a capgun pop; college going among high school graduates has dropped from 50 percent to 43 percent; and all across the land higher learning institutions are cutting costs, trimming staff, and, in some instances, fighting grimly for survival.

How should we in higher learning meet this stark reversal in our fortunes? There are, of course, no easy answers. But I have an intuition that any new surge in education will be linked to something called creative management.

Of course, this word "management" falls gratingly on the academic ear.

1. "Hope for America," *Look,* Dec. 1, 1970.

It conjures up such notions as control and output and bureaucratic mechanization at its worst. But for purposes of discussion here, I shall not draw sharp or subtle distinctions between management and the more traditional concepts of administration, governance, and leadership—terms which I prefer. In this context, what I mean by good management is the process by which objectives are fulfilled with the minimum waste. And *creative* management means not only efficiency but effectiveness as well. What we are considering, then, is the exercise of more rational judgment based on reliable facts—administration by perspective rather than by panic.

To achieve creative management is easier said than done. It requires a very special style that may be described as the capacity to live with and reconcile the tensions and counterpulls of higher learning. Rather than discuss management in the abstract, I should like to identify four real-life management problems facing our colleges and universities and present a suggestion or two for how they might be overcome.

SERVING TRADITIONAL AND NEW STUDENTS

First, creative management means finding better ways to educate traditional students while at the same time getting ready to serve a new clientele.

Historically, the span of human life has been chopped up into slices like a great salami, with each section having a special flavor all its own. First, there was the thin slice of early childhood: the time of happy play. Then came a thicker slice—twelve to twenty years perhaps—devoted almost exclusively to full-time learning. Next was the still thicker chunk of full-time work. And, finally, came retirement, the little nubbin at the end. In this typical life cycle of the past, the stages of existence were kept rigidly apart, each clanking along behind the other like a string of freight cars. The individual moved on from stage to stage, seldom looking back.

What does all of this have to do with higher education? Much indeed, for throughout the years colleges and universities have accommodated fully to this long tradition. For example:

- College catalogues and brochures are usually addressed to the young, suggesting that students come in just four sizes—eighteen, nineteen, twenty, and twenty-one.
- Classes are scheduled mainly Monday through Friday, usually nine to four, colliding head-on with the world of work.
- The academic year has been broken into chunks of study called semes-

ters, with time off in the summer so students can go home to tend the crops.
- Students are expected to "finish" college before entering the world of work, never to return.
- In this arrangement, the campus has become a place where older people seem like strangers in a foreign land.
- Adult students are viewed largely as retreads engaged in a kind of salvage operation, sadly out-of-step with the learning cycle and even with the cycle of life itself.

So, through the patterns of our institutions, we have locked this neatly ordered view of life into an iron vise of custom. The campus has become a kind of youth ghetto. We are geared to serve best the young high school graduate, our principal client.

But now this pattern has begun to change, and we must respond.

- Today, about 40 percent of all American boys and girls enroll in pre-school programs before they go to kindergarten, and older children mature physically two years earlier than their grandparents did a half a century ago.
- The neat and tidy adult work is also breaking up. In 1900, the average work week in America was sixty-two hours long, by 1945 it had dropped to forty-three hours, and today it is thirty-seven and one-half hours. And the four-day and even three-day work weeks are serious proposi-tions, along with six-month intensive work periods, followed by six months of leisure, in some fields.
- Life expectancy also has increased from forty-seven years in 1900 to seventy-one years today, and it is estimated that by the year 2000 nearly 30 percent of all Americans will be over fifty.

My point is this: For years we have assumed that life was neatly divided into chunks. Colleges and universities were to serve principally the young and unattached. Now, with the birthrate falling off, we are inclined to panic, fearing a loss of our supposedly natural clientele. But even though the population explosion is now an implosion, there are actually *more* people to be served: workers who have more leisure time, technicians who face early obsolescence, executives who need new skills, older people who retire earlier, change careers, live longer, and remain active and alert.

For the first time in our history, higher education may now be viewed not as a prework ritual but as a process to be pursued from seventeen to seventy. The time has come to set forth new objectives which focus not only on traditional students but also on the new clienteles. This, I am convinced, is the first step to creative management.

Living with Collegial and Hierarchic Governance

Second, creative management in education means living with a complex and sometimes confusing decision-making structure.

For years educators have been ambivalent about how a college should be governed. On the one hand, we have had a long-standing love affair with the so-called collegial decision-making pattern. We have emulated the New England town meeting in which everyone met and talked together to find the truth. Collegial government won renewed popularity during the 1960s, when demands for consensus arrangements became intense. Campuswide senates, involving administrators, faculty, and students, sprang up like mushrooms and, soon after, the push toward collective bargaining by some faculties added a special variation to the participatory theme.

But we in higher education have also had a long-standing, often unstated, fondness for a hierarchic form of governance. Our respect for power wielded at the top expands measurably when that power brings in more money and more prestige. While few faculty senate handbooks quote Alexander Hamilton's dictum that "energy in the executive is the leading element in good government," there is nonetheless a grudging recognition that strong leadership makes a difference. Such university presidents as Andrew White, Charles Eliot, David Starr Jordan, Nicholas Murray Butler, and William Rainey Harper are regarded as men of strength and vision whose institutional influence was immense. And, in fact, it was.

I do not propose, of course, that we return to one-man rule. Nor am I amused by the British vice-chancellor who loved to quip that he was "in full charge of his faculties." But I do suggest that our commitment to town-meeting governance on campus has, throughout the years, collided somewhat with our respect for a strong, bold leader.

And there's the rub. Creative management in the university means that we must understand this ambivalence in our notions about how colleges should be governed. Rather than forcing a choice between the so-called hierarchic and collegiate models, we should recognize that both decision-making patterns have a place and that one can and must complement the other. Some decisions can be reached through informal consultations; others, through traditional senate structures; and still other issues will be settled through the process of negotiation. These various forms of governance can flourish side by side. Indeed, they must.

Power in an academic setting, more than in any other institutions perhaps, is both fluid and elusive. The person who tries to fix it free of ambiguity and of subtle shifts will find it slipping away like sand in the face of pounding waves.

One more point. It has to do with people. While flow charts and the fixing of authority seem inevitable in large organizations (which include many higher learning institutions), how men and women carry on within the structure will make all the difference. If people talk frequently and easily with each other, if ideas from all levels are encouraged and rewarded, then faculty, administrators, and students will come out of their bureaucratic boxes and trust the system regardless of the so-called decision-making model. After all, an organization exists only in our heads, and how people feel about the structure—their perception of whether it is there to support them or suppress them—is what truly matters.

The Carnegie Commission in its final report suggested that "the governance of higher education is more a matter of how good decisions can be made than it is one of any single clear principle to be followed."[2] Understanding that truth is central to creative management.

BALANCING AUTONOMY AND ACCOUNTABILITY

Third, creative management must reconcile the growing tension between autonomy and accountability.

Higher education's commitment to the autonomy of each college and university is old and deep. Most educators are convinced that the university is a unique institution and that any intrusion from without is a fundamental threat. I agree, of course, with the spirit of this stance. The essential integrity of the university must be guarded at all costs. And yet, it is also true that decision-makers are increasingly expected to account to the public for their decisions; and, during the coming decade, nearly everything we do will be subject to closer outside scrutiny. Within reasonable limits this trend is justified: Educators cannot demand that more dollars flow to them with no questions asked, especially since education is now so closely linked to the health and vitality of the nation.

Indeed, it seems ironic that higher education, so committed to the study of other institutions and to the open exchange of information, is reluctant

2. *Priorities for Action: Final Report of the Carnegie Commission on Higher Education* (New York: McGraw-Hill, 1973), p. 57.

to study and assess itself and to reveal the facts and objectives of its operation. This is all the more surprising since better information can help spark responsible social change. The Supreme Court's famous Brown decision of 1954, for example, was unanimous and enduring precisely because it was based upon massive data proving that segregation damages both its victims and its perpetrators. The planned parenthood movement has gained credibility because of increased information about population growth, pollution, and world famine. The antipoverty program in this nation was, to a large extent, kicked off by Michael Harrington's forceful argument of hidden pockets of poverty in the midst of vaunted affluence. And, certainly, measures for greater auto safety were sparked by Ralph Nader's revelations. Higher education should learn from all of this. We too need better information and responsible self-scrutiny to understand where we are and where we should be going.

I know well the hazards implied. The push for data can, as Stephen K. Bailey, vice-president of the American Council on Education, puts it, "slip into overbearing bureaucratic regulations which frequently reduce themselves to mindless record keeping, and to the harassment of academic life style into joyless and mechanical pedantry."[3] But it is also true that improved information can lead to improved credibility and more rational decision making. We cannot use our cherished independence, rightly and jealously though we defend it, to justify ambiguity or, worse, sheer ignorance.

The point is this: The autonomy-accountability dichotomy is no longer an either-or proposition; we must learn to live with both. Rather than resist blindly all forms of accountability, we should give much more thought to the central questions of "accountability to whom?" and "accountability for what?" We should stress that certain parts of the university operation are measurable and other parts are not, and we must be smart enough to tell the difference.

To manage creatively in the future requires a careful and thoughtful balance between the need for freedom to teach and to carry on research and the demands for stewardship imposed by those who pay the bills. Colleges and universities must accept the obligation to explain how their resources are being used and why; and at the same time they must all resist the suffocating surveillance of the state.

Yet another aspect of accountability must be faced. College leaders

3. "Higher Education American Style," *American Education,* August/September 1974, p. 28.

should also answer to those whom they presume to lead. I believe that this process of evaluation might be formalized on every campus. At almost every higher learning institution, when a new president is selected, students and faculty are included on the search committee. But when the final choice is made, the relationship changes abruptly. The president, in a legal and official sense, becomes the trustees' man (rarely woman, I regret to say), and faculty and students are no longer involved in evaluation except in crude and informal ways. As a result there seems to be an unwritten rule that the other campus constituencies should keep the president off balance—through letters in the student press, occasional votes of no confidence, and the like—lest he stay on forever.

The situation would improve, I feel, if presidents were named for terms of service and then evaluated formally by the faculty and students. Under this scheme, the president would be obliged to state his program and would be given sufficient time—five or six years perhaps—to pursue these goals. Campus constituencies might be more inclined to give the president respectful support because they will later have an opportunity to appraise his efforts. The president at the end of his term would review his accomplishments and shortcomings, and the faculty and students, joining with trustees, would compare their views of his tenure with the president's own. Such an arrangement could, in my view, improve the relation between the administrator and those he seeks to lead. Creative management would be achieved through improved accountability to constituencies inside the institution, as well as to those beyond.

PROMOTING STABILITY AND CHANGE

Finally, creative management means building an administrative structure that both sustains and challenges the status quo.

As I look at our organizational charts, it strikes me that they are geared to reinforce the status quo. The president is at the top and beneath are vice-presidents and deans who answer phones, respond to memos, and valiantly put out brush fires wherever they flare up. Stability and smooth growth within the structure as it now exists is the order of the day. Obviously, unless we want chaos and confusion, this is necessary business, and only by sitting in one of these hot seats for a day or two can one fully realize just how crucial such routine is to the well-being of colleges and universities.

But keeping the ship afloat is not enough. We must also move forward and call in from time to time at new ports. Yet under present patterns most administrators—even the most conscientious and enlightened—are so consumed by day-to-day demands that creative planning often is postponed. For most of us, the important is smothered by the urgent.

Therefore, the big question is: How does the creative educational manager hold a college or university intact, while also charting new directions? I have come to believe that we need to *institutionalize* the process of change by assigning people and money to the job full time. Industry refers to this as the research and development function—R&D—and someone once proposed a department of heresy at each college. And wasn't it Robert Hutchins who suggested that every college should be burned down every twenty years so that our educational functions could break out of their concrete forms?

My own suggestion is more modest. I propose that each president employ staff officers whose job it is to work exclusively on new programs. The specific charge would be to identify emerging trends, shape proposals to test new assumptions, and develop specific fiscal and calendar steps to implement the plans. There is danger in this idea. Such people—let's call them the "new directions officers"—may become separate islands removed from senior line administrators who manage the institution day to day and whose inclinations to look to the present tasks may be reinforced. This danger can be overcome so long as the chief administrators concerned with budgets, buildings, academic programs, and the like remain a committee of the whole, with the new directions officers assisting the line administrators with planning and responses to their suggestions. The office should help, not compete with, the formal decision-making structure.

The recent move to organize affirmative action offices at our institutions may be a helpful illustration. Here we have a pioneering attempt to solve an urgent problem, to implement a purpose to which nearly all administrators are committed. A separate office should not isolate the effort but rather make its efforts felt in each of the traditional areas of academic life.

Creative leadership thus calls for a structure that both stabilizes and stimulates the institution. Since the day-to-day process of business, almost by definition, tends to shore up the status quo, change will not emerge by chance. Unless we give aggressive, if not equal, attention—in the form of time and money—to programs for the future, academic leaders will continue to be engulfed by chicken dinners and suffocated by their daily mail. Our institutions will lack purpose precisely because they will have lost perspective.

ELEMENTS IN THE PROCESS OF CREATIVE MANAGEMENT

I wish to close where I began. Higher education since World War II catapulted upward but now is caterwauling downward. The current crisis can be overcome in part, and the direction again reversed, by something called creative management.

Machines and formulas may improve this process, but they can never replace it. For in our move toward better leadership, it is the human equation that matters most. The key ingredient is an intelligent person who can reconcile, with some degree of equanimity, inherent conflicts between serving traditional and nontraditional students, between central and shared authority, between autonomy and accountability, and between stability and change.

A note of optimism, I feel, must be struck. During the last three decades higher education responded magnificently to unprecedented demands from outside. Today, many colleges and universities are still responding to new needs, and there is every reason to believe this process will persist.

John Gardner has said that "sometimes institutions are simply the sum of the historical accidents that have happened to them. Like the sand dunes in the desert, they are shaped by influences but not by purposes." But Gardner goes on to suggest that "men can shape their institutions to suit their purposes . . . provided that they are not too gravely afflicted with the diseases of which institutions die—among them complacency, myopia, and unwillingness to choose."[4]

Some wit may sum up by saying that, since we have a postwar bulge behind us and are at loose ends, we need either a corset or some push-ups to get ourselves in trim. I would suggest that we indeed have bulges to the rear and that with energy and luck we can shape our ends, but tightrope walking rather than waist tightening or push-ups may be a more appropriate exercise for those who have the audacity to try.

4. John Gardner, "The Future of the University," Address at the inauguration of President James Perkins, Cornell University, Oct. 4, 1963.

Factoring the Concept of Creative Management

G. M. SAWYER

LET US ASSUME from the start that we all have a working definition of the term *creative management*. Suffice it to add that management can be creative only when managers themselves are creative. Even the very best set of management guidelines in the hands of an insensitive and rigid organization officer can place strictures on operations that impede rather than facilitate the organization's development.

Moreover, it is obvious that no set of regulations or rules can cover every possible condition. The procedural manual which accommodates more than half the situations that actually arise within an institution is unusual. The creative manager is one who is skillful at adapting individual responses to general institutional demands. This is what the administrator is paid for—not for applying overly structured procedures intended to be all-inclusive or totally exclusive. At either extreme, only problems can result.

It may be concluded at this point that two factors characterize creative management, sine qua non. It is *people-centered,* depending for its actualization on people more than on procedures; and it is *dynamic,* requiring adjustments and accommodations between and among discrete sets of guidelines.

If the person is critical to a valid concept of creative management, then the nucleus of regulatory judgments upon which the manager's behavior is based must also be people-centered. Thus, to make the concept of creative management operational is to bring into productive interaction a *person* with other *persons.* Parenthetically, but by no means inconsequentially, when one takes into account certain contemporary responses to the human condition, one begins the approach toward creative management by bringing people with "hang-ups"—managers—into contact with groups of people with "hang-ups"—institutional members. Creativity can hardly be expected to cascade, Niagara-fashion, from such a union. Nonetheless, it must emanate from these interactions if it is to exist at all.

There are at least three categories of issues with which management in our universities must be concerned: (1) the universal state of all institutions, (2) the general requirements for creative management in government, business, and education, and (3) the special application of creative management techniques to selected issues in international relations. I will discuss each of these points and conclude with a delineation of several characteristics of creative management.

Overcoming Our Failures in Management

First, I would propose that the deterioration that so generally characterizes our contemporary social, political, and economic institutions can only be arrested and reversed by bringing together all people involved in group processes in a strong and dedicated effort to effectuate a creative approach to management. The goal of such an approach must be a greater accommodation of the human condition in the practical matters of generating wealth, assuring a just and orderly society, and educating the world citizen.

The special-interest decisions that have resulted in the interminable imbroglio of Watergate were made by university graduates. The implication is grave: The quality of management—or, in this instance, mismanagement—is more or less the direct function of higher education. And the prescription for remedying the situation is clear: As our universities educate students in the specialized skills needed for leadership, they must also make the *ethic of consequences* a strong component of management preparation.

Arnold R. Weber, dean of the Graduate School of Industrial Administration at Carnegie-Mellon University, was careful to emphasize to his graduates at the June 1974 commencement that they had been exposed to an intensive experience with quantitative materials but that the university had not directly attempted to give them those qualitative exposures which would temper their assimilated information with a sense of morality. This, he said, the graduates must achieve for themselves. I applaud the recognition of a basic problem by such an influential educator. I cannot but lament the necessity for his admonition.

This much is clear: Higher education in America must acknowledge a responsibility for the kind of management decisions that generally characterize our volatile existence, but more important, higher education must itself become more creative in fashioning the kind of leadership experiences that will complement the demands of academia.

It is hardly incidental that the American public has taken to the classic presentation of factors in management described by Robert Crichton in his best-selling novel, *The Camerons*.[1] Briefly, the plot is as follows: The Earl of Fyffe, owner of a coal mine, and his manager Brothcock are locked in fierce conflict with workers' representative Gillon Cameron because of administrative and supervisory practices that take little or no account of the miserable human conditions resulting from the mining operations at Pitmungo, Scotland. Some idea of the extent to which relations have deteriorated can be gleaned from the advice given to Gillon by his mentor, Keir Hardie, as Gillon prepares for an obligatory confrontation with the Earl. "You have much to lose; they have more. You have much to lose in character by giving in; they have little."

The wide readership of Crichton's book is almost certainly in large part attributable to our identification of his managers with managers as we meet them in everyday life. That is, they have little or no character. In the end, however—whether in real life or in the pages of a historical novel—all people and their general state must be taken into proper regard in the creative management process.

MANAGEMENT IN ECONOMIC AND GOVERNMENTAL INSTITUTIONS

The second concern for trainers of managers lies in the area of economic endeavors. The goal of economic institutions, for example, is the generation of wealth in a rather narrow sense of the word.[2] More precisely, the concern of the corporation or the business enterprise is to make a profit—to make money and to distribute that money through salaries, benefits, dividends, philanthropy, and so forth—which in turn contributes to the wealth of the community, which in principle resides in its human capability.

Although the goal of our economic institutions may be twofold—at short range, the increase in usable income and, at longer range, the generation of greater wealth through human enrichment—it is the former that has most meaning in this discussion, if for no other reason than because these institutions devote incalculable energies toward increasing profits. They shift emphases, change directions, alter products, and modify operations endlessly as such actions contribute to the margin of profit. Inordinate attention to the profit margin can, and sometimes does, become most troublesome. Likewise, governance—from the family unit to the international sphere—tends to focus upon short-range goals, with minimum regard

1. New York: Warner Paperback Library, January 1974.
2. See Alan Watts, "Wealth Versus Money," *Does It Matter? Essays on Man's Relations to Materiality* (New York: Vintage Books, 1971), pp. 3–24.

for consequences, in the interest of maintaining or establishing order to assure continuity of expedient matters.

I have recently experienced, both in the corporate world of business and finance and in government circles, the application of management tactics which can only be described as callous or insensitive; some bordered on punitiveness. The withdrawal of support for social service programs and the increase in support for enterprises that train rather than educate are real-life manifestations of management that can only create problems to be resolved by some future crisis.

Perhaps the most unfortunate legacy of Watergate is that it preoccupies the policy-makers and leaves decisions to the managers whose very mentality is made up of short-lived, quick-run, brief-bred programmatic concerns which seem to be increasingly separated from human aspirations. For goals they substitute strategies, and for goal-related objectives they prefer the intrigue of procedural details.

The "manager mentality" advocates a return to the rural areas when migration to the city is being intensified by the energy shortage and accompanying inflation. The manager mentality advocates a penalty for accepting food when one lives on the verge of starvation, unless the food is provided through "legitimate" means. Such attempts at managing the affairs of national and local governments cannot meet the minimum criteria for creative management. Alas, they speak of man's inhumanity to man in the processes of the "bureau." Again, in *The Camerons,* Brothcock's manager mentality reveals itself in his response to the legitimate complaints of the miners: "It's the system doon here, man." More poignant, despite their tinge of vulgarity, are these lines from a British ditty quoted by Nicholas Monsarrat:

> The working class can kiss my arse
> I've got the foreman's job at last.[3]

MANAGEMENT FOR INTERNATIONAL ORDER

The third issue which I wish to touch on before settling finally on the specifics of management in the educational enterprise is the implication of creative management in two areas of international concerns. Last June I was privileged to participate in two international conferences: a Symposium on Population and Law in Tunis, Tunisia, North Africa, and a Pan African Congress at Dar es Salaam, Tanzania. I was not at all surprised

3. *Life Is A Four-Letter Word* (London: Pan Books, 1972), p. 30.

to find that both forums focused their attention upon the relationship between the quality of decision making on the part of governments and the quality of life for the peoples of the world. When one thinks in terms of a doubling of the world's population in twenty-five years and of competition for the earth's shrinking resources, the final horrors of ill-conceived and unconscionably applied management decisions in government become apocalyptically real.

At the Tunis conference, Reuben R. Cavoy, mayor of Cagayan de Oro City in the Philippines, spoke in detail about a Model City Population Project conducted in a "typically Philippine urban community of 150,000." He reported that the study points to at least one indisputable conclusion: "That the local government as a political entity has the means to effectively carry out national population policies and programmes at the grassroots level."[4] Mr. Cavoy is correct when he suggests that such troublesome problems as global inflation, political instability, illiteracy, malnutrition, and overpopulation can be talked about in international forums but that their resolution depends upon viable and creative management in local governments. But given the tendency of bureaucracy to feed upon itself, such management is not easily come by. Local governments are hardly meeting the problems at home with necessary creativity.

At a recent workshop on teaching population dynamics, several participants in one session emphasized that decisions must be influenced by respect for human rights. On the other hand, "one participant felt that a government, facing pressing problems, must adopt a pragmatic approach."[5] But management practices—at the local, national, or global levels—that do not accommodate human rights could result in unspeakable conditions. One participant at the Tunis conference told of the possible resort to genetically transmittable diseases as a tool of management. I am somewhat relieved to see at least some open discussion in a world forum on this biogenetic engineering possibility.

At the Sixth Pan African Congress, which was called to "help mobilize and organize one of our most important assets: our own manpower,"[6] my concern was twofold: (1) to learn firsthand the strategies and projections

4. "The Local Government as a Direct Participant in Population Activities," Paper presented at the United Nations Symposium on Law and Population, Tunis, North Africa, June 17–21, 1974, p. 1.

5. "Summary Record of the Proceedings of the Workshop on the Teaching of Population Dynamics in Law School," sponsored by the United Nations Educational, Scientific, and Cultural Organization, Paris, France, February 18–22, 1974, p. 3.

6. Courtland V. Cox, "Sixth Pan African Congress," *Africa,* September 1973, p. 22.

for human and economic development in the less developed countries and
(2) to ascertain the extent to which the established programs and practices of an American university can accommodate the critical needs arising out of newly acquired political and economic freedoms.

Obviously, I view the second concern as extremely important insofar as creative management of our educational enterprises requires that new expressions of human concerns—in whatever form and in whatever place—be resolved within the context of our existing academic structures and of whatever more responsive structures we can bring into being. To omit these human concerns from our programmatic arrangements is to relegate life-determining decisions to managers with limited skills and experience.

My intent is not to be theoretical in this presentation but rather to present some real substance to which the vague concept of creative management can be anchored. To leap forward into prescriptions for creative management without first setting forth some fundamental notions about the conditions under which such management decisions will be applied is to prescribe a poorly understood remedy for an unknown malady. At the least, the cure must not be worse than the disease.

FREEDOM FOR CREATIVE MANAGEMENT IN THE UNIVERSITY

Basic to creative management in our educational institutions is the need for greater degrees of institutional freedom. Universities must be free to educate for more responsible and responsive leadership, to produce capable and humane managers to develop our human enterprises. At present we in higher education are not assured such freedom. More often than that, we can service only those needs which are supported by special constituencies. The chief administrators of universities, then, are forced to exercise those limited degrees of freedom available to them so that management functions within their institutions are performed at optimal levels in all activities.

With respect to the problems of black colleges, for example, every management decision must be based on the proposition that the institution's purpose is to move black and other enrollees into the mainstream of national life, not only in terms of greater economic sufficiency but also in the larger sense of increased adequacy as human beings. Traditionally, this has been the specialized function of the black colleges, and the creativity and ingenuity which their leaders brought to the job have been nothing short of phenomenal.

As a group, black college presidents have had to demonstrate consummate skill at managing their institutions, institutions which exist in at least two different worlds: the one from which their students come and the other to which they want to go. This schizoid existence required the ultimate in flexibility, innovation, and adaptability. At the same time, black college presidents are knowingly constrained by certain intractables which make their jobs a continuous search for realistic alternatives that carries them on excursions into unfriendly and even hostile territories.

That they have been successful is without question. The educational community is the poorer because their successes have not been sufficiently codified; their own desire to systematize their operations has been thwarted by very limited opportunity and the perpetual shortage of funds. It would be a worthwhile venture to assemble periodically a select group of recently retired black presidents to document the components of their management techniques. All of us would have much to gain from such an exercise. I would hypothesize that such analysis would yield a set of salient factors such as *empathy, acceptance, integrity,* and *awareness.* These, then, I propose as the essential components of creative management.

Empathy and Acceptance in Institutional Management

The manager who would be creative in his or her approach to melding individual aims and aspirations with the goals and functions of the institution must be able to identify with the personal aspirations of his/her constituencies. The creative manager would be particularly advantaged by having not only broad personal experiences but also some specific experiences that parallel those of the clients. Where this is not possible, a willingness to put oneself in the other's place is helpful.

Although a sensitive manager can assume vicariously the internal reference of such clients, the hard lines of cultural separation have made it difficult for this to be done with the care and effectiveness that certain ethnic conditions require. An institution which establishes a reputation as empathizing with the student as a learning organism is most certain to establish an above-average record of service. Conversely, the institution that is dispassionate and remote from the human experience—voluntarily or involuntarily—will inevitably incur the disfavor, and perhaps even the wrath, of those whom it purports to serve.

Creative management *accepts* the client, the student, the worker, as incomplete individuals in an incomplete organizational arrangement. Neither is complete nor completable—each depends on the other for growth experiences that will afford to both specified degrees of maturation. The burden here, of course, rests with management. There must be institutionalized at selected points in the organizational structure those practices and procedures which will be perceived by the individual as existing to accept him or her as a person.

Everyone who becomes a part of an institution, or who otherwise identifies with it, has the right to certain arrangements which clearly set forth the assurance that he/she is acceptable within his/her own capabilities. If this acceptance is not possible, the person should not be permitted to remain a part of the institution. Acceptance in this sense goes far beyond the constraints of an admissions system, for example. Formal acceptance into an institution is preliminary to acceptance on a psychological level. This is where it really matters; whether it be a government worker frustrated by bureaucracy, a young business executive struggling to achieve upward mobility, a woman thwarted in her aspirations in a male-dominated enterprise, or a student who has never had the security of an unfettered opportunity to develop his/her basic intelligence. Such people have undreamed-of potential for enriching the life of any institution they might serve, given optimal conditions of acceptance.

Integrity in Institutional Management

Creative management has an identifiable integrity, both in the sense of wholeness and in the sense of ethical behavior. The larger and more complex an organization, the greater the need and the responsibility for communicating itself to its constituencies as an entity. The individual who must perform tasks in a vaguely defined set of relationships may develop a sense of isolation from the total organization, and this feeling may have markedly negative effects, including low morale, high anxiety, and absenteeism. The university is obligated, in its management training courses, to see that the managers-to-be can function with the necessary security in a situation where the overall picture of the organization is as familiar to the worker as it is to them.

In the sense of ethical character, integrity means that there are certain things the institution does not do because they are morally wrong. No matter what ends are sought, some means should not be employed. To turn again to *The Camerons,* the miners have little or nothing to give them relief from the drudgery of the mines, and when they finally lose patience and demand relief from intolerable conditions, management responds by taking away their one source of recreation—a soccer field. This is clearly the act of a manager mentality without integrity, without character, and without a sense of right and wrong.

The government that gives preferential treatment to some citizens at the expense of others, the business or corporation that increases its profits at the cost of human dignity, the charity organization that preys upon even those that it purports to serve are all alike in kind: a set of management functions without conscience. Creative management is democratic in its blessings of citizenship, fair in its profit taking, and judicious in the selection of enterprises that it supports.

Awareness in Creative Management

Finally, creative management is characterized by *awareness*. In this context, awareness describes the quality of relatedness, of a sense of history.

We speak of short-term gains and long-range goals with the understanding that we are talking about linear, time-related conditions. Looking forward for five years or twenty-five years, for example, is a good indicator of planning that is accepted as important to good management practice. A review of the past is likewise desirable. As salient as these applications may be, they are, in my judgment at least, eclipsed by the need for management to look around and to take into account items and circumstances as they coexist and interact in the same time frame.

Progression is as much horizontal as it is vertical; thus, decisions at *x, y,* and *z* placed in the same time plane are related whether we want them so or not. It would be far better if our management decisions were, at the outset and by design, related to a wide spectrum of human efforts rather than being forcibly adjusted later so that they include what has been overlooked or ignored and exclude what has proved excessive or injurious. Consequently, a decision to support a class of institutions—white colleges, for example—and not support black colleges is a management decision void of necessary awareness. Awareness in this sensitive instance would take into account the demonstrated and differential strengths of black colleges, such accounting would most certainly affect the ultimate decision.

On a larger scale, I am yet intrigued by the provincialism of much of our decision making in higher education: too often our judgments are based on immediate situations and circumstances. I have had occasion to observe the behavior of American students in international encounters.

Their perceptions, and hence their communications, leave much to be desired with respect to an awareness of the requirements for participation in world dialectics. It appears that our curriculum managers need to review their individual and collective behaviors with the recognition that centers of human interests are shifting and that a corresponding flexibility is needed in the academic exposures of American students. I have seen a large number of American students on their own in Europe, Africa, and parts of Asia. Almost without exception, they evidence a greater awareness of global conditions than many of their peers who follow the rigid outlines of Sociology 300 or Political Science 450. I speak here of students in general. Students in black colleges are even more restricted in outlook, as is consistent with the deprivation that has characterized their existence.

Even so, I, for one, feel a special obligation to lead the way in helping our curriculum managers overcome this deficit by establishing and maintaining communication at many levels in national and international arenas. This has been important all the while, but more creative behavior from our curriculum managers is increasingly a grave necessity. For I sense a concretizing of forces around the world that could lead to innumerable polarities to the detriment of world harmony. More than all other institutions, the university comes closest to having the expertise to offset such circumstances.

The University: A Model for Creative Management

Creative management would seem to be the cure for many, if not all, of the miseries that plague our existence. The university is uniquely qualified and experienced to produce creative managers who will direct institutional functions to greater humanizing capabilities. To do so, however, universities must become better models of management themselves; they must provide more creative curricular experiences for their end products.

In the closing pages of *The Camerons,* Gillon wins his suit against a noncreative management. The miners get improved work conditions and certain other rights guaranteed them through a union. Gillon is awarded reasonable damages for injuries suffered in the line of duty. The price? Death for Gillon's brother and dissolution of his proud family.

Creative management would be dedicated to avoid such consequences for its constituencies.

Management as a Political Process: Overt versus Covert

ANN SCOTT

DURING A RECENT interview, John Gardner said that the aspect of our national life most challenging to us as individuals is how to make the huge and dehumanizing institutions whose decisions affect our lives open, accessible, accountable, and responsive to our needs.

If *creative* and *management* are not to be two mutually exclusive terms, then the management of higher education—along with that of business, industry, and government—must meet and conquer this challenge. We are already on that battlefield. We may not be agreed upon the tactics.

In this paper I shall argue that institutions of higher education are as political in their internal workings as any other institutions but that their internal politics are generally more covert than overt; I shall argue that it is in the interests of management, faculty, and students to make that internal political process (whatever process is used on a given campus) open and explicit; and, finally, I shall propose an office based on advocacy politics as a possible means for achieving responsiveness.

First, a warning: This is not a scholarly paper in the field of higher education. It is an informal opinion paper; perhaps some would even think it opinionated. Although I was a member of a faculty for some years, I come here more directly from the world of pressure or issue (as distinct from electoral) politics, as the lobbyist and campaign strategist for NOW, the National Organization for Women. My political experience is practical, not theoretical; I have had some interesting on-the-job training doing NOW's grassroots organizing in half the country to pass the Equal Rights Amendment and in the other half to oppose the forced pregnancy amendments pending in Congress. My vocabulary is that of an adversarial politician, and I shall occasionally employ the X-rated terms of my avocation—*constituency, lobbying, self-interest, handles, raising the issue, building a base campaign, wins and losses*—even though these terms and the kind of thinking they represent meet with a good deal of resistance among educators.

Second, as I think about defining *management* plain or fancy, I confront the task of specifying the functions of what one is managing: in this

49

case, of course, the functions of higher education. I intend to avoid that question entirely and to operate on the assumption that academe has a plurality of functions or that the specification of function lies in the eye, if not in the teeth, of the beholder.

Finally, I define *management* broadly as "the system by which decisions are made and implemented and the procedures by which operations are carried on." I do not intend to argue for one management system or model over another. I would not know how. Instead, I am concerned with the nature of the *processes* by which management manages, under whatever system or lack of system, and I speak of the desirability of applying to those systems the criteria of openness, accessibility, accountability, and responsiveness.

MANAGEMENT AS A POLITICAL PROCESS

Managing anything is a political process. No institution can be free from politics whenever individuals or groups vie for decision-making power over the allocation of scarce resources. In the world of academe, scarce resources include such things as academic status, control over budget and personnel and students, the attention and time of the powerful. Getting published can be a political process. Getting tenure is a political process. Getting a larger share of line positions for your department, a new program funded, a course accepted as a prerequisite are all political processes. Deciding the ground rules under which decisions will be made is a political process. Politics in academe, as elsewhere, consists in exercising power, consolidating power, or effecting a change in power relationships—or, more crudely, in working the system to get what you need.

That a political process is not overt and explicit does not mean that it does not exist; it simply means that it is covert, underground, informal, hidden, called by some other name. To say, as I have heard it said, that "politics has no place in the university" or that "our system is collegial, not political," is naïve at best, dishonest at worst.

I have stated that in my experience the political processes of decision making in academe are largely covert. In their recent book, March and Cohen have delightfully identified some academic decision-making models,[1] defining the process itself as a "garbage-can" into which problems and solutions (choice opportunities) are dumped and mixed to see if any of them stick to each other. But the process is covert in that it is informal.

1. James March and Michael D. Cohen, *Leadership and Ambiguity: The American College President* (New York: McGraw-Hill, 1974), chap. 5, passim.

The precise ways in which decisions are arrived at are not definable and predictable.[2]

For example, suppose that a new faculty member wants to get a budget item considered for a new community outreach program. No manual is available to her that describes how to get access to the budget-making process. She has to ask around, and people will probably be more inclined to make snap judgments about the process ("Oh, a new faculty member couldn't get to first base with a new idea"), or to guess ("Well, I suppose you could go to the Office of the Vice-President for ———"), than to give specific directions ("First, consult the comptroller to see if there are any funds available that can be legally used that way, then go to see ———").

I am not arguing that schools should produce *The Intelligent Faculty Rat's Guide through the Institutional Maze to a Just Reward;* writing it down solidifies it, and solidification of process can be a death or certainly a deterrent to useful change. Further, there may be more than one route to the food pellet—such as jumping over the walls of the maze. But I am arguing that management must find some way to allow the faculty member access to the system. She may have a good idea and a considerable professional stake riding on her program. The institution owes it to her—and to itself—not to thwart her with an incomprehensible system or with blank indifference, but to give her a chance to shoot her best shot.

Further—and most important—undefined and unpredictable processes favor the existing power structure, because the chances are that they operate through personal networks and informal tradition: "John Bartlett might know what to do about this. I found him useful in my department . . ." or "What did the last president do about that? Didn't it go to some bylaws committee?"

Those within the various kinds of informal systems often call them "collegial" or "consensual"; those outside of them frequently use the term "the old-boy system." The possible advantages of the collegial, consensual, old-boy system are that it is comfortable, flexible, based on trust or knowledge; it can move fast if it needs to, can work with a minimum of strain, and holds high rewards for those within it. Its disadvantages are that it can be exclusionary, self-protecting, patronizing, nonaccessible, nonaccountable; it can create suspicion of the "ins" on the part of the "outs" and it can allow misconceptions about power roles. (Students and faculty, for

2. This of course does not mean that processes are deliberately or maliciously hidden: though March and Cohen's comparison is odorous, it is not redolent of sulphur and brimstone. This is not the world of Machiavelli.

example, generally attribute more power to the president than he actually wields.[3]) There is nothing wrong with a consensual system if it works—if everyone who has a legitimate stake in its decisions are part of the consensus. My experience is that this generally is not the case.

To return to John Gardner's words: Institutions whose decisions affect our lives should be open (accountable, accessible, responsive). A covert system is none of those things.

CRITERIA FOR RESPONSIVE MANAGEMENT

I shall try to define these four criteria, with the reminder that I am not speaking for or against any particular system but only posing these criteria as useful for testing a system's humanizing quotient.

Openness means that the deliberations that affect the lives of people take place in the full view of those people.

Recent informal inquiries on my part have elicited information that many academic institutions (especially the public ones) are trying to achieve more openness in their decision making by, for example, allowing the public to attend meetings of the board of trustees or by holding open budget hearings. This is certainly desirable.

But openness is a toddler's step rather than a full sprint. What use can someone make of openness once it is there? Do open meetings mean, for example, that a faculty member can get the board of trustees to do away with an antiquated antinepotism policy? No. What it does mean is that faculty members interested in abolishing an antinepotism rule (a constituency) can monitor the board to see how it operates, what its jurisdiction is, who has the power; can learn whether the board lines up in blocs, rubber-stamps the president, is "liberal" or "conservative." But openness alone does not assure accessibility or accountability or responsiveness, though it is necessary if they are to be achieved.

Accessibility means that individuals or constituencies have the capacity to provide genuine input to the decision-making process: that they can, for example, get the antinepotism item included on the board's agenda, present a written report, make the case in person, bring in a panel; that they have time to lobby board members for their votes or, in the case of a rubber-stamp board, time to pressure the president to make the case.

Accessibility does not mean simply having someone sit on the board or the committee. For example, a board can, and usually does these days,

3. March and Cohen, *Leadership and Ambiguity,* pp. 115–18.

include a token woman, but if her opinion is dismissed because she is just the token woman, then women as a constituency have no access. In fact, they are worse off than if there were no woman on the board at all, since simply having her sit there keeps up an appearance of accessibility.

Even on campuses where, as a result of the unrest of the sixties, attempts have been made to ensure (usually) student representation on committees, we often hear complaints such as, "But the students don't show up or fill the seats. They're not interested." I suggest that such a comment points to openness without access. The students fail to attend because they cannot perceive how their self-interest can be served on such committees.

Accountability means that once constituencies know who makes the decisions and how, they can call the decision-makers to account to them for those decisions that affect their lives. They can raise publicly the question of whether the decision-maker is living up to his word or not, is acting in what they perceive to be the best interests of the institution. Of course, beliefs about what constitutes "the best interests" may differ; if so, the issues should be publicly debated.

How decision-makers are called to account is a somewhat dodgy business. For example, imagine a situation in which a new president is being selected. A constituency of faculty that wants antinepotism policies eliminated makes it a point to meet with each of three finalists in the presidential sweepstakes and to get a public statement on how he or she stands on the issue. They publicize these stands in the campus paper and support the candidate with the position most to their liking. The person ultimately chosen by the board publicly favors abolishing the antinepotism rule. Once chosen, however, he never pushes to get the policy change on the agenda. And when agenda time is secured through other channels, he votes against the change.

The interested faculty members must now hold him to account and demand an explanation. Since the president's position as a candidate was publicly stated, they can go to the campus paper, or they can demonstrate, protest to the governor, ask to be heard by the board, file a grievance, or sue. Whatever they do, the president will have to explain why he changed his publicly stated position, on the strength of which people supported his appointment. He may have very good reasons which ultimately convince most people. If he does not, people may lose confidence in his word, the faculty senate may censure him, or he may be forced to resign. Whatever happens, people are entitled to an accounting.

Responsiveness is what follows when the other three criteria have been satisfied: That is, when management becomes open, accessible, and accountable, it will become responsive. People know whom to ask, what to ask, how to ask it, and what it is possible to get. They are not put off by difficulties or by the fear of making waves that may drown them. They have the opportunity to raise the issues and to make their best case; then, if it is possible, management will find a way.

You might say that, at a few institutions, such conditions exist now, and perhaps they do if one knows one's way around and has the political sophistication and staying power to mount a campaign. But the atmosphere on most campuses, especially the big ones, does not favor boat rocking. The institution is just too big and impersonal and complicated—too unknown. One can get hurt. The part-time student is overwhelmed; the graduate student is afraid of getting bad recommendations; the junior faculty member is worried about tenure.

Openness, accessibility, accountability, responsiveness are ideals, adding up to the perfect institution. But human beings—including those who manage institutions—are no more perfect than Adam; Beulah Land is not to be found on any earthly campus, nor will it ever be. Most likely it is not even possible. What is possible and necessary is the constant striving, the constant pressure by those who do not have control of the decision-making power to keep the processes of management open, accountable, accessible, responsive. All political histories could be viewed as such a struggle.

OFFICE OF TECHNICAL ASSISTANCE IN CONSTITUENT LOBBYING—A PROPOSAL

I am now going to propose a model for "working the system," a way for people to get from decision-makers the decisions that answer their needs. My model is an office of Technical Assistance in Constituent Lobbying (TACL) and is based on advocacy politics. There is one caveat, the one under which any advocacy process must function: It is that both sides must agree on the premise that they want the system to work.

A TACL office would serve constituent groups in the institution by helping them to learn how to "work the system." Constituent groups are composed of individuals loosely bound together by self-interest; for example, junior faculty, students living on campus, members of fraternities and sororities, the physics department, bookstore workers, and people interested in karate.

A TACL office differs from an ombudsperson in that the ombudsperson actually represents the interests of the individual to the institutions. A TACL office would act more as community organizer, training a constituent group in how to idenitify what it wants, what can be done, and who can grant it; in how the group can rally allies, develop a lobbying strategy and tactics to approach the decision-makers, find handles to convince them, and decide what to hold out for and what to agree upon.

Let me present a matched pair of scenarios to illustrate what happens to a constituent group without access to expertise in working the system and what happens to one with such access.

Two students taking an English class at a large state university are in their fifties. They feel—and are—somewhat set apart from the younger students and start having lunch together. They agree that there must be many more on campus like themselves. It would be pleasant for these older students to be able to get together, to feel a part of a group with common interests. Perhaps, they speculate, older students could have a small building on the edge of the campus where they could meet, talk, have coffee.

The two write a letter to the campus paper suggesting that such a building be provided. Two weeks later the manager of the student union writes a letter to the paper stating that he would be happy to arrange a meeting room for older students. Our friends set up a Thursday lunch meeting and run a notice in the campus paper; about twenty-five older students show up. As they discuss the idea of the building, it comes out that some of them have commuting problems: It is too expensive, parking space is scarce, some of them find it a hardship to walk from the parking lots in winter. A building of their own where they could also park might work. If only they could get the university to act.

Several students ask for a meeting with the dean of students, whom one of them knows. The dean tells them that the budget committee would have to consider their request but that budget meetings are closed, and he cannot predict how the committee will act. Anyway, the institution is worried this year about funds. The dean of students does not hold out much hope.

Discouraged, the students report at next Thursday's lunch. The end of the semester is coming up and attendance at lunch dribbles off. The following semester no one gets around to scheduling the room, and no one is left to articulate or deal with a genuine problem.

The second scenario takes up after the first day's discussion of shared problems. Someone suggests that the TACL office be invited to talk over with them the idea of the building. Listening carefully to the discussion, the TACL liaison helps them clarify what they really want: a place to hold meetings regularly. She informs them that all funds for buildings are frozen by the state but that a request for a regular permanent lounge and office for older students in the student union might have a chance.

From the discussion of commuting and parking problems emerges the idea of car pools and of priority parking places closer to campus buildings for the car pools. But how can people be put together in pools? Ads? Flyers? Word of mouth? The TACL liaison suggests that they need computer matching and that they could ask the university to develop a program. Off-campus students could register for the car pools in the Older Students' Lounge. Of course, a staff person would be needed, so the expense must be calculated and justified.

First they need to build a constituent base among those who have a self-interest in the issue: the campus police are urging car pools; the Ecology Club should be interested. They design and hand out flyers in the parking lots; they talk to people. As word of a specific program gets out, support grows. They do research to find out how many older students there are on campus, and they put together a budget, which, because of the computer programming ($2,000) and time ($100 per hour), is large enough to be frightening. Their requests now constitute a major budget item. How can it ever be approved?

The TACL liaison suggests they build their arguments on the basis of the university's self-interest. Part-time enrollment is down; the program, if publicized, could pay off in recruiting, as well as demonstrate to the community the university's genuine concern with serving the community's needs. The next step is to make their case publicly and to identify who has the power to grant what they want.

The TACL liaisons help them get a story in the campus paper. The local papers pick it up and turn it into a public issue. A delegation makes an appointment to meet with the president and, at the suggestion of the TACL liaison, with the vice-president for operations, who must present such requests to the budget committee for transmittal to the board of trustees for final approval. Both administrators are interested enough to present the request but point out that, while the budget committee might go along, the board has declared that it will approve no "unnecessary" expenditures this year. The board, then, is the problem. With the TACL liaison, the students in the group attend board meetings, research and analyze every member for possible support or opposition, and go out to get commitments. They see board members formally and informally, count heads, and find they are one vote shy. But just before the board meeting, the TACL office helps them come up with a break; one of their opponents on the board is married to a man, now retired, who is a part-time student. They find out who has a class with him, make contact, present their arguments, and win his support; he, in turn, lobbies his wife. The president gets their proposal put on the board agenda for a panel presentation and debate. Since the vote is to be on the record in an open meeting, they monitor to see whether board members honor their commitments. They win by one vote.

In one way, this story is not unusual. Such organizing goes on every day in local communities. What is unusual is that, here, a university, recognizing its size and complexity make it inhospitable to those whose voices are not easily heard, has instituted its own means to teach those voices how to speak effectively. What is more unusual is that the TACL office achieves a fair amount of accessibility and accountability. The older students have built a good program that serves both their needs and the university's, have done the research that enables them to make a good case, have enjoyed working hard to get the program accepted, and are proud of their accomplishment.

Lone individuals speaking to their needs arc usually crushed or ignored by institutions. But those concerns that affect numbers of people similarly deserve to be, and must be, articulated. This can happen only through organization, and it is the ability to organize constituencies based on shared self-interest that is not encouraged on campuses, and should be. Effective political organizing is a highly technical skill. It does not just happen by instinct. The skill must be made available to potential constituencies if the management of higher education really wants to be responsive to the genuine needs of those it serves.

Finally, I turn again to what John Gardner said: Making the great dehumanizing institutions responsive to our needs is the major challenge in our national life. Why should educational institutions be different? In fact, why should they not, using themselves as laboratories, provide the technical training that equips people to meet the challenge of, and to make their needs known to, federal, state, and local governments, corporations, political parties, media, unions?

In a country capable of Watergate—and of finding a way to remedy it —such training could be the most useful preparation that higher education can offer.

Higher Education in a Low-Growth, High-Inflation Economy

JUANITA M. KREPS

"PLANNING FOR THE STEADY STATE" directs attention to the probable condition of higher education during the last quarter of this century. The no-growth framework is specified because the college-age population will level off in the second half of the 1970s and decline through the two subsequent decades. The proportion of this age group enrolled in institutions of higher education has changed very little thus far in the 1970s, and the annual increase of enrollments has dropped significantly.[1]

Projections of college enrollments from population size are not altogether reliable inasmuch as factors other than the numbers of 18–24-year-olds affect the demand for higher education. Prior to the 1970s, the percentage of youth attending college rose markedly during two decades of high economic growth. Beginning in 1950 with an enrollment rate of only 14 percent, the proportion climbed steadily to 32.1 percent in 1970, dropping slightly to a 1972 rate of 31.0 percent. If the next two decades should see another doubling in the proportion of this age group attending college—so that two-thirds of all youth rather than one-third were in school—higher education would continue to be a growth industry. As Bowen has pointed out, an increase in the enrollment rates of particular groups in the society could have a marked effect on the total demand for higher education.[2]

The prospect of offsetting declining numbers of youth by increasing their

1. Bureau of the Census, *Current Population Reports*, Series P-25, Nos. 311, 483, and 490.
2. Howard Bowen, "Higher Education: A Growth Industry?" mimeographed (April 1974).

58

proportions in college (and the proportions of other age groups as well) has great appeal, not only for the institutions facing severely reduced enrollments, but also for those persons who have long advocated the extension of higher education to all who seek it, irrespective of socioeconomic status. How much offset can actually be achieved is, of course, difficult to predict. But an examination of the forces that will bring an increase or a decrease in the aggregate demand for higher education is entirely in order here, even though the context of this discussion somewhat presumes the direction of change by specifying a concern for steady-state conditions. By special dispensation I am allowed to discuss, not the management of institutions under the expected no-growth set of circumstances, but, rather, the macroeconomic factors that will influence the movement toward or away from steady state in higher education.

Economic Growth and the Demand for Higher Education

Preoccupation with the numbers of persons in the age group from which colleges and universities draw the bulk of their students makes it easy to forget that institutions of higher education are subject to the whims of the marketplace in much the same way as other industries; that these market forces influence not only endowments but also enrollments, particularly in the private institutions; that the influence of economic growth on the demand for higher education, although difficult to disentangle from other factors, needs to be written into planning calculations. Current discussions of whether continued economic growth is possible or desirable are thus fundamental to any appraisal of the steady-state condition hypothesized here. Following a review of the growth/no-growth debate, it is well to draw a distinction between the initial and the subsequent effect of slowed growth on an "industry" such as higher education.

Beyond growth questions, the threat of continued inflation reduces institutional planning to something of a guessing game. Hedges against price increases are less and less reliable as equity markets, responding to inflation and high interest rates, steadily worsen. It is important to address the inflation question in today's discussion, not because there is something new to say, but because expectations are now being shaped by the belief that high rates of price increase lie ahead. Since higher education is an enterprise that must be responsive to expectations, it needs to examine the link between people's perception of their financial future and their willingness to make educational investments in that future.

On the economic growth debate

Few readers have been spared the gloomy model of tomorrow's possible disaster drawn by the Club of Rome's Project on the Predicament of Mankind.[3] Yet a summary reminder sets the scene.

> Within the next century, man may face choices from a four-pronged dilemma—suppression of modern industrial society by a natural resource shortage; decline of world population from changes wrought by pollution; population limitation by food shortage; or population collapse from war, disease, and social stresses caused by physical and psychological crowding. We may now be living in a "golden age" when, in spite of a widely acknowledged feeling of malaise, the quality of life is, on the average, higher than ever before in history and higher now than the future offers.[4]

In the wake of such warnings, the question of future economic growth in the United States becomes more than an academic exercise. Although economists have sharply questioned the assumptions underlying the Doomsday Models,[5] almost none have questioned the probability that there will be a limit to aggregate growth. Discussion turns on the technical question of when the limit will be reached, given the present growth rate, and the social policy question of what should be done to retard the rate of movement toward that limit and thus prevent the ultimate collapse described in the Club of Rome model. True, this nation is slow to invoke policies designed to move it to zero growth in the near future. A number of compelling arguments for continued growth can be cited, not only on behalf of that large portion of the earth where subsistence levels of living call for a continuation of improved technology and increased output, but also as a means for improving the lot of the bottom fifth of this country's income recipients.

These valid arguments in favor of continued high growth notwithstanding, there are unmistakable signs that resource constraints will force some change in the rate and pattern of growth. And although it would be easy to assume the problem away by proposing that the economy could grow without consuming resources too rapidly or destroying the environment by

3. D. H. Meadows et al., *The Limits of Growth* (New York: Universe Books, 1972).

4. Jay Forrester, *World Dynamics* (Cambridge, Mass.: Wright-Allen Press, 1971).

5. See, especially, Robert Solow, "Is the End of the World at Hand?" in *The Economic Growth Controversy*, ed. Andrew Weintraub et al. (New York: International Arts and Sciences Press, 1973), pp. 39–61.

shifting from goods production, with all its waste and pollution, to services
—which presumably use only "clean" human resources—Lester Thurow
reminds us that

> While it's quite true that services don't pollute directly, they generate a lot
> of indirect pollution. . . . Take education. Who is the largest consumer of
> electricity in the Boston area? . . . MIT. Who is the second largest? . . . The
> Affiliated Hospitals of Harvard. It's not at all obvious that we can have lots
> of health care and lots of education and still not have pollution or use of re-
> sources. It may be that when we add the direct and indirect aspects of these
> activities, they are, in fact, great polluters. . . . Until hard information is
> developed on who pollutes, and who doesn't, who uses resources and who
> doesn't, no growth should mean no growth for everyone.[6]

In short, there seems to be no easy way to take the purifying medicine
of zero growth without suffering certain side effects. So the ecologists are
forced to face the trade-offs of increased output versus decreased pollution. What society and the ecologists have to face is the additional set of
constraints imposed by natural resources and the supply of capital which
together specify the rate at which growth *can* take place, once the desired
pace has been determined. Within these boundaries, society will then have
to reconsider the problem of income and work allocation. For when the
rate of growth changes, the total output shifts, and the former division of
that output among different groups of people is no longer necessarily appropriate or even acceptable.

Implications for incomes and educational expenditures

These growth questions have important implications for higher education now and in the future. The zero growth which has already hit academia because of demographic developments has brought with it a set of
problems that may well signify things to come in the rest of the economy.
Any educational goal must now be considered within the context of this
steady state in which educational resources are already underutilized. For
example, productivity improvements that reduce the requirements for educational manpower worsen the faculty demand-supply imbalance. Realistic
appraisal of economies in higher education thus have to take into account
a human resource imbalance and its probable impact on institutional
capacity to reap substantial savings even when productivity improvements
are achieved.

6. Lester Thurow, "Zero Economic Growth and Income Distribution," in Weintraub, *Economic Growth Controversy*, p. 145.

But long-run effects of slowed economic growth on higher education may differ significantly from the effects resulting from the decline in college-age population. The latter shrinks the available pool of students and may or may not be offset later by changes in the proportions of the population served; the former affects the aggregate real income throughout the society and may well influence the distribution of that income as well. In addition, a slowing growth is likely to produce differential rates of change in the various sectors; for example, services may gain relative to goods production in total value of output. Public sector spending will probably gain relative to that in the private sector. Within the services area, higher education's share could grow or diminish.

We have not looked at the future aggregates for higher education under the assumption that economic growth will slow, possibly to zero. Yet the rate of growth will surely set the course of higher education far more dramatically than will changes in age structure (which in turn affect growth and the composition of demand for most goods and services). To pose the central question of what happens to the distribution of income in a no-growth society is to realize that the changes could be quite profound. Lester Thurow argues that income will be distributed less evenly under no-growth conditions (and given women's liberation, that income will be less evenly apportioned under growth as well); the only circumstance in which no-growth produces redistribution in favor of the poor is one in which a substantial negative rate of growth collapses the current structure and allows for drastic social change such as occurred in the depression in the 1930s.[7]

During the Second World War, a high-growth era, the degree of income inequality was reduced by full employment and high wages. Very little redistribution has occurred since that decade. Significant reductions in the number of poor people and in the percentage of the population classified as poor by the commonly used market-basket definition have taken place, nevertheless, because growth in output enabled many low-income families to earn additional income. The question of whether this gradual decrease in the incidence of extreme poverty will continue in the absence of further growth is important to ask in any attempt to estimate the proportion of the population that will have access to higher education.

In addition to the distribution question, it is important to remember that higher education has made vast strides in recent decades (as measured by

7. Ibid., pp. 152–53.

the numbers and proportions of all youth attending college) because the rise in aggregate real income enabled the nation to pay for education without undue sacrifice of other goods and services. Moreover, since the major cost of education was the student's forgone income and since the return to investments in education has been quite high, there have been strong incentives to spend for higher education. Such incentives will probably be lessened by slowed growth; families will not continue to have rising real incomes, and the student's prospective increase in lifetime earnings will not be as great. On the other hand, if slowed growth reduces job opportunities for youth to the point that governments allocate more public funds for education as a means of keeping a better balance between jobs and job-seekers, higher education might well find that it is providing education to a larger proportion of youth than is now being served. If the job market worsens, both education and retirement will be extended, and the trend toward shortening the male's work life will continue.[8]

Stages of economic nongrowth[9]

In view of the possible magnitude of changes in incomes and in expenditures for higher education that could result from slowed economic growth, we in higher education would do well to direct careful study to the forces impeding or spurring economic activity, and to ways the educational needs of the society might be met under income conditions less favorable than have been projected. To view the demand for higher education as a function of the size of the traditional age group obscures our vision of a much more pervasive set of issues. Other distinctions also need to be made. In particular, we should try to identify those aspects of the approaching steady state that are peculiar to the turn-around period, as distinct from the characteristics of the industry once no-growth has become the norm. Further, it is important to differentiate between an industry whose size is stable and the position of any single institution whose size may be growing or declining.

To deal with the stage of growth or decline in an industry, we may resort to the principle of acceleration which holds that investment depends on the rate of change in income. In applying the principle to higher edu-

---

8. Juanita M. Kreps, *Lifetime Allocation of Work and Income* (Durham, N.C.: Duke University Press, 1972).

9. With apologies to W. W. Rostow, whose noted book *The Stages of Economic Growth* (London and New York: Cambridge University Press, 1971) emphasized that each of the stages of development generated forces that led to its demise.

cation, one observes that while the demand for college education was increasing, college and university investment expenditures raced ahead, generating heavy commitments for physical plant and more or less permanent (tenured) human capital. But accelerated investment cannot continue unless demand continues to increase; once demand stabilizes, net investment spending drops to zero. Thus total educational outlays decline even when student enrollments are constant. When the industry has become stabilized, these sharp swings in accelerated (and then decelerated) investments do not occur: long-term investments in faculty are less frequent, expansions in plant capacity are not made, and so on. The pattern of spending in the steady state will therefore differ with the length of time stability has ensued. Many of the financial difficulties confronting universities in the early 1970s were peculiar to that transition stage.

The distinction between a no-growth industry and the position of a single institution within the industry is an obvious one. Yet confusions arise because different firms have different rates of growth and, as a result, steady state arrives on varying schedules. Many institutions continue to be besieged with applicants even while others are closing their doors for lack of students. The differential effect of shifts in total student demand makes it difficult to speak with one voice on the issues before educational institutions. But there is general agreement among educators that competition for students is healthy and that public support to the student should be provided in a form that allows him a wide range of institutional options. As a result, an institution's enrollment will depend primarily on its ability to bid against other institutions for the limited group of students. As in any competitive industry, the number of institutions is likely to decline in a period of reduced demand. Agreements to share the market, although well known to industries with some degree of market control, have not yet been invoked by colleges and universities.

PLANNING FOR INFLATION

To live with inflation is never to catch up. When the rate of price increase is itself rising, the dilemma is doubled, tempting decisions that would not in stable times be entertained by entrepreneurs, not to say educators. In an era so uncertain as to threaten the one known hedge against inflation—investments in equities—earlier rules for the management of endowment incomes no longer apply. Nor is the pattern of adding to the endowment at all predictable. On the budgetary side, only the most heroic attempts to keep pace with costs are successful, and even these successes are contingent on letting staff lose real income or maintenance go unfunded or programs be cut.

As a permanent route to balancing the budget, these shortcuts are obviously unacceptable. Yet the cost escalation is unlikely to abate. The question of how to manage an educational institution in an era of permanent inflationary pressure cannot be answered by studying the behavior of business firms, for in the business sector price is expected to cover all costs plus a return on investment, and prices can be raised to cover cost increase. Unless the consumer is willing to pay the entire costs, the product or service is not available to him. But higher education financing is peculiar in one important respect: the consumer pays only a portion of the costs, the percentage ranging from insignificant to substantial. Thus when costs rise, they must be passed on, not just to the consumer, but to others as well—the taxpayer, the donor, and in part to the student's parents.

Reluctance to transmit cost increases to the student even in a period of rising family incomes reflects a belief that education should be subsidized if not free and that the return to the society justifies the social expenditure. But inflation brings another dimension to the three-way exchange between the university, the student, and other public and private sources of support. Inflation insists that either the second or the third party make much heavier payments for education, although the returns from that education will not be forthcoming for some years, and even then real returns are far less predictable than in stable times. Alternative sources of investment may well appear to offer better rates of return in an inflationary period. For although the time lag between the expenditure and the return is captured by discounting that return, expected rises in the rate of interest tend to divert funds into shorter-term commitments.

In the past three years we have experienced extremely high rates of inflation. Despite repeated reassurances to the contrary, high rates will surely continue and the university's costs will escalate, along with other costs. We in higher education need to adjust our thinking to this source of instability, and this need suggests a certain danger in dwelling long on the steady-state condition. Steady state implies stability, which is not possible in an inflationary period. Inflation distorts existing financial interrelationships and reallocates income and asset ownership; otherwise, it would not be a source of concern.

Ultimately, the financial fate of higher education turns, of course, on the amount expended for that service. Spending for education in an inflationary era would appear to be highly satisfactory inasmuch as one is investing dollars of declining purchasing power in income-producing capital. One possible deterrent to continued investment in education, however (beyond the decreasing numbers of students now being written into the projections), is the shortage of dollars, even cheap dollars, to invest. Capital shortages are not unique to educational endeavor; consider, for example, the plight of the housing industry. Capital is short everywhere, and the shortage is reflected in the rates charged. As the different sectors of the economy bid against one another for capital, universities will need to write high rates of inflation into their long-run budgeting and then persuade the student and the public that even such additional costs constitute a wise investment.

FOREBODING, NO MATTER WHAT

Economists are a gloomy lot. We bear out the proposition that "There is a strain in human thinking that calls for eternal foreboding no matter what."[10] Pessimism should not be allowed to run rampant, however, lest it help to create the problems we fear. For although a look ahead tells one how the forces are shaping up, it cannot predict the outcome of interventions conceived by man when he is quite determined to reshape those forces.

In weighing the probable consequences of slowed or zero growth for incomes, spending patterns, and, in particular, spending for postsecondary education, one needs to apply what he knows of economic forces to predict where the cutbacks will occur if no intervening action is taken. Then he needs to postulate a series of policy decisions and trace the probable impact of each on the outcome. The second step is far more difficult, because it requires the imagination to conceptualize new approaches to financing education and the skill and persuasiveness to launch the necessary programs. In short, although growth and inflation problems make a healthy environment for higher education elusive, they do not make it impossible.

As the economic scene shifts, the kinds of interventions educators offer will change as well. On the higher education street corners, where the trade gossip is exchanged, one now hears some fairly astounding suggestions. The schemes are not clear, but the same terms keep cropping up: lifetime learning, blue-collar sabbaticals, prepayment for college, drawing accounts of time and money. All of these new terms emerge from an

10. Jeb Fowles, "Humanity and Its Gloom-Doom Prophets," *The Futurist,* June 1974, p. 135.

implicit belief that we have reached a stage of economic development that permits a far greater expenditure of time and effort on education than has been available in the past. All reflect attempts to find ways to translate economic capacity into improved educational performance.

The future of higher education turns largely on how accurately we appraise both the constraints and the potentials of today's economy. On the constraint side, it is foolhardy not to recognize the slowed pace of growth and the increased rate of inflation. Aggregate real income is simply not going to rise at its past rate and neither is the size of the college-age population. On the other hand, the potential for expanding the proportion of the total population who share in postsecondary education and for improving the quality of education offered is greater than ever before precisely because past growth rates and relative price stability have brought the economy to an extremely advanced stage. Not to recognize the range of options that lie ahead—to concentrate instead on the decline in traditional markets—is to continue to be "Guided . . . by ideas that are relevant to another world; and as a . . . result do many things that are unnecessary, some that are unwise, and a few that are insane."[11]

11. John Kenneth Galbraith, *The Affluent Society* (Boston: Houghton Mifflin, 1958), p. 3.

Management Talents Required for the Steady State

ELMER JAGOW

THE CHALLENGE ahead for postsecondary education is a new phenomenon for most administrators. Few of them have professional experience that predates World War II and therefore a large majority have spent their careers in managing expansion. The steady state can be a frightening prospect; certainly it will ask for new and different emphases in their work as educators.

Only the oldsters, professionally speaking, recall the veteran bulge of the late 1940s. More will have dealt with the building boom on campuses as both public and private institutions anticipated coping with the predicted millions more college students in the future. Budgets expanded over the years to a degree hardly contemplated in wild dreams; indeed, education during these years became truly "big business." As the portion of tax dollars going to support education increased, so also the political significance rose, so that now the spotlight focuses brightly and often on education, particularly the postsecondary levels. Government, both state and federal, have become partners in the enterprise, albeit not always cooperative partners.

Faculty and other professional staff rosters have expanded greatly as new specialties, new degree programs, and more positions needed occupants. Services to students and others grew especially in the fields of counseling and caring about personal and emotional problems. A large university encompasses almost all the services needed to live after high school throughout life. Doing more things for more people has seemed the route most schools pursued.

Grantsmen, in their successful pursuit of support from heretofore often unknown sources, reigned high in the pyramid of entrepreneurs and frequently outdid scholars as all vied for executive favor. The virtually independent and resourceful faculty member with a pocket full of luscious grants was for a long while the envy of the regulars at the faculty club luncheon table. But even they have returned to earth and now too compete for funds from the sparse discretionary pittances of operating budgets.

The heyday of higher education has come to an abrupt halt and, within the past few years, a new reality has emerged. The switch results from the popular rejection of the notion that education is *the* solution to world societal problems, a view that powered the post-Sputnik boom for colleges and now brings us to the quizzical inquiry and search for proof of the real values, economic especially, of baccalaureate education, not to mention the viability of graduate study fields.

"Steady state" is a relatively new term and stage, and education is suddenly competing in a marketplace that includes welfare, health, social service, and a growing tax burden. Inflation introduces a whole additional set of factors which exacerbate the newly realized reduction in the college-age population. Education *must,* without choice, retool for the steady state ahead by refining some dusty old management talents too long shelved and now somewhat atrophied principally from lack of use and regular application.

Constrained resources for education in the years ahead call for a new management style. The student of management might have observed our habits of the past and characterized management behavior as practicing "solution by addition," or trotting up the presumed steady growth trend as though it were the permanent incline, or as postponing facing up to difficulties because time would solve the problem, so, just wait. So long have administrators dealt with the scarcity syndrome of space and personnel that they do not really know how to cope with a plethora of assorted Ph.D.'s. The expansion psychology so long permitted us to surround ineffectiveness with competence by applying more people and more dollars to solve problems that we have forgotten how to use the eradicator for incompetence.

A New Focus for Administration

What then, can be done? Which talents do we need to exercise and bring back into fuller use? I suggest clarification of missions, the refinement of organizations, the redefinition of responsibilities, and the exercise of improved and prudent control of the entire educational enterprise. We must accelerate the corporate tempo of decision making and perfect our ability to be flexible enough to change the course and emphasis of our programs. In the future, as in the past, but even more *now,* institutional health and, yes, survival will result more from maximizing opportunities as they embryonically become apparent than from carefully avoiding major errors. The challenge ahead is exciting—if it doesn't kill you along the way.

Planning as a way of life, rather than as a particular published plan, will focus on clear objectives that are useful for the society, timed to capture the changing scene, and attainable from where we now are; each element is indeed critical. The entire organization needs to participate actively in this planning, in contrast to an esoteric staff function by specialists or visionary platitudes that are impressive in a glossy brochure but not as part of the fiber of the organization. Nor should the institutional objective be "survival-plus-one" or "plus-two" as a modus operandi for the next twelve or twenty-four months.

Planning must focus on student career objectives in the light of demographic and occupational data now available. To be successful, it cannot bend with the fad or whim of the moment. Nor can it longer indulge the professional preferences of faculty and staff or model the institution for the convenience of the payroll. Our accountability for planning is to the truly best interest of the customers, the students. Even though universities and colleges move slowly, as managers we must develop a more responsive steering mechanism.

Thus we come to the subject of organization and the framework needed to keep a college as a whole well balanced during a period when no growth or even shrinkage takes place. How an institution is manned during periods of size change is a key task for the successful administrator. I have come to conclude that optimum size for a college cannot be expressed in enrollment terms. As change occurs, the important criterion is to keep the balance reasonably level. Most fatalities have occurred where educational institutions have been over-facultied and under-managed, and where members' role definitions have not been clear or understood.

In education, structures are generally "bottom-heavy." Through the years we have placed a premium on numbers, usually at modest salaries with limited ability to manage.

Faculties, anxious to share with everyone "a piece of the action," have developed vast committee networks in which responsibility is fuzzy, progress is slow, matters are discussed to near extinction, innovation has been subjected to the rigor mortis of the status quo. No wonder that the public has become frustrated with educators and institutions. Has everybody lost sight of the difference between information sharing and decision making? Many administrators, following their egalitarian bent, have distributed so much of the authority for decisions that the ship, in some cases, will sink before the power can be reconcentrated. As Dumke has observed, "Attempts have been made throughout history to pin . . . responsibility on groups, committees, cabals, and legislative bodies, but in practically every case that I can think of, the result eventually has been to return to the individual who can be held accountable for operations and progress."[1] I join him in a strong plea for centralizing authority and responsibility in education as we gear up for the future.

POINTERS FOR MANAGERS

Granted the premise for strong responsible leadership, just examined, what talents of control will be useful, obviously in appropriate orchestration, as educational institutions enter further into the steady state? I choose to cite ten.

1. Glenn S. Dumke, *Accountability in Action,* Paper presented at the 13th Annual Meeting of the American Association of State Colleges and Universities, November 1973 (Washington: The Association, December 1973), p. 1.

1. For the college administrator of the future, management skills are a prerequisite. Beyond a sympathy for education and for people young in heart and mind, he must understand what motivates people to respond to incentive. He must be competent in the science and art of managing large organizations, drawing to each task the variety of talents needed. He must understand the difference between a business organization and an educational enterprise, and the difference in the orientation and goals of each. *A presidency is a management job.*

2. Being "computer-literate" (but not necessarily specialist) seems to me to be an indispensable competency for the steady state. Some college administrators have been so sidetracked in one-upping their colleagues in faster and larger hardware that they have lost perspective on what the computer can really provide in meaningful management data for decision making. We have all seen executives show off reams of printouts, yet be unable to explain the significance of the data for the future of the college. Without overreacting and becoming only bottom-line managers, we must avoid getting more information than we need. The manager must learn to become the master of the process lest education indeed be managed by the manager of the computer center, or even the programmers.

3. The able executive is characterized by the ability to discern significant data in perspective. In education, we tend more to worship information for its mass than to cultivate measuring it for critical relationships or ratios to guide and control the organization. Data integrated into a viable, often simple, data system focused on management, as well as fiduciary information, will help the manager use the decision-making activity to keep his desk relatively clear to the extent that the matched walnut grain can be appreciated. Too few educators can recall the color of their desk tops.

4. In the search for alternatives, the search for alternative models of curricular design is an activity in which educators can well afford to engage. One thing is sure: changes will occur, whether they come from external pressures forced by panic circumstances or, more happily, as purposeful pursuit of desirable changes by design. The prospect for *successful* change obviously favors the latter method.

The greatest challenge may come in trying to preserve the values of basic educational tradition which, though sometimes arduous in mastery, have proved worthwhile in the ultimate, and at the same time capturing the sprightly inspiration and fervor of seeing learning in a new, even uncharted way. Maintaining the fragile balance of these divergent or even opposing approaches asks for the sage ability of the seasoned and able college administrator. To be the successful manager of meaningful change on a campus is a prize worthy of great effort.

Coordinating segments of change into an integrated whole provides, then, the bright capstone of the dynamic institution.

5. It is reasonable to ask that the person who aspires to top executive responsibility exhibit the ability to add leverage to personal performance by educating others to join efforts in creating a team of effective steady-state managers to help lead the enterprise. On any campus, this team will include both traditional administrators and key faculty and staff who, see-ing the objectives and mission clearly, will explore and even initiate sug-gestions to improve the institution's management.

Participatory management, if focused sharply on agreed-upon objectives and geared to the plan for success of the college, can bring into the corps of leaders important faculty, trustees, alumni, students, all pulling in the same direction. Any efforts expended in successfully sharing the load as well as the limelight of gratification will pay dividends. Although I cer-tainly advocate strong leadership and favor centralized control, it is critically important that the plan of operation be endorsed, fostered, and participated in by as large a group of the organization as possible.

It is not necessary to draw a distinction between administrators and faculty members, especially if the organization is unified and pulling to-gether. Mutual trust will permit a fuzzy line of demarcation without incur-ring confusion and working at cross-purposes.

6. In many small colleges, we find the supposition that the size of the college assures adequate communications on matters of academic and administrative policy and procedure. Large institutions are aware that special efforts and devices must be employed to get the word around. In these days, and in the future, when economic pressures will impinge espe-cially upon the smaller institutions, candid and full disclosure about the financial facts to faculty and other significant groups is imperative. Sound management advises that faculty and staff respond better to honest adverse news than to suspicious utterances about the good shape the college is in.

After all, the able college administrator finds himself more mobile and marketable these days than the relatively able faculty member in one of the surplus supply specialties. In these times, the college manager ought to be sympathetic and helpful toward the understandably anxious members of the college teaching professions. A manager can be loved for a kind at-titude.

7. When times become difficult and accountability becomes crucial, critics as well as supporters look for the person in charge. When success seems almost inevitable in days of plenty, there is an ample supply of persons to take the bows. But with the opportunity to be counted also must be coupled the chance and clout to correct errors and to chart better paths toward solutions.

Good management criteria augur for clear-cut job delineations so that when success sets in, it can be measured objectively, whether expressed in organizational terms or personal standards of performance. Education is rife with examples of confused job assignments and unquantified narratives of platitudes regarding teaching, learning, or counseling. It seems unusually difficult to detect various levels of success throughout a college or university organization. Because the worker is unsure of what is expected, because the public is miscued about the job to be done, because the donors are distrustful of what seems to be unclear activity, education falls short in the progress it could make. Support follows confidence in an enterprise. An administrator must be sure to pin both the glory and the blame as individually as possible.

8. In any enterprise, the manager has the prime responsibility to keep it alive and afloat. The loyalty involved in this kind of commitment is highly important to others in the organization. All members need to feel convinced that the executive leaders hold a high degree of commitment to the college in order to develop their own full commitment.

Second, a manager ought to plan and be able to help the organization move closer to success as a result of his or her own management effort. Loyalty frowns on sniping, back-biting, and other familiar forms of behavior which tear down. Denigration cannot be tolerated at the top-management level.

A survey of institutions that are moving forward will support the finding that good morale exists throughout the staff. A healthy climate combined with the faith that success is attainable and will be reached is a giant forward step toward the goal.

9. As we near the end of this list, it should be possible to discern a logical sequence of dynamic characteristics that ought to be innate in a well-qualified college manager. Often, in setting things in the organization in order and in eliminating ambiguities wherever possible, the focus is on the one individual who is charged with the responsibility for that portion of the operation. At this point we separate the ones who are willing to act from the larger crowd who are willing only to discuss, refine, refer to

committee, and hope problems will go away. A willingness to act and make decisions even on ticklish or difficult matters is a surprisingly rare characteristic among executives. Without being rash or arbitrary, the leader who will put himself on the line in making decisions is usually greatly admired.

All too often subordinates wholeheartedly wish to achieve but are frustrated and become less effective because a boss cannot or will not make decisions. Education seems to have an ample supply of the latter. We must grant the possibility of an occasional failure in exchange for the prospect that successful decisions will outweigh the failures and that the organization will progress as a result.

The future will, I predict, not allow for a snail's pace and success at the same time. The alternative, then, is clear. It is in favor of action-oriented management.

10. The ability to focus on those organizational areas that hold the key to the future is critical to a college manager. The list, I suppose, is in continual flux for any institution through time, but for the immediate future certain areas can easily be agreed upon, and these are the ones the top administrator should watch closely and try to influence in a constructive direction for his institution:

College enrollments seem now to occupy the attention-getting space of the education press and platform. Recruiting students (hardly "admissions" these days) is the lead topic of professional conversation. The private, tuition-dependent school obviously must devote top-management time and talent to the sales effort. Seeking public appropriations based on enrollment is, of course, equally strategic.

Support by voluntary gifts and grants has changed during the past several years. More public desert areas and fewer oases for education exist now than earlier. Donors must have and keep the faith that a dual system of postsecondary education is critically important to preserve and support. We need to do the job of delineating mission and cultivating support even better than before.

Relations with government agencies, in growing variety, have long been in the domain of managers of public education. In recent years the private colleges and universities have become recipients of various large allocations of public funds, whether as loans and grants to students or the institution, as research grants of various sorts, or as indirect agency monies used at the campuses.

Being comfortable and knowledgeable in the political arena now is on the desired capability listing for most top educator-managers. So much new legislation is proposed and frequently passed which impinges importantly on the educational institution that the manager is required to spend much time and effort in bringing appropriate information and influence to bear on matters before the legislative bodies. After a bill is passed, contact continues ad infinitum as the provisions of the law are implemented.

Hardly anyone can hold a significant position in education without having some governmental relations involved in his job activity.

The *management of student services* has become so important and significant a portion of the administrative budget that it requires careful scrutiny and attention. The steady-state constraints ahead will force greater justification for these and other areas of expanded service to students. Colleges have become service-oriented to an extent that the costs of the added functions have come under sharp criticism.

This area will warrant use of the careful eye of the capable manager.

Financial exigency will push administrators toward a dynamic position in encouraging changes or the study of changes in program design. The traditional degree program is under fire from a variety of sources as being too rigid, too long, not relevant, too conservative for tomorrow's world. In assisting faculties to consider new and better formats for learning, responsible leadership will display a sympathy for and understanding of the components of good education and the learning process. Educational innovation mixed with an appreciation of sound traditional values must be on the agenda of each forward-looking educator-manager in the steady state.

In administrative affairs, the successful college executive must be a competent utilizer of administrative personnel and, as coach and manager, be able to muster a superior result from those who provide support services to the teaching and learning functions of education.

TRUSTEES AND FACULTY

The foregoing discussion has dealt principally with the educator-manager in postsecondary education and viewed management talents required from that point of view. Two other groups will interact in the process, namely, faculty and trustees. A few words with respect to their orientation to steady-state issues may help to maximize their positive effect on the success of their institutions.

First, the faculty as managers of constrained resources will be helped if they can consider change by substitution as they engage in the management of curriculum. The proliferation of courses and the adjustment of teaching loads has a tremendous effect on college costs. To understand these inter-relationships in economic as well as philosophic terms will facilitate greatly the ability to engage in change for improvement.

It seems inevitable that, in the decentralized university or college, the administration will be forced to accept a more central role in which leadership and control gravitate centrally as the stringencies increase. Some experts argue that this development can even be conducive to improved teaching quality.

The anticipated rate of faculty turnover could seriously affect the nimbleness of the college to embrace innovation into fields requiring new academic specialties. Therefore, care ought to be exercised and configurations of the faculty projected to avoid a "locked-in" obligation format that makes the management of change extremely difficult.

Faculties will need to be aware that the most costly resources employed in education are, indeed, themselves.

Second, trustees will serve their roles best by taking a sharp look at their institution's mission and their understanding of an academic enterprise. After engaging a capable president to manage the programs, the board should restrict itself to policy matters and clearly refrain from day-to-day administration. In times of anticipated stress, the relationships within an organization need to be clearly defined so that the institution can weather the rough seas of financial difficulty and academic threat on an even keel or certainly, if rocking, without capsizing.

The centralizing of authority in the president's office will be greatly enhanced if it has the support of the board.

In summary, the management talents required for the steady state may best be described as basic elements that have long served organizations well: planning, organizing, and controlling. During most of the "years of plenty" for higher education, there was enough slack available within the parameters of acceptable progress that it was not paramount, nor popular practice, to streamline the organization or purge the operations of fuzzy or sloppy procedures. In the years ahead, colleges and universities will no longer have the luxury of anything less than running in the spartan but healthy mode of a lean and nimble team. If the managers for the future can give attention to some of the suggestions in this paper, the chances for success will surely be enhanced.

Managing the Faculty Resource in the Steady State

ALBERT H. BOWKER

THE MANAGING OF FACULTY RESOURCES has captured much attention in recent years as higher education has entered the no-growth era. Particularly, some have suggested the desirability or need to impose quotas on the number of tenured faculty, partly to ensure flexibility to undertake new programs and enter new fields, and partly to avoid long-term commitments when enrollments are uncertain. The Carnegie Commission on Higher Education admonished institutions to provide flexibility in the faculty deployment against times when funds for new programs are hard to come by. More recently, Furniss has cited the literature and provided a good statement of the issues and policy alternatives.[1] I need not repeat the argument about tenure and quotas for I am sure it is widely familiar. The crunch comes when the promotion of assistant professors to tenure is blocked by factors other than merit.

Here I shall describe how the faculty resource is managed at the University of California, Berkeley—an example of a large and probably stable institution—and how we believe we have managed to avoid a tenure quota. Although we arrived at our technique by an indirect route (described below), in essence it provides that a sizable portion (8–10 percent) of our budgeted faculty resources are not available for ladder appointments; this pool is used for temporary, part-time, and visiting faculty. Our nontenured faculty consists of two groups: first, assistant professors who are on the lowest rung of the ladder and can expect to make the tenure rung if favorably reviewed, and, second, a group of temporary lecturers, associates, and visitors who are not on probationary status.

THE STEADY STATE AT BERKELEY

On analysis, the basic assumption at Berkeley has been that the number of students and the number of faculty are likely to remain relatively stable. As the first and parent institution in a statewide, nine-campus system, we believe we can count overall on a steady state and not be faced with en-

1. W. Todd Furniss, "Steady-State Staffing: Issues for 1974," *Educational Record*, Spring 1974, pp. 87–95.

rollment cutbacks. However, we must be prepared for changes in enrollment mix.

The enrollment at Berkeley is targeted at approximately 27,000, with 9,000 graduate students and 18,000 undergraduate students. At the graduate level, enrollment seems quite secure. We are inundated with graduate applications in areas of national popularity such as law and architecture, and also have four or five applications for places in most other graduate schools and departments. Most recently there has been some shift toward professional degrees, away from the Ph.D.

At the undergraduate level, the university is limited by state policy to admit as freshmen those who are in the upper 12.5 percent of their high school graduating class in California. We do not have the policy option, open to many other institutions, of lowering admission requirements to achieve a bigger freshman class. On the other hand, we accept transfer students who maintain a *C* average in community colleges. The demand for undergraduate admissions from these two primary sources is far greater than we can accommodate, although over time it may become somewhat less strong than the graduate demand. Nevertheless, we feel comfortable that Berkeley's popularity will continue over the next five to ten years despite the national decline in the college attendance rate.

Another assumption we make at Berkeley is that the number of faculty positions will remain about what it has been for the last few years. As I have suggested, some institutions may not be able to make this assumption. Our student-faculty ratio is targeted at 16.5 to 1, not particularly generous for a campus with one-third graduate students and with some professional schools like engineering and architecture, which characteristically require richer ratios.

This assumption of stability is at the heart of our planning process. One must remember that austerity hit in California at about the same time it hit the Middle West and that we are as far along in austerity as they are. The state is just finishing the eight-year term of a governor who was elected on the platform of holding down the growth of public expenditures. Indeed, for the last several years, the state has had substantial surpluses, some of which have led to tax refunds. There may have been a particularly critical eye cast at the university's budget in the first year or two of the governor's first term, but I think there has been no special attention in recent years. However, as with most state services here, the University of California system has for eight years been budgeted on a very tight rein. Anyway, my impression is that the austerity era may have bottomed out in California. The budget for 1974–75 does contain new faculty positions and some new programs.

ATTAINING FLEXIBILITY WITHIN THE PERSONNEL SYSTEM

Given these assumptions and observations, it has been possible to devise for our campus and, for two academic years, put into practice a system of faculty and promotion policies which provide adequate flexibility, yet which continue the present fairly high tenure ratio.

In the University of California system, the number of faculty positions is a control point in the budget. When I arrived at Berkeley in summer 1971, I found that the faculty budget had just been cut by 110 positions because of austere state support and the need for those positions on growing campuses elsewhere in the system. The 110 positions represented 6 percent of Berkeley's total faculty resources, but, more seriously, it represented almost 40 percent of the resources not permanently committed to regular ladder-faculty members. Although our present planning is based on a fixed number of faculty positions, for the first year the availability of resources not permanently committed to regular ladder faculty made it possible, though not desirable, to absorb the cut within the so-called temporary (nonladder) budget.

Through the 1960s, the Berkeley departments had averaged about 110 new regular rank appointments per year. The budget cut in 1971 left only about 160 uncommitted positions. Moreover, turnover was evidently declining in the new, slower employment market. Obviously, the appointment rate we had enjoyed could not be sustained.

Thus the first major decision I had to make was that the 160 positions still not committed to faculty members on the regular ladder be recaptured, and held centrally in uncommitted status. Since that time they have been used as a reserve cushion under a redesigned regular faculty recruitment program and then allocated flexibly every year to provide nonladder staff where required. Understand, the positions in our temporary budget are used every year for lecturers, visitors, and associates, but allocation of permanent slots (or FTE, as we know them) to the rank of assistant, associate, or full professor is controlled very carefully according to the model I shall describe.

I must emphasize how vitally important to the management of our faculty resource this uncommitted, flexible pool of 160 positions is. Given the peaks and valleys of our faculty flow, there is no way we could manage without it. Remember also that many of our present distinguished faculty arrived at Berkeley *together* in the mid-1950s, at a time of very rapid growth, and they have moved up the professorial ladder together. Our temporary pool will enable us to manage the faculty flow for the next few years until that "bump" or "wave" of professors who arrived together begins to retire.

For my part, I am grateful that the leadership of our academic senate could see the wisdom of this plan and particularly that our various schools and departments did not balk when it became necessary to "recapture" uncommitted positions into a central pool. The creation of this flexible pool was a controversial but necessary action which I would have been obliged to take, even over faculty objection should it have developed. Fortunately, it did not.

Our second major problem was to devise a plan that would maintain the dynamics of Berkeley's regular faculty personnel system—that is, regulate the system so that we would be able continually to bring in new, young ladder-faculty members—but would reallocate resources in accordance with an agreed-upon plan of programmatic development without seriously changing the system and without increasing the resources committed to regular faculty ranks.

Throughout its history, Berkeley's academic personnel program has been governed by a policy under which each new nontenured appointee to the professional ladder ranks is guaranteed continuous, systematic progression up the regular faculty ladder and eventual accession to tenured rank provided only that performance in teaching and scholarship meet, and continue to meet, the standards applicable in the field of competence at Berkeley, as adjudged by professional peers. There has never been a fixed quota for promotion to tenure.

Peer review is, of course, standard academic practice in many institutions, but it is extremely well performed by the Berkeley faculty. The maintenance of the rigor of this review process is absolutely central to our plan if we are to avoid the necessity of a tenure quota. I cannot emphasize this point too strongly.

COMPUTER-ASSISTED DECISIONS

We use a computer-based model which is designed to demonstrate four variables under steady-state conditions: (1) how appointment advancement and separation rates determine the distribution of faculty among the ranks and, particularly, the distribution between tenure and nontenure ranks; (2) how the redistribution can be changed by manipulating these rates; (3) what combinations of rates will have to pertain to achieve prescribed distributions; and (4) the resource implications of selected rates.

The model simulates in complete detail the progression of faculty members through the ranks and steps of the regular ladder personnel system from the point of initial appointment through the highest rank and step attainable. Its components are a data base and a series of transitional probabilities for faculty transactions not in the data base, for example, promotions and resignations from the university. These operate on the data base to project the consequences of different sets of input.

The data base is an extensive accumulation of data, comprising all appointments, advancements, resignations, retirements, and deaths, year by year, at Berkeley since 1962–63 for all individuals on the regular ladder. That is, it records the year-by-year progress of each individual who has held a regular ladder appointment at Berkeley since 1962–63.

The mathematical operation employs a model which converts historical patterns of progression into parameters that can be used in various combinations for projective purposes. The output is in the form of numerical matrices that display the faculty distributions in ranks and steps for any given time period, past, present, or future. The matrices, produced in a historical mode, reveal trends in rates of appointment and advancement that are useful in policy review. Produced in a projective mode, the matrices demonstrate the consequences of alternative policy decisions.

Upon applying our model at Berkeley, we found out some things that turned out to be fortunate. For instance, we found that to attain our objectives with respect to turnover, we did not have to seek any marked reduction in the rate of promotion from nontenure to tenure other than that which has pertained historically. We are targeting promotions to tenure at a per-year average of 12.3 percent of the nontenured population. This is close to the mean for the period 1962–63 through 1971–72, but below the actual record for the closing years of the decade. Our 12.3 percent figure represents a 55 percent probability that a new nontenured appointee will attain tenure. In other words, for whatever the reason, about one out of two don't make it at Berkeley; this rate is solely a function of the rigor of the review process upon which I have earlier commented.

By the same token, we have not been obliged to specify any marked change in the rate of nontenure separations. Our target is 10.4 percent of the nontenured population per year, also close to the mean for the period 1962–63 through 1971–72. This proportion is slightly below the actual record in the late 1960s and allows for the reduced mobility of the profession in the 1970s.

Our model permits us to make 70 new appointments per year. We have decided to adopt a fixed annual rate although this involves some over-commitment of resources against future releases. There is, hence, some marginal cannibalization of our reserves through 1980–81 until the rate of retirements increases—as it will—significantly in the 1980s. The figure of 70 represents a 5 percent turnover, which I find quite satisfactory. To achieve that turnover, however, we found that we must hold down the number of new appointments made directly into tenure ranks. About 35 percent of all new appointments made in the latter half of the 1960s were to tenure ranks. This we have had to force down. Our ceiling is now 20 percent per year (only 14 of our target of 70 recruitments). And as a matter of year-by-year implementation, we are trying to hold below this figure, to the extent that the requirements of our academic and affirmative action program permit.

In the two years we have been following our model, it has proved remarkably reliable as a predictive tool. In both 1972–73 and 1973–74 we have bettered the targets because we thoroughly understand the policy limits it has set for us.

The policies and values I have described are particular to Berkeley's situation in the steady state. Two observations with respect to the policy limits established by our model should, however, be mentioned as being of more general application.

GENERALIZATIONS FROM EXPERIENCE

First, the matter of turnover. Our target is 5 percent per year. In the lingering nostalgia for the 1960s that still persists, this rate has seemed low to some people. Personally, I fell that replacing 50 percent of a faculty every ten years to be about the right rate. But leaving judgment aside, the model makes clear that the range of attainable turnover is quite narrow. Given the distribution of our Berkeley population, for instance, we would be able to exceed 6 percent per year only if we were willing to modify our promotion policies in quite drastic (and probably undesirable) ways. The principle of "selective progression" certainly could not survive; that is, we could not make to the aspiring faculty member—as we now can—the commitment that he will be promoted to tenure on the basis of his merit and that there will be no tenure quotas operative.

Second, as far as the sensitivity of our model to the variables, my observation is that most people concerned about the management of the faculty resource seem to think that it is almost exclusively a matter of appointment policy and, particularly, of policy governing new appointments to tenure. Our model tells us, however, that in fact the turnover rate for a steady-state faculty population is much more sensitive to the applicable promotion rate than to any other parameter. In successive tests we have found that a quite marginal increase in the promotion rate reduces the attainable turnover figure significantly. Thus, managing the faculty resource calls for rather careful regulation of faculty promotions. Again, we at Berkeley are most fortunate, because our faculty-based review procedures are very rigorous.

To conclude then, managing the facutly resource in the steady state— in my experience—means:

1. Establishing a reserve of faculty resources to provide a cushion for the steady-state system and to finance the temporary, nonregular staff that each institution needs in order to retain annual flexibility.
2. Understanding the dynamics of the regular faculty personnel system in all its aspects in order to ensure the development of policies that will achieve an optimum balance between the objectives of institutional personnel policy and those of resource policy.
3. Central direction and monitoring of the process.

There is a further component, an ancillary process of academic review and analysis whose purpose is to determine the priorities in allocating the resources freed by the steady-state personnel scheme. But this is a matter outside the scope of this paper. Suffice it to say that 70 new faculty appointments a year do permit the gradual phasing out of some programs and introduction of some new ones. Some professors may get caught in this process. It is also clear that individual schools and departments may still be highly tenured and lack the ability to bring in young faculty. In some cases, we have had to overallocate to a unit and in some cases have had to live with a relatively unsatisfactory faculty mix.

But we have managed to protect tenure and the integrity of the promotion policy on our campus.

Part Two

ALTERNATIVES FOR FINANCING HIGHER EDUCATION

Current Issues in Fund Raising

DAVID ALEXANDER

RECENTLY, IN AN ANONYMOUS ENVELOPE, I received several carefully cut out coupons of the sort one sees in magazines and receives by direct mail advertising. Because these coupons have a cash redemption value of one-twentieth of one cent, I could only assume that some kindhearted person was generously offering to help in my institution's unending quest for funds, and that here was an innovative method of fund raising for higher education. If church groups and interest groups can do it, why not colleges and universities?

This incident, in a sense, points up the difficulty of considering innovations in fund raising and current issues in institutional finance. I suppose, however, the only things we really have not tried, beyond the illegal and the immoral, are the bake sale and the sale of work, but then there must be illustrations of fund raising by these means in colleges and universities.

The realities are ineluctable: get more money or spend less. Both means will accomplish positive results in the bottom line of institutional financial reports, but spending less, especially in a time of severe inflation, may seriously damage the effectiveness of the institution. The Council for Financial Aid to Education (CFAE) has stated that "In 1972–73, for the first time since 1968–69, the percentage increase in voluntary support was greater than the percentage increase in total expenditures."[1] Perhaps, then, voluntary support of higher education has brought in more money than before. But perhaps, too, efficiencies in management may have diminished the growth rate of expenditures, while inflation has eroded the value of the gifts themselves. One notes with great regret the comment made by the National Commission on the Financing of Postsecondary Education that the newly won balance in postsecondary education budgets seems to have been achieved at the expense of compensation to the staff: "If so, the

1. *Voluntary Support of Education 1972–73* (New York: Council of Financial Aid to Education, 1974), p. 5.

colleges and universities appear to be coming full circle since 1960 when the second Eisenhower report urged that faculty members no longer be asked to subsidize their institutions through low salaries."[2]

This paper will now attempt to examine three current issues in fund raising: fund management and accountability, voluntary support, and governmental support.

FUND MANAGEMENT AS A FUND-RAISING TOOL

"Fund management," used in this sense, refers to the broadest range of the institutional activities that generate funds internally. Revenues such as tuition and fees, which are under the control of the institution, can be raised to produce more income. Shifting budget allocations, reducing and eliminating support to programs, and reorganizing budgets themselves can have the effect of reducing costs. Making auxiliary enterprises self-supporting and "profit" making can generate additional revenues and increase institutional funding.

Another means of raising funds within the institution itself is through revised investment strategy. Since the Ford Foundation's work on educational endowments and its advocacy of total return, which includes ordinary income and capital appreciation, many colleges and universities have adopted the concept. Increases in funds available for operations have been realized, and this strategy seems to be producing desired results. Its theory is correct; its timing is disastrous in the great stock market sell-off. *Fortune Magazine* in its directory of the 500 largest U.S. industrial corporations for 1973 reports that the total return to investors was negative for 385 of the 500 corporations and that the median total return was minus 25.49 percent.[3] Yet, as the Ford Foundation's Advisory Committee said, total return in investments will, in the long run, result in larger annual contributions to operations and greater long-term growth, as well as offer a significant increase in the safety of the endowment.[4] Other investment strategies which have been widely noted, but infrequently followed, are direct investment in industries, limitation of the number of equities in a portfolio, and special high-risk investment opportunities taken by trustees

---

2. *Financing Postsecondary Education in the United States* (Washington: Government Printing Office, December 1973), p. 189. See also *AAUP Bulletin,* June 1974, p. 171.

3. May 1974, p. 230.

4. *Managing Educational Endowments,* A Report by the Advisory Committee on Endowment Management to the Ford Foundation (New York: The Foundation, 1969), p. 45.

or other benefactors under which the college is protected from loss while being offered much greater return than would be possible on lower-risk investments.

One wonders, however, what even the most sophisticated investment strategies can do to raise funds for institutions that have tiny endowment funds. Jellema found that, among the colleges in his 1969 study, the median market value of true endowment was just under $2 million. One-quarter of the reporting institutions had endowments amounting to $1.25 million or less.[5] The figures developed by the Carnegie Commission staff indicate that aggregated institutional income from endowment for 1970–71 was $500 million, or 3.1 percent of total educational income, and in the private sector was $430 million, or 8.6 percent of total private educational funds.[6] It is difficult to see that much leverage for additional aggregate institutional income can be gained from endowments of such a low base. Efforts like the Common Fund are to be applauded for enabling smaller institutions to participate in more sophisticated fund management of both their endowment funds and short-term assets.

Managing funds so as to produce additional income or so as not to spend money cannot be considered fund raising in a normal sense. Yet such management is essential to fund raising in its traditional sense because it is closely linked to the principle of accountability, which is being widely talked about, advocated, and adopted in new ways by American higher education. (Mind you, I do not abjectly confess that American higher education has not been accountable in the past.) This new kind of accountability may well move institutions toward the nationally standardized reporting mechanisms for improved comparability, as the National Commission on the Financing of Postsecondary Education rightly has insisted.

Accountability in its new dress can itself become an effective fund-raising tool. Donors and officials alike enjoy seeing their money used well, and they can justly claim the right to know what happened to their gifts and grants. Money which is used well and appropriately within the interests and restrictions of donor or grantor sets an example that is appealing to the donor and grantor and is likely to be persuasive to others— reason enough to underscore the paramount importance of reporting. We

5. William W. Jellema, *From Red to Black?* (San Francisco: Jossey-Bass, 1973), p. 75.
6. Carnegie Commission on Higher Education, *Higher Education: Who Pays? Who Benefits? Who Should Pay?* (New York: McGraw-Hill, 1973), p. 22.

may be good at proposal writing and public advocacy; we must also be good at reporting the uses to which the funds were put. One need not enlarge on the real reasons for accountability, which are decency, gratitude, and integrity.

FUND RAISING THROUGH PHILANTHROPY

Fund raising is, by definition, the generation of philanthropy. Individuals, groups of individuals, business corporations, religious denominations, and foundations are philanthropists who in 1972–73 contributed an estimated $2.24 billion to higher education, a record high. The CFAE estimates show an increase of 10.9 percent over the amount received in 1971–72.[7] Such cheerful figures may suggest that higher education is doing its job of fund raising well. Surely, however, there is immense room for improvement, two examples of which are alumni giving and deferred giving.

Among alumni, the givers, as a proportion of those solicited, constitute a response so low as to be dismaying. Among the seventy colleges, universities, and professional and specialized schools cited in the American Alumni Council's honor roll of achievement in alumni giving in 1972–73, only eight institutions received responses from more than half of those solicited. The median response for the seventy institutions is one-third of alumni solicited. Twelve institutions received gifts from fewer than one in five whom they solicited.[8] The national average for all institutions was a participation rate of 17.6 percent and an average gift of $68.47.[9] If all students are actually subsidized, as statistics indicate, institutions must become more effective in asking alumni to help their alma maters by repaying the difference between tuition and fee revenues and the cost of education. *A fortiori,* the substantial number of alumni, especially in private institutions, who received direct financial aid ought to feel obliged to repay at least interest on the grants which enabled them to attend. Both public and private institutions would have here a virtually untapped resource for both annual funds and capital gifts. Although alumni giving has increased, why has higher education been unable to reach more alumni? Neither the "I gave at the office" argument ("We gave to my husband's school" or "I went to four different institutions for undergraduate and professional education") nor alumni dissatisfaction with alma mater suffices as a reason

7. CFAE, *Voluntary Support 1972–73,* p. 4.
8. Ibid., pp. 68 ff.
9. Ibid., p. 10. These figures also include the independent schools in the survey.

for such low response levels. Surely every alumni and development office in the country must set about raising the response level by improving relations with alumni, offering them incentives to give, and communicating a greater sense of responsibility to those from whom funds are solicited.

Deferred giving and bequests form another area of individual philanthropy that deserves attention. The CFAE reports that all forms of deferred giving reached new highs, increasing in 1972–73 by 56.7 percent to a total of $80 million, an amount equal to 9 percent of all voluntary support.[10] Bequests remained virtually constant for the two most recent reporting years. Deferred giving remains an unexploited resource for much of American higher education. It is a highly technical field and combines trust law, tax law, and special investment responsibilities. After the 1969 Tax Reform Act and during the subsequent debate about regulations for charitable remainder trusts, which were not published in final form until August 23, 1972, deferred giving had suffered a decline. Levi and Steinbach concluded that some $50 million were lost because after 1967–68 the 7.4 percent deferred-giving proportion of all individual giving did not persist through the three succeeding fiscal periods, and that "these costly injuries to American higher education have not been balanced by demonstrable benefit to the Federal Treasury."[11]

Although deferred giving has now reached a historic high percentage of total individual voluntary support, it has room to grow. Institutions without deferred-giving programs (more than three-quarters of all those reporting to the CFAE) act with understandable hesitancy in trying to establish deferred-giving programs. The well-known disadvantages and difficulties require no elaboration here: the cost-benefit relationship necessitates using current funds to sustain a program whose benefits lie in the future; trained personnel are lacking; annual fund exigencies and staff time for current needs lie in the present; and humility is generated by the awesome complexities of trust and tax laws. Deferred-giving programs, when well administered, bear a positive influence on both direct gifts and gifts by bequest. One major caution about deferred giving: because it is so highly technical, an institution that embarks inexpertly on a program faces serious liabilities to its reputation, and to all of higher education.

Although some colleges and universities may decide not to become sub-

10. Ibid., p. 12.
11. Julian H. Levi and Sheldon Elliot Steinbach, *Patterns of Giving to Higher Education: II, An Analysis of Voluntary Support of American Colleges and Universities, 1970–71* (Washington: American Council on Education, 1973), p. 25.

stantially involved in deferred-giving programs, every institution should recognize that educating the advisory professions—lawyers, trust officers of banks, investment counselors and brokers—in aspects of charitable giving is imperative. It is by no means uniformly true that these professionals are well informed about charitable giving, and institutions can be helpful in this respect. In this enterprise, it is vital to involve trustees, for typically they have friends and business colleagues in the advisory professions. While some see the advisory professions as having a self-interest that conflicts with charitable giving, experience suggests otherwise, and the education of professional financial advisers helps reduce the conflicts and allay the fears.

GOVERNMENTS AS PHILANTHROPISTS

It seems incongruous to think of governmental entities—whether federal, state, or local, whether legislators, administrators, or the voters themselves—as donors to higher education. "Philanthropy" and "donor" are terms rarely applied in dealing with official bodies. Yet educators from both the private and the public sectors may well meet one another frequently in legislative halls and in meeting rooms of the political policy-makers. It is by no means inapposite to label these activities as fund raising and to speak of officials, as well as the public, as benefactors and donors—in short, as philanthropists. Public higher education and private higher education are closer than siblings; they are twins, for private institutions are seeking greater levels of public support, and public institutions are highly successful in attracting private money. The National Commission on Financing estimates that the fifty states and the District of Columbia provided $185 million in measurable direct and indirect aid to private institutions in 1971–72, and the value of tax exemptions, tax credits, and tax incentives (which operate for the benefit of both public and private institutions) must be added to such direct and indirect aid.[12] That year, so the CFAE reports, public universities in their survey received $356 million in voluntary support, and in 1972–73 received $382 million.[13] The University of California system, the University of Michigan, the University of Wisconsin, and like institutions perennially are listed among the twenty colleges and universities reporting the highest totals of voluntary support. On the other side, the Education Commission of the States reported that thirty-nine states make public support available to private

12. *Financing Postsecondary Education*, pp. 88, 94.
13. *Voluntary Support 1972–73*, p. 6.

higher education and that eighteen states provide direct aid to private colleges and universities.[14] Of course, one may also note that some states grant private institutions the authority to issue tax-exempt bonds. Seen in this light, legislative and administrative advocacy by the public and private sectors become forms of fund raising: sauce for goose and gander.

One of the most significant areas of advocacy as related to fund raising is tax reform. The CFAE's paper "Voluntarism, Tax Reform, and Higher Education" lists the several tax reform proposals of 1972, and on January 3, 1973, Representative James Corman of California introduced the Tax Equity Act of 1973, H.R. 1040. Among the "loopholes" cited by Congressman Corman to be closed by H.R. 1040 is the favorable treatment accorded charitable gifts of appreciated property. The Council for Financial Aid to Education, the American Council on Education, and many other organizations and individuals are vigorously defending the existing provisions in the tax laws. They argue that changing these provisions will produce little or no additional tax revenue because taxpayers can escape the new tax treatment by not making gifts. They point out further that "there would almost certainly be a large decrease in the voluntary support of higher education and other public charities."[15]

The discussion of late has taken an even more challenging turn. Professor Surrey's recent *Pathways to Tax Reform* expands his concept of tax expenditures and the tax expenditure budget. He characterizes deductions and tax preferences as government subsidies or "tax expenditures" of $60–$65 billion, which are "buried"[16] in the tax system. Surrey and others have as their overriding concern the simplification of the current tax structure, with the concomitant effects of reducing tax inequities while increasing tax revenues. Professor Surrey powerfully objects to the present "upside-down" system of what he calls "support of private philanthropy": the wealthy benefit and the poor do not. He argues that under the current tax rate structure a gift may cost a donor nothing and may actually increase his net worth.[17]

14. Reported in *Chronicle of Higher Education*, April 1, 1974, p. 7.

15. Council for Financial Aid to Education, "Voluntarism, Tax Reform and Higher Education" (New York: The Council, November 1973), p. 17. The paper also analyzes the declining growth rate of philanthropy from 1965–66 to 1971–72 and estimates the "loss" to higher education at $800 million in gift income in 1971–72—more than $300,000 per institution (p. 28).

16. Stanley S. Surrey, *Pathways to Tax Reform: The Concept of Tax Expenditures* (Cambridge, Mass.: Harvard University Press, 1973), p. ix.

17. Chap. 7 of *Pathways to Tax Reform* must be read *in extenso*, pp. 223 ff. and pp. 371 ff.

The CFAE argues to the contrary that:

> Since voluntarism is an alternative to reliance on government, charitable gifts may be thought of as a voluntary tax which, like the progressive income tax itself, results in a redistribution of income from the rich to the poor. Most charitable giving directly or indirectly benefits the low and middle income segments of society more than the wealthy. Therefore, by stimulating the wealthy to give more, this provision in the tax law results in a beneficial discrimination in favor of the low income taxpayers and those whose incomes are so low they pay no taxes at all.[18]

This argument is valid provided the "voluntary taxes" flow to sectors of social activity which are not in themselves discriminatory and which meet genuine and general public needs. One of the criticisms of voluntarism has been that a donor *as donor* can control his or her funds in a way a taxpayer *as taxpayer* cannot, and that tax-subsidized gifts are inherently unfair and regressive.[19] The tax subsidy that donors enjoy can represent a private modification of the public interest and can conceivably actually operate against the public interest. This dark side of the pluralism argument is important, and higher education in its advocacy of pluralism and tax incentives must make certain that no special interests and parochial concerns divert money from the public interest. The substitution theory of voluntarism (private support replaces direct public subvention) suffers from the danger of being perceived as a means of imposing private will on the public, a privilege denied the poorer segments of society under current tax policy. While Plato's Guardians in the *Republic* might have known better than the rest what was good for all, contemporary American political thought and practice would dispute such a contention. Higher education must be alert in answering these criticisms, and not resile from its proper claim to having made major contributions to the welfare of the state as a whole.

Professor Surrey recognizes the significance of private philanthropy and places it in the category of tax expenditures requiring substitute direct assistance under specially structured programs which have not yet been fully devised. He suggests that colleges and universities should join in the effort to develop alternatives joining "with those who recognize the instability and unfairness of the tax expenditure approach and seek to devise more lasting and productive alternatives."[20] One such alternative, sug-

18. "Voluntarism, Tax Reform, and Higher Education," p. 16, fn. 6.
19. Cf. Surrey, *Pathways to Tax Reform,* p. 373, fn. 62.
20. Ibid., p. 232.

gested by Professor Paul McDaniel and discussed at length by Mr. Surrey, is a system of direct matching grants by which the government would match charitable contributions under a formula.[21] One must raise four kinds of questions about such proposals:

1. Would a replacement program provide as much money as current voluntary support? Would a replacement program provide funds which can be used at the absolute choice of the institution? Now one tends not to raise money for purposes of low priority, and priorities will vary widely from institution to institution. Will the replacement of tax expenditures by direct aid allow institutions to be assured that matching grants from the government may be used for precisely the same purpose as the private donor intended? It must be seen that the relationship with a donor is direct and usually personal, whereas relationships with government are typically diffuse, remote, and, perforce, impersonal. Will the institution lose flexibility for the utilization of the direct grant?[22]

2. Is there any danger to institutional diversity in a direct aid program? Here I mean not so much any attack on freedom of the institution as an imposition of bureaucratic preferences on availability of aid.

3. While one can see how the tax expenditure theory works in general and how charitable deductions benefit donors (a point surely never in contention), how does the "federal assistance" in fact come to the institution? Is it that the donor gives *more* because it costs him *less*? Surrey states that:

> The provisions involve federal assistance in that the contributors are allowed to reduce their tax liabilities through deduction of contributions made to their charitable donees. The amounts involved in the tax liabilities forgone are shifted away from the Federal Government to the charities through the mechanism of the charitable gift and the allowance of that personal gift as a deduction from gross income.[23]

The argument, then, is that there is benefit to the donor and corresponding loss to the government through tax expenditure. The charity, however, actually receives only the amount of the donor's gift, although Surrey claims, for example, "If a person in the first [tax] bracket contributes $86

---

21. Ibid., p. 230 et passim.
22. Professor Surrey notes this point: "For while the assistance to philanthropy comes from the Federal Government, its allocation is privately directed—the Government funds are paid to particular institutions at the direction of private persons. *Moreover, the assistance is blanket, automatic, no-strings attached, open-ended aid*" (ibid., p. 225; emphasis added).
23. Ibid., pp. 224–25.

to a philanthropy, the government contributes $14 to that same philanthropy (he makes a gift of $100 and obtains a deduction worth $14)."[24] Worth $14 to whom? The college which receives the donor's check for $100 gets $100; yet Surrey states that: "Today a donor's gift in effect consists of two checks—his own and the Government's, the latter being the tax reduction brought about by the charitable deduction."[25] Surely, from the institution's standpoint, this is a hyperbole: the tax deduction flows to the donor and not to the charity. Similarly, the treatment of charitable gifts of appreciated property results in the *transfer* of the capital appreciation to the charity. Thus in the ACE illustration discussed by Professor Surrey,[26] the securities which cost the donor $100,000 are worth $500,000 *to the charity*, and this transferral of appreciation accrues to the benefit of the charity entirely apart from tax considerations. Such questions relating to the benefit enjoyed by the charity have to be asked of any direct aid proposal, which, in my judgment, is unlikely to replace the full value of either cash gifts or gifts of appreciated property, to say nothing of deferred gifts.

The encouragement to the donor in the tax treatment of charitable gifts is historical in that it has always been present in federal income tax policy. One readily admits, indeed, that there are incentives to giving in present tax policy, and one argues that the benefits to the government outweigh the costs. Will some new system which replaces the present tax expenditure system with, say, direct matching grants be more cost effective to society? In attempting to answer this question, one must remember that federal support for higher education has not always reached even appropriated amounts, and that the task of advocating large appropriations has proved to be politically difficult, and, finally, that voluntary support is *in addition to* existing direct grants. It is not difficult to doubt that direct grants would fully replace what is called the "tax expenditure." Moreover, the really fundamental issue transcends tax questions. The American concept of voluntarism is based on the notion that the people's money is given for the benefit of the people. As Goheen has pointed out, philanthropy should be considered money "that still belongs to the people, considered severally and in voluntary associations."[27]

Two final observations: philanthropy, whether private or public, must be truly philanthropic. That is, it must be disinterested, unselfish, and

24. Ibid., pp. 226–27.
25. Ibid., p. 231.
26. Ibid., pp. 374–75.
27. Robert F. Goheen, "Is Private Philanthropy 'Government Money'?" *University*, Spring 1974, p. 16.

directed toward the benefit of society. Tax concessions, however important they are, should not obscure the philanthropic motives and should not ignore that donors are alienating their property or allocating funds under their direction for the benefit of a public good. The second observation relates to the first. It is not in the public interest to support moribund, weakened, or directionless enterprises. Although money can be raised in the short run to save an institution, it too will run out, leaving the unimproved institution in distress, back where it was.

Higher education should raise its funds on the basis of a sense of mission and value to society. If too much is cut out and too much is attenuated, the advancement of learning and the transmission of knowledge and values of civilization will not prosper, and higher education will not deserve to be supported by anyone. If one is looking for innovation in fund raising, the most innovative way to proceed might be to talk again about education more than management, about knowledge more than curricula, and about ends more than means.

Financing Private Higher Education: Assessment and Suggestions

PEGGY HEIM

THE PURPOSE of this paper is twofold: first, to discuss some of the broad factors affecting the financing of higher education; second, to analyze factors contributing to the generally deteriorating financial position of private institutions and to explore solutions. Although some views expressed here parallel those of the NCICU Task Force on Financing Higher Education, others either did not come within the purview of Task Force discussions or are strictly the writer's.[1]

---

1. *A National Policy for Private Higher Education: The Report of a Task Force of the National Council of Independent Colleges and Universities* (Washington: Association of American Colleges, 1974). The author served as director of the Task Force.

GROWTH IN ENROLLMENT AND OPERATING FUNDS

In recent years higher education in the United States has been characterized by unusually rapid growth—rapid growth in enrollment and in the funds used to finance expenditures. As table 1 indicates, from 1949 to 1959 enrollment in public and private institutions together increased by 1.1 million, or 48 percent. In the next decade the rate of growth was much higher, 121 percent, or another 4.1 million students. The increase in enrollment in the 1960s exceeded that of the preceding two centuries. Operating funds to finance the expenditures rose even more sharply than enrollments.[2] From 1949 to 1959, funds more than doubled (an increase of $2.1 million) and then quadrupled in the next decade (an increase of $10.8 million). Most of the growth occurred in the latter half of the decade. Almost as much extra money was required to finance the increase in expenditures for one year at the end of the 1960s as to finance

TABLE 1

DEGREE-CREDIT ENROLLMENT AND CURRENT EDUCATIONAL FUNDS
FOR INSTITUTIONS OF HIGHER EDUCATION, 1949–50 TO 1971–72

(In millions)

Year	Degree-Credit Enrollment			Current Educational Funds		
	Total	Public	Private	Total	Public	Private
1949–50	2.3[a]	1.2[a]	1.1[a]	$ 1,567	$ 848	$ 719
1959–60	3.4	2.0	1.4	3,712	2,211	1,501
1961–62	3.9	2.4	1.5	4,655	2,736	1,919
1963–64	4.5	2.0	1.7	5,914	3,520	2,394
1965–66	5.6	3.7	1.9	8,163	5,016	3,148
1967–68	6.2	4.4	2.0	10,907	7,113	3,796
1969–70	7.5	5.4	2.1	14,498	9,933	4,565
1970–71	7.9	5.8	2.1	16,059	11,076	4,983
1971–72	8.2	6.1	2.1	n.a.[b]	n.a.	n.a.

SOURCES: Enrollments from American Council on Education, *A Fact Book on Higher Education*, First Issue, 1974. Current educational funds from Carnegie Commission on Higher Education, *Higher Education: Who Pays? Who Benefits? Who Should Pay?* (New York: McGraw-Hill, 1973), pp. 22–23, 139–61.

NOTE: From institutional accounts were deducted activities having little to do with the educational function: auxiliary enterprises, student aid income, income from related activities (e.g., athletic events and adult nondegree programs), sales of services, and 75 percent of the federal payment for research and service. The Carnegie Commission believed the remaining 25 percent (an admittedly arbitrary figure) was so closely related to the educational process that it would have to be obtained from some other source to provide the same educational service.

a) Comparable degree-credit enrollment data are not readily available for 1949–50; figures here are for 1950–51. All are opening fall enrollments.
b) n.a. = not available.

2. Although expenditure data are preferable to income figures, comparability over time is more important than having the perfect statistic. A long time series is available on the income of institutions but not on expenditures. The two vary primarily by the size of the surplus or deficit. Inasmuch as institutional surpluses and deficits cancel out to some extent for the sector as a whole and approximations meet our needs, we shall use current fund figures as a proxy for outlays.

the growth occurring in higher education for the decade of the 1950s. The escalating demand for funds was persistent and it was shocking.

The public institutions needed four and a half times as much money in 1969 as in 1959; the private institutions, three times as much. The dollar amounts were even more impressive: a growth component of $7.7 billion in the public sector as compared with $3.1 billion in the private sector.[3]

Both sectors turned to their traditional primary sources of revenue. Of the $7.7 billion of new money needed by the public sector over the decade of the 1960s, 66 percent was provided by state and local governments. The private sector called on its clients—the students and their parents—for almost as large a share of its increased revenue needs (61 percent) as the public sector elicited in subsidy from state and local governments.[4]

What are the shock effects of rapid escalation in the requirements for money? I hypothesize that a rapid escalation in the requirements for new funds is likely to be disquieting at best, shattering at worst, and disorganizing in between. I suspect higher education is in the zone between.

Those called upon to provide unusually large amounts of funds experience shock. In the public sector, the primary funders are the state and local governments giving the public subsidy; the secondary funders, the students and parents paying tuitions and fees. The broad financing trends for the public sector are shown in tables 2 and 3. From 1949 to 1959, the increase in state and local government contributions averaged about $100 million a year, and from 1959 to 1969, about $500 million a year. By 1970 the increase in state and local payments to public institutions

TABLE 2

AGGREGATE INCOME ACCOUNTS FOR PUBLIC INSTITUTIONS,
1949–50 TO 1970–71

(In millions*)

Source	1940–50	1959–60	1969–70	1970–71
Tuition and fees	$102	$ 332	$1,640	$ 1,887
State and local governments	524	1,500	6,580	7,494
Adjusted federal	194	274	1,303	1,295
Endowment income	9	20	50	70
Gifts	19	86	360	330
Total educational funds	$848	$2,211	$9,933	$11,076

* May not add to total because of rounding.

3. Although the amounts are small when compared with the gross national product, they are significant when related to the base.

4. Calculated from Carnegie Commission on Higher Education, *Higher Education: Who Pays? Who Benefits? Who Should Pay?* (New York: McGraw-Hill, 1973), pp. 150–51, 160–61.

TABLE 3

SOURCES OF EDUCATIONAL INCOME, PUBLIC INSTITUTIONS,
1949–50 TO 1970–71

Source	Percentage			
	1949–50	1959–60	1969–70	1970–71
Tuition and fees	12	15	17	17
State and local governments	62	68	66	68
Adjusted federal	23	12	13	12
Endowment income	01	01	01	01
Gifts	02	04	04	03
Total educational funds	100	100	100	100

amounted to about $900 million over the preceding year. Although one might argue that these sums should be related to payment capacity—for example, national income—people ordinarily do not think in these terms. It is the absolute dollar amount, not a sophisticated statistic, which imparts the psychological impact. Moreover, people generally fail to adjust the amounts for changes in the value of the dollar except after a considerable time lag.

Federal payments to institutions showed the same general trend as state and local contributions, but, as table 4 indicates, the growth was less pronounced. In the 1950s the increase in federal payments to public and private institutions combined, including the total research and service component, averaged $52 million a year; in the 1960s, $260 million a year. By 1969 federal payments to institutions were three and a half times as high as in 1960. The trend was disquieting.

From the standpoint of federal, state, and local governments the ap-

TABLE 4

AGGREGATE FEDERAL FUNDS TO PUBLIC AND PRIVATE
INSTITUTIONS, 1949–50 TO 1970–71

(In millions)

Academic Year	Federal Funds
1949–50	$ 524
1959–60	1,041
1961–62	1,542
1963–64	2,171
1965–66	2,672
1967–68	3,363
1969–70	3,640
1970–71	3,790

SOURCE: Carnegie Commission, *Who Pays? Who Benefits?* pp. 22–23, 139–61. See note to table 1; funds in this table include the full research and service payment.

petite of colleges and universities for educational and research funds seemed insatiable. Where would it end? The components of government naturally began to take a second look. The federal government economized. First, it scrutinized research; next, it cut back on certain forms of student aid. State governments, though with many exceptions, reviewed more carefully the budget requests submitted by public institutions and sought management techniques to determine appropriate levels of funding. One theme occurs again and again. What funding is reasonable?

ATTEMPTING TOO MUCH?

How did higher education get to its present position in which government is reacting to what it considers excessive educational demands and excessive expenditures? I hypothesize that higher education tried to do too much and that it failed to estimate the financial implications of the total program. The higher education community attempted to raise significantly the percentage of young people enrolled in higher education, both on the graduate and undergraduate levels. At the same time, the college-age cohort was increasing rapidly. From 1960 to 1970 the population cohort age 18–24 increased about 52 percent. The contrast with the previous decade was enormous. In the 1950s the number of college-age people actually declined about 1 percent. We in higher education were gulping a large mouthful and we were unaccustomed to so large an intake.

Those of us in higher education were also forgetting the lesson our mothers taught us: Do not take a large bite before you swallow what you have. Higher education had already started another costly activity: the enthusiastic promotion of research, sponsored and nonsponsored. Indeed, as we climbed into the 1960s we almost made a fetish of research and publication. This activity had various ramifications, most of which were cost enhancing—more complex equipment, more released time, more research assistants, more books and more journals which any self-respecting library had to buy, higher salaries and more perquisites to land the scholars and superscholars, and more effort to get grants. In universities, sponsored research, financed mostly by government, became a large part of the budget. The effort to promote research did not extend just to the proven few— proven few institutions and proven few scholars. Everyone wanted his chance or felt obliged to try. The same applied to institutions. Higher education was convinced that publication and research were the epitome of what is important. Research could be done more expeditiously with graduate students and graduate programs. Four-year colleges added master's programs and five-year institutions added doctoral programs. This trend was especially pronounced in the public sector, but wherever it occurred, the new programs added greatly to cost.

While all this was happening, higher education was implementing another objective which in industry is called "product improvement." Higher education too was busily engaged in improving its product. As in industry, it is not clear to what extent all the improvements were in the best interest of the student, or at least were desired by the student when the cost was considered. We deepened, broadened, and enriched programs (to a large extent at the behest of faculty), promoted individual study, established January Plans and mini-mesters, pushed the idea of work-study, launched semesters here, there, and everywhere, added complex equipment—costly to buy and costly to maintain—expanded computer centers, dotted the campus with terminals, computerized this, that, and everything else so that we then needed still larger computers. These are just a few of the "improvements," mostly in the academic area. In student services, changes were equally extensive. In addition to the usual medical services, colleges expanded psychological counseling and occupational counseling, and added sex-life counseling, gynecological counseling, and drug counseling. Cultural events and guest lectures were piled ever higher on the college calendar. We now enrich students' cultural, intellectual, and political life so much that they can barely find time to read books. Most of these changes cost money.

With these cost-enhancing forces converging at the same time, there is little wonder that the need for funds to finance higher education rose dramatically. There is also little wonder that the various major funders were disquieted by the trend. In both the public and private sectors the pace of financial growth became increasingly difficult to maintain. Institutional financial stress intensified.

DETERIORATION IN THE SITUATION OF PRIVATE INSTITUTIONS

As institutions entered the 1970s, deficits became more common in the private sector and they grew in size.[5] The financial distress was ably documented in the studies by Jenny and Wynn, by Cheit, and by Jellema.[6] In

5. This and the following sections draw on the NCICU Task Force report, *A National Policy for Private Higher Education*. The author and the Task Force are especially indebted to Howard R. Bowen for his suggestions.

6. Hans Jenny and G. Richard Wynn, *The Golden Years* (Wooster, Ohio: College of Wooster, 1970); Earl F. Cheit, *The New Depression in Higher Education* (New York: McGraw-Hill, 1971); William W. Jellema, *The Red and the Black* (Washington: Association of American Colleges, 1971).

response to the deficits, institutions tightened their belts, and many deferred maintenance expenditures. Some raised more money. Deficits declined or disappeared.[7] The new situation was described by Cheit as one of "fragile stability."[8]

The precariousness of the situation has not been communicated clearly by the private sector. Current periodic data are not available, and institutions are reluctant to announce their plight lest they discourage donors and students and demoralize faculty. But much scattered evidence indicates that the situation is deteriorating for hundreds of colleges. Even with stepped-up recruitment, the number of applications and the quality of students are declining, and in some colleges enrollments are falling. The need for student aid is rising more rapidly than tuitions. Endowment income is financing a shrinking portion of expenditures, and colleges are having difficulty raising tuitions without losing students. They are postponing maintenance and replacement, falling behind in wage and salary increases, and cutting other expenditures. As Wynn points out, there is evidence that expenditures per student may, on the average, have declined. In effect, despite higher tuitions, students may be getting fewer resources in real terms than they had previously.[9]

CAUSES OF THE DECLINING HEALTH OF THE PRIVATE SECTOR

While it would be unrealistic to say that none of the schools could benefit from improved administration or from redevelopment of program, the problems confronting private colleges and universities are essentially not of their own making. These institutions continue to serve society well. Their major problems arise from influences beyond their control. The basic problem is that private higher education has been subjected to a radical increase in competition from an active competitor which, because of heavy public subsidies, can sell its product at one-fourth of cost. Although the private sector can survive with a significantly higher price, it cannot survive with a tuition differential that averages more than $1,500 and is growing every year.

As the NCICU Task Force points out, the causes of the distress are (1)

7. William W. Jellema, *From Red to Black?* (San Francisco: Jossey-Bass, 1973).
8. Earl F. Cheit, *The New Depression in Higher Education—Two Years Later* (New York: McGraw-Hill, 1973), pp. 71–72.
9. The Wynn technique of measuring constant dollar outlay per student resembles the adjustment of consumer incomes for changes in the cost of living. Wynn sought to adjust outlays per student for price changes as they relate to the expenditures of private liberal arts colleges. His price index is a significant contribution to financial studies. G. Richard Wynn, *At the Crossroads* (Ann Arbor: University of Michigan, Center for the Study of Higher Education, April 1974).

the ever-widening dollar gap between public and private tuitions, (2) provisions in student aid programs that make them less useful to private than to public institutions, (3) the establishment of new public institutions competitive with well-established private institutions, (4) actual or threatened changes in tax laws affecting philanthropic giving, (5) costs that escalate more rapidly than institutions can increase revenue from endowment income and current gifts, and (6) demographic changes that reduce the rate of growth in the student-age population.[10] Except for the last two factors, the conditions that make questionable the continued existence of many private colleges are the result of public policy.

Here, I shall discuss briefly only the first two points. Those seeking elaboration should refer to the Task Force report.

THE TUITION GAP

The tuition gap may be looked at in two ways: (1) as a ratio between public and private tuitions, or (2) as a dollar difference between the two. In 1927–28, the ratio between all public and private tuitions combined was about three to one. This approximate ratio continued until about 1951–52. Thereafter it rose steadily until, by 1971–72, it was almost five to one, where it has remained.[11]

To the consumer the dollar differential is even more important. He is impressed by absolute magnitudes. Over the seven-year period 1966–67 to 1972–73, the dollar gap between average tuition in all public and in all private institutions increased almost $600 (table 5), or an annual compound rate of about 8 percent.

Barring significant changes in public policy, the differential between

TABLE 5

TUITION AND FEES IN PUBLIC AND PRIVATE INSTITUTIONS,
1956–57 TO 1972–73

Year	Private Institutions	Public Institutions	Dollar Gap	Ratio
1956–57	$ 610	$175	$ 435	3.5
1961–62	906	218	688	5.2
1966–67	1,233	275	958	4.5
1971–72	1,781	367	1,414	4.9
1972–73 (est.)	1,919	392	1,527	4.9

SOURCES: U.S. Office of Education, *Projections of Educational Statistics* (Washington: Government Printing Office, 1967 ed., p. 94; 1968 ed., pp. 98–99; 1970 ed., pp. 109–10; 1971 ed., pp. 106–7.

10. NCICU Task Force, *A National Policy for Private Higher Education*, chap. 3.
11. From materials supplied to the Task Force by Howard R. Bowen.

public and private tuitions threatens to grow worse rather than better. Because of the nature of the industry and the things it buys, cost increases in higher education exceed those for the national economy. This factor combined with present two-digit general inflation will quite likely escalate the differential. Unless higher education opts to pursue the backward wage and salary policies of the late 1940s and the 1950s, cost increases over the next three years (1974–75 to 1976–77) are not likely to be less than 30 percent and may run much higher than that. With average private tuitions of about $1,900 in 1973–74 and cost per student above that figure, private institutions will probably need, on the average, an additional tuition increase of at least $500 over the three years. (An average increase of $600 would not be surprising.) Because of public subsidies, the increase in public tuitions will not be nearly as great as that of private tuitions. The dollar differential will be likely to grow more rapidly than in the past. The fact that both public and private institutions will have to raise room and board charges will probably affect private institutions more severely than public institutions. The total price of attending a private institution will be forced ever further beyond the level which middle-class families can afford.

The implications of such large potential cost increases to the private sector are clear. Institutions can hold down cost increases temporarily by forgoing wage and salary increases, but this action eventually leads to demoralization and affects staff quality. They can hold down other expenditures, but program and plant will begin to show obvious signs of deterioration as new frugality is heaped on top of past economies.[12] As program deteriorates and the niceties of life disappear, students will be less attracted to private colleges. The slippage in their clientele will be intensified by the rapidly growing public-private tuition differential. The stage is set for the withering away, not as Karl Marx said, of the state, but of the private college.

STUDENT AID PROGRAMS

Student aid measures have favored the public institutions. Because of heavily subsidized public tuitions, limited grants to cover student costs (such as the $1,400 Basic Educational Opportunity Grants program) generally go further in public than in private institutions. The figures in table 6 illustrate the amount of unmet need with different levels of income and proposed parental contributions for 1974–75 BEOG's. Two points are

12. Or the colleges can live off endowment. This merely postpones the fateful day.

TABLE 6

UNMET STUDENT NEED UNDER THE BEOG
FORMULA FOR SELECTED ADJUSTED FAMILY
INCOMES AND PARENTAL NET CAPITAL ASSETS EQUAL TO INCOME

(With maximum BEOG of $1,400)

Adjusted Family Income	Average Public Four-Year College	Average Private Four-Year College	Difference, Private over Public
$ 9,000	$1,200	$2,639	$1,439
12,000	733	2,372	1,639
15,000	(139)[a]	1,500	1,639
18,000	(1,132)[a]	507	1,639

NOTE: Illustrations assume four dependents, proposed family contribution schedules for 1974–75, and average total cost to the student in four-year colleges (as reported by the College Scholarship Service of the College Entrance Examination Board, *Student Expenses at Postsecondary Institutions 1974–75*) for 1974–75 of $2,400 in public institutions and $4,039 in private institutions. A grant is available for only the $9,000 income level.

a) Figures in parentheses indicate the amount by which the expected parental contribution exceeds cost to the student, and represents a surplus which the family would have for other uses.

apparent. (1) Unless there is supplementary assistance, the average private institution must spend considerably more on student aid to enroll low-income students than middle-income students. For example, the student with $15,000 of family income has $1,500 of unmet need, whereas the student with $9,000 of income needs $1,100 more than that. (2) Even middle-income students—the customary market of many private institutions—require considerable amounts of assistance. For example, the contribution schedule of BEOG's has not been revised to reflect inflation. Even with these obsolete schedules, students from families with incomes of $15,000–$18,000 may have $1,500–$500 of unmet need if they want to attend a private four-year college with costs to the student equal to the average.[13] In view of the pressures of inflation on the family and on the institutions, adequate governmental assistance will become even more critical if students of low- and middle-income groups are to retain choice of institution and the private sector is to be preserved.

SOME SOLUTIONS TO THE PROBLEM

Basically the problem is one of closing the public-private tuition gap. The differential might be reduced by raising public tuitions. This technique is not recommended. It would tend to reduce access to higher education. Or the gap might be closed by providing funds to help defray tuitions in private institutions.

13. In 1974–75, the total cost to the student attending the average private four-year college is $4,039. There are many colleges where costs are significantly higher than that.

Funds for tuition reduction might be paid to the institution or they might be paid to the student and credited against his tuition. There is much to be said for channeling aid directly to the student, even though the institution serves as the delivery agent to facilitate administration. The market directs the payments.

Tuition offset payments might be paid to all students without regard to need, or they might be based on a means test. There are many disadvantages to means tests, not the least of which is their administrative clumsiness. Moreover, if means tests are not applied to determine the eligibility of students for the tuition subsidy in public institutions, equity would indicate they could not be required for students to qualify for tuition offsets in the private sector.

The NCICU Task Force recognizes, however, that there are various reasons a means test might be preferred. For one thing it would help minimize cost to the government.

The public-private tuition differential might also be reduced on a selective basis. One way of doing this is to modify the student aid programs to provide supplementary cost-of-education grants to students in private colleges. The grants would help offset the subsidization of tuitions in public institutions. But if grants are provided, some formula is needed. The formula might be one-half of the subsidy of instructional costs in public institutions. This formula gives government control over the subsidy, and it relates the subsidy to the public sector. The subsidy is determined by costs in the public institutions and by the level of public tuitions.

These are only some of the proposed solutions. Other Task Force recommendations can be found in the document itself. But this much is clear. The private sector was already in a precarious state before the recent inflation. The inflation can serve only to exacerbate its plight by widening further the public-private tuition gap and by placing private institutions even further beyond the means of the lower- and middle income groups. The time is rapidly approaching when our society must decide whether it wants to preserve the private sector as a major force in our higher education system and take steps to assure this outcome.

Higher Education Finance: Health and Distress

HANS H. JENNY

WHEN ONE PREPARES a manuscript on any phase of finance and knows it is to be discussed several months later, he experiences a certain apprehension. Either the text will be somewhat dated or the essay will be so broadly couched that it would suit almost any occasion. Further, any brief discussion of a subject so vast as higher education finance must leave many facets unmentioned. When I considered which aspects I might best select, my choice fell to a subject that I had pursued when I was associated with the research staff of the National Commission on the Financing of Postsecondary Education during the summer of 1973.

The topic can be phrased as follows: *How would it be determined whether higher education in general, specific segments of the higher education enterprise, or specific higher educational institutions are in sound financial health or find themselves in a state of financial distress?*

This question is not likely to lose any of its interest soon.

FINANCIAL HEALTH, EDUCATIONAL HEALTH, AND ACCOUNTABILITY

The financial health of educational institutions is important because without it there cannot be educational health. It is appropriate also to suggest that educational health is more important than financial health. If these two propositions are seen in proper perspective, no confusion need arise. But what is the proper perspective? I do not suggest that what follows *is* the proper perspective, but I trust that my thoughts will point in the right direction.

There has been some puzzlement that the National Commission's report[1]

I am grateful to several people and organizations without whose help this paper could not have come about. G. Richard Wynn permitted me to use the materials on inflation, taken from his "Inflation Indicators in Liberal Arts Colleges" (Ph.D. diss., University of Michigan, 1974). A grant to the College of Wooster from the Ford Foundation helped underwrite Mr. Wynn's work as well as my own research into higher education productivity and inflation. The Commission on Philanthropy and Public Needs allowed me to use data prepared for a study on the effects of voluntary support in higher education. Finally, I want to thank Earl F. Cheit, Ben Lawrence, and George Weathersby, whose friendship and support made this work possible.

1. National Commission on the Financing of Postsecondary Education, *Financing Postsecondary Education in the United States* (Washington: Government Printing Office, 1973).

did not flatly state what most people in the enterprise know: higher education is in a state of crisis. The Commission did not reach such a conclusion simply because it could not make a convincing case. The evidence may have been out there in college and university land, but it either remained intractable or had to be taken on faith.

There exists today only a vague consensus on how to determine whether an educational institution is financially sound, particularly when the caveat is added *that it be simultaneously sound in its educational endeavors*. Using this broader context, I shall try to set forth the essential elements of sound financial health:

1. Financial resources must be adequate to accomplish the institution's articulated missions and must include both funds for current operations and sufficient capital to provide functional plant, appropriate equipment, and up-to-date teaching and learning technology.

2. The expression "articulated mission" requires that the institution define who its clients shall be and what services it will render.

3. Once it is decided that scarce monetary resources (as well as scarce natural ones) are to be allocated in order to support and render these services, the question to be answered is how well the services are being performed.

Although the National Commission's report might have been more blunt, behind its deliberations on institutional financial health and distress lay the more fundamental question of whether the huge expenditures really accomplish something of value. And, of course, the question then arises of who shall determine what is of value.

Recently there has been talk about cost-effectiveness. Almost everyone in higher education tends to be touchy when the word "efficiency" enters the conversation. I have always been convinced that the defensive reaction stems largely from an inability to articulate what higher education is up to. Academics and managers of academe are likely to be past masters at verbalizing. But are they equally adept at identifying specific educational outcomes to which they then assign their meager resources for optimum effect? Frank Newman stated the case well, and Warren Martin issued a warning when he referred to "The Ethical Crisis in Education."[2]

Granted, much in higher education is not measurable. But merely be-

2. *The Second Newman Report: National Policy and Higher Education,* Report of a Special Task Force to the Secretary of Health, Education, and Welfare (Cambridge, Mass.: MIT Press, 1973), see especially chap. 1; Martin in *Change,* June 1974, pp. 28–33.

cause much is not measurable, we in higher education are not thereby warranted in behaving as if it were not there. On the other hand, much more is definable and measurable than we have been willing to acknowledge: studies of institutional goals and inventory analyses as well as institutional research of a nonfinancial character testify to the many and exciting possibilities. Still, little official consensus has emerged, and until it does, public confidence in our credibility will continue to suffer or may even decline further.

Closely linked to financial health is the issue of accountability. Usually accountability is viewed in a narrow financial and quantitative framework but gives rise to a variety of worries, among them anxiety about control. Yet, why should we have concerns about accountability? We are engaged in professional activities; we are spending other people's money; and we protest that our activities are essential and good.

In the best sense, then, accountability simply means to " 'fess up." Let me explain. It has seemed to me that the financial case for higher education would be bettered considerably if we could find improved ways to document what is happening to students and other users of our services. The need is not always for new devices; rather, the need is to reach some agreement on how to document educational outcomes. One possibility, though difficult, is the concept of "value added," for which contract learning and functional testing offer useful models. *The essence of accountability lies in documenting how well specific services are being performed.*

Accountability is but incidentally a financial matter. Money and other resources such as faculty, laboratories, and complex campuses and administrative structures are means to an end. But in the absence of accountability for quality and outcomes, financial accountability will assume dominance. The broader concept of financial health, whether applied to the higher education enterprise or to educational institutions, urges us to look behind money into the real world of educational activity. It is this world that we must present and make real to the public.

From the start, all higher educational institutions are creatures of the state, and what the public grants, it can take away. As institutions respond to and affect a great variety of publics, institutional missions and program outcomes elicit differing responses, depending on who looks at them. In this way, all of higher education, whether public or private, sooner or later becomes the public's business. Beyond this, educational missions are being increasingly determined, though in varying degree, by public policy, not all of which has to do with education.

EDUCATIONAL OBJECTIVES AS A RESPONSE TO NATIONAL POLICY

When the matter of serious financial distress came before the National Commission, the membership established early in the discussion that individual institutional finance trouble was not the issue. Further, it concluded, national policy about higher education should not and could not be formulated solely as a response to disarray in institutional management or finances. The Commission insisted that financial weakness matters only if broadly accepted public policy objectives are not being achieved. But the same constraint could apply to institutional policy. The Commission was referring primarily to national policy, but its philosophy is valid for state and local governments as well. National policy may serve to guide funders generally, especially foundations, corporate donors, and, indirectly, even students.

Thus it is essential to determine which publics and which public policies are at issue in a given situation or at a given moment. The next step is to assess what specific objectives—public or other—are in question and how well or badly they are being achieved. Finally, it becomes essential to establish whether the reason for nonachievement is lack of money or whether there are other causes. Higher education is thus given a formidable challenge, particularly when we consider how backward it is in the art of evaluating its own performance.

Although the National Commission did not establish a framework of analysis, it did suggest how the several elements—finances, program and activity data, and information concerning the student and other clients of higher educational institutions—might be fitted together.

APPROACH TO THE EVALUATION OF FINANCIAL HEALTH

It may be useful to consider that colleges and universities, like the general economy, are going through different stages in their financial lives. At a given moment, individual institutions will find themselves at different stages of financial health, whereas, on other occasions, higher education as a whole or important segments of the industry or large numbers of institutions of all types may experience similar financial circumstances. The purpose of the analysis proposed by the National Commission[3] is to determine when and how institutions are moving from one stage to another and, on aggregate levels, when higher education in general, important seg-

---

3. National Commission, *Financing Postsecondary Education*, pp. 218 ff.

ments of it, or groups of institutions are moving from one stage of financial health to another.

The analysis would start with the distinction among four stages of financial health: First, the condition "sound financial health" is to be understood in the broad sense defined earlier. Second, there is the stage of "deteriorating" financial health which, if it continues, may lead to "financial distress," the third stage. This stage may lead to institutional "disappearance" (or bankruptcy) or to significant "program transformation." If the latter is successful there may be a "turnaround," the fourth stage, leading in turn to improving and, it is hoped, eventually sound financial health.

The higher education enterprise, major sectors of it, or groups of comparable or different institutions may be going through such stages in a type of financial evolution or cycle. Today there is nothing to help education planners and managers—and especially members and staffs of legislatures concerned with educational matters—make an intelligent judgment along such lines. I believe that information can be gathered and that a consensus can be worked out for such an analysis. The American Council on Education and the National Association of College and University Business Officers might become the instruments in such an effort, particularly if the Council's Office of Administrative Affairs and Educational Statistics, under Dr. Lyle H. Lanier's able direction, can help develop the necessary theoretical framework.

The variables that jointly describe the behavior of higher educational institutions are one building block for such a theory, and elsewhere I have illustrated what might be included.[4] The list of potential indicators of evolving financial health in the broad sense defined is not particularly unusual; what may be novel are the types of variables that must be studied simultaneously. For instance, as stated in the National Commission report, at least three types of indicators (or variables) must be monitored: (1) indicators describing the nature, objectives, and scope of those for whom educational services are performed; foremost among those served are students, but also included are those who purchase other higher education services, such as research and public services; (2) indicators describing the financial condition proper, including current operational and balance sheet data; and (3) indicators describing changes in budgets and programs of educational institutions.

Until now, most studies of higher education financial health have con-

---

4. Hans H. Jenny, "Indicators of Financial Distress in Higher Education" (Paper delivered at the Annual Meeting of the Pennsylvania Association of Higher Education, Harrisburg, Spring 1974).

centrated on elements in current financial operations and, additionally, some attention has been given to indebtedness and to changing student profiles. Yet, by and large, still lacking are comprehensive and simultaneous analyses of key customer, program, and finance data.

Of course, a mammoth data-gathering effort has been carried on. Both the Higher Education General Information Survey (HEGIS) and the American Council's own extensive statistical work make available to researchers, institutions, and trade organizations large amounts of information. Until this year, however, the HEGIS material in particular has not become available until three or four years after the fact. Furthermore, the data being collected regularly are not based on an accepted formal theory. As a result, much of what is available is not being used, and perhaps as much that might be useful is not being collected.

One weakness in current statistical efforts is the absence of carefully defined information concerning the evolving net asset structure of higher education finance, including a detailed overview of the capital debt, of the maturity structure of the debt, and of the institutional interest cost burden. Also, although HEGIS collects annual endowment statistics, no systematic effort is made to assemble periodic information on comparative endowment investment performance. And the almost total absence of national reporting on meaningful educational budget, program, and outcomes data (which then should be carefully correlated with the financial and client profiles) is perhaps the weakest link in the present statistical efforts. As Dr. Frank Newman's task force has pointed out, the key to sound higher education statistics is not merely in assembling numbers, but in doing it within an agreed-upon framework of theory.[5]

The Measurement of Inflation in Higher Education

An illustration of how theory and statistics are related is provided by how inflation is measured. The National Commission, in its recommendations on the analysis of financial health in higher education, suggested that a series of price deflators be developed for higher educational institutions and for their clients.[6] Specifically, it recommended three types of price indices: one describing the "cost of living" of colleges and universities, a second measuring the changing purchasing power of dollars for plant construction and equipment purchases, and a third describing the changing cost to students of attending higher educational institutions.

---

5. "Data and Decision Making," *Chronicle of Higher Education,* March 12, 1973, p. 25.
6. National Commission, *Financing Postsecondary Education,* pp. 222–23.

Recently, several efforts have been under way in price index construction for higher education. I shall present some illustrations from one endeavor. Most of the findings are based on a recent University of Michigan dissertation by G. Richard Wynn.[7]

The Wynn index series, as now defined, pertains to four-year liberal arts colleges, but it can be modified and readily adapted to reflect the market baskets of other educational institutions. As described in careful detail in the dissertation, the Wynn index derives from studies of price changes extending over more than forty major expenditure groupings conventionally found in college and university financial statements. The initial price data were assembled from a pilot institution. The specific prices that institution paid or expenditures it incurred during a ten-year period (1964–73) were checked against established time series for commodities, services, and wages as published by federal agencies. Each set of price deflations developed was then connected with the appropriate corresponding expenditures of some twenty colleges.

The evolution of inflation and of the changing institutional purchasing power for the pilot college as well as for the twenty-college sample that Mr. Wynn assembled make possible some simple, not always surprising, but always noteworthy generalizations:

1. Between 1964 and 1973, inflation in higher education was steeper than in the economy as a whole.

2. Inflation in the colleges was greater chiefly because, at first, wages in higher education were catching up to those elsewhere in the economy and, later, because competition for personnnel brought about rates that exceeded those in other wage sectors. The wage and salary component represents, on average, 55–60 percent of total expenditures.

3. If student aid is included as a cost to institutions (income forgone), the rate of inflation in higher education increases still further.

4. Deflated price series *without the wage and student aid components* show that, on balance, *price* inflation in higher education did not differ significantly from that suffered elsewhere in the economy; if anything, at times price inflation in colleges seems to have been slightly less than that expressed by the Consumers Price Index (CPI). But it must be remembered that the CPI includes wages for services such as medical care and pertains to an entirely different market basket than that encountered by colleges and universities.

7. See opening footnote.

5. The price deflators can be used in analyzing institutional financial health. When specific deflators are applied to appropriate expenditures in the sample institutions, it becomes clear how differently each institution may have been affected. Some colleges show significant financial strength in the broad sense in which the term is used here whereas others give evidence of, at times, drastic program retrenchment. Thus, the deflators become important indicators of what institutions are doing in *real* rather than monetary terms.

6. Often the deflated series reveal surprises to institutions and funders alike. Overall, real expenditures per student have been static or declining for several years. Although some program redundancies must have existed at the height of higher education's recent prosperity, the deflated time series indicate the urgent need to ask *how much further real per student expenditures should be allowed to drop.*

7. When the deflated data are applied to income and expenditures for large groups of institutions on a state or national basis, they can reveal, by comparison, whether higher education programs are developing in a balanced or an uneven fashion.

8. An interesting statistic pertains to gifts for operations, which play an important role in both public and private institutions but especially in the latter. The aggregate purchasing power of all gifts reported in 1973, a year of record giving, is not much greater now than that of the much smaller sum reported in 1964. As for plant gifts, the total amount received by colleges and universities in 1973 buys much less than did a smaller amount in 1964. Gifts, then, overall represent not only a smaller percentage of total income, but also what there is, all of it, buys less educational activity now than it did ten years ago.

These, then, are a few of the many conclusions that derive from the application of the Wynn index to higher educational income and expenditure data. There will be disagreement on whether Wynn used the proper methodology, and some will question whether his computations are accurate. One important issue will be whether his flexible market basket is a better indicator of higher education inflation than could be obtained with a fixed market basket. There are various schools of thought in the realm of price or cost index construction.

In the final analysis, I believe the specific methodology will be less important than getting on with the task of establishing an official, generally accepted measure of higher education inflation.

I have been able to monitor Mr. Wynn's efforts and believe that his methodology and results are eminently satisfactory. At the same time I see no disadvantage in pursuing other avenues provided we desert the drawing board in favor of an official higher education index of institutional costs.

Even a dirty (or imperfect) index can quickly became a useful instrument in guiding educational policy. For instance, when *real* economic activity does not grow for two consecutive calendar quarters, or when the growth rate turns negative, economists term the result a recession. When the situation persists long enough, they call it contraction and, eventually, a depression.

In higher education, many real expenditure trends prove to have turned negative. This condition has existed for three or four years overall, and in many institutions it has been a fact of life even longer. If we had had a set of credible price deflators for higher education in 1973, the National Commission could have come to a more fiery conclusion about whether financial distress existed in the higher education enterprise generally or somewhere within it. Today the news that such distress exists surprises no one. Nor would higher education be an exception. Today two-digit inflation is blanketing the economy, and we are all in a recession.

COOPERATIVE EFFORT

The preceding findings are, of course, tentative, for there does not now exist a generally applicable and accepted cost deflator for higher education. Nor would such a deflator answer all the questions raised earlier in this paper. The index for higher education is, nevertheless, one relatively simple way to get behind the money veil to see what is happening—at least in broad terms—to real-life educational activities and programs. It shows whether they are expanding, standing still, or shrinking by means of documentation that is essential and can be understood by funders. And it represents a step in the direction suggested by the National Commission.

Many institutions will probably be asked relatively soon whether they will participate in an effort to gather institutional data for cost index construction as well as in a more complex analysis of performance and financial viability such as that sketched above. Within recent months, interest in such indicators as those noted has increased considerably. I hope that, when the time comes, the institutions will cooperate not only by providing the data requested but also by subjecting themselves to the needed analysis.

Beyond organized public efforts in this direction, ample institutional expertise is available to develop appropriate theory and data for internal use. There is no need to wait for others. Useful results can be achieved within and on behalf of individual colleges and universities.

To those in the private sector of higher education, let me suggest that the responsibility to come up with useful policy-directed intelligence is ours before it is that of the federal government. Repeatedly it has been said that institutions cannot afford to spend the sums of money required to gear up a functional, policy-oriented statistical effort. Since higher education is, among other things, in the research and development business, is it not high time that we annually allocate an adequate sum of internal resources for public statistical and analytical purposes? If it is sound practice for industrial and commercial firms to spend vast sums annually to improve their performance, why should it not be equally sound for colleges and universities to report each year how much they are spending for research and development designed to improve their performance? The task is admittedly more complex than industrial and commercial R&D, but this should make it all the more challenging and worthwhile.

The reason such an effort should be undertaken has nothing to do with the present financial condition. My own observation is that higher education has never been without financial crises. Unfortunately, there are many among us who do not remember the good old days when we all did things with shoestrings and mirrors. Too many of us have been brought up during the golden years—an exceptional period, mostly likely an aberration. Now that we are back to normalcy, the shoe will pinch, the pockets will be frayed, and genteel decay may once again become the hallmark of higher education.

It further occurs to me that *then* there seemed to be more confidence in the quality of what we were doing. And on the subject of crises, there seems to have been less of a confidence crisis. "The pursuit of excellence" had a noble ring. To some, it may have had a somewhat snooty connotation, but if we are honest and fair, "the pursuit of excellence" is an honorable endeavor and worth going after. Now that so many have tasted the fruit of higher education, familiarity may have bred a certain contempt. It is up to us to renew both the challenge and our reputation. We must make ourselves respectable once again. Public accountability for what we are doing, for how we are doing it, and to those for whom we are doing it is one means. And a prerequisite for such accountability is proper self-study and analyses of the kind I have sketched here.

A Quid pro Quo Approach to Tuition

JOHN E. CORBALLY, JR.

IT IS A RARE education meeting or journal today that does not in some way or another touch on the "tuition question." It is equally rare to find a discussion that bothers to define what the question is. In fact, most such discussions deal almost exclusively with subjects that are, at best, peripherally related to tuition, and, in many cases, not related to tuition at all. Once again, it seems to me, we educators have taken a term that has some basic, long-run meanings and used it to discuss a whole range of short-run, cyclical, transitory problems.

For better or worse, our economy passes through periods of inflation and of deflation; our local, county, state, and federal tax systems reflect the concepts of ability to pay and of benefit theory to varying degrees; the priority given higher education by the American people and their elected representatives shifts from high to less than high; and the health and wealth of public and private higher education institutions go from better to worse and worse to better. Particularly when these and other swings in society combine to inflict what we regard as a cumulative negative effect on our institutions, we search out the quick solution to reverse those impacts.

In the last few years, we have been especially adept at finding these quick avenues to salvation. Our courses are not relevant? Let's add students to our curriculum-making bodies; although this move may not make us relevant, it will at least make us more popular with part of our constituency. Our curricula have gaps? Let's not improve and update what we have but instead add whole new curricula, departments, schools, and what have you, which—in spite of their obvious deficiencies—will permit us to proclaim our alertness to current events. We have financial and enrollment and even survival problems? Let's avoid discussion of the root causes and talk about tuition.

118

I have little quarrel with those consistent voices which, over the years in our nation, have been opposed in principle to the public subsidy of higher education. Those voices have spoken through prosperity and depression, through inflation and deflation, through good years and bad to a basic philosophy and to a basic understanding of the meaning of free enterprise in our democracy. I do not agree with them, but I understand them and respect their logic and their consistency.

I am also able to understand those who speak on behalf of full or total subsidies for higher education in our nation, who believe that among the essential public services to be provided by our government is free higher education. Such voices have also been consistent throughout our history; they have not varied their theme with variations in economic, educational, or other conditions.

But today, much of the so-called tuition debate has little to do with either of these consistent and opposing fundamental positions. Educators, business leaders, legislators, taxpayers, students, and many others are using the terminology of tuition to argue about other matters. Such arguments are lent the dignity of charts, graphs, and mathematical presentations as if subjective discussions of expediencies can become precise and objective statements of principle through the magic of statistics. In Illinois, we discuss with seriousness—and with charts—the philosophical differences between tuition as one-third of instructional costs and tuition as, say, one-fourth of instructional costs. My illustration reveals my public education bias; we also discuss with the same degree of thoroughness the difference between one-third and one-half. A deputy in the Illinois Bureau of the Budget and one of my colleagues on this panel, President Cyert, both compare state support of public higher education with the possibility that the state provide a free automobile to each taxpayer. Both fail to move on into the much more pertinent analysis of local, state, and federal support of public transportation or of highway construction, but such is the nature of the debate and of its analogies.

My purpose here is not to provide answers to what I perceive to be a set of nonquestions but rather to attempt to rephrase the question and to focus the discussion of tuition on the subject of tuition. Let me list just a few items which I believe have nothing whatsoever to do with tuition:

1. Is there really a dual system of higher education in the United States?
2. Is a dual system necessary? Why?
3. If a dual system is not necessary, should the single system be public

(that is, heavily subsidized and greatly controlled through government) or private (that is, minimally subsidized and minimally controlled through government)? Why?

4. Are our local, county, state, and federal tax systems in and of themselves and in the aggregate equitable?

These and other questions are important—perhaps crucial—but they are not tuition questions. Tuition questions arise only if one concludes either that a dual system is needed or that a single, public system is needed. In either event, it is assumed that public higher education is an appropriate, perhaps even a necessary, public service in the United States.

Next, one must define the nature of that public service and specify how the service shall be provided. Unfortunately, we in public higher education have not spent much time asking "we the people" what that public service should be. We have assumed a great deal, have accepted various assignments (and funds) from the federal government and from foundations, and have assured the people through our testimony before state legislative bodies that they need what we are providing. Our assumptions may be right, though a major debate today at the state level revolves around questions concerning how much service the people really do want from us. But, for the moment, let us assume that the dimensions and components of our public service are known and accepted and that they include some combination of teaching, research, and public service which shall be offered by some system or systems of colleges and universities.

One then moves into the public finance question, which influences decisions about a whole host of public services. The question is, How shall we the people through our governments pay for public services? and the set of subquestions is, How shall we the people pay for public services *A, B, C,* and so forth?

And here is where tuition enters the picture. Tuition is nothing more or less than one way in which some individuals pay for something. In the public sector, tuition is not too different from carfare or from the gas taxes used for highway construction. It is a payment made by a person who happens to make use of a public service at the moment, but it is not a payment which in the aggregate supports the full cost of that public service. Thus, though I live in Urbana, my state income tax payment in part supports the Chicago Transit Authority. In addition, the "user tax" I pay may or may not relate directly to my use of the public service. If I move to Chicago and pay forty-five cents to ride a crowded, multicar elevated train to the Loop, I am paying more than necessary, were it not for those nearly empty trains that run at midnight. I am sort of an undergraduate train rider helping to support a graduate-level train. As a transit rider, my best bet is to live in Chicago, to be poor enough to pay no taxes, and always to ride nearly empty trains. This arrangement would make me sort of a Ph.D.-level train passenger.

The tuition question, then, is not much different from the carfare question, the gas tax question, the admission-fee-for-a-state-park question, or the social security tax question. We make it different because our professional pride leads us to believe that our public service function is of a much higher order than are other public service functions. But nonetheless the basic question is really of the same order.

Incidentally, I know of no proposals to raise carfares on a public transit system to preserve a private system, to raise admission fees to state parks to preserve commercial picnic grounds, or to raise social security taxes to make private pension funds more attractive. But this ignorance leads me astray from my main point.

The key question is as follows: If the provision of higher education is determined to be a necessary public service, subject to public control and supported by public financing, how much "carfare" shall the "riders" pay? How much tuition shall the students pay? And a second question, the quid pro quo question is: For what is the rider paying? If public higher education is deemed a necessary public service, what portion of the cost of that service shall be borne by the small segment of the public which, for the moment, is directly involved in at least a portion of the service offered?

I wish I knew the answer to that question, for if I did, I could solve a whole series of public finance questions. I could, with certainty and objectivity, establish carfares, park fees, tuitions, public university short-course fees, rates for municipal garbage collection services, gas taxes, and a number of other user fees for public services. All I do know is that, in general, the greater the general public's real or imagined need for a public service, the lower the user fee for that service. Or, to put it another way, the greater the real or imagined need for a public service, the more that service is subsidized.

Thus, I cannot help but conclude that user fees for public higher education are far more a function of the value that the public places on public higher education than of any other factor. One can develop all kinds of philosophical frameworks for discussing tuition; the actual determinants of tuition levels in public higher education are the levels of the subsidies provided by local, state, and federal governments and the level of costs of providing such public higher education.

While I am not sure that Howard Bowen would agree with my paraphrases, what I hear as the basic message in his thoughtful address to the Association of American Colleges in January 1974[1] is that we stop wasting our time discussing tuition and move on to think about and to discuss higher education. Tuition is a false issue, and I agree with Bowen and others that there is no answer to the so-called tuition question which speaks to the significant questions which face us as participants in either public or private higher education. Just as the problems of mass transit will not be solved by discussing carfare questions or the problems of squalor in our cities by adjusting garbage collection fees, so the problems of higher education will not be solved by tinkering with tuition levels or by arguing about whether tuition should equal some specific percentage of an almost-impossible-to-determine measure of cost.

As I consider the tuition question, I am reminded of the great debates in which some educators engaged in the late 1940s and the early 1950s on whether federal funds should be involved in public education. All the time the debate was going on, a program of federal aid to education was being designed and implemented by a few educators and a host of politicians. In the same way, while we debate tuition matters, other forces in society are dealing with the real questions that, in the long run and inevitably, will determine tuition levels.

We were asked, in preparing these papers, to "address issues and solutions rather than engage in lengthy background discussions of the issues." The objective was to produce a "lively exchange of views on the merits of specific alternative solutions to the issues." Because I have ignored the announced title "Public and Private Tuitions" (finding it more appropriate in May than in July), I certainly do not want to ignore my instructions. My specific alternative solution to the issue of tuition is as follows:

1. Let us swear (or affirm) to spend at least one year without including the topic on any conference agenda or journal contents page.
2. Let us consider, instead, one or more of the following topics, preferably in our own institutions with our own people and with a commitment to act on our answers.

1. See Howard R. Bowen, "Financing Higher Education: The Current State of the Debate," *Liberal Education,* March 1974, pp. 27–48.

a) What do we think our institution is doing, and who—besides us— thinks anyone needs what we are doing?

b) For whom do we think we are doing whatever it is we are doing? Do those "whoms" seem interested in buying what we are doing for them?

c) Who asked us to do whatever we are doing, and have we checked with them lately to see if they remember asking?

d) If we suddenly find that no one except us wants what we are doing —and if even we are not too thrilled about it—what is the honorable thing to do?

This is but a sample of good topics. Each of you could think of many more. But as long as we are content to talk about tuition, we won't have to worry about any of the important issues. We can continue to talk about carfare on a bus that fewer and fewer people want to ride and that isn't going anywhere very important anyway.

The Market Approach to Higher Education

RICHARD M. CYERT

EVERYONE IN HIGHER education and everyone using higher educational facilities recognizes that something is happening in the education market. In every state that has a significant proportion of private colleges and universities, there is a crisis with respect to the financing of higher education. It is no longer uncommon to read about private schools going out of business. Hence, it is clear that a broader understanding of the problem is necessary. The purpose here is to analyze the problem and to propose some solutions.

I wish to thank Professors Lucas, McGuire, Simon, and Van Horn of Carnegie-Mellon University for their criticisms of an earlier draft of this paper. I wish to thank also Chancellor Allen Wallis of the University of Rochester for his many suggestions for improvement.

THE ROOT OF THE PROBLEM

In any attempt to get to the root of the problem, it must be recognized that the educational services produced by colleges and universities are capable of being analyzed by economic methods. The services carry a price or prices. There are quality differences among the services being produced. The product, like many others, has some externalities that call for analyzing government's role in the production process. It seems entirely reasonable, therefore, in analyzing the current and future problems, to view tuition (including fees) as a price.

The education market can be characterized broadly as composed of the public and the private sectors. It is clear that the difference in the prices of public and of private institutions—the tuition gap—has been increasing.[1]

The problem of the growing gap in tuition results from several factors. A major one is inflation in the economy. This inflation affects private institutions by causing an increase in operating costs, a need for higher faculty and staff salaries, and similar factors. New sources of income, however, have not been adequately forthcoming. Endowment income, which typically amounts to about 30 percent of income exclusive of such elements as auxiliary enterprises and research grants, either has not increased because of the stock market situation or has not increased at a rate adequate to cover the inflationary effect. Gifts and grants from individuals and foundations have not been growing significantly. Overhead from research has dropped off or flattened out because of changes in government research policy and because of limits on the amount of research support faculty members can accept. Thus, the private institution finds itself with rising costs and no compensating increases in income. The one source over which it has control is tuition. As the pressure of increased costs mounts, the tendency is to raise tuition in an attempt to maintain a balanced budget.

The public university is, of course, subject to the same inflationary pressures: Its costs also increase significantly, but so does its income from tax revenues. In an effort to maintain a policy of low tuition, state legislatures increase the amount of the subsidy to the public university, or they may refuse to approve a tuition increase, the result being a degradation of the quality of education. Whatever the method, the outcome is one in which the private institutions must increase tuition and the public institu-

1. Carnegie Commission on Higher Education, *Higher Education: Who Pays? Who Benefits? Who Should Pay?* (New York: McGraw-Hill, 1973), pp. 61–65.

tions are either forbidden to raise prices or given an increased subsidy so that they are not forced to raise prices.

There are other reasons for the gap. Even without inflation, it is entirely possible that tuition would have to rise. Education is a labor-intensive industry; it has not shown any great inclination to increase its productivity. At the same time, the thrust of our economic system is to raise standards of living; thus wages and salaries rise on the basis of increased productivity in the industries that produce goods by nonhuman capital. The tendency is for the prices of products produced by the latter process to fall and for the prices of labor-intensive products to rise.

In addition, the gap in tuitions might increase without inflation because of the attempts by private institutions to differentiate their products. More specifically, one virtue of the market pressure is to make each school conscious of the need to improve its quality if it is to remain viable. Because such improvements increase costs, they are likely to result in increased prices.

THE THREAT TO PRIVATE EDUCATION

Low public tuition has a significantly negative effect on the private sector. As the gap between the cost of attending public and private institutions widens, private colleges and universities fail roughly in reverse order to the size of their endowments for a given level of financial obligations. Because of the tuition differential, students who, in the past, attended private institutions are now enrolling in public colleges and universities. Reduction in enrollment leads to serious financial trouble, and an increasing number of private institutions are being forced to close their doors. The eventual result will be excess educational facilities. At the same time that a policy leading to such a result is being followed, states are spending public funds to increase the capacity of public institutions through construction of new buildings. In the long run, unless the methods of financing public education change significantly, all private institutions will be affected adversely regardless of quality and size of endowment.

To see the reality of the threat to private education, it is useful to look at some trends in higher education. One striking statistic is the change from 1961 to 1971 in the number of bachelor's degrees conferred by public and by private institutions. In 1961, private institutions accounted for about 44 percent of the degrees awarded nationally. By 1971, when the degrees granted had doubled (402,000 to 840,000), private institutions were awarding only 34 percent. Part of the reason for this drop is that many private institutions did not try to expand, but a more sub-stantial reason is that the number of low-tuition public institutions had increased. In the fall of 1961, about 56 percent of all students enrolling in four-year colleges were in public institutions. In 1972, this figure had risen to about 69 percent. By 1981, it is projected at 74 percent.[2] Clearly, these developments must be of concern to our society if our mixed system is one we want to maintain.

The trends are, of course, no different from what could be expected if any private industry had to compete with a government-sponsored industry that was subsidized with public funds. Suppose that the government en-tered the automobile business to produce a low-priced car, and suppose further that it was decided to subsidize the factories so that the poor could have cheap automobiles. The government factories would not be required to show a competitive return on investment, nor to account for deprecia-tion, nor even to recover all out-of-pocket costs in the prices that they charged. In a very short time, private manufacturers would have to with-draw from the production of low-cost automobiles. Neither Ford Motor Company nor General Motors could compete with the federal government if it were producing automobiles under these conditions. It should be noted that the subsidized automobiles would be sold not only to the poor but also to anyone else who wished to buy one. Thus, this would be a wasteful way of supplying automobiles to the poor. Private companies would pro-duce only expensive, high-quality automobiles. As the gap in price between the high-quality automobiles and the low-quality, publicly produced auto-mobiles became greater, production by private companies of the high-quality product would have to be significantly reduced. Public and private higher education institutions are now involved in a comparable situation.

WHY PRIVATE INSTITUTIONS?

At this point, it is proper to question why private universities should continue to exist.[3] To those of us who have been in private education most of our lives, it may come as a shock to realize that almost all of the uni-versities of the world are dependent upon governments for support. Private

2. National Center for Educational Statistics, U.S. Office of Education, *Projec-tions of Educational Statistics to 1981–82* (Washington: Government Printing Office, 1973), p. 42.
3. For much of this information, I am indebted to the "Report of the Committee on Private Universities and Private Giving," *University of Chicago Record*, April 21, 1973.

universities are in the minority. Even in the United States, two-thirds of all college and university faculty are employed in the public sector.

The argument for maintaining private institutions is based on their role in providing leadership and high quality in education. It is fair to say that the private universities have been of significant importance in the history of higher education and research in America, particularly as a source of innovation. They have also led in experimentation and curriculum development in undergraduate education. The initial impetus toward graduate education and research came from private universities. And, in each of the five volumes since 1925 that has ranked the quality of graduate education, the private universities have had a majority of the strongest departments in most fields.[4] Most of the institutions of highest quality have been private universities.

Other kinds of evidence substantiate the importance of private institutions. In 1970, for example, although fewer than half of all graduate degrees were granted by private institutions, roughly 71 percent of the professors in the five strongest departments in each field were from private institutions—again, an indication that private institutions have remained vigorous. An analysis of Nobel Prize winners leads to the same conclusion: Sixty-six Americans received the Nobel Prize between 1946 and 1971, and of these, approximately two-thirds received their most advanced degree at a private university, only 13 percent at a public university, and 20 percent at a foreign university. (Most of the last were naturalized citizens.)

Thus, the private sector is vital not only to the quality of higher education but also to the diversity necessary to make further progress in research and education. The United States has been a leader in research because of the quality of its private institutions. It is generally recognized, too, that public universities are of a better quality than they would be without the competition of private universities. And they are better because of the great contributions of the private universities to innovative education, to graduate training, and to research.

A more subtle point relates to the diversity in institutions provided by an industry that must be sensitive to the market. The private sector in education offers a wide range of alternatives in size, quality, and religious ideology from which a student may choose. This diversity is in marked contrast to the homogeneity of public institutions, with a few exceptions.

4. The most recent ranking is: Kenneth D. Roose and Charles J. Andersen, *A Rating of Graduate Programs* (Washington: American Council on Education, 1970).

But the point is not to make invidious comparisons; rather it is to stress the need to develop a solution that will maintain diversity.

It should be clear that if the private sector were to disappear, American education would be the poorer in many different ways.

A Solution to the Problem: Full-Cost Pricing

The problem clearly resolves itself into a simple prescription: Given the current system of state subsidization of education and given inflation, private institutions, if they are to survive in the long run, must find an income source that is independent of tuition. One possible source of funds is savings from more efficient management. Because of the financial pressures on them and because of the nature of their organization, private institutions are probably better managed than public institutions. Nevertheless, further savings can undoubtedly be made. But these alone will not solve the problem. It is unlikely that, over the years, the savings achieved by decreasing cost through improving efficiency can keep up with the pace of inflation. A second possible step is to increase the amount of income from endowments. Again, it is unlikely that increased return on endowments, even with the utilization of capital gains, will enable private universities to make their tuitions competitive.

The third and most decisive change that should take place is in the way that the state finances public education. If we are to maintain a mixed system of private and public education, state governments must move to the concept of giving public funds directly to students, thereby enabling those students to attend the college or university of their choice.

The solution to the problem should start from the assumption that we want to create a market in which both private and public institutions can continue to exist. We also want a market in which all qualified persons, regardless of income, have an opportunity to attend a college or university and in which all persons of equal qualifications have the same freedom of choice of institution.

Given this statement of the problem, one can prescribe a straightforward solution. That solution consists of eliminating the subsidy to institutions and substituting in its stead a subsidy to individuals in the form of scholarship grants. The grants should be made prior to the time the student chooses a college and should be based on the need and quality of the student. The income cutoff point can obviously be set as high as society wants it to be. Thus, the familiar cry that the middle class cannot afford college can be easily remedied. Each institution can then decide its pricing strategy as it desires. It can also decide the type of institution it wishes to be with respect both to the qualifications of the students it admits and to the areas in which it will produce educational services. Such an approach will allow each school to put its long-run survival in the hands of the market. From the standpoint of society, the allocation of resources will become rational again. The student from the lower-income family will have the same freedom of choice that the student from the high-income family now has. The state will no longer be in the position of telling low-income students that they have the opportunity of going to college, but only if they choose one of the colleges the state provides. The total cost should be less than is currently spent because the subsidy now given to the high-income student will be eliminated as will the "pork barrel" aspects of new buildings for public universities. Further, the subsidies to private institutions that many states now incorporate can be eliminated. Such subsidies are a poor solution to the problem in that they do not effect a student redistribution and they keep some schools viable that the market would otherwise eliminate.

There are other virtues to such a system. For one, the interests of public and private institutions would be unified. All institutions would have a common interest in making the financial grants to students as large as possible and as widely distributed as possible. Thus, the market could well increase. Another factor leading to an increasing market would come from the supplements that parents and students might make. Currently if the state gives an education that costs $3,000 for which the tuition is $500, the student who wants a $4,000 education has to find an additional $3,500. Under the system I have described, the student would get the $3,000 directly and would need only an additional $1,000.

Even more important in many respects is that, through this system, public institutions could escape the political influences of state legislatures. Under current funding patterns of direct state aid to institutions, politicians can attach constraints to the expenditures. More subtly, knowing the kinds of questions that powerful legislators ask and the positions they take, the president of a public institution may well modify the behavior of the institution. But once the funds are given directly to students, the public institution will have to become responsive to its potential clientele. The legislature can effectively transfer its concerns over curricula and similar matters to the control stemming from students' free choice of which school they will attend. Public institutions will have to meet the test of the market and submit to the controls involved in such a process. At the same time, direct aid to students will provide real accountability for the effective use of public funds. Students will have a strong incentive to make the best use of their money and, despite the problems of making a free choice of a complex product, will do better choosing for themselves than by having others choose for them.

ANSWERS TO POSSIBLE OBJECTIONS

To evaluate the proposed solution more effectively, it is desirable to examine some of the objections to a market solution. Howard Bowen, for example, has written, "I can live with the Carnegie program, whereas I cannot accept many other proposals—especially those of economists who are in love with the price system but have not thought through all aspects of the problems and needs of higher education."[5]

Dr. Bowen is particularly concerned about increases in tuition but acknowledges that inadequate tax support and gifts to institutions make higher tuitions necessary. Though he does not, in the document quoted, make explicit his objections to a market solution, it is clear from his other writings that the question of equity is important to him.

There are two aspects to the equity question. One has to do with equity among individuals with different incomes: Should the individual with the $50,000-per-year income receive the same subsidy as the individual with the $5,000 income? Such is the case when the state subsidy goes to the institution and the individual with the higher income decides to attend. The second aspect relates to the proportion of the total cost of education that the state should pay. The argument that the state should pay some portion is based on the assumption that society as well as the individual captures benefits from the education of the individual; thus, the society should subsidize the individual's education to the extent of the benefits it receives. In any event, one should note that the system of giving grants to individuals can be made to satisfy the notion of equity. A market system that does not include direct grants to individuals, however, could not deal effectively with the equity problem.[6] The two aspects should be kept distinct. The use of prices for allocation, along with direct grants, can achieve equity within any reasonable definition of the term.

5. The remark occurs in a letter to Allan W. Ostar of the American Association of State Colleges and Universities that constitutes Attachment B in Carnegie Commission on Higher Education, *Tuition: A Supplemental Statement to the Report on "Who Pays? Who Benefits? Who Should Pay?"* (Berkeley: Carnegie Commission on Higher Education, April 1974), p. 84.

6. See "What Price Education?" and "Financing Higher Education," *Wall Street Journal,* May 1 and May 4, 1959, cited by John D. Millett, "The Role of Student Charges," in *Financing Higher Education, 1960–70,* ed. Dexter M. Keezer (New York: McGraw-Hill, 1959), p. 181.

A related concern expressed by some is that a system of full-cost tuition that depends on direct grants to students from the legislature is unstable. It is asserted that legislators can reduce or eliminate such grants more easily than grants to institutions. This objection can be neither substantiated nor disproved. It is difficult, however, to see why it should be true.

Another possible objection emanates from the fear that, if students have free choice, they will desert the public institution in favor of the private. Such a possibility is unlikely because of limitations on physical capacity. Any such trend would result in an overcrowding of private institutions, making them less desirable and encouraging students to move back to public institutions.

A variant of this argument is that the "best" students will go to the private institutions, and the publics will be left with the remainder. As a result, the quality differences between publics and privates will grow larger in favor of the privates. We will have replaced a tuition gap with a quality gap. We will have accentuated the socioeconomic inequalities already existing, since there is some evidence that the measurements of student quality are correlated with income. We will have accelerated already existing trends toward elitism in our society.[7] This argument assumes that, because of the redistribution of students following the new method of financing, private institutions will have the superior financial capacity to attract the best faculty. But it is unlikely that the redistribution would be great enough to cause such a shift in financial capacity and thus give private institutions the capability to monopolize the top students. If there were such a shift, many methods are available for equalization, including capital grants to public institutions from the legislature.

OTHER SOLUTIONS

Though the logical strength of the argument for a market solution is great, there are political forces that discourage optimism. Pennsylvania has a small system of grants to students as well as a system of subsidies to institutions. A recent study of the Pennsylvania legislature in relation to the financing of higher education indicates some reasons why legislators do not want to move from subsidizing institutions to direct grants to individuals:

> Under present conditions, the possibility of enacting a much broader

7. See James Tobin, "On Limiting the Domain of Inequality," *Journal of Law and Economics,* October 1970, pp. 271–73, for a discussion of the effects of a voucher system on elementary and secondary education.

scholarship program seems unlikely for several reasons. Many legislators do not want to vest so much power in PHEAA [the agency currently administering the grants-in-aid to students], which is still a controversial agency. They also fear that the general public will react adversely if increasing the PHEAA appropriation means cutting direct aid to public institutions. The general public can readily recognize a $200 increase in tuition at a state school; it is not as easy, however, to comprehend how that additional money will affect the tuition for needy students. Moreover, higher income students who are receiving aid by attending public institutions now would not qualify for comparable aid under a voucher system.

Another problem affecting the feasibility of an expanded voucher system in Pennsylvania is the strength of the lobby groups maintained by the public institutions. Many are permanently stationed in Harrisburg; consequently, they influence the legislature greatly.[8]

One solution that has been supported by many private colleges and universities is a system of direct subsidies to private institutions on the basis of their student population or on some similar basis. This form of aid has appeal because it gives immediate help. It is not a long-run solution because it does not affect the allocation of students among institutions. In fact, it does not change the allocation of resources in the proper way. It allows the continued existence of some private institutions that would be eliminated by the market just as the current system continues the existence of some public institutions that the market would eliminate.

The only solutions that can have an impact are those that reduce the gap between public and private tuitions. Thus a two-valued scholarship program is a move in the right direction. Such a scholarship, which has a higher value when used in a private institution than in a public institution, can reduce the gap.

I have tried to demonstrate that tuition is a price and that the gap between the prices for public and for private institutions is growing larger. Quality difference may reduce the influence of the gap.[9] It must be expected, however, that a growing gap will have an increasing effect. As Spies says, "Most students are willing to pay a great deal for a superior education. The question is: How much should we ask them to pay?"[10]

8. David Hand et al., "Financing Postsecondary Education in Pennsylvania," Working Paper, School of Urban and Public Affairs, Carnegie-Mellon University, June 1974, pp. 134–35.

9. Richard R. Spies, *The Future of Private Colleges* (Princeton, N.J.: Princeton University, Industrial Relations Section, 1973).

10. Ibid., p. 62.

The gap will affect those private institutions first that cannot claim superiority over their public rivals. Eventually the gap must affect enrollments even at private institutions giving high-quality education.

The emphasis here has been on the development of a market environment in which the best private and public institutions can continue to exist. The question of equity or the proper role of government is not dealt with.[11] The proposed solution assumes the use of public funds but for persons rather than institutions. It is also a system that can achieve equity as reasonably defined. The solution is an example of the power of using the price system to affect resource allocation and of using direct grants to consumers to achieve equity.

11. For a good discussion of this topic, see Robert W. Hartman, *The Rationale for Federal Support for Higher Education* (Washington: Brookings Institution, 1974), General Series Reprint 283.

Needed: A National Cost Adjustment Factor for Higher Education

G. THEODORE MITAU

ANY DISCUSSION of the financing of postsecondary education must, in my judgment, be prefaced with a brief reference to this country's public policy commitment to mass higher education. The historical development of that commitment—from the Morrill Act of 1862 to the Education Amendments of 1972—is well known. But the relevance of that commitment to current and future national goals and requirements is worth emphasizing, especially in light of simplistic analyses which suggest that the capacity and productivity of our postsecondary institutions have expanded beyond the manpower and educational requirements of the nation's economy.

To those who measure the value of postsecondary education policy only in its bearing on job-related training requirements, I suggest that the world is in the midst of several revolutions—technological, political, economic—

affecting every country, every class, every citizen. Many people—including myself—would assert that postsecondary education has not fully realized its potential in leading and assisting the analysis and explication of contemporary problems; certainly, few would deny the need to expand the knowledge of the citizenry on such issues as the energy crisis and its consequences for employment and unemployment, international economic relationships and the balance of trade, ethics and the public service, individual and institutional racism and sexism, and the rebuilding of urban and rural communities. Clearly, these issues (and many others) transcend narrow career-oriented training. Moreover, they have pertinence for all citizens, not just the 18–22-year-old on-campus student.

The Fiscal Crisis and Its Consequences

At the very time when postsecondary education should be expanding its horizons to include the needs of a broader clientele, many institutions face forced retrenchment and constriction of program scope. This situation results from two concurrent factors: (a) inflation, which has created increasingly severe economic strains, and (b) the leveling-off, and in some cases the substantial decline, in on-campus enrollments.

The effect of inflation is obvious when we consider that inflation approximated 10.7 percent in just the twelve-month period May 1973—May 1974. At that rate, the purchasing power of the funds available for financing higher education has declined by almost $1.3 billion. Few states (if any) have provided for such an inflationary rate in their appropriations for public institutions. The consequences—increases in tuition, reductions in programs, and the erosion of faculty and staff salaries—have been obvious. In some instances, the burden shifted onto students has been particularly heavy. In Minnesota, for example, a well-established policy that tuition should equal 30 percent of operating costs results in a direct connection between inflation and the cost of postsecondary education to the consumer.

The effects of stable or declining enrollments are equally evident. The enrollment-related budget appropriation formulae utilized in most states have assumed a whole new dimension as enrollment trends have reversed. The imperfections of incremental budgeting, which were readily tolerated in an era of increasing enrollments, now elicit cries of anguish. Understandably, few legislatures have demonstrated a ready willingness to change the rules of the game in the present environment.

Worst of all, the inflationary spiral and its consequences for tuition tend to exacerbate the enrollment situation. While the National Commission on the Financing of Postsecondary Education estimated that each $100 increase in tuition would depress enrollments by 1–3 percent,[1] empirical data from a recent Wisconsin study by Jacob Stampen indicated an actual effect of 4.8–12.2 percent.[2] Moreover, a study soon to be released in Minnesota shows substantial elasticity in student demand for four-year institutions located outside metropolitan centers.[3] The why of the case becomes evident when we examine the economic status of students in the Minnesota State College System:

89 percent come from families with incomes under $15,000;
74 percent come from families with incomes under $12,000;
41 percent come from families with incomes under $9,000;
19 percent come from families with incomes under $7,500.

A recent study of students who dropped out of Minnesota state colleges indicates that, of those who listed lack of financial resources as a major factor in their decision:

70 percent came from families with incomes under $7,500;
51 percent came from families with incomes under $3,000.[4]

Beyond the deleterious effect that increasing tuition has on currently enrolled students is the forgone opportunity to serve a broader clientele. In an address to the Association of Governing Boards, Howard Bowen reported that, in 1972, only 15 percent of college-age youth from the lowest-income group (under $3,000) were enrolled in postsecondary institutions, whereas 56 percent from higher-income groups (over $15,000) were enrolled. He pointed out that if women enrolled in postsecondary institutions at the same rate as men, and if low-income people enrolled at the same rate as high-income people, total enrollments would be increased by six to seven million students.[5]

1. *Financing Postsecondary Education in the United States* (Washington: Government Printing Office, December 1973).
2. "The University of Wisconsin Center System Experiment in Low Fees, 1973–74" (Special Projects, University of Wisconsin, Madison, April 1974).
3. School of Public Affairs, University of Minnesota, "The Pricing of Postsecondary Education in Minnesota" (Minneapolis: University of Minnesota, in preparation).
4. Office of the Chancellor, Minnesota State College System, *Student Dropout Study* (St. Paul, Minn.: Minnesota State College System, August 1972).
5. Howard R. Bowen and Stephen K. Bailey, *The Effective Use of Resources: Financial and Human* (Washington: Association of Governing Boards of Colleges and Universities, 1974), pp. 7–8.

SCOPE OF THE NATIONAL DISCUSSION

As we all know, the growing seriousness of the challenge presented by these facts has led to a national discussion of the entire question of financing postsecondary education. Not only have many knowledgeable persons been involved in this discussion, but also such prestigious bodies as the National Commission on the Financing of Postsecondary Education, the Committee for Economic Development, and the Carnegie Commission on Higher Education have presented reports and recommendations. Although many of these reports have been useful in explicating analytical bases for the complex issues involved, no consensus on appropriate public policy directions has emerged.

The major issue to come out of the discussion so far centers on the question, Should the "pricing" structure of postsecondary education be fundamentally altered so as to redistribute public tax support? Those who answer this question affirmatively make two basic recommendations. First, tuition ("cost") in public institutions should be greatly increased so as to reflect more closely the cost of providing the services involved. Second, to offset the impact of such increases, greatly increased financial aid should be made available to students in need of assistance.

Such a two-pronged approach, it is argued, would provide the most effective utilization of public resources in that tax monies would be targeted to students in need of financial assistance instead of being used to keep tuition low for all students, regardless of their financial condition; moreover, it would increase students' options because tax support would not go directly to institutions but would be portable. Additional desirable results are anticipated in the improved competitive position of private institutions and in changed access patterns.

Those opposed to such a fundamental restructuring of existing relationships foresee problems of unacceptable magnitude:

· The burden of redistribution will fall most heavily on the middle class, a group already hard-pressed by inflation.
· Making tax support portable by targeting it to students rather than institutions ignores the multipurpose nature of public institutions, which provide a range of public services extending far beyond classroom instruction.
· Because of the complexities of disposable income analysis, the determination of "financial need" is an imprecise and often inequitable process.
· The lowered age of majority in many states and the growing propor-

tions of students who declare themselves "emancipated" from parental support and control further complicate analysis of financial need.

- The *perceived* barrier of high tuitions will prevent many students from applying for admission and for a determination of eligibility for financial aid.
- A significant proportion of the population—particularly middle-class persons—finds the very concept of seeking financial aid unacceptable.

These, then, are some of the concerns expressed by proponents of low tuition in public institutions. On their side, they are firm in three major convictions. First, low tuition is the best guarantee of the widest possible access to postsecondary educational opportunity. Second, tuition should not be used as a mechanism for income redistribution when more equitable means (such as the federal income tax) are available for the purpose. And, finally, reliance on direct financial aid to students as an offset to high tuition presents severe problems in perception and equity.

AN INTERIM SOLUTION

Although the discussion of appropriate public policy directions in the financing of postsecondary education continues and intensifies, it seems clear that no consensus is in sight. With inflation approaching an annual rate of 12 percent, I submit that to defer action until all parties agree is to ensure further tuition increases, more program reductions, and the possible demise of many institutions.

What is required, then, is an interim solution to the immediate fiscal realities confronting students and institutions—an interim solution which recognizes the urgency of the current situation as well as the complexity of the issues under discussion. Such a solution might be structured as follows:

1. Fiscal year 1973–74 would be designated as the base year of a National Higher Education Cost Adjustment Factor. That Cost Adjustment Factor would establish the national average educational cost per student in public two-year colleges, four-year colleges, and universities through the formula for institutional aid provided in Section 419 of the Higher Education Act of 1972.

2. Since 70–80 percent of educational costs reflect salary expenditures, and since salaries generally follow trends in the cost of living, the Cost Adjustment Factor would be "tied" to the cost of living index computed by the U.S. Department of Labor.

3. The annual percentage change in the cost of living index would be applied to the Cost Adjustment Factor; the resulting dollar amount would represent the per-student institutional aid to be made available to all colleges and universities, public and private.

4. So that aid would be timely, the index change would be computed for the calendar year (January through December), and payments would be issued each March on the basis of the previous fall's enrollment. Such a time frame would enable institutions to estimate and budget the aid on a current fiscal year basis.

5. States, local government units, and private institutions would be required to maintain per-student support at the 1973–74 level unless unusual circumstances were demonstrated to the satisfaction of the U.S. Office of Education.

The above proposal, then, would provide direct federal assistance to every public and private postsecondary institution in an equitable manner. It requires no complex and difficult value judgments—only the recognition that the inflationary spiral is having a severe and adverse effect on an increasingly fragile and hard-pressed endeavor.

The proposal *does not* address itself to the fundamental and complex issues which have plagued the debate over the financing of postsecondary education. It does not

- consider the basic roles of federal, state, and local units in the financing of education
- seek to redirect currently existing federal funding patterns
- seek to alter the current cost and tuition differentials between public and private institutions
- address the issue of altering student access and subsidy patterns through a retargeting of the existing tax support on a state and local level

What the proposal *does* represent is a limited but practical effort to address a fiscal crisis that endangers this country's postsecondary educational enterprises and activities. It recognizes that Congress may be reluctant to transform radically established financing patterns to a philosophically more symmetrical but politically less likely basis. Such reluctance is, of course, understandable in the absence of any consensus in the educational community itself. The proposal does

- accept and continue a pluralistic approach to the financing of post-secondary education, an approach whereby diverse funding strategies

have evolved through the give-and-take of the political and social processes
- reflect a commitment to preserving diversity and multiple options within the postsecondary spectrum
- seek to maintain relatively wide student access to multiple options

Beyond fiscal considerations, there remain still greater challenges to all of us. As educational partners, we are all engaged in a common enterprise of enormous consequence. Only the future will tell whether we are possessed of sufficient imagination, intelligence, sensitivity, good will, and administrative competence to make the curricular changes that need to be made; whether we are strong enough to break with uncritically accepted instructional concepts and practices; whether we are wise enough to learn from what concerned young people are trying to tell us about academic relevance and integrity of conviction; whether we are creative enough to discover ways to eradicate the evils of violence and war, of poverty and disease, of environmental pollution and social waste; and whether we are courageous enough to fashion an educational commonwealth dedicated to human brotherhood and dignity.

Don't Forget the "Student" in Student Assistance

JOHN D. PHILLIPS

ALL THOSE who write, read, criticize, and file or discard the position papers for the ACE Annual Meeting on "The Search for Alternatives" can readily recite the sixteen-year history of the federal government's growing involvement in the field of general student assistance. It begins with the limited programs of loans and fellowships authorized by the National Defense Education Act of 1958, continues with addition of the Work-Study Program by authority of the Economic Opportunity Act of 1964, continues further with the addition of Educational Opportunity Grants and Guaranteed Student Loans by authority of the Higher Education Act of 1965, and concludes, at least for the present, with the addition of Basic Educational Opportunity Grants and State Student Incentive Grants by authority of the Education Amendments of 1972.

Such a recitation, of course, omits the hundreds of program adjustments that have taken place over the sixteen years, as well as the accumulation of rules, regulations, guidelines, application materials, and other statutory and bureaucratic notations, each new set of which sends its tidal wave of paper spilling into the offices of presidents, financial aid administrators, business officers, and government relations officers in every postsecondary institution in the nation.

When I say "accumulation," that is exactly what I mean. With the single exception that the old Educational Opportunity Grants were technically superseded by the Basic and Supplemental Grants in the Education Amendments of 1972, federal programs have multiplied at every turn and nothing has been discarded in these last sixteen years. The result is an incredible cafeteria line-up of federal student aid programs which threatens to make gluttons of its patrons without ever providing a balanced diet of financial sustenance.

The "patrons" for whom these federal student assistance programs are mandated to provide balanced financial sustenance are, of course, the students who need money to finance their education. Such an elemental observation may seem pedestrian, but in my view this fundamental purpose has not always been clearly recognized and understood in discussions about federal student assistance programs. In fact, I sometimes sense that these programs are perceived in certain quarters as having been mandated to provide balanced financial sustenance not just for the students, but for many others as well.

All of us in postsecondary education and government realize that subsidizing consumers of postsecondary educational services has a decidedly positive effect on the sales of those services—in much the same way that welfare payments stimulate supermarket sales and help defray a market's cost of doing business. But that does not mean we should start thinking about student subsidies mainly as a means of financing postsecondary educational institutions—any more than we should start thinking about welfare payments mainly as a way to finance supermarkets. It is hard enough to make federal student assistance programs work effectively in financing needy students without trying to make them responsible for financing institutions as well.

Despite all the earnest efforts of the last sixteen years, the central objective of providing balanced financial sustenance for needy students remains far from achievement. In fact, it seems that each time we begin to make progress toward that achievement, forces and events conspire to move the oasis still further away, and we are left pursuing a constantly receding mirage. The present situation is instructive, if not encouraging.

INFLATION HITS "NEEDS"

Five of the six federal student assistance programs carry a statutory requirement that monies be made available according to the dimensions of a student's "need"—a dollar figure produced by subtracting an expected contribution of the student and his family from the student's budgeted cost of education.[1] This procedure sounds simple and straightforward, but it isn't. To begin, need analysis is a subject complex and cumbersome, contentious and controversial. And no matter how ardently the proprietors

---

1. The most recent statutory changes in the Guaranteed Student Loan program permit students to borrow beyond their calculated "need" provided such borrowings do not raise their assistance from all sources above their budgeted cost of education.

and proponents of the several major need analysis systems protest their absolute objectivity, need analysis procedures simply cannot be insulated from economic, political, and clientele pressures. For example, the College Scholarship Service recently announced sweeping changes in its system, and noted that the changes were being made "in response to strongly voiced concerns of parents, students, and the CSS constituency regarding the expected parental ability to pay for postsecondary education in the face of a continuing inflationary economy."[2]

Since the CSS constituency includes more than five thousand postsecondary institutions and agencies, the changes in the CSS system provide a semiofficial sanction for sizable reductions in expected family contributions at all income levels, which in turn generate sizable increases in the documented "need" for student assistance.[3] And with congressional mailbags overflowing with stinging reminders from inflation-weary constituents about the plight of middle-income students, the changes in the CSS system also generate pressure to liberalize the Family Contribution Schedules for the Basic Grants program, which would drive the full-funding costs of that program further and further out of reach.

On the other side of the need analysis equation, the costs of education to the student are bounding upward at a staggering rate, while prestigious study groups such as the Committee on Economic Development and the Carnegie Commission on Higher Education plump for tuition increases as a matter of public policy instead of mere economic necessity.

The result is obvious and discouraging. With declining contributions from students and their families and rising costs of education assigned to them for payment, need analysis procedures are generating ever larger dimensions of documented "need" to be filled by the federal student assistance programs. Nobody knows exactly what the aggregation of individual student needs might be for 1975–76, but all concerned parties

2. A "Dear Colleague" letter dated Aug. 15, 1974, from College Scholarship Service, College Entrance Examination Board, New York, N.Y.

3. It is estimated that the reductions in expected family contributions for the 600,000 students who traditionally have qualified for federal student assistance on the basis of the CSS system will generate additional documented "need" of $300–$350 million for 1975–76. For the 600,000–1,000,000 additional students who are newly qualified for need-based assistance by the CSS reductions in expected family contributions, the additional documented "need" could run anywhere from $300 million to $550 million for 1975–76. Altogether, then, the changes in the CSS need analysis system are expected to generate additional "need" for student assistance of at least $600 million for 1975–76, and the bill could run as high as $900 million.

know that aggregate need[4] will exceed aggregate resources by a much wider margin than in 1974–75. And this despite commitments from both the administration and the Congress to supply over $2 billion for next year's program operations. We seem to be pursuing a mirage.

There is also an increasing restiveness with the whole concept of need-based student assistance. Since the rules governing need analysis change continually in response to political, economic, and organizational pressures, it is always a complex, imperfect guessing process, capable of visiting inequities on individuals and on whole classes of cases. There is, too, a growing sentiment that it is simply wrong-headed for the federal government to sanction procedures that force students and their families "to humiliate themselves in front of some bureaucrat" in order to become eligible for the assistance. This sentiment was recently summarized by Howard Bowen when he declared that "the means test is essentially undemocratic, bureaucratic, arbitrary and open to evasion."[5]

Whatever the merits of this argument, it must be recognized in advance that liberalization or removal of current "need" requirements for financial assistance under the federal programs would tear the lid completely off the already rapidly escalating demand for student assistance and send the mirage so far out of sight that it could easily recede out of mind as well. Moreover, given inflation as Public Enemy Number One, and the national battle against it as requiring sharply limited growth in all federal expenditures, including federal expenditures for student assistance, tearing the lid off the demand for student assistance would simply heighten the frustrations of everybody concerned, particularly students and their families.

4. Although individual "need" has long been analyzed, only recently have systematic approaches been developed for aggregate need analysis. The Southern Regional Education Board has completed a ground-breaking study, *Student Financial Aid Needs and Resources in the SREB States: A Comparative Analysis* (Atlanta, Ga.: SREB, 1974), but it covers only the enrolled undergraduate portion of the student universe. Until the techniques of aggregate need analysis are further developed, refined, and applied throughout the nation, postsecondary education will remain unable to provide an answer to the critically important question of what is really needed to do the job in student assistance. The inability to answer that question undermines postsecondary education's credibility in the annual negotiation of student assistance budget requests and appropriations, and places it in the unappealing position of arguing, in effect, that "we don't know how much we need but we want more." Many observers are now suggesting that the new Section 1202 State Commissions should be encouraged to use their Section 1203 Comprehensive Planning Grant monies to develop statewide aggregate need analysis techniques and undertake state-by-state assessments of student assistance needs and resources.

5. Howard R. Bowen, *Financing Higher Education: The Current State of the Debate* (Washington: Association of American Colleges, 1974), p. 21.

SOCIAL POLICY AND AID POLICY

Clearly, however, there are far more critical issues involved here than simply balancing up the accounts of student assistance supply and demand. The sixteen-year experience indicates that there is likely always to be some shortfall of student assistance resources relative to the demand—however demand may be defined. We are, therefore, always confronted with the necessity of making unpleasant, discomforting choices among competing claims for limited resources. The concept of need-based student assistance and the need analysis procedures which support that concept in five of the six federal programs both reflect a social choice and a social commitment of long standing: to apply the limited resources first to those students who need them most to secure access to postsecondary education. This commitment has become the source of increasing controversy in recent years, and my own view is that the growing contentions over need analysis procedures are really only symptoms of an underlying and ever-deepening division over social goals and priorities.

On the one side, it is argued that if federal student assistance resources are likely to remain limited, the commitment to target those resources on the students who need them most must, of necessity, be modified. Why? Because, it is argued, this social commitment is having the effect of assuring access to postsecondary education only for the very poor and the very rich, leaving the great bulk of students, those from middle-income circumstances, to fend for themselves in the face of rapidly increasing educational costs. This logic suggests that it would be far better to "do something for everybody" than to persist in social policies that are essentially discriminatory, if not undemocratic.[6] On the other side, it is argued with equal force that the concentration of federal student assistance resources on the students who need them most is the essence of democracy: it endeavors to equalize the chances and opportunities for the poor to catch up with students from middle- and higher-income circumstances in gaining access to the benefits of postsecondary education; much, much more remains to be done before the critical social goal of equalizing opportunities for the poor

6. The changes in the CSS need analysis system provide significant reinforcement for this line of argument by greatly expanding both the dollar amounts of documented "need" and the universe of students who can claim to be needy. This procedure, in turn, greatly expands the gap between needs and resources and virtually invites institutional aid administrators to reconcile the conflicting pressures by simply funding everybody at a uniform percentage of their documented "need." The whole business is reminiscent of the story about the lifeguard who worked all day to bring everybody in closer to the dock, but saved nobody.

to accede to and succeed in postsecondary education is achieved; and instead of drawing back from our commitment of resources to achieve this goal, we should be broadening and deepening that commitment.[7] Or, as Peter Finley Dunne observed a long time ago, "The trouble is that the poor, who need the money the most, are the very ones who don't have any."

BASIC GRANTS UNDERMINED

Two years ago, the Congress and the administration collaborated in an effort to allay this social policy debate by amending the Higher Education Act of 1965 to establish a basic student assistance "entitlement" which, in the language of the Conference Report, would serve as "the foundation upon which all other federal student assistance programs are based."[8] The Basic Educational Opportunity Grants program was intended to provide a guarantee of universal access through a variable amount of grant assistance up to $1,400 or one-half the total cost of education (whichever is less), based on the difference between the total cost of the education desired and the expected contribution of the student and his family to the payment of those costs. In effect, the Basic Grants legislation took the long-standing commitment to provide grant assistance for students in accordance with the dimensions of their "need" and extended that principle to cover all students within a fairly broad eligibility range. As such, the program held promise for resolving the debate by doing something for everybody but at the same time doing most for those who need it the most. It was to be the meat and potatoes in the cafeteria line-up of federal student assistance programs, providing the staples in a balanced diet of financial sustenance.

Unfortunately, the great promise of the Basic Grants program has not yet been fully realized. Essentially, the program which was intended to serve as the entrée at the federal student assistance cafeteria has been funded with leftovers. From the outset, it has operated under the aggregate weight of (a) the statutory requirement that funding could be provided for Basic Grants only after the three campus-based programs had been funded at "threshhold" levels,[9] (b) the determination of postsecondary

---

7. The most persuasive presentation of this line of argument in recent years is the report of the Panel on Financing Low-Income and Minority Students in Higher Education, *Toward Equal Opportunity for Higher Education,* sponsored by the College Entrance Examination Board (New York: CEEB, 1973).

8. Education Amendments of 1972, *Conference Report* (To Accompany S. 659), p. 167.

9. The required minimum levels are $130,093,000 for Supplemental Educational Opportunity Grants, $237,400,000 for Work-Study, and $286,000,000 for National Direct Student Loans (ibid., p. 168).

institutions to resist any diversion of resources from the campus-based programs, and, indeed, to expand them further, (c) the pressure exerted by state postsecondary agencies for funding of State Student Incentive Grants, and (d) the truly frightening escalation of resource allocations required to finance subsidies, special allowances, and insurance claims (defaults) on Guaranteed Student Loans.

In each of the last three years, the administration has come forth with budget proposals for full funding of Basic Grants and Guaranteed Student Loans, plus $250 million for Work-Study, thereby setting the overall ceiling for student assistance expenditures. By way of response, the Congress has each year deducted monies for SEOG, CWSP, NDSL, GSLP, and SSIG from the budget ceiling, and left the funding of Basic Grants to move upward on a closely measured basis. If the administration had not raised the ceiling each year to accommodate the increasing costs for full funding of Basic Grants and Guaranteed Loans, the program could hardly have got under way at all.

Even now, as administrative processes are being completed to place some $525 million of Basic Grants in the hands of an estimated 700,000 first- and second-year students for 1974–75, it is painfully clear (a) that the ceiling on federal student assistance expenditures simply cannot be raised much further, (b) that Congress continues to find what it regards as good and sufficient reasons for annual deductions from the ceiling to finance SSIG and the campus-based programs, (c) that the runaway costs of Guaranteed Student Loans are cutting deeper and deeper into the expenditure ceiling, and, therefore, (d) that the growth of appropriations for Basic Grants could be adversely affected in the next few appropriations cycles. There simply aren't enough leftovers to go around.

These circumstances, combined with growing pressures to liberalize the Family Contribution Schedules and expand the universe of students eligible to receive Basic Grants, will require that the funds be rationed in smaller and smaller individual awards until the bold promise of an income-equalizing "entitlement" becomes the meek reality of an incidental "allowance" that buys little in either postsecondary education or social justice. Back at the cafeteria, the lengthening lines of students and their families will be faced with fighting their way from station to station in the bureaucratic chain of federal, state, institutional, and private "servers," pausing at each station to fill out another application and submit to another means test in order to retrieve another morsel of funding, only to discover finally that they have been treated unevenly along the way and that the accumulated morsels simply do not add up to a balanced diet of financial sustenance.

THE SEARCH FOR ALTERNATIVES

If we—in postsecondary education and in government—wish or intend to improve this bleak prospect before it becomes reality, we must use the months before the federal student assistance authorizations expire next June to refine our thinking about the purposes of student assistance, about the resources required to advance those purposes, about the programs we are relying on to advance those purposes, and about proper, efficient management of student assistance resources and programs.

With respect to purposes, my own view is that the nation still has promises to keep in equalizing opportunities for students from low-income circumstances to accede to and succeed in postsecondary education, and that this objective should remain central in all our thinking about student assistance. Of course, not all student assistance should be concentrated on this objective, nor even should all student assistance be based on "need." Instead of perpetually playing around with need analysis standards and procedures in a thinly veiled effort to bring everybody up (or down) to a technical condition of possessing "documented need," some very knowledgeable observers are wondering increasingly whether the range of need-based student assistance might be narrowed so that the means test applies only to federal grant assistance and it is simply assumed that the student who applies for work or loans must have some unmet need.[10] In this way, it is argued, serious attention could be given to the widely held objective of providing "something for everybody" without diluting the primary commitment of federal grant resources to those who not only need them most but who are also historically least able to work or borrow while they go to school.

With respect to resources, it seems clear enough that the federal government cannot be expected to carry very much more of the student assistance load, and that even the existing federal resource commitments will be subject to annual reappraisals by both the administration and the Congress, with an eye to limiting either total federal program expenditures or the federal share of total program expenditures, or both. Also clearly, the state governments will continue as major resource providers in the field of student assistance and, indeed, the states may well be the principal growth

10. The idea that a distinction be drawn between "documented need" for grant assistance and "assumed need" for work and loan assistance has been advanced primarily by Richard L. Tombaugh, former director of financial aid at Purdue University and George Washington University. Mr. Tombaugh argues that such a distinction is desirable not only to help resolve overall questions of social purpose, but also to help resolve some of the knotty problems posed by the increasing numbers of students who are claiming self-supporting status.

sector for the next few years.[11] But increasing state appropriations will not begin to close the overall gap between needs and resources. To reach this goal will require a corresponding growth of resources provided by the institutional and private sectors of the student assistance economy. And that imperative will force many institutions to abandon the notion that student assistance budgets will be financed primarily from government contributions, and require them instead to make systematic efforts to expand their own student assistance resources.

With respect to the federal programs which the nation relies on to advance its purposes, it is my view that we should continue the drive toward full funding of the Basic Grants program under current or only slightly liberalized Family Contribution Schedules, while continuing to explore possibilities for modifications to disentangle the program from the "high tuition–low tuition" debate and establish it as the sturdy foundation in a balanced configuration of grant, work, and loan programs. This basic conceptual framework, of course, contains within it a number of specific issues and alternatives that need elaboration beyond the scope of this discussion.

With respect to proper and efficient management of the resources and programs, I see an immediate imperative to complete work on a common application form which students and their families can fill out once and submit to all of the various sources of possible assistance. I see an immediate need to synchronize the deliveries of monies under the various programs, building in a sequential and timely fashion upon the foundation of the Basic Grant. I see, in short, an immediate need for a working partnership of federal, state, institutional, and private parties. And oh, yes, don't forget the students.

11. For a succinct summary of state activities, see John Mathews, "The States Move In on Student Aid," *Compact,* May-June, 1974, pp. 25–26.

Federal Student Assistance: Title IV Revisited

LOIS D. RICE

THE Higher Education Act of 1965 will expire in June of 1976, forcing Congress once again to consider federal policy for the support of postsecondary education.[1]

In one sense, this reconsideration comes too soon. Several new and promising programs authorized in the 1972 legislation are still unfunded, underfunded, or barely operational; and several funded programs still lack governing regulations. Therefore, we do not and cannot yet know their impact on the behavior of individuals, institutions, or state governments.

In another sense, the reconsideration may come too late. Some of the programs contained in the 1972 amendments demand immediate scrutiny and prompt change. Recognizing these needs, the House Special Subcommittee on Education (recently joined by the Senate Subcommittee on Education) has begun searching hearings on federal policy toward postsecondary education, but the nature of the process is such that its results will not be felt for several more academic years.

In reconsidering the higher education legislation, Congress has three options: (*a*) simply extend the law now on the books for an additional number of years; (*b*) refine programs in a manner similar to the revisions in 1968, which were sandwiched between the major higher education efforts of 1965 and 1972; or, (*c*) make substantive changes in the legislation, possibly redirecting the federal role in financing postsecondary education.

No one can predict the congressional strategy with certainty, but one thing is clear: the upcoming debate will focus on the title IV student assistance programs of the Higher Education Act, for they are the principal vehicle by which the federal government has intervened in the process called postsecondary education. The 1972 amendments also placed major

The opinions expressed herein are those of the author and do not reflect any position or policy of the College Entrance Examination Board.

1. Public Law 93-380 automatically extended the Higher Education Act until June 1976.

emphasis on student assistance—emphasis further reinforced by recent budgetary trends.[2]

Like much federal legislation, title IV developed by accretion.[3] It is the packaged accumulation of separate programs authorized and periodically revised over a decade and a half to meet the urgent and changing needs of American higher education. It is the product of congressional compromise and concession and of often unrelated policy decisions. The regrettable consequences are incoherence and little apparent connection among programs; inequity in a set of programs intended to bring about national equity in the financing of needy students;[4] and confusion on the part of institutions, students, and the public about federal student assistance effort.

In this paper, I will first summarize the current debate (which began in the 1960s, when equal educational opportunity was finally recognized as one of the primary goals of federal policy), concentrating on a set of concerns that are particularly divisive and rankling. Then, within this context, I will suggest some possible solutions that could lead to a more coherent and rational federal policy. My particular focus is on the grant programs, though I shall also deal briefly with loan programs and with the College Work-Study program. My suggestions for needed changes in the federal student aid programs have four objectives:

- To sustain the momentum of the landmark Education Amendments of 1972, which emphasized student assistance as the principal means of achieving equality of educational opportunity;
- To extend eligibility for federal student aid to a wider population of students;

---

2. Excluding the category of research support, about 74 percent of all federal education expenditures (outlays) in FY 1974 were in the form of student aid; in FY 1975 the percentage will rise to about 78 percent. Counting only monies administered by the Office of Education, approximately 90 percent of the FY 1975 higher education budget—and 33 percent of OE's total budget—is for the title IV student assistance programs of the Higher Education Act.

3. Title IV contains six student financial aid programs: Basic Educational Opportunity Grants (BEOG); Supplemental Educational Opportunity Grants (SEOG); State Student Incentive Grants (SSIG); College Work-Study (CWS); National Direct Student Loans (NDSL); and Guaranteed Student Loans (GSL).

4. These and other problems in the student assistance programs are discussed in College Entrance Examination Board, Washington Office, "Title IV of the Higher Education Act: A Technical Analysis of Six Student Financial Aid Programs," mimeographed (August 1974).

- To simplify and improve the equity of the federal student assistance programs; and
- To bring federal and state policies into harmony.

THE CURRENT DEBATE

In the 1960s, Congress authorized programs to improve access for new classes of students whose aspirations for higher education were soaring: the children of the poor, of blue-collar workers, of minorities. The federal government had to intervene not because the states are somehow malevolent but because, by themselves, they are incapable of meeting societal demands that cut across state lines, because they vary so in their resources, and because their efforts are often so diverse that they compound rather than ameliorate existing inequities. But although the new federal programs were numerous, and the rhetoric that accompanied them profuse, the social commitment to reorder priorities and focus scarce resources on the objective of equal opportunity was lacking.

Equal educational opportunity remains an unachieved goal, part of the unfinished business of our time. The college participation rates of high-ability young people from low-income and moderate-income families remain substantially below those of moderate- and low-ability students from higher-income families. As table 1 indicates, low-income students are only one-fifth as likely to be enrolled in college as are middle- and upper-middle-income students. Nor has the situation improved over time: In 1967, 13 percent of families with incomes under $3,000 had dependent children enrolled in college; by 1969, the proportion rose to a high of nearly 16 percent, but in 1970 it dropped to about 14 percent, and it has remained

TABLE 1

PARTICIPATION IN HIGHER EDUCATION, BY INCOME LEVEL, FALL 1970

Family Income	Percentage	
	18–24-Year-Old Dependents Attending College	Families with One or More 18–24-Year-Old Dependents Attending College Full-Time
Below $3,000	13	n.a.
$3,000–$4,999	19	32
$5,000–$7,499	31	41
$7,500–$9,999	37	36
$10,000–$14,999	45	45
$15,000 and over	61	62

SOURCE: Calculated from U.S. Bureau of the Census, *Current Population Reports*, Series P-20, No. 222, "School Enrollment: October 1970" (Washington: Government Printing Office, 1971).

TABLE 2

DISTRIBUTION OF FULL-TIME FRESHMEN AMONG TYPES
OF INSTITUTIONS, BY INCOME LEVEL

Family Income	Percentage					
	2-Year Colleges		4-Year Colleges		Universities	
	Public	Private	Public	Private	Public	Private
Below $3,000	54	4	17	15	7	2
$3,000–$5,999	52	4	19	15	9	2
$6,000–$9,999	47	3	19	15	13	3
$10,000–$14,999	42	2	20	14	17	3
$15,000–$19,999	35	3	22	15	21	5
$20,000–$24,999	29	2	22	16	24	6
$25,000 and over	21	3	17	23	25	11
All incomes	38	3	20	16	18	5

SOURCE: Computed from Alexander W. Astin et al., *The American Freshman: National Norms for Fall 1973* (Los Angeles: American Council on Education and University of California, Los Angeles, Cooperative Research Program, n.d.).
NOTE: Rows may not add to 100 percent due to rounding.

fairly steady at that level. Furthermore, low-income and minority students are heavily concentrated in low-cost institutions and in vocational schools; thus, institutional choice, another dimension of equal opportunity, suffers. Table 2 shows the distribution of students, by family income level, among institutional types.

Recognizing these inequities, the Congress provided, in the Education Amendments of 1972, mechanisms to achieve equal opportunity primarily through new and expanded student assistance programs. Now that these mechanisms are in place, the goals and focus of that legislation are being intensively questioned. A growing set of concerns—some new and some old—divide people, polarize thought, and threaten the current federal strategy. Many of these concerns emanate from worries about the fiscal viability of institutions. But institutional survival and equal opportunity are not mutually exclusive objectives, as we shall see. Student assistance programs can be part of the cure for, rather than a cause of, each of the concerns, so long as the terms are defined sensibly and so long as all participants in the debate are willing to listen to each other. What are these concerns?

The first is "the plight of the middle class," which has been so widely publicized that many people forget it is outweighed by "the plight of the lower classes." The lower classes are hit hardest by inflation not only because they are poor, but also because they are usually least able to give any upward push to their incomes in response to rising prices. They are also hardest hit by unemployment.

In recent years the costs of postsecondary education have risen even faster than prices in general, and this trend may continue into the indefinite future. Thus the plea that eligibility for federal student assistance, including grants, be extended upward into the middle-income range is warranted. *But any such expansion of eligibility absolutely must be accompanied by increased funding for federal student assistance.* Otherwise, the necessary result will be to take money from the desperate in order to help those who are merely miserable. As colleges competing for students are very well aware, middle-income families face the question, What college? Poor families face the question, Whether college?

Unfortunately there is little agreement on the definition of *middle income.* In 1973 the median income in the United States was $12,051. While *middle income* might be defined realistically as between $10,000 and $15,000, and liberally as between $10,000 and $20,000 a year, it is a debasement of words to consider (as some do) the 15 percent of families with incomes above $20,000 a year as middle-income families. Although they may indeed have some difficulty meeting the costs of postsecondary education or readjusting their spending priorities, it is hard to defend a federal policy that would utilize scarce subsidies to support a choice that these families would make without subsidies. Moreover, these families have a real option which is only theoretically available to low- and middle-income families: a choice between the public and the private sectors of postsecondary education.

The second major concern, low tuition, is also confused by definitional problems: Is low tuition simply maintenance of the status quo in pricing? Or does it mean moving to zero tuition, the only principled position for its advocates? Definitional problems aside, those who advocate continuing high levels of subsidy for all students in the form of low tuition claim that students from low-income families will come into the fold when tuitions are kept low for everybody. Manifestly this has not happened in past years when tuition was lower or at a zero level, as, for example, at the City College of New York. The plain fact of the matter is that low tuition is not enough. The noninstructional costs of attendance—room, board, personal expenses, and forgone earnings—suffice to bar access, even to zero-tuition institutions, and compel a continuing and strong focus on student aid.

A third concern is institutional aid. Some participants in the policy debate contend that institutions need general assistance to help themselves out of financial distress. While these proponents of institutional aid give lip service to the need for aid directed at students as well, all too often the effect of their advocacy is to pit institutional aid against student aid, to the irritation and confusion of legislators and to the detriment of all appropriations for higher education. Such warfare is unnecessary and ruinous.

Policy arguments for or against institutional aid aside, it seems obvious that aid to students does, in fact, benefit institutions by allowing them to direct their own student aid funds to other institutional needs. Moreover, since the college participation rates of middle-income and high-income students are leveling off at a fairly high plateau, any reversal in the declining growth of enrollments can be achieved only by increasing the college enrollments of students whose current participation rates are low. These low-income and moderate-income students carry with them state or federal aid, most of which will come to the institutions in the form of tuition payments. It has often been asserted, but never demonstrated, that the costs of educating these incremental students exceed the extra revenues they bring. Only if and when such a demonstration is made will it be time to choose between added payments to students and new payments to institutions.

The final concern underlying the current debate has to do with the emancipation of students. Many prophets of doom claim that the lowering of the age of majority is a prelude to the destruction of financial aid based on parental income. I disagree with such dire predictions. None of us knows exactly where our society is headed, but I refuse to believe we will end up with a federal policy that treats those who are poverty-stricken by choice as if they were no different from those who are poverty-stricken by circumstance. In any event, the prospective difficulty of the issue is not grounds for ignoring the present reality that talented young people from low-income families do not yet have equal opportunity for postsecondary education.

A Revised Strategy for Grants

Any future federal strategy for student assistance must accommodate the social goals of the 1960s, the evolving concerns of the 1970s, and the momentum of traditional roles in financing postsecondary education. Although few generalizations apply to the gamut of American postsecondary education, it can be said that, traditionally: (1) instructional costs have been borne by a combination of state, private donor, and family resources;

(2) noneducational costs have been met by students and their families; and (3) costs of students' time have largely been contributed by the students themselves.

The following suggestions for change in the current federal student aid strategy build on these traditional financing roles. They may, however, assign a different weight to the sources of support within each category of costs.

Historically, grant programs—like other forms of student aid—consider both instructional and noninstructional costs as components of "cost of attendance." The programs then try to help needy students meet some or all of these costs. But the effort to meet both types of costs may dilute the impact that student aid programs (and grant programs, in particular) have on the behavior of students. Further, the effort may obscure the purposes of the programs and the relationship among them.

A better approach would be to design grant programs for specific purposes and for specific categories of costs. For example, grant programs designed to improve access by inducing new enrollments could focus on the noninstructional costs that all students face, whatever the type of institution. Inability to meet these costs, even at zero-tuition institutions, may well be the major deterrent to the enrollment and retention of needy students in postsecondary education. Conversely, grant programs designed to provide choice and maintain a desired institutional diversity might focus primarily on instructional costs.

Except for the growing number of state scholarship programs, states do not subsidize noninstructional costs of attendance, concentrating instead on heavy subsidies for instructional costs in the form of low tuition. Inasmuch as states and institutions have reasonably complete command of tuition and pricing policies, and virtually no control over noninstructional costs, we can assume that states will continue to place primary emphasis on subsidizing instructional costs, whether through support of institutions or of students. For example, New York State's new Tuition Assistance Program, as its name implies, considers only the tuition costs of eligible students. (At the same time, New York, like other states, continues to subsidize heavily all students enrolled in its public institutions.) New York's Tuition Assistance Program may well be a model that other states should adopt, for it could augur a much more effective federal-state partnership in providing help to students *if* the major federal grant program—Basic Educational Opportunity Grants (BEOG)—were to focus on noninstruc-

TABLE 3

AVERAGE NONINSTRUCTIONAL COSTS (ROOM AND BOARD,
TRANSPORTATION, BOOKS, ETC.) OF COLLEGE ATTENDANCE,
1974–75

Type of Institution	Resident Costs	Commuter Costs
Public two-year college	$1,866	$1,635
Private two-year college	2,039	1,709
Public four-year college	1,859	1,544
Private four-year college	2,080	1,603
Proprietary school	2,166	1,763

SOURCE: College Scholarship Service, College Entrance Examination Board, *Student Expenses at Postsecondary Institutions, 1974–75*.

tional costs.[5] Additional federal grant dollars, such as Supplemental Educational Opportunity Grants (SEOG) and State Student Incentive Grants (SSIG), could then be used to provide wider institutional choice to students and to supplement state efforts in helping pay for instructional costs. These suggestions reflect two facts of postsecondary finance:

1. Tuition levels are not determined by the federal government and probably never can be or should be; there is a real question, too, about the extent to which federal policies and programs should influence institutional pricing.

2. Noninstructional costs are the most uniform set of costs across state lines and across sectors of postsecondary education, as table 3 indicates. This uniformity lends itself to a far more equitable, as well as a simpler, federal role, particularly for BEOG's, which could be related to the average of these costs.

BEOG: A program for access

The Basic Educational Opportunity Grants program, authorized in the Education Amendments of 1972, was intended to open college doors to any qualified young person, the amount of the grant being determined by need, irrespective of whether the student lives in Arkansas or Connecticut or where he/she seeks postsecondary education. Supplemented by other types of aid, BEOG's could also assure eligible students a choice among types of institutions. As the Conference Report on the 1972 amendments states: "This program is viewed as the foundation upon which all other Federal student assistance programs are based." Framers of the legislation wanted the program to be equitable and simple so that eligible students

5. The implications of such a program are discussed by Robert W. Hartman in Edward R. Fried et al., *Setting National Priorities: The 1974 Budget* (Washington: Brookings Institution, 1973), pp. 154–60.

would have early and certain knowledge of their entitlements; this, they felt, might induce new groups of students to pursue opportunities for post-secondary education.

The program was not intended:

- To foster higher tuitions (although at full funding it may);
- To discriminate against lower-income students (although it does through its half-cost provisions and methods for reducing grants when the program is less than fully funded);
- To restrict eligibility for the program to a narrow population (although this is a result of the $1,400 award maximum, coupled with the Family Contribution Schedule developed by the Office of Education);
- To discourage needy students from participating in the program (although this is the effect of the complex application procedures developed by OE).

The following suggestions for change in BEOG seek to maximize its intended purposes and minimize its unintended effects:

Suggestion 1: The maximum grant under the BEOG program should be directly related to the *average* noninstructional expenses of students and adjusted annually for inflation in these costs.

Noninstructional expenses include room and board, books, transportation, and so forth. Resident and commuter students, full-time and half-time students, would be treated alike.[6] The grant would meet all or part of the average noninstructional costs after a determination of family contribution. Families or students who could pay all of the average noninstructional costs would be excluded from the program.

At full funding the maximum grant would *equal* average noninstructional cost *minus* family contribution. At less than full funding, grant amounts would be reduced either by an equal dollar amount for all eligible students or by the imposition of an additional family contribution as a fixed percentage of family income.[7]

---

6. Since some portion of the students' earnings would reduce entitlements, part-time students who work would receive reduced grants.

7. These two alternatives for reducing grant amounts at less than full funding of BEOG's, and their effects on grant recipients, were elaborated by Robert Hartman, who concludes that either alternative is far preferable to the complex ratable reduction formulas contained in the present law. I agree. See Hartman, "Higher Education Subsidies: An Analysis of Selected Programs in Current Legislation," in *The Economics of Federal Subsidy Programs,* a compendium of papers submitted to the Joint Economic Committee, Part 4, *Higher Education and Manpower Studies,* 92nd Congress, Second Session, 1972, pp. 465–96.

Grants would not be ratably reduced (as they are now) because such percentage reductions are most damaging to students with the largest entitlements—to those who can least afford them.

Suggestion 2: The current half-cost limitation on grant payments should be eliminated under all circumstances.

The provision is inequitable in that it discriminates against low-income and moderate-income students who attend lost-cost institutions, but it has no negative effect on students who attend high-cost (tuition charge over $2,800) institutions. The half-cost provision has no rationale if BEOG's are related to noninstructional costs.

Suggestion 3: Special educational benefits from other public programs (for example, Social Security) should continue to be deducted from the grant entitlements; the amount deducted should, however, be fixed.

As it stands now, families or students receiving Social Security Educational Benefits must report on the application form the amount of these benefits that are attributable to the student. But this procedure makes no sense, since applicants often err in giving this information (sometimes, for instance, reporting these benefits twice, both as family income and as student income). Instead, a standard amount could be fixed by law or regulation; thus, students receiving Social Security Educational Benefits would have a fixed amount (say, $500) deducted from their entitlement.

Suggestion 4: The application form and the Family Contribution Schedule should be simplified so that students and their families can understand them and not be deterred (as they are now) from applying for a grant under the program.

Under present procedures, determination of the family contribution is greatly complicated by the inclusion of a "tax" on assets. Though the asset tax has the merit of excluding students who come from a high-wealth but low-income background (the fabled millionaire businessman who always shows a loss), the price paid is heavy indeed. Families are led to believe that their homes will be confiscated; they may be tempted to cheat in estimating the market value of real assets; they may be induced to invest in nontaxed assets. The asset tax ought to be either eliminated or vastly simplified (for example, anyone with assets over a given level—say, $25,000 or possibly $50,000—is ineligible). At worst a few odd-ball cases would become eligible; but if the millionaire can really keep his income low, the remedy lies in federal taxation, not in the BEOG program.

The biggest drawback to the present procedure is that the forms and accompanying instructions are forbidding. Families must report adjusted gross income (which has to be readjusted if the parents are divorced or separated after the application is filed), child support, taxable income, income tax paid, earnings of both parents, medical and other unusual expenses, losses or theft, and so on, at tedious length. Most of these items could be eliminated, and the form simplified, if only taxable income were reported and used to determine the family contribution.[8]

Suggestion 5: The year of income used in calculating the family contribution should be changed from current-year income either to prior-year income or to estimated income for the year in which the grant will be used.

Families must now report on the application form certain items from their tax or W-2 forms for the tax year immediately preceding the academic year when the student will use a Basic Grant. In effect, this requirement bars families from applying for the program until they have filed a tax form; for most Americans, that is on April 15. Thus, students cannot receive notice of their grant eligibility until the late spring or summer.

Reporting prior-year income is preferable to reporting estimated income because such reports will be accurate. Either alternative, however, permits students to apply for the program earlier and to receive notice of their eligibility for grants in reasonable time.

Early and certain knowledge of grant eligibility, and in what amount, maximizes the enrollment of students in the target population. Furthermore, with earlier information institutions can begin to build a package of aid for grant recipients, and Basic Grants could finally become the foundation for other forms of student aid, as they were intended to be.

Suggestion 6: Better definitions of the term *independent student* should be developed.

Currently, a student is considered to have independent status if he has not and will not be claimed as a dependent for tax purposes or received more than $600 from his parents for two consecutive years prior to the

8. New York State uses taxable income in its means test. A report of the New York Board of Regents found high correlations between net taxable income and gross income: ".81 for the families of students at private colleges, .82 for the families of students at State university campuses, and .80 for the families of students at community colleges." The report noted, "Families rarely receive more than $2,000 in non-taxable income and inclusion of non-taxable income in the State means test would have major impact on low-income Social Security holders . . . or families where the principal wage earner is deceased or retired."

academic year in which the grant will be used, and if he has not spent more than two consecutive weeks in a calendar year with his parents. With no great ingenuity, the student can circumvent the last requirement by spending one night every other week with a friend.

These requirements are intended to prevent the "instant emancipation" of students who could not qualify for grants if their families' income and assets were considered. But this danger would be lessened and the program made simpler, if more stable and more easily measured criteria were used. For instance, independent status might be assigned automatically to veterans, married students, orphans, wards of a state, and students over twenty-five years of age (or some other specified age level).

These six suggestions for change in the BEOG program would have several advantages.

First, they would allow for a higher—and more rationally based—grant ceiling. In 1972, the figure of $1,400 as a maximum was plucked out of the air, the result of bargaining and compromise in the Senate subcommittee. Later it was justified as roughly approximating the minimal amount required to assure access to the lowest-priced institution or as the amount that the average family could contribute to educational costs. Neither is true today.

If, however, the maximum grant were related to average noninstructional costs, it would finally have a rational basis, and—unlike the current ceiling—one that lends itself to annual adjustments in response to changes in the cost of living. As the cost of living increases, so would the maximum grant. For instance, the grant ceiling for the 1974–75 academic year would be raised from the current $1,400 to somewhere between $1,600 to $2,000 (Table 3). Coincidentally, this happens to be the range of grants that several panels and commissions have agreed is necessary to improve the access and participation of low- and moderate-income students in postsecondary education.[9]

A second advantage is that the suggested changes would make for greater simplicity, from the standpoint of both applicants and institutions. When average noninstructional costs are used to establish the maximum grant, BEOG's can begin to function as a voucher system. Since entitlements are simply average costs minus family contribution, eligible students applying for the program would receive promptly a certified chit indicating

9. Among these are the College Entrance Examination Board Panel on Financing Low-Income and Minority Students in Higher Education, the Carnegie Commission on Higher Education, and the HEW (Rivlin) Task Force.

their grant amounts. Upon enrollment, they would simply present these chits to the institutions for payment or credit against institutional charges.

The voucher system would also simplify the program for institutions in that they would no longer have to determine "actual costs of attendance" for each individual student or category of students before making preliminary and final calculations of BEOG entitlements. A recent OE circular provides an example of the complicated tasks that institutions must perform before setting students' grant levels:

> It has come to our attention that many institutions have board plans which do not cover a full week. In those cases, we have established a mechanism for calculating those students' total costs by pro-rating the board charges to cover the full school year. For example, a school has room and board charges of $1,100 per academic year and the cost for board is $300 covering five days per week. The school would determine the per-week charge for a five-day week which, in this example, is $15. Then, the school would prorate this amount on a daily basis ($3.00) and multiply the daily rate by the number of days not covered under the board plan (2 days × $3.00 = $6.00). This $6.00 charge would be added to the weekly rates ($6.00 + $15.00 = $21.00), multiplied by the number of weeks of the term and included with the total cost for the student. While this procedure may appear to be cumbersome, it is, we believe, the most equitable manner of determining these students' actual costs of attendance.

Relating BEOG's to average noninstructional costs not only eases the burden on institutions but also gets the federal government out of the business of auditing "actual costs of attendance," a practice that seems inevitable under existing legislation.

A final advantage is that the suggested higher grant level automatically increases the pool of eligible students, even without any change in the current BEOG Family Contribution Schedule. With each $200 increase in the grant ceiling, the income level at which families become eligible increases by about $800. Thus, if the grant ceiling were $1,800, the family income eligibility would be about $14,000 instead of the current $11,500. On the other hand, if the maximum grant remains at $1,400, then the current BEOG Contribution Schedule will have to be lowered by about 15 percent for all families in order to bring into the program students who would become eligible if the grant ceiling were raised by $200; the family contribution would have to be lowered by 25 percent to bring in students who would become eligible if the maximum grant were raised by $400.

Some critics argue that tying BEOG's to average noninstructional costs and eliminating the half-cost provisions from the program would give a "free ride" to recipients at zero-tuition institutions. But this is true only if (a) the program is fully funded (unlikely in the immediate future) and (b) the student qualifies for the maximum grant. Since only the neediest students receive the maximum grant, I argue that it may be not only desirable but also necessary social policy to offer low-income students special inducements to enroll in college, for higher education may be their only hope for upward economic and social mobility. These same critics consider some "self-help" inviolate and urge its inclusion in the suggested program. The simplest and fairest way to do so is to set the maximum grant for all students at average noninstructional costs minus $400 (or some other specified amount of self-help) and not to make self-help depend implicitly on a grant that cannot exceed one-half the student's cost of attendance. But introducing a self-help component into a program that relates the maximum grant to noninstructional costs simply reduces the grant maximum and at full funding—perhaps again to the $1,400 level—an indefensible ceiling, as we have seen.

Others argue that relating grants to average noninstructional costs will turn BEOG's into a welfare program or an income-maintenance program and that is not acceptable politically. I remind them that noninstructional costs are currently considered in all need-based student aid programs— federal, state, and institutional—and no one complains. I wonder, too, why many of these same critics view education subsidies to the low- and moderate-income students as welfare but regard subsidies to middle- and upper-income students, in the form of low tuition, as embodied virtue.

While the suggested changes in the BEOG program would improve access to public institutions, they do not open the door very wide at most high-cost private institutions. Equal opportunity has two dimensions: access and choice. Mere access to the postsecondary system without regard to the type of access is not enough, for opportunity is inherently unequal unless students are able to choose the institutions best suited to their abilities, needs, and aspirations. A CEEB Panel on Financing Low-Income and Minority Students in Higher Education stated:

> Public policy grounded in a narrow concept of access implies that class status rather than individual attributes and achievements would determine opportunities for higher education; and that the higher education system would become more stratified than it is now on the basis of income and social class.
>
> It is an unstated but frequent assumption that a poor first generation college-goer should enter the local community college or vocational school, his children might enroll in a state college or public university, and the following generation might finally go to a prestigious private college or uni-

versity. In other words, the poor should rise only one rung at a time up the "ladder" of institutional types. The panel rejects such thinking as alien to a society that claims to be free of the arbitrary privileges of class.

Because access to higher economic and social positions is influenced by the kind of institution one attends, opportunities for higher education cannot be equal until the poor and minority students are assured not only equality of access but also equality of options among programs and institutions.[10]

Since the panel made its report, this two-dimensional definition of equal opportunity—access and choice—has begun to take hold, reinforced most recently by the report of the National Commission on the Financing of Postsecondary Education and by a policy statement from the American Council on Education. Still earlier, the 1972 amendments recognized—implicitly at least—that BEOG's, supplemented by the Supplementary Educational Opportunity Grants program (SEOG, a revised and renamed version of EOG) and by the newly authorized State Student Incentive Grants program (SSIG) could ensure eligible students a range of institutional choices. At the same time, these programs—together with the form that the amendments gave to payments to institutions—could help preserve a diverse postsecondary system, particularly a vital private sector. Clearly the Congress attached importance to two goals: equal opportunity and institutional diversity. Both of these goals could be achieved more effectively if SSIG's were expanded and SEOG's restructured to reflect more clearly the legislative intent.

SEOG and SSIG: Programs for choice

Although its title and its placement (following BEOG) in title IV imply that grants under Supplemental Educational Opportunity Grants are to be additive to Basic Grants, the statutory language and legislative history suggest that these grants should be available to two groups of students: (*a*) those who receive a Basic Grant but need more help and (*b*) those who are ineligible for a Basic Grant but still need help. Keeping in mind these target populations, and the objectives of SEOG's discussed above, I would suggest the following program changes:

Suggestion 1: At least 50 percent of SEOG monies should be focused on high-cost private institutions to aid needy students.

When BEOG's are fully funded, the first of the two target populations for SEOG's (BEOG recipients who need more help) will be enrolled

10. *Toward Equal Opportunity for Higher Education* (New York: College Entrance Examination Board, 1973), p. 8.

primarily in high-cost private institutions. If at least half the SEOG funds were allotted to private institutions,[11] SEOG's would foster two national objectives: equal opportunity and preservation of a vital private sector. Moreover, the program could finally live up to the designation of "supplementary": with BEOG's related to average noninstructional costs, then logically SEOG's could be related to tuition or instructional costs.

An institution's eligibility for these funds would be determined by the level of its tuition or instructional costs. So that the program would not encourage tuition increases, institutions would be eligible only if their instructional costs or tuitions in a *prior* base year exceeded a specified *average* of these costs for the private sector. SEOG funds could then be distributed among eligible institutions according to the number of BEOG recipients they enroll. Student eligibility, however, would not be restricted to BEOG recipients. The grant ceiling for the individual student would have a rational basis, reflecting either the average tuition ($1,800 in 1974–75) or one-half the average instructional costs in the private sector (an estimated $3,600 in 1974–75).

Suggestion 2: Another 50 percent of SEOG monies should be distributed among *all* institutions according to the needs of low- and moderate-income students.

Any national program of direct grants, such as BEOG's, is arbitrary and inflexible. Some low-income and moderate-income students simply get cut out. These funds, then, would aid the second target population (students not receiving BEOG's). A recent study by the Washington Office of the CEEB indicates that, were BEOG's to supplant SEOG's, about 5 percent of the current recipients of SEOG's would get reduced or no supplementary grants. To assure that this does not happen, and to counter the inflexibility of the BEOG program, about half of SEOG monies should be allotted to all institutions, private and public.

The allocation of these SEOG monies is a vexing problem. Current state allotments for SEOG's and the other campus-based programs are clearly inequitable. For example, in 1973–74, twenty-three states received only 42.6 percent of their panel-approved requests for SEOG's, while twenty-eight states did considerably better; indeed, one got 100 percent. I have no immediate solution to the allocation problem, but I know a new and more equitable solution must be found.

11. During the 1973–74 academic year, private institutions (excluding proprietary and vocational schools) received 32 percent of SEOG allocations compared with 38 percent in the 1970–71 academic year.

Some participants in the current policy debate suggest that SEOG's and SSIG's be consolidated, related to instructional costs, administered by states, and targeted on students attending private institutions. Although this strategy may be desirable in the future, I consider it premature. SSIG's is one of the most promising programs authorized in the Education Amendments of 1972; it portends a new federal-state partnership in aiding needy students and sustaining a viable private sector. Not until the 1974–75 academic year did the SSIG program finally come into being. It should be given a chance to live at least through infancy and early childhood so that it can be tested to determine its impact on states, students, and institutions and to assess its interaction with other federal and state programs.

It is not yet clear whether state scholarship programs, designed to meet differing state objectives, can be made to meet national objectives. These programs vary markedly from state to state. Some are based purely on need, while others are based on a combination of ability and need. Some restrict aid to students attending a particular sector of postsecondary education, public or private, while others aid students at both public and private institutions. Few accept the broad federal definition of postsecondary education and thus provide aid to students in proprietary, technical, and vocational schools, and few allow recipients to use their grants at out-of-state institutions. Furthermore, state scholarship programs vary widely in their resources and patterns of expenditures—imbalances often compounded by imbalances in student aid resources at institutions within each state.

In short, the SSIG program should be allowed to expand, and state scholarship programs to develop; then we can consider whether it makes sense to mesh SSIG's and SEOG's.

A Note on Loan Programs

With subsidies scarce, grants have to be rationed among students whose backgrounds and incomes would otherwise preclude access and choice. Loans, on the other hand, are repayable investments and should be available to all students wishing to borrow, without consideration of their need. Nor should loans be related to specific categories of costs, as has been suggested for BEOG's and SEOG's.

It is generally accepted that the government must play a role in assuring that all students or their families have access to credit resources so that they may finance higher education out of future rather than current income. Present federal efforts through National Direct Student Loans (NDSL) and the Guaranteed Student Loan program (GSLP) are not adequate to fulfill this role. Furthermore, the programs are inequitable. Who determines which student should receive a 3 percent NDSL, which a 7 percent GSL? Who determines whether freshmen, women, minorities, and nondepositors are eligible to participate in GSLP? Not the law, certainly. It is too soon to know whether the new secondary market established for guaranteed loans will have significant impact, although it clearly could.

Other remedies must be considered, such as meshing the NDSL and GSL programs, with institutions or states to act as lenders, or establishing a national student loan bank (perhaps evolving out of Sallie Mae), which would raise its own capital to make loans to students, with the government providing insurance against losses. Eliminating interest subsidies and allowing more flexible repayment terms (long term and income contingent rather than fixed obligation) might also be considered.

A Note on College Work-Study

At the risk of challenging a sacred cow of the current federal student assistance effort, I must state that, in my view, the College Work-Study program (CWS) is not a student aid program.

During the recent House hearings, CWS received more acclaim than any other title IV program. It was applauded by students, institutions, employers, corporate executives, and members of Congress. And it was the one college-based program for which the administration has requested funding since the 1972 amendments were passed.

Perhaps everyone likes CWS because it is in keeping with the work ethic and with the traditional belief that "working one's way through college"—at least in part these days—has moral value exceeded only by motherhood and apple pie.

Students like Work-Study because it is an accepted form of the traditional student assistance package: grants, loans, and work. Further, they need not seek employment; instead, institutions find them jobs.

Institutions and employers like College Work-Study probably because the federal government pays 80 percent of the cost of employing individuals in necessary jobs and because Work-Study students are often cheap labor. But the question then arises, Who is receiving the subsidy, employers or students? While there is nothing wrong with subsidizing institutions and nonprofit organizations, this was not the intent of the program.

Work-Study is a form of employment, of payment for services provided; and, if that premise is accepted, College Work-Study students should be treated no differently from other students who use work as a means of meeting the college bill. But they are treated differently.

The earnings of CWS students are taxed at a rate of 100 percent; that is, if work is filling the student's need gap, all of his or her earnings are applied to the cost of education. On the other hand, the student who earns wages outside the College Work-Study program is not required to apply all earnings to educational costs. For example, if a full-time student earns $950 (the current average for full-time students) and if his/her need gap is $650, he/she can save $300 and apply it to expenses for the following academic year. According to current needs analysis, however, the student's expected contribution from these savings is approximately 30 percent instead of the 100 percent required of CWS students. In addition, full-time students who work at outside employment earn, on the average, about $300 more than full-time College Work-Study students; part-time students who are employed outside earn about $700 more than part-time students in the College Work-Study program.

College Work-Study emerged from poverty legislation of the 1960s as a program directed at low-income students, who frequently had to work for low pay in jobs unrelated to their programs of study. Historically, the program has penalized the poor, whose participation in CWS was—and often still is—a condition of their receiving other forms of student assistance.

While the 1972 amendments deleted the low-income provision from College Work-Study, they stated that preference should be given "to students with the greatest financial need." If work and study benefit some students, it should follow that work and study benefit all students. I therefore suggest that the needs test be eliminated from College Work-Study and that the program be expanded to all students, rich and poor, dependent only on their interest in combining work with study or career objectives. Their earnings would not be regarded as student aid but as student income and would be treated exactly like other student income in determining eligibility for other forms of financial aid. To hold down the costs of the proposed program, the federal share, now 80 percent, could be greatly reduced.

Relating BEOG's to average noninstructional costs makes the program more equitable, comprehensible, and rational; it becomes a voucher scheme, thus simplifying matters for both applicants and institutions. Because of the higher grant ceiling, a wider population becomes eligible;

low-income students no longer suffer the inequities of ratable reduction or the current half-cost provisions. Further, relating the program to noninstructional costs keeps the "feds" out of the business of influencing the costs of instruction. A new federal-state partnership in financing needy students may eventually evolve. These were my stated objectives.

The Supplemental Educational Opportunity Grant program would focus on instructional costs and, with the State Scholarship Incentive Grants program, would supplement BEOG's and provide wider institutional choice to eligible students. Finally, a new loan structure should be considered, and College Work-Study would cease to be seen as a student aid program.

Some might argue that these changes in federal student aid programs are unnecessary and that all we need is more money and better administration of the existing programs. The simplicity of this contention gives it an appealing plausibility. Yet neither additional funds nor improved management can free the program of its present shortcomings or resolve the incoherence that results from the legislation itself; nor can either cure the inequities that are inevitable when student eligibility is determined partly by law and partly by chance, by accident of geography or of institutional participation. Neither can cure the problem of state allotments and their resulting inequities; neither can right the inequities that I have identified in the BEOG program.

Others, claiming that the student assistance program requires far more sweeping change than I have suggested, present dramatic and costly proposals which are doomed to oblivion. The Ford administration has already indicated that it will certainly seek a slowdown in the growth of expenditures for education; indeed, it may insist on cutbacks. Tax dollars are needed for a multitude of worthy causes, and added billions of government support for postsecondary education simply are not going to materialize in the near future.

The alternatives that I have proposed are actually a bit conservative. They assume that parents still have the obligation to meet some of the costs of their children's education; they focus on change in *existing* programs; they sustain the goals of the 1972 amendments and recognize the continuing social needs of the 1960s and the concerns of the 1970s; they build on the traditional roles of postsecondary finance. In the search for alternatives, however, we do not need utopian solutions. Instead, we need to place before the Congress for its upcoming debate imaginative and pragmatic solutions to the real problems which plague the current federal student assistance programs.

Grants for Students Based on Their Own Income

GEORGE B. WEATHERSBY

VIRTUALLY EVERYONE who attends postsecondary education is an adult, and, from the viewpoint of physical and psychological development, has been acknowledged so for some time. Recently a variety of statutes and court decisions have given legal affirmation to eighteen-year-old majority. However, federal and state student aid policies have divided adults attending postsecondary education into two categories: young people who are financially dependent on their parents and who attend school full time, and other people who are older, or financially independent of their parents, or attend school part time. Furthermore, federal and state student aid policies and regulations have treated persons in these two categories quite differently, with the bulk of student aid going to young, full-time, financially dependent students. I argue here that this discrimination is unjust (largely a legal and moral argument) and, perhaps more persuasively to public policy, that this discrimination is unnecessary (largely an analytical argument).

I advocate two propositions: (1) Public financial assistance should be provided on a just and equitable basis to all students attending postsecondary education. (2) Governments should base their decisions regarding the amount of, and the eligibility for, student financial assistance on the impact on enrollment rather than on arbitrarily defined "financial need." Equity and effectiveness in public policy are hardly radical notions, but their application to student financial assistance would require substantial changes in public views as well as public policies. I argue further that distributing student financial assistance on the basis of individual income and individually borne costs of education would be equitable and effective.

POSTSECONDARY EDUCATION: THE EMERGING CONTEXT

To understand the implications of distributing student financial assistance on the basis of individual income necessitates being alert to the emerging context of postsecondary education. As public policy has expanded its focus from higher education to postsecondary education, some of the stereotypes have become myths with but a shadow of reality.

TABLE 1

DISTRIBUTION OF HIGHER EDUCATION
ENROLLMENTS, BY AGE GROUP, 1970

Age	Enrollment	Percentage
Under 18	59,946	0.8
18–21	4,266,874	56.7
22–24	1,333,898	17.7
25–34	1,393,841	18.5
35–49	366,056	4.9
50–over	103,966	1.4

SOURCE: *Financing Part-time Students: The New Majority in Postsecondary Education*, Report of the Committee on the Financing of Higher Education for Adult Students to the Office of Governmental Relations, American Council on Education (Washington: The Council, 1974), p. 23.

One pervasive notion is that the vast majority of students are in the 18–21 age group. But the facts belie this perception: 42.5 percent of higher education students in 1970 were twenty-two years old or older (see table 1). In 1972, of all 18–24-year-olds who did not report family income, 26 percent were enrolled in the collegiate sector.[1] In the same year, 31 percent of all college graduates and 23 percent of all adults who had completed some college work were enrolled in one or more continuing education programs. In other words, in 1972, the proportion of adult college graduates enrolled in a program of continuing education was greater than the proportion of young adults enrolled in a collegiate program seeking a degree.[2]

Still another myth, and probably one more difficult to dispel, is that a majority of students attend full time. But the enterprise is really comprised of an equal number of part-time and full-time students. The American Council on Education's Committee on the Financing of Higher Education for Adult Students came up with these findings about part-time students: (1) "Since 1969 more students have participated in postsecondary education on a part-time basis (credit and noncredit) than on a full-time basis . . . (55.0 percent vs. 45 percent in 1969 and 57.5 percent vs. 42.5 percent in 1972). Between 1969 and 1972 . . . part-time students . . . increased at a rate 2.3 times faster than full-time students (20.4 percent

1. U.S. Bureau of the Census, *Current Population Survey* (October 1972), quoted in National Commission on the Financing of Postsecondary Education, *Financing Postsecondary Education in the United States* (Washington: Government Printing Office, 1973), p. 137. The age range 18–24 is used because comparable 18–21 statistics are not available.

2. Dorothy M. Gilford, "The Noncollegiate Sector: Statistical Snapshots of Adult Continuing Education" (Paper presented at the American Association for Higher Education, March 12, 1974), p. 12.

part time vs. 8.8 percent full time).'' (2) In the collegiate sector, the rate of increase of part-time students was 35.3 percent, or 3.5 times greater than for full-time students (10.1 percent increase). (3) Approximately one-half of students in collegiate institutions in 1972 were part time.[3]

In short, postsecondary education today actually encompasses both degree and nondegree programs for all organized learning opportunities beyond secondary school; it serves adults of all ages; it includes collegiate and noncollegiate institutions and community organizations. It serves a grand total of 25 million students in about 78,000 institutions: 66,700 adult education, 8,182 accredited noncollegiate institutions, and 2,948 collegiate.[4] It is in this context that we must evaluate the impacts of alternative student financial assistance policies.

FINANCIAL NEED VERSUS ENROLLMENT PRICE RESPONSIVENESS

For the purposes of analysis, it is important to separate two concepts: "financial need," based on either student or family income; and "price responsiveness," based on observed individual behavior.

Financial need is an arbitrary means of deciding who should (*not* who will) bear the cost of an individual's attendance at a postsecondary educational institution. The Family Contribution Schedule established by the federal government is intended to be a consistent set of assumptions about how much support parents should (*not* will) provide toward meeting a student's cost of education. This expected contribution is then used as a basis for a consistent distribution of public funds in the form of student grants. However, there is little evidence that financial need is related to student enrollment decisions and, therefore, to access.[5] A recent College Scholarship Service report on the results of administering its Student Resource Surveys in California, Washington, and Oregon, observed:

> Perhaps the most surprising finding in all three West Coast Student Resource Surveys is the large discrepancy between the theory of parent and student financing of higher education and the reality.
> The theory behind student financial aid and financial need analysis asserts that parents will contribute towards college costs to the best of their

---

3. *Financing Part-time Students: The New Majority in Postsecondary Education,* Report of the Committee on the Financing of Higher Education for Adult Students to the Office of Governmental Relations, American Council on Education (Washington: The Council, 1974), pp. 2, 40.

4. Gilford, "The Noncollegiate Sector."

5. For a discussion of the evidence on student access, choice, and opportunity, see *Financing Postsecondary Education,* pp. 134–36.

financial ability. The parental contribution is considered as the primary source of funds for college. . . .

In practice, the parental contribution seems to be the final step in the financing equation. First, the student works (and borrows), then he/she may apply for financial aid, and finally the parent (acting as a family aid officer) may fill the gap between those resources and the student's need.

Indicative of this pattern (and also of a more disquieting pattern) is the discrepancy between expected parental contribution (as derived from college scholarship service contribution tables) and student reported parental support.

. . . it still appears as if better than 40 percent of the parents in the total SRS survey are making little or no contribution towards college.[6]

Of the $4.4 billion spent by all sources on student aid in 1971–72, $3.9 billion (or 88 percent) was provided by the federal government.[7] As Cartter puts it: "The new federal philosophy, expressed in the Education Amendments of 1972 (although not yet fully implemented), establishes as a federal responsibility the basic funding of a system of universal access to higher education, and selects direct student aid as the means of implementation."[8]

The two largest federal student aid programs, representing over $3 billion in 1973 federal obligations, are administered by the Veterans Administration[9] and the Social Security Administration. The remaining financial aid programs include need-based student grants, work subsidies, loans, and programs targeted for particular segments of the student population. The need-based grants, loans, and other aid, totaling over $1 billion in 1973 federal obligations, include: Basic Educational Opportunity Grants (BEOG), Supplemental Educational Opportunity Grants (SEOG), Guaranteed Student Loans (GSL), College Work-Study (CWS), and others.[10]

In federal statutes establishing these need-based programs and in Office of Education regulations administering them, two categories of students— dependent and independent—are used in determining eligibility. For in-

6. Dick Dent et al., *Oregon Student Resource Survey* (Salem: Oregon Educational Coordinating Council, June 1973), p. xvii.

7. *Financing Postsecondary Education*, p. 69.

8. Allan M. Cartter, "The Future Financing of Postsecondary Education," in *Education and the State,* ed. John F. Hughes (Washington: American Council on Education, 1975), p. 52.

9. The GI Bill provides (*a*) assistance for up to thirty-six months of full-time schooling or on-the-job training for eligible veterans and service personnel; (*b*) educational assistance for war orphans and widows; and (*c*) vocational rehabilitation training for disabled veterans, which provides for the cost of books, tuition, fees, and training supplies, among other items.

10. U.S. Office of Education, Bureau of Higher Education, *Factbook: Summary Program Information Through FY 1973* (Washington: Government Printing Office, 1974).

stance, for BEOG purposes, all students are assumed to be dependent on their parents, unless, through a series of tests, they can prove themselves to be independent. One among the tests is that the student not receive more than $600 per year in support from the parents, and have not been declared as a dependent on the parents' tax forms. (Note that neither "dependent" nor "independent" is as yet strictly defined in the same terms across all student aid programs.)

The amount of aid to which a dependent student is entitled is based on the parents' income and assets; for instance, Basic Educational Opportunity Grants determine the eligibility of dependent students for aid by "using a standard 'family contribution schedule' which assesses each family's expected contribution toward a student's eligible costs and expectations." (Under the BEOG provisions, the dependent student gets a maximum of $1,400 minus his own assets and the expected parental contribution.) For determining a dependent student's eligibility for Supplemental Educational Opportunity Grants, the "expected family income shall be considered." To be eligible for a subsidized Guaranteed Student Loan, a dependent student's "adjusted family income" is required to be less than $15,000. Furthermore, to be eligible for Social Security survivor's benefits, students must count themselves dependent upon parents. In making the award, the government puts full-time students, ages 18–22 only, through a postsecondary education—on the assumption that death, retirement, or disability has prevented the parents eligible for Social Security benefits from meeting this obligation.

Today, most students seem to count themselves as dependents. The Office of Education reports that, of 1974–75 applicants, 82 percent were dependent students, and 18 percent were independent. But a 1973 survey completed for the College Scholarship Service Western Regional Subcommittee on Need Assessment reports an increase in the number of students claiming themselves independent of parental support. The subcommittee found that beyond just the desire that an increasing number of young people have for claiming independence from parents, the institutions' procedures for testing "economic independence" have a definite influence on the numbers declaring independence. Institutions requiring affidavits that parents are not providing support, the study concluded, have lower-than-average proportions of students claiming to be independent for student aid purposes.[11]

For most students, then, family financial resources, described by statute

11. Dent, *Oregon Student Resource Survey*, p. xvii.

TABLE 2

WEIGHTED NATIONAL NORMS FOR ALL FRESHMEN,
ALL INSTITUTIONS, FALL 1975

Income Group	Percentage	
	Parental Income	Student Income
Under $3,000	3.7	94.3
$3,000–$9,999	22.4	4.8
$10,000–$14,999	29.6	0.9
$15,000 and over	44.2	

SOURCE: Alexander W. Astin et al., *The American Freshman: National Norms for Fall 1973* (Los Angeles: American Council on Education and University of California, Los Angeles, Cooperative Research Program, n.d.), pp. 41–42.

or by agency regulations, are the central test for eligibility for federal student aid. The Congress's and the Office of Education's point of view is that financial support is primarily the responsibility of the student's family.

The percentage of students eligible for student aid would increase dramatically if, based on the OE need schedules for independent students, student income rather than the parental income were the measure. As table 2 shows, only 3.7 percent of collegiate freshmen surveyed by the American Council on Education estimated their parents' income at under $3,000. At the same time, 94.3 percent of this freshman group said their own income—independent of their parents—was under $3,000. Thus, by these measures, a 90 percent or more increase in the number eligible for student aid is conceivable.

Using these estimates of student income under grant limitations of $1,400 or 50 percent cost of instruction, whichever is less, and using the BEOG contribution schedule for "independent students with no dependents," approximately 7.5 million students would have qualified in 1972–73 for about $8 billion in grants. That sum is equivalent to total federal expenditures in postsecondary education in 1972. However, the unmet need approach is misleading for two reasons: (1) Many currently enrolled students experience a substantial, unmet need that bears no relationship to their decision to attend postsecondary educational institutions.[12] (2) There is no information on the effect that additional grants might have on the access of individuals not now enrolled.

In addition to being only loosely related to public policy objectives of student access, choice, and opportunity, the unmet need approach leaves

12. Massachusetts estimates $78 million in unmet needs for just over 200,000 currently enrolled students. See Peter Edelman, *Equal Opportunity Pool Proposal* (Massachusetts Public and Private Forum, 1974).

open a still unresolved legal and ethical question of equity. Basing the distribution of public financial aid to students on the presumption of family financial support creates a special problem for those who do not receive the anticipated financial support from the families, which the Oregon Student Resource Survey showed is increasingly the case. The key question here is whether or not the federal adoption of a Family Contribution Schedule creates a legally enforceable claim that a student could exercise against his or her parents. If the family contribution schedule is legally enforceable and if students received less family support than the federal government said they should receive, they could sue their parents. On the other hand, if the Family Contribution Schedule is not legally enforceable, then its use by the federal government to determine both student eligibility for financial aid and the amount of award may seem to violate the equal protection amendment to the Constitution. In other words, current need-based programs that are based on family income presume a specified level of family support, even though students are not assured of receiving that support and evidence suggests that its level is falling. Given the choice of encouraging students to sue the parents or encouraging the government to reconsider its presumptions, I prefer the latter.

A second analysis compares what would happen if the same amount in student grants were distributed in two different ways—one based on family income and one based on student income. Using the estimated price responsiveness of persons according to their income bracket,[13] one can predict what effect the two approaches would have on enrollment and, therefore, the effect on access. This approach is reported below.

This analysis uses the same institutional categories, projected base-line enrollments, and family income distributions that were used in *Financing Postsecondary Education in the United States*. This analysis also uses the other parameters and assumptions described in *A Framework for Analyzing Postsecondary Education Financing Policies*. In addition, in the absence of any representative data, this analysis assumes that student income is distributed similarly among all institutional types, and the figures used are intentionally conservative—50 percent earning less than $3,000, 80 percent earning less than $5,000, and 96 percent earning less than $10,000 (see table 3).

13. See Daryl Carlson, James Farmer, and George Weathersby, *A Framework for Analyzing Postsecondary Education Financing Policies* (Washington: Government Printing Office, May 1974) for a discussion of the evidence on price responsiveness.

TABLE 3

ASSUMED DISTRIBUTION OF UNDERGRADUATES
IN POSTSECONDARY EDUCATION,
BY INCOME CATEGORY, 1974

Student Income	Percentage	Cumulative Percentage
Under $1,000	10.0	10.0
$ 1,000–$1,999	15.0	25.0
2,000–2,999	25.0	50.0
3,000–3,999	17.5	67.5
4,000–4,999	13.0	80.5
5,000–5,999	8.0	88.5
6,000–7,499	5.0	93.5
7,500–9,999	3.0	96.5
10,000–14,999	2.0	98.5
15,000–24,999	1.0	99.5
25,000 and over	0.5	100.0
	100.0	

SOURCE: Calculations by staff of the National Commission on the Financing of Postsecondary Education.

NOTE: This distribution shows slightly higher incomes overall than those for freshmen shown in Table 2, because it covers students of all ages at all levels of undergraduate schools.

The assumed income distribution is especially conservative when one recognizes that about one-half of the students in postsecondary education are part time, and of these, many work full time and almost one-half are over twenty-two years old. The conservative income distribution was chosen to understate the effectiveness of need-based financial aid reckoned from student income.

Without proposing to change any other financing programs, this analysis examines the effects of the following plan:

1. $1.6 billion in 1977 and $1.8 billion in 1980 are made available in additional student grants.
2. These grants are distributed to all eligible students (incomes less than $15,000) in proportion to their "need," that is, proportional to the tuition of an institutional sector and inversely proportional to the individual or family income.[14]

The following discussion refers to the two alternative plans as "Family Income Need Based" (FINB) and "Student Income Need Based" (SINB); the only difference is the income distribution used to determine the eligibility for the grants and their distribution pattern.

The fundamental conclusion of this analysis (see tables 4–6) is that,

14. See *A Framework for Analyzing Postsecondary Education Financing Policies,* pp. 67, 75–77.

under the conservative assumptions specified above, a student income need based grant program will be more effective in increasing student access and choice than will a family income need based grant program, for the same expenditure. Table 4 shows that SINB grants would increase enrollments at public four-year, at private, and at noncollegiate institutions more than would FINB grants. The percentage increase in low-income enrollments (under $10,000) is less with SINB than FINB grants only because 96 percent of all students are assumed to earn less than $10,000 and, therefore, the SINB denominator is markedly larger than for FINB. As shown in table 5, SINB grants would increase enrollments by about 100,000 students more than would FINB grants; and, for the same amount of additional public funds, the cost per additional student is $1,300 less per year.

Table 6 shows the estimated average grant per student. Under current family income distributions and with $1.6 billion to $1.8 billion additional expenditures, just over 6 million students would be eligible each year and

TABLE 4

ESTIMATED ENROLLMENT AND FINANCIAL IMPACT
OF FAMILY AND STUDENT INCOME NEED BASED GRANT PROGRAMS,
FOR $1.6 BILLION ADDITIONAL IN 1977 AND $1.8 BILLION
ADDITIONAL IN 1980

Enrollment Category	Percentage Changes from Base-line Enrollment			
	Family Income Need Based		Student Income Need Based	
	1977	1980	1977	1980
Public				
Two year	−1.08	−1.16	−1.25	−1.35
Four year, lower division	0.77	0.83	1.21	1.31
Four year, upper division	1.84	1.99	2.74	2.96
Four year, graduate	0.0	0.0	0.0	0.0
Private				
Undergraduate	6.61	7.12	10.94	11.82
Graduate	0.0	0.0	0.0	0.0
Noncollegiate	5.31	5.71	5.93	6.40
Undergraduate				
Under $10,000	5.88	6.27	3.76	4.03
$10,000–$15,000	0.97	1.03	0.32	0.34
Over $15,000	0.0	0.0	0.0	0.0

Source of Support	Projected Cost per Additional Student			
Federal government	$3,843	$3,894	$2,513	$2,544
State government	197	226	217	252
Local government	0	0	0	0
Student or family	863	1,023	824	977
Private sources	233	273	251	295
Total	$5,136	$5,416	$3,806	$4,066

SOURCE: NCFPE staff calculations.

TABLE 5

ESTIMATED NUMBER OF STUDENTS, BY INCOME, GIVEN
AN ADDITIONAL $1.6 BILLION IN STUDENT GRANTS IN 1977,
AND AN ADDITIONAL $1.8 BILLION IN 1980

| Income Level | Number of Students (thousands) | | | |
| | Family Income | | Student Income | |
	1977	1980	1977	1980
Under $1,000	71	75	930	971
$ 1,000–$1,999	155	164	1,412	1,475
2,000–2,999	224	236	2,307	2,408
3,000–3,999	342	359	1,599	1,667
4,000–4,999	418	438	1,180	1,230
5,000–5,999	429	449	723	754
6,000–7,499	678	710	451	469
7,500–9,999	1,223	1,275	267	278
10,000–14,999	2,641	2,754	178	185
15,000–24,999	2,009	2,086	89	92
25,000 and over	889	918	44	46
Total[a]	9,080	9,464	9,180	9,576

SOURCE: NCFPE staff calculations.

a) Totals computed separately; columns may not add to total because of rounding.

TABLE 6

ESTIMATED GRANT PER STUDENT, BY INCOME, GIVEN
AN ADDITIONAL $1.6 BILLION IN STUDENT GRANTS IN 1977
AND AN ADDITIONAL $1.8 BILLION IN 1980

| Income Level | Average Grant | | | |
| | Family Income | | Student Income | |
	1977	1980	1977	1980
Under $1,000	$705	$764	$201	$218
$ 1,000–$1,999	918	997	254	276
2,000–2,999	684	737	166	180
3,000–3,999	458	494	124	134
4,000–4,999	299	324	98	107
5,000–5,999	274	295	82	88
6,000–7,499	231	249	67	73
7,500–9,999	168	181	52	56
10,000–14,999	115	124	37	42
15,000–24,999	0	0	0	0
25,000 and over	0	0	0	0
Average grant	$259	$279	$177	$191

SOURCE: NCFPE staff calculations.

the average grant would range from $260 to $280, with a high of about $1,000. However, under the assumed student income distribution, but with the same eligibility cut-off at $15,000 maximum income, the number of eligible students increases by about 50 percent to over 9 million; and the grants fall a corresponding 33 percent, averaging between $180 and $190 per person, with a maximum of about $275.

GRANTS BASED ON STUDENT INCOME *Weathersby* 179

With the grant pattern shown in table 6, one might assume that FINB grants ranging up to $1,000 and averaging $280 should have a greater effect on access than SINB grants ranging up to $275 and averaging $190. This assumption would appear reasonable: a larger student grant would increase the likelihood that an individual would attend a postsecondary education institution. However, the average grant awards shown in table 6 would be applied to the very different income distributions shown in table 5. Although the average SINB grants range from one-fourth to one-third of the average FINB grants by income level, SINB grant recipients with below $6,000 income are approximately two to ten times as numerous as the same category of FINB recipients. In other words, under SINB, a smaller grant is available to a larger, low-income (and, therefore, more price responsive) population; SINB grants thereby have a greater effect than FINB grants.

Some observers are concerned that using student income instead of family income would dilute much of the current effort to aid students from low-income families. Even worse, some fear that basing student aid on student income would work to the disadvantage of persons from low-income families who must help support the family. Although little information exists on the relationship between student and family income, a 1973 survey revealed that the earning power of first-time, full-time freshmen was very similar, independent of family income.[15] Therefore, while SINB grants would not discriminate in favor of students from low-income families, neither would they discriminate against students from low-income families. In fact, SINB grants appear to be relatively neutral with respect to family income and much more responsive to student income.

15. Special tabulations from the fall 1973 freshman survey of the Cooperative Institutional Research Program, Alexander W. Astin, director, sponsored by the American Council on Education, administered by the Higher Education Laboratory, University of California, Los Angeles.

Differentiated Aid Programs
for Today's Emancipated Students

RICHARD A. FULTON

A LACK OF CANDOR permeates both the philosophy and the practice of America's most institutionalized cottage industry, the administration of student financial aid. The otherwise emancipated student of today still is inhibited—and possibly even intimidated—by an array of undifferentiated financial aid programs.

The philosophy of some programs is clearly linked with the cultural heritage of parental financial responsibility. Other programs may be the result of political compromise or budgetary duplicity. Fortunately the scheduled 1976 expiration of the Higher Education Act of 1965—which first proclaimed the principle of "student entitlement"—offers Congress the opportunity to make that principle practicable through a comprehensive redefinition and differentiation of all the title IV student aid programs.

Except for the administration of financial aid, today's student is emancipated, as was succinctly noted in a recent issue of *Financial Aid News:*

> *Age of Majority.* As Congress rethinks the guaranteed loan program and considers changes in other federal student aid, attention may increasingly focus on the implications of the age of majority. According to the Council of State Governments, since 1970 over 40 states have lowered the age of legal adulthood to 18 (19 in a few states), which in most cases means that 18-year-olds now have the right to sign legal contracts in their own behalf. This development has stimulated questions about the traditional concept of parental responsibility in need-based student financial aid programs. Although no one has a crystal ball, some observers maintain it is only a matter of time before the courts bar government programs that allocate benefits to legally adult students on the basis of need defined in terms of their parents' financial status.[1]

Resort to the courts by students dissatisfied with the administration of student financial aid programs is neither novel nor isolated. Nearly 4 percent of student debtors under the Guaranteed Student Loan program (GSLP) have successfully sought relief in bankruptcy. A move by the New York Higher Education Assistance Authority to deny new applicants

---

1. College Entrance Examination Board, 1974.

insured student loans because of the "unacceptable" default rate of previous student borrowers at the same eligible institutions was judicially denied.

Accreditation as an element of institutional eligibility is the subject of two student-supported lawsuits against the Accrediting Commission of the Association of Independent Colleges and Schools (AICS), of which I am general counsel. In South Carolina, AICS has been subjected to a $1 million damage claim by students who allege that the accrediting agency failed to timely withdraw accreditation of the institution.[2] Conversely, in California, AICS has been sued by a class of students who seek to preserve their eligibility for student aid by asking the court to prohibit withdrawal of institutional accreditation by the Accrediting Commission.[3]

THE FALLACY OF DESIGNATIONS

The question is not whether suit will be brought by some emancipated student; it is, rather, under what program and against whom. My own prediction is that one of the so-called college-based programs, such as Supplemental Educational Opportunity Grants (SEOG) or National Direct Student Loans (NDSL) rather than Basic Educational Opportunity Grants (BEOG) will be involved. This is not because parental financial status is less important in BEOG but because the institution, which supposedly has a more direct exercise of discretion in the college-based programs, is also a less formidable defendant than the federal government. (Under BEOG, the institution is merely a disbursing agent instead of a grantor, as in the college-based programs.)

Even the term *college-based programs* is itself nothing short of a euphemism, one more example of the lack of candor in denominating programs of financial aid to students. Such an artifice avoids useful differentiation of title IV student aid programs into at least two distinct categories: (1) the college-based programs, comprising SEOG, NDSL, and College Work-Study (CWS), in which the student is an incident of the institution's discretion to award federally funded largesse; and (2) BEOG and the Guaranteed Student Loan Program (GSLP), in which the institution is, theoretically, merely an incident of the student's decision to enroll, under the entitlement rationale of both programs.

2. *Alfred Jacobs et al.* vs. *Association of Independent Colleges and Schools,* No. 44-CP-23-882, in the Court of Common Pleas, State of South Carolina, County of Greeneville (1974).
3. *Rockland Institute and Belinda Ortega et al.* vs. *Association of Independent Colleges and Schools,* No. CV 74-2712, C.D. California (1974).

The ascription of only the most laudable intent to both the institution and the student pretermits the possibility of an indiscrete (and indiscreet!) motive on the part of either. The student may be seeking nonquantifiable equality of institutional choice rather than homogenized equality of educational access. Presumably the institution is succoring a budding scholar rather than suckering, through an aggressive recruitment program, another body to help fill a half-empty dormitory in this no-growth era.

Parental financial status is, of course, only part of the impedimenta both of access to postsecondary education and of institutional choice. The explicit parental financial responsibility in the present title IV statutory language was as equally implicit in the not-so-subtle advertising of the insurance industry dating back at least to the 1920s.

If we were dealing only with the aspirations of middle-class students, the currency of the concept of parental financial status might go unquestioned. It would be consonant with the cultural heritage of privately financed insurance programs or publicly funded grants. But since we have opened postsecondary education to additional "publics," the utility of the concept as it applies to each student aid program is an appropriate policy item for Congress to consider in reviewing higher education legislation.

Two eras of student financial aid and college recruiting are touchingly contrasted by John Egerton. He describes the colorful "Uncle Billy" Hill, a field representative of Western Kentucky State College in the 1950s:

> Unencumbered by the arcane intricacies of the standardized aptitude test, he was free to grant admission—and often scholarship assistance—to students his instinct told him would succeed in college, and to those favored prospects he became in fact a surrogate uncle. At any given time during his career, a hundred or more of "his" students were enrolled, and he always knew which ones were on the dean's list, or in academic difficulty, or in debt at the bursar's office. . . .
>
> In the spring of 1974, the Office of University-School Relations at Western Kentucky University looked as busy as the floor of the New York Stock Exchange. A full-scale campaign to recruit new students was nearing its climax. Computer printouts listing every candidate for graduation from a Kentucky high school in 1974 were being pored over by the staff. The printouts yielded a wealth of information: American College Test scores, college choice in one-two-three order, preferred fields of study, special talents (debate, music, athletics, even cheerleading). A three-member professional staff and a team of secretaries, with help from committees of faculty members and administrators, were busily pursuing the best potential enrollees by mail and by personal visit. Two of the staff members had been on the road three or four days a week since the previous October, trying to get their prize

prospects "signed" before some competing college or university beat them to it.

The stark contrast between the recruiting style of Will B. Hill and that of the computer-armed professionals and technicians of 1974 aptly symbolizes the difference between Western Kentucky State College and Western Kentucky University. But more arresting than the contrast—and perhaps more significant—is an underlying similarity: when Western was in the midst of its transformation from a small college to a large university, it had no need at all for field representatives of any kind. Its biggest problem was not finding students, but finding places for them—building dormitories and classrooms quickly enough to meet the demand. Now it has come full circle, in a sense: in order to keep its enrollment from shrinking, it must send out recruiters to engage in intense competition for new students.[4]

CONTRAPUNTAL NONHARMONICS OF THE GSLP

In contrast to Sir Winston's pudding, which was taken away because it lacked theme, the Guaranteed Student Loan program survives apparently because of its chameleonlike adaptability to the political coloration of any theme currently in vogue.

The GSLP has its conceptual roots deep into the past of a simpler American society where fewer than 10 percent and probably closer to 5 percent of the nation's youth went off to college. A loan from the hometown banker was a personal transaction by which the student's commitment to the system was made manifest. Such was superficially the rationale which justified the proposal's being favorably reported out by the Senate Subcommittee on Education in 1964.[5] That the measure did not exclude students in proprietary, business, trade, and technical schools was either not noted by academics or deemed unworthy of comment.

A 1964 survey of guidance counselors by the Senate subcommittee led to the erroneous prediction that "students from lower income families are less likely to accept Federal student loans or guaranteed commercial loans than students from higher income families."[6] (In fact, according to ACE's Policy Analysis Service, "low-income students are overrepresented, and high-income students underrepresented, among loan-takers."[7])

Thus, the stage was set to publicize the program as providing "loans of convenience for middle-class students." Such a theme ignored the fact that this would be the only USOE-administered student aid program available

4. Egerton, "Western Kentucky University: Facing the No-Growth Era," *Change,* September 1974, p. 36.
5. Senate Report No. 1486 to accompany S. 3140, Aug. 19, 1964.
6. Ibid., p. 8.
7. See "Student Aid Programs," ACE/PAS Fact Sheet #3, June 20, 1974.

to students in proprietary institutions. In a statement to the Senate sub-committee, Dr. Kenneth B. Hoty, then president-elect of the American Personnel and Guidance Association, characterized such students as coming "from families of a lower-income socioenomic [sic] background."[8]

What was conceived out of an age of educational innocence became law in 1965 as the result of a political response to the Ribicoff-Dominick tax-credit-for-tuition proposal, which had appreciable private college support and middle-class momentum. Actually there were two guaranteed student loan programs enacted in 1965. The better-known program in the Higher Education Act was for years explicitly characterized by both the executive and the Congress as "loans of convenience." Little noted was the National Vocational Student Loan Insurance Act (P.L. 89-287), which was destined to provide loans of necessity for nondegree vocational students, including those in proprietary schools. No other program was open to these vocational students.

By 1968 the two divergent GSL programs were consolidated statutorily, if not philosophically, into section 435 of the Higher Education Amendments. Then, in the first Nixon Administration, what had been called *loans of convenience* came to be styled *loans of necessity*. What was enacted as a political ploy was perpetuated to keep some $5 billion out of the federal budget.

In 1972 the GSLP had grafted upon it the necessity for a computation of adjusted family income so that the student borrower might be eligible for the payment of the interest on his loan (of convenience or of necessity?). A detailed statutory comment on the resulting contretemps between Congress and HEW can be found in the *Harvard Journal on Legislation.*[9]

Rather than ascribing a mere lack of candor, this discerning HEW lawyer (writing in his private capacity) concludes:

> Far from being susceptible to a number of conflicting but reasonable interpretations, *the new interest subsidy eligibility provisions are much more accurately described as gobbledegook.* As if to affirm this characterization, the members of Congress who expressed their thoughts on the meaning of the new provisions almost uniformly avoided discussing the language of the provisions: instead, they expounded on what their "intent" was in adopting them. Even if HEW had had the benefit of all these post hoc statements of

8. See Hearings on S. 600, Senate Subcommittee on Education, June 3, 1965, p. 1083.

9. Harold Jenkins, "Statutory Comment: Legislative-Executive Disagreement: Interpreting the 1972 Amendments to the Guaranteed Student Loan Program," *Harvard Journal on Legislation,* April 1973.

intent, to the extent that they embodied concepts which were obviously absent from the law and in many cases contradicted each other, it is uncertain how HEW would have implemented the statute. Such uncertainty would seem to be inevitable whenever legislators attempt to use statements of intent not to supplement statutory provisions but to serve as substitutes for drafting provisions clearly.[10]

As GSLP default rates continue to climb, a host of proposals are aborning to reform the program and its administration. These include: eliminating the interest subsidy; abandoning the program itself; and imposing stringent new restrictions on "high-default schools,"[11] such as (*a*) strict prorated refund formulas for student dropouts, (*b*) enforced negative recruiting techniques, and (*c*) proof of job placement for graduates.

Completely ignored are the following issues:

· As yet, the "high-default student" has not been publicly profiled. After all, students—not schools—borrow the money.
· As yet, the "high-default bank" has not been publicly profiled. After all, banks—not schools—lend the money.

To have a stable future, the GSLP must be endowed with an explicit and consistent theme unambiguously articulated by Congress to be unequivocally administered by HEW-USOE. Otherwise the GSLP will continue to be the Flying Dutchman of student financial aid, doomed to sail endlessly on an uncertain course in search of an undefined anchorage.

CONSPIRACY THEORIES

To assert a lack of candor in student aid is not necessarily to imply an overt conspiracy against the student by society, Congress, the Office of Education, or academe. It could be merely the result of that ingenuous consensus so often manifested by higher education spokesmen when the legislation was formulated and enacted during the Icarian Sixties. This is not to say that some elements of academe were not more ingenious than others during this same period. The steady demise of private nonprofit colleges testifies to that!

Commentators on secondary and postsecondary education seem to encourage the inference of social conspiracy against students when polemiciz-

10. Ibid., p. 484; emphasis added.
11. Currently this code term means all proprietary schools whether or not students at that particular school have a high default rate. A new term will have to be found when statistics are available on the state guarantee agency increments of GSLP and on NDSL, which appears to have a delinquency rate double that of GSLP.

ing against "the legitimacy of the system that abused them." For some students, they say: "There is no place to go. No place now, no place ever. For the lower half of the school population—the general course, the voc-ed course, the yet to be certified losers with their low-C grades, the high school is like a refugee camp, a camp for displaced persons waiting for something to happen."[12]

According to Peterson, however, the emancipation of the postsecondary student is possible by the time he has enrolled in either the community college or the great university. If dissatisfied, these

> voiceless students vote with their feet. . . . Scores of youths leave community colleges after just a year—one semester in good standing and one on probation—with their hopes for a college education dashed. Some then enroll in proprietary schools (if they can afford to), others join the military, many find jobs where they do not need to read or write or multiply, and others take to the streets.[13]

Similarly, the great university

> being what it is, extensive curricular restructuring is not likely to be forthcoming. Not a few students in consequence will choose to seek their educational fortunes in other settings.
>   Moral: If you let the students go elsewhere, they will.[14]

The conspiracy theory has strong support from Karabel, who points out, according to *Higher Education Daily,* that

> the student response to vocational training in the community college "has been less than enthusiastic" and that many students drop out once they realize they are being programmed to fill modified working-class slots. In response to the failure of these colleges to cool students' ambitions toward a college degree, the "national educational planning establishment" has begun a new movement stressing "no-nonsense" vocational education. . . . This movement, unlike the open admissions movement, originated from the "top" of our society—the foundations, the established educational associations, educational planners, government at the Federal and state level, and "education-minded business executives."[15]

12. Peter Schrag, "Growing Up on Mechanic Street," *Saturday Review,* March 21, 1970, p. 78.
13. Richard E. Peterson, "Institutional Goals and Curriculum Planning," *Findings,* Vol. 1, No. 2 (Princeton, N.J.: Educational Testing Service, 1974), p. 6.
14. Ibid., p. 7.
15. *Higher Education Daily,* July 29, 1974, p. 6. See Jerome Karabel, "Protecting the Portals: Class and the Community College," *Social Policy,* May-June, 1974, pp. 12–18.

THE CHOSEN INSTRUMENT AND LOW-TUITION POLICY

Given the evidence of the emancipated student's mobility and the allegations of a high-level societal conspiracy that community colleges serve as an escape valve for public pressures to open the doors of higher education to all while actually tending to reinforce the status quo of a class-based society, there is a sound basis to question the wisdom either of designating the community college as a "chosen instrument" or of reverting to "low-tuition/institutional subsidy" proposals offered as alternatives to a flexible and fully funded student aid program.

Discussing the Supplemental Educational Opportunity Grants (SEOG) in a committee report, the Joint Student Aid Committee of the Association of American Universities and the National Association of State Universities and Land-Grant Colleges eloquently state the case for the pluralism of postsecondary institutions and the mobility of the emancipated student.

> In all, the eligibility criteria of SEOG covers a wider population than BEOG. This explains the unique contribution Supplementary Grants make to the ability of all students—including those also receiving a Basic Grant—to attend the university of their choice. It enables the student to realistically choose between a tuition-free community college and a public university which charges tuition. It places the student who wishes to attend a public university in another state on more equal footing with a student who is a resident of that state. It enables students to consider attending a high cost private university without having to borrow simultaneously through the GSLP and NDSL programs and working an unreasonable number of hours at a part-time job.
>
> We in this country deem the pluralistic character of our society among its highest virtues. Pluralism is reflected in our institutions of post-secondary education and in the students who attend them.
>
> The Supplementary Grant Program helps maintain the healthy equilibrium in the cost competition among institutions from community colleges to state universities to the private institutions. One of the simplest and surest ways to drive the middle income group from the higher cost institutions and thereby render them havens for the very poor and the affluent, is to allow the authorizations for the SEOG Program to lapse in 1975.[16]

Equality of access without equality of choice for institutions or students is a Hobson's choice. Exercise of discretion should be available both to the student and to the institution. Given functional identity to each of the ex-

16. "A Study of Federal Student Assistance Programs," July 8, 1974, p. 10.

isting programs, such dual discretion could become a reality. In such a system the mobility of the emancipated student voting with his feet will contribute to the preservation of a pluralistic postsecondary educational system.

The alternatives I would propose for student aid are not sweeping changes but candid attributions of functional identity to each of the existing programs of student financial aid, coupled with balanced funding. Differentiation of programs by function would encourage an accommodation for the motives of both the student and the institution. It is not a cost allocation system. It candidly would take into account the selfless and selfish motives of people and of institutions.

Part Three

STRATEGIES FOR IMPROVING PROGRAMS IN HIGHER EDUCATION

The Elusive Goal of Educational Equality

K. PATRICIA CROSS

IF I COULD have my choice of when to live and work in the world of higher education, I would choose the 1970s as the most interesting era in the past fifty years or probably within the next fifty. I believe higher education now stands at a significant crossroads. Sometime around 1970, we could look back on a system that took as its major claim to fame a truly remarkable physical growth. Few questioned either the desirability or the direction of that growth.

The final report of the Carnegie Commission on Higher Education refers to the post-World War II years as the Golden Age of higher education,[1] but I wonder whether history will not find those years more akin to the turbulence of adolescence than to the golden years of maturity and wisdom. In many ways, higher education has had a difficult adolescence. The entire enterprise has experienced rapid physical growth—growth so demanding that little time or energy has been left for raising more profound questions about the future. We have faced the encouraging, but still adolescent, problems of integrating parts that were growing at different rates. Like most adolescents, we have bumped against the problems of authority in the form of taxpayers and legislators and alumni who felt we may have grown too big for our britches. We even struggled briefly with the acne of campus eruptions. They were good years in many ways, full of the exuberance and energy and natural optimism of youth, but they were not the golden years, and I am not sorry to see them pass.

The decade of the 1970s will not, I think, be the golden years either. They are more likely to be the seeking years in which we in higher education will face the problems of our own identity. Who are we and what does

1. *Priorities for Action: Final Report of the Carnegie Commission on Higher Education* (New York: McGraw-Hill, 1973).

191

the future hold for us? Like postadolescents who have attained physical maturity, we are likely to waver between brashness and timidity as we seek to find our place in the world. These will be the years of self-study and evaluation. While it is hard to see what lies ahead for individual institutions, we have great faith in the collectivity that is higher education. Some institutions, like some young people, will make it big; others will teeter on the brink of insecurity and self-doubt. Some of the decisions made in these years will be wrong—some fatally so—but most institutions appear to possess the vitality to profit from errors, to grow in maturity and self-confidence, and to develop uniquely and distinctively—free to establish their own identity.

Such freedom has not been characteristic of higher education in the past. We are constantly reminded of the increasing homogeneity of higher education.[2] Again, like insecure adolescents, we seem to feel more comfortable trying to look and act like everyone else. But things are changing now. Research shows that people perceive real differences in the emphases and priorities of different kinds of colleges,[3] and there is a growing interest in educational innovation as colleges seek distinctiveness. Many colleges are now more interested in what Empire State College or Ottawa University in Kansas or El Centro Community College are doing than they are in what the older prestige models of Harvard or Stanford are doing. The present plateau in physical growth is giving higher education the opportunity to "get itself together" and to think seriously about goals and purposes. For most colleges, these years of the 1970s are raising profound questions about identity.

Higher education, individually and collectively, derives its identity from three sources: Some comes as a heritage; some is a product of the times in which we live, but, mostly, the identity is a function of decisions we make. If I do say so myself, our inherited identity is good; we come from good stock. There are not many rascals among our ancestors, no incurable heritable strains of disease, and only an occasional eccentric aunt or odd uncle. As to the identity that has been thrust upon us, we can acknowledge that we are the offspring of parents that have been considered pillars of society; people look to us for leadership in solving all manner of problems

2. W. B. Martin, *Conformity: Standards and Change in Higher Education* (San Francisco: Jossey-Bass, 1969); H. L. Hodgkinson, *Institutions in Transition,* Carnegie Commission on Higher Education Sponsored Research Studies (New York: McGraw-Hill, 1971).
3. R. E. Peterson, *Goals for California Higher Education: A Survey of 116 College Communities* (Princeton, N.J.: Educational Testing Service, 1973).

of the community. They expect us to be knowledgeable (sometimes beyond our capabilities) and they expect us to be generous (sometimes beyond our resources). For the most part, people expect today's institutions to be like the older generation of colleges, preserving their standards in the face of social change which has been rapid enough to make some standards unwise and others impossible.

There is much concern today about the preservation of academic standards. But there is considerable truth in the wisdom that reminds us that we can never go home. Standards we surely need, but the problem lies not so much in the preservation of the old as in the creation of standards more in tune with our emerging identity.

FROM MERITOCRACY TO EGALITARIANISM

Our problem with identity is this: In the meritocratic era of the 1950s and 1960s we had, or quite universally aspired to, an identity of academic excellence. And as long as the demand exceeded the supply and the egalitarian conscience of the public lay dormant, we could select students who would enhance and strengthen our image. The identity crisis came when we could no longer select the student body that created the image we wished to project. The image of the higher education establishment is threatened, not so much by the highly visible issues of affirmative action and civil rights, as by the relatively quiet influx of large numbers of students with poor academic records into open-door colleges. In discussing "new students," I am referring, *not* to the ethnic minorities or to women or to older part-time students, but rather to students of any color or age who are ill-prepared for traditional college study. This is the group that presents the threat to our older image. For *educational* egalitarianism has a flavor of mediocrity about it that is a jolt to a self-image that aspires to academic excellence.

If the nostalgia that surrounds the pleasant ring of the words "academic excellence" is blown away, the unpalatable truth emerges that the identification with academic excellence was more the result of the work of the admissions office than of the teaching faculty. The lesson learned during the meritocracy was that if you start with quality you will end with quality if you do nothing to destroy it. But today we need to be imaginative educators because we can no longer select the student body that makes us look good by conforming to what we know how to do.

Education is beginning to place the emphasis on process rather than on selection. We are entering an era that challenges us as teachers and educators. We admittedly know little about the teaching-learning process, but we are beginning to experiment. A new excitement permeates the air as classroom teachers talk across disciplines with one another about the Keller Plan and PSI (personalized system of instruction) and self-paced, modular learning. But underneath a prevailing spirit that shows a new willingness to tackle the *means* of education lurks the uneasy feeling that we have lost sight of the *ends*. What is it that higher education is supposed to do for everyone who decides to go to college?

As I study various programs designed for new learners, I discern three quite different assumptions about the ends of egalitarian education. The earliest and still quite prevalent assumption is that equality of opportunity should lead to equality of outcome—that if we can somehow provide the opportunity, the new learners will end up with the achievements and rewards enjoyed by traditional college graduates in the past.

The means to this end is to provide remediation until the new learners can profit from the same type of education that has been offered in the past to selected student bodies. This mode of thought arises quite naturally from the old meritocratic concept that faculty in the academic disciplines have a right to expect that the students they teach will be selected—or corrected—until they are ready to learn what the faculty member is prepared to teach. Remedial programs today often are segregated educational ghettos with a faculty and a mission quite different from that of the parent institution. By and large, the attitude has been that if remedial programs can get students ready for college, we can go about business as usual, secure in our conscience that we are providing equality of educational opportunity and that academic egalitarianism is just a matter of time.

NEW MODES UNDER THE MERITOCRATIC STANDARD

Model I, the Remediation Model, approaches egalitarian higher education a little embarrassed by individual differences. It attempts to "correct" individual differences at the point of entry into college. This approach to academic egalitarianism is not unlike our earlier approaches to social egalitarianism in which we tried to blend ethnic differences into the melting pot. The best tactic for the ethnic caught in the melting-pot approach to equality was to attempt to "pass" into the majority culture—a task considerably easier for the white or light ethnic than for those of more distinctive color.

Despite its obvious limitations, the melting-pot approach was not the total failure that is sometimes assumed from today's perspective. Thousands of immigrants did pass into the majority culture, and many of us are testimony to the fact that equality *can* be achieved through eradicating cultural differences. But it works only for those who are close to the borderline. The Irish passed more completely than the Jews, who were assimilated more easily than the Chinese, who, in turn, faced fewer problems than the blacks.

The analogy for education is obvious. Remedial education will help those on the borderline of acceptable academic achievement to pass into the standard curriculum. But there are some students—from rich homes and poor, from white homes and black, from suburbs and reservations—who cannot or will not be assimilated into the academic mainstream. For these students, remediation is not the answer to educational equality. We have enough experience and enough research now to know that it is not a question of whether remediation works or does not work. Rather, we can conclude that it works for some—to date, a disappointingly small minority—and not for others.

And so we are just starting a second major experiment with egalitarian education. Model II accepts individual differences as an educational challenge. It permits individual differences at entry to college and then attempts to devise multiple processes and treatments that will reduce or eliminate differences upon exit from college.

There are at present two major approaches to our latest frank acceptance of individual differences in learning. One acknowledges differences in the amount of time required by individual learners; the other recognizes differences in learning styles. The acceptance of individual differences in learning rates is promoting such innovations as flexible scheduling, self-paced modules, and mastery learning. Differences in learning styles or preferences are recognized through the introduction of such alternatives as computer-assisted instruction (CAI), the use of peer tutors and faculty mentors, and experimentation with a wide variety of learning media and teaching strategies.

These new concerns for individualizing instruction are a direct outgrowth of the search for ways to deal with the increasing diversity of mass postsecondary education. They are understandably popular answers to academic egalitarianism because they concentrate on the elimination of invidious comparisons by varying the treatment and proclaiming eventual equality for all who attain the desired level of mastery. I label Model II the Educator's Model because it comes to grips with the teaching-learning process while striving to preserve traditional academic standards.

I want to discuss Model II because it is an important and emerging approach to egalitarian education. While it is not the final answer to equality of educational opportunity, I would like to encourage the growth of this model. As far as I can see, its only problem is that it does not go far enough. Like remedial education, it is unlikely to bring about the equality that it promises, but no doubt it will help another group of people to pass into the academic mainstream.

The concept of mastery learning is the basic ingredient of Model II. Benjamin Bloom, hailed as the father of mastery learning, claims that "95 percent of the students . . . can learn a subject to a high level of mastery (for example, an *A* grade) if given sufficient learning time and appropriate types of help."[4] The optimistic ring of this kind of statement has tremendous appeal to academic egalitarians, and there is more to mastery learning than idealistic promise. It works—for some students in some subjects.

At the level of higher education, the concept of mastery learning has been incorporated into a more sophisticated learning model known as PSI (personalized system of instruction) or the Keller Plan.[5] The Keller Plan has swept across the country and across academic disciplines at a phenomenal rate. To the delight of some of us who occasionally grow cynical about the relevance of much of the content of higher education to the practical problems of today, the Keller Plan was devised by a psychologist who simply applied his academic knowledge about human learning to his teaching. An overly brief synopsis of the Keller Plan would be as follows. It breaks the material into small, clearly defined objectives, permits each student to proceed at his own pace, requires mastery of one unit before proceeding to the next, furnishes immediate positive reinforcement, and provides for the personal-social interactions that are important to motivation. Research evaluations are generally positive. Students are enthusiastic, and learning and retention of context are as good as or better than those occurring in conventional classrooms. Thus, there are scientific as well as humanistic reasons for promoting PSI and other derivations of modular mastery learning.

Equality through mastery learning is predicated on the assumption that

4. B. S. Bloom, "Mastery Learning," in *Mastery Learning: Theory and Practice,* ed. J. H. Block (New York: Holt, Rinehart, & Winston, 1971), p. 51.
5. F. S. Keller, "Good-bye Teacher," *Journal of Applied Behavior Analysis,* Spring 1968, pp. 79–89.

although the time required for learning may vary, the final result will not. Through the simple expedient of diversifying the treatment, we can proclaim equality in the outcome. But the time required for learning does categorize people into fast and slow learners, and pragmatic employers, if given a choice between two equally competent people, are quite likely to give the good jobs to the fast learners and the lesser jobs to the slow learners. Furthermore, the dimension of time is as biased as any other measure yet devised to categorize learners. What is perceived as equality today because it permits people to reach equal academic attainments may be seen as inequality tomorrow because some must spend five years in college whereas others may graduate in three years.

In the strange world of higher education, it is not these limitations, however, that are impeding the advance of mastery learning. Rather it is the very idea that 95 percent of the students in a course could be worth an *A*. Ironically, it is the notion of academic equality itself that is disturbing. But even the most thoroughgoing advocate of the traditional educational meritocracy must be bothered by the existing situation in which a student in the top 1 percent of the college-going population can make a *C* at a highly selective college while his lowest quarter peer may make an *A* at a less prestigious institution. Nevertheless, all logic to the contrary, the concept of mastery learning is experiencing rough treatment in some colleges because it comes into direct conflict with grades and the sorting functions traditionally performed by higher education.

More recent than the attempts to vary the time for learning are the attempts to deal with the different learning styles of students. Although research on cognitive styles is at least twenty-five years old, its application to education is quite new and frankly experimental. Researchers concerned with cognitive styles are studying individualistic ways of perceiving, remembering, thinking, and solving problems. For example, some learners perceive the elements in a situation, processing information methodically and analytically, whereas others perceive the whole and take an intuitive approach to problem solving. Such learning preferences are relatively stable throughout life, and their importance to education is obvious. Herman Witkin, a colleague in the Educational Testing Service and a pioneer in research on cognitive styles, maintains that "While relatively little research has been done compared to what is possible and needed, it is already clear that cognitive style is a potent variable in students' academic choices and vocational preferences; in students' academic development through their school career; in how students learn and teachers teach, and in how students and teachers interact in the classroom."[6]

The notion of learning styles has two highly appealing features that make its emergence now especially welcome. In the first place, it recognizes that teachers, too, have distinctive cognitive styles that affect their teaching. Some outstanding faculty lecturers, for example, are justifiably irate over being told that lectures are "out" and discussion groups are "in" for the "new students." The concept of learning styles permits maximum opportunity for both students and teachers to develop the teaching-learning styles that are effective for them. Some teachers, however, are challenged by *how* students learn; they might be called "cognitive strategists."

The second attractive feature of the concept of learning styles is that it is the best answer yet to our quest for egalitarian education. Measuring education on a bell-shaped grading curve is increasingly unpalatable because it condemns half the class to below-average status. The mastery learning approach of permitting *time* rather than *achievement* to vary has admirable educational advantages, but it still fails to meet egalitarian demands, since we know that a fast learner is better than a slow learner. But cognitive styles, for the moment at least, are value free. We cannot really say whether an intuitive learner is better than an analytical learner. Each style has its merits.

The point I wish to make, however, is that educators working with cognitive styles or with mastery learning share a common goal: to attain equality of output through varying the process. In either case, academic standards would be preserved by the expedient of varying time or method or both.

ALTERNATIVE MEANS, ALTERNATIVE GOALS

Model III may be labeled the "Pluralistic Model" for egalitarian education. Whereas Model I recognizes individual differences upon entrance to college and tries through remediation to erase such differences before the end of the first year, Model II permits individual differences throughout the college years, but hopes to certify that there are no differences upon exit from college. Model III, however, proclaims that equality and individual differences can coexist compatibly, that learners can enter college with differences, can proceed through college in varied ways, and can

---

6. H. A. Witkin, "The Role of Cognitive Style in Academic Performance and in Teacher-Student Relations," *Research Bulletin* RB-73-11 (Princeton, N.J.: Educational Testing Service, February 1973), p. 1.

exist from college with different competencies. To use the melting-pot analogy, Model I does not care for lumps in the melting pot; if they are not dissolved in a year, they must be cast aside. Model II dislikes lumps also, but it recognizes that some lumps can be melted by higher temperatures and some by longer cooking. But Model III likes lumps. It aims, not for the melting pot, but for the salad bowl as an end product; differences in texture and flavor are clear, but they work together to enhance and complement one another in the total product.

Our experimentation with truly pluralistic educational outcomes is just beginning. The bridge between Model II and Model III is under construction now and is popularly known as nontraditional education. The many experiments classified, for want of a better term, as "nontraditional" originally came into being in response to pressures for more egalitarian access to higher education. But nontraditional study is more than an access model. With its roots in Model II, it recognizes individualistic learning needs by proclaiming that if the life styles of learners cannot be adapted to the life styles of colleges, no harm will be done by putting some of the burden for adjustment on the colleges. To date, the majority of the nontraditionalists have concentrated on new ways of making available a rather traditional curriculum to a previously excluded clientele.[7] This moderate wing of the nontraditional party represents a form of Model II education, for it stresses maximum flexibility in the processes and procedures of education while insisting on traditional standards of output. Understandably, many nontraditionalists are especially concerned about the preservation of academic standards, on the probably quite realistic grounds that until their alternative methods are accepted, the quality of their output must be above question.

But once the educational focus is on the learner, as it is in Model II, it is hard not to proceed to Model III. And there is a rapidly growing liberal wing of the nontraditional party that encourages going all the way in recognizing individual differences. They point out that society and individuals would be better served by the development of the widest possible diversity of talent—affective and social as well as cognitive. Experiential education, learning contracts, competency-based education, and project learning are examples of approaches that can promote the development of individual talents. Although out-of-class learning can be tied to the tradi-

7. J. Ruyle and L. A. Geiselman, "Non-Traditional Opportunities and Programs," in *Planning Non-Traditional Programs: An Analysis of the Issues for Postsecondary Education,* K. P. Cross et al. (San Francisco: Jossey-Bass, 1974), pp. 53–94.

tional curriculum by granting credit only for the standard academic components of the learning, such a limitation is not necessary and is more characteristic of Model II than Model III education. Pluralistic education emphasizes individual initiative in setting learning goals and, at its best, it leads the student into lifelong, self-directed learning.

Pluralistic education, by its very nature, defies measurement along a single dimension, and the performance of one student cannot easily be compared with that of another. Thus, it is sometimes charged that pluralism has no standards. But comparison is no more essential to educational pluralism than it is to cultural pluralism. There is no need to say that one culture is better than another, only that each strives to be the best of its kind and that it is true to its own nature. The standard for pluralistic education is individual excellence, a goal sadly missing from much of today's mass education. Model I and Model II students are usually urged to meet *minimal* standards of academic achievement. They can, and frequently do, consider their education completed upon meeting the basic requirements for the degree. But Model III students, educated to the pursuit of excellence, find that education does not end with the degree. When personal achievement and development are internalized as goals, the motivation for learning is lifelong.

The foregoing continuum is one of increasing recognition of individual differences in learners. But Models I, II, and III also move along a continuum of institutional change. The Remedial Model demands only that resources be allocated to remedial programs whose task it is to prepare students so that the rest of us can do what we have always done. Model II, the Educator's Model, demands massive change in procedures and in instructional methods, but it leaves academic departments and disciplines intact. Model III, Pluralistic Education, requires all of the changes incorporated into Models I and II, but also requires new alternatives in the curricula, new measures of achievement, and new standards for individual accomplishment.

This is a tall order for change, involving profound and difficult questions about the future of higher education. The big questions seem always to return to the search for identity. What should be taught, and how can new standards be developed that will guide us in doing it well? Colleges cannot do everything. What are the tasks to which we can legitimately give our attention? How can we offer a curriculum of substance that will give each student a realistic opportunity for self-realization through striving toward some form of high personal achievement? There are no easy answers to the implementation of Model III, but I am convinced that we owe it to ourselves and our world to make a serious study of the alternatives.

There are many ways to organize the search for alternatives. I believe that the goal of educational equality is the prime mover of educational change. Egalitarian motives stimulated the search for alternate routes of access to college. An egalitarian motive is still pushing the search for alternatives in the instructional process, for it is now apparent that access alone will not result in equal educational opportunity. In the near future, I believe that the search for the elusive goal of educational equality will move us into greater encouragement of alternative outcomes for education.

The Evergreen State College: An Alternative

EDWARD J. KORMONDY

THE Evergreen State College, chartered in 1967 as the first new four-year public college in the state of Washington in over seventy years, opened its doors in the fall of 1971 with 55 faculty members and 1,000 students. This fall, the student body has grown to 2,300 and the faculty to 120. The legislative intent in founding Evergreen was that it not be a carbon copy of the state's other four-year colleges but rather that it offer an alternative in higher education. Alternatives provide opportunities for choice on the part of students, faculty, and staff; alternatives provide opportunities to meet the diverse needs of a diverse populace; alternatives provide opportunities to avoid needless duplication. But *an* alternative is not *the* alternative. Evergreen is not *the* alternative for all students, nor for all faculty or staff—it is but one. If its role is pertinent to higher education, it is as the demonstration of one conception of an alternative scheme.

At the outset, it should be said that the alternative that is Evergreen is singular not in its parts—none of which is unique and all of which are or were alternatives available elsewhere—but in its whole. Interdisciplinary studies, off-campus internships, independent or contracted study are neither new modes of learning nor peculiar to Evergreen. Absence of departments, of tenure, of faculty ranks, of merit salary scales, and of faculty senates are neither new governance structures nor peculiar to Evergreen. The replacement of alpha-numeric grades by narrative evaluations and the replacement of large lecture courses by tutorials and seminars are neither new practices nor peculiar to Evergreen. What is new and unique is the particular configuration afforded by the totality of all of these as a system, the particular form and function which encompass these components of the system. It is the concatenation and interaction of these parts and processes that constitute Evergreen as a dramatic alternative in higher education. Most crucially, it is in the intimate relationship of program and structure that the brew of success—if you will allow that judgment—has fermented in so short a time.

This central point about the significance of form and function, part and process, derives from my teaching and research experience as a life scientist: A particular kind of organism (a species) is successful if it has a structure and physiology conducive to meeting the exigencies of its environment. Success is defined in terms of survival. If the species survives, it is succeeding. It succeeds if it has the proper structural design to facilitate processes of survival under existing, as well as changed or changing, conditions. This analogy to the survival of a new species cannot be taken too far in the educational world, for there are certainly vast numbers of colleges and universities whose survival is because they are; that is, they survive because of what they are or have been, or—more often—because they are part of a larger system in which all kinds of homeostatic crutches obtain.

But more to the central point, Evergreen is succeeding in providing an alternative in higher education because its structure supports its program and its program is consonant with its structure. The very peculiar linkages of program and structure make questionable the possibility of Evergreen's programs being transferred in toto. This matter is of concern inasmuch as one of the secondary functions of an alternative is to be a model for change, an exemplar whose bones and flesh can be scrutinized to determine what and how much might be transplanted or infused elsewhere.

To apply the central point to a few focal issues—community cooperation, meeting the needs of adult and mid-career students and students with particular vocational and career-oriented goals—it is necessary to sketch the curricular structure that has grown out of the founding philosophical rhetoric. That philosophy posits a unity to life: The world is a whole, each individual's life is a whole. This is the nature of nature, this is the nature of the student, this must also be the nature of the curriculum. It, too, must be a whole. This holistic conception has been implemented in the form of broadly conceived, problem- or theme-oriented, largely year-long interdisciplinary studies in which the student and faculty are immersed 100 percent both in time and effort. Neither the faculty nor the students are fractioned among several concurrent, and often conflicting, courses. In these coordinated studies, as we term them, science, social science, humanities, and art interact, interdigitate, interweave in a fashion similar to their interaction and interweaving in the "real world." These are the forces of men's minds working in concert—sometimes symphonically, sometimes cacophonously, always authentically. Some 60 percent of the students and faculty are engaged in some twenty different coordinated studies at basic, intermediate, and advanced levels this fall.

A curriculum must, perforce, speak to individual goals and directions, aspirations and expectations; it must provide opportunities for developing specific skills and enlarging particular competencies in preparation for particular vocations or continued study—that is, it must offer an opportunity for specialization without compromise of individuality. A learning contract or a small-group contract provides that opportunity. Herein a small group or an individual may concentrate on a particular problem with a clearly articulated and limited set of objectives, procedures, and evaluation methods spelled out.

Another major philosophic foundation of Evergreen is that, for a curriculum to remain viable, it must be sensitive to the world outside and responsive to its changes by having the inherent capacity for modifiability. This is achieved by a system of annual self-destruction. Programs are, with few exceptions, designed and offered for a given year; to be repeated, a program must justify a need to be served. There are no guarantees of continued existence and hence no fossilizing of the curriculum. Survival is of the kind, not of the individual; not of a particular coordinated studies program, but of coordinated studies in general.

In building on still another philosophic cornerstone, the curriculum is designed to "reflect the nature of the real world, where none of the problems man faces is single and where none of the parts becomes, in its own conception, more important than the whole." In large measure, this objective is accomplished through two major avenues: (1) direct curricular involvement in real-world problems and (2) individual off-campus learning experiences, or internships. In the former, for example, one program focused on the nature of the state of Washington in the year 2000; another undertook surveys in behalf of a community mental health group; yet another developed a comprehensive land-use plan (subsequently adopted by the county); and still another is investigating the tussock moth–Douglas fir–DDT complex. A program in urban planning provides a more specific instance. After several months of "hitting the books," the group accepted an invitation to assist in a study dealing with the relocation of a small community about to be dislocated as a proposed new dam was completed. Not only was the project real, but also the proposals that came out of it are being continued and implemented; several of the students serve on the relocation board.

An internship may vary in concentration and length of time from several to forty hours a week or from a few weeks to an entire year. The student is under the direct, daily supervision of a person who earns his living by the occupation that intern is seeking to learn about—as a banker, a research chemist, a lawyer, an agency administrator. A sponsoring faculty member carefully articulates this "real world" experience with concurrent academic experience in reading, researching, report writing, and tutorial conferences.

These several kinds of curricular structures are not independent of governance and organizational structures; rather, they are intimately tied to them. A team of faculty and students can work concertedly and uninterruptedly, for all programs are of the full-immersion sort. There are no class bells to break up a seminar discussion, no conflicting class obligations to preclude extended field trips, no deterrents to devoting oneself full time and with full effort and concentration.

The absence of departments and divisions means that interdisciplinary studies can operate without the problem of dues paying or other allegiances to the department source of bread and butter: promotion in rank or to tenure, merit salary adjustments. There are no promotions in rank because there are no ranks—every faculty member bears the nonhierarchial title "Member of the Faculty"; there is no tenure but rather three-year renewable appointments; there is no merit salary—there is a salary schedule along which one moves based on years of experience. The kinds of forces that are so often divisive and petty irritants are removed; the faculty can work truly as equals, as members of teams learning from one another not only substance but, just as important, pedagogy. Faculty are assigned to programs according to institutional needs as reflected by overall curricular design and by student acceptance through program enrollment. This means that curriculum—not departmental survival—comes first.

The dynamics of a flexible and responsive system is supported further by a rotation system of faculty members to deans, health sciences counselors to faculty members. Constituencies have difficulty being built, and all have a better appreciation of mutual roles under such a scheme.

Finally, this kind of dynamic and demanding system has yet another key component: The absence of the usual support structures, such as a department with which a faculty member can identify and be assessed, the absence of grades and rankings by which a student can compare his work with that of others, may seem to imply a concomitant absence of assessment. This is not so. Given this kind of system, the function of assessment is in fact the more important, and the structure that produces it is narrative evaluation, with particular emphasis on self-evaluation. A student's self-evaluation is reacted and responded to by the faculty member who has worked with the student in depth and in a long-term relationship; the faculty member's self-evaluation is reacted and responded to by his faculty team and by his dean; a dean's self-evaluation is reacted and responded to by his faculty group, his fellow deans, and the provost. The function of this process is not to determine pass-fail, credit–no credit for the student, or contract renewal for the faculty member. Its function is, instead, growth and development; its aim is to help the student be the kind of student he aspires to be, to achieve his particular set of goals; its aim is to help a faculty member teach better and an administrator to administer better.

In sum, I posit that alternatives in education must have a coincident structure that supports, facilitates, and enables. Processes and outcomes are dependent upon the form of governance and organization, and the latter must be an outgrowth of the former if the former are to operate successfully. Function—purpose, if you will—precedes and must determine form, not the other way around, which is the traditional way. The success of an Evergreen, which is now entering its fourth year not only without having succumbed by reversion but also with every indication of being progressively more healthy, has in no small measure been a function of its form. I commend to you the position that, in seeking reform and innovation in education, one must look beyond a program or proposal to the structures which are critical to its execution, implementation, and survival.

Articulation of Vocational and Career-Oriented Programs at the Postsecondary Level

JOHN W. PORTER

FOR THE United States, the ten years from 1958 to 1968 can be thought of as the Education Decade. Although the historic Supreme Court decision on racial segregation was handed down in 1954, the passage of the National Defense Education Act of 1958 focused the country's attention on the need for a modern education system. This federal emphasis continued with almost annual enactments and amendments, the better known being the Elementary and Secondary Act of 1965 and the Higher Education Act of the same year. The 1968 Vocational Education Amendments were, until 1972, the last in a decade of federal responses to the cry for an up-to-date educational system.

In the past few years the ferment of that decade has settled. The Vietnam war drained off funds needed to fulfill earlier education commitments and denied funds for later commitments. The innovative ideas of the Education Decade have not yet transformed education delivery systems in any specific way. But perhaps most ubiquitous is the uncertainty about the role and place of vocational and career-oriented programs in a society that can put man on the moon but cannot control poverty, pollution, and population.

According to the National Commission on the Financing of Postsecondary Education, of which I was pleased to be a member, postsecondary education comprises four major sectors: the collegiate sector (colleges, universities, professional schools), the noncollegiate sector (occupational schools, mostly proprietary, eligible for participation in a federal student aid program), other postsecondary institutions (occupational schools not included in the noncollegiate sector), and other learning opportunities (formal and informal learning opportunities offered by agencies and institutions not primarily engaged in providing structured educational programs). The commission observed that, while 10 million Americans were engaged in the collegiate and noncollegiate sectors, an additional 32 million were involved in the fourth sector.[1]

Discussing the role of postsecondary education in a changing society, the commission identified nontraditional education as one of fifteen critical issues that will affect postsecondary institutions during the remainder of this century. A major assumption was that: "A growing number of off-campus educational programs will be available to students of all ages in their local communities, in their homes, and at their places of work."[2]

The commission went on to note:

The present system of postsecondary education, particularly the collegiate sector, is, as the Newman task force observed, "oriented to the young and

1. National Commission on the Financing of Postsecondary Education, *Financing Postsecondary Education in the United States* (Washington: Government Printing Office, 1973), p. 37.
2. Ibid.

the mobile." Although extension courses, part-time enrollment, internships, and evening programs have grown significantly over the past two decades, postsecondary education remains firmly rooted in the campus, whether it be a college or a university or a proprietary school. The Newman task force has proposed that, in order to reach many potential students who are now inadequately served or not served at all, the resources for postsecondary education be provided "to the community as separate services in order that individuals and groups can find their own way to an education." Others have made similar proposals in the past several years and, in fact, a strong impetus has developed behind expansion of credit by examination, "open" universities, the "external degree," and other forms of what has been termed "nontraditional" education.

Thus, a major movement appears to be underway, one that is likely to continue at least through the 1970s. Yet there are many formidable obstacles to this movement: the problem of accreditation for off-campus programs, resistance from those who fear that the limited resources will be drawn away from traditional programs, the necessity for careful planning, and what one observer has described as a tendency to "talk the nontraditional concern to death" before it has really been tried. Perhaps the most important obstacle of all, however, is uncertainty about the real demand for off-campus programs. Several recent surveys have indicated that there are a great many persons of all ages who would like to participate in various forms of off-campus learning. But it is not certain that when these persons are forced to make real decisions about how they will spend their time and money, they will give education priority over additional employment, recreation, and other alternatives.[3]

The commission concluded its review of nontraditional education by observing: "If an increasing number of persons are to be brought into postsecondary education for part-time study on or off campus, it will be essential that federal student aid programs treat part-time students equally (on a *pro rata* basis) with full-time students."[4]

Here, the discussion of nontraditional approaches to education will be delimited to the contribution that postsecondary institutions can make to career development and career preparation, the two prongs of career education. My purpose is to examine thoroughly the diffusion of the intent of traditional education philosophy with respect to contemporary needs of students by increasing, without penalty, learning options through *quality* nontraditional offerings. Expanding the availability of learning opportunities does not call for eliminating either the philosophical connotations of the country's excellent liberal arts base or the new emphasis on job-re-

3. Ibid., pp. 37–38.
4. Ibid., p. 38.

lated training. A nontraditional approach to postsecondary education may well balance both forces. Those of us who have undergone traditional collegiate academic gymnastics are still few in number—no more than 10 percent of the population. To suggest that we offer those people who have not completed college but who might wish further education the goodies of traditional academia seems foolhardy.

THE NONTRADITIONAL APPROACH: THE STICK AND THE CARROT

The nontraditional approach, utilizing jobs and career-oriented programs as the stick and the carrot, seems a viable alternative since what most Americans apparently desire, whether rightly or wrongly, is a job sufficient to provide income for food, clothing, shelter, health, welfare, and the good life. The last item can be defined any way one pleases.

Vocational and career-oriented education programs are responsive to this desire. Moreover, such programs present to members of the higher education community a new way of thinking and behaving, whether it be as individuals, as institutional representatives, or as government officials. For example, such programs can meet the desperate need that exists for more responsive secondary schools everywhere, particularly in the big cities. James M. O'Hara cites in "Disadvantaged Newcomers to the City" the possibility that poor communication contributes to poor career-oriented offerings in urban education centers. He observes that before the city schools can begin to cope with their large share of the rural migrant problem, they must know what attitudes rural migrant children are likely to have toward formal education.[5] If self-realization for these urban residents is to be achieved, vocational and career-oriented programs must be designed to reinforce individuality. Secondary programs must be flexible enough to take all learners from where they are to the desired acceptable standard without bias or prejudice. Postsecondary institutions cannot be oblivious to the problems faced by secondary schools if articulation between secondary and postsecondary education is to be successful.

The interlocking role of postsecondary vocational-technical education for lifelong careers must constantly be strengthened. Such education has to be adapted to meet the accelerated pace of change brought about by the increasing demands for educational opportunity beyond the secondary level. Correctly perceived, under the aegis of career education, the secondary program, the comprehensive community college program, and

5. In *Readings in Curriculum,* ed. Glenn Hass and Kimball Wiles (Boston: Allyn & Bacon, 1966), pp. 97–100.

college and university programs must complement each other, not compete with each other.

Our approach to self-realization for learners insists that the curriculum must meet all students on their own level, then guide them progressively toward reaching their potential.[6] Students' successful attainment of outcomes is determined by carefully assessing their needs in order to tailor a curriculum to meet those needs. This approach is specific enough to assure the proper blending of general, exploratory, vocational, and cooperative education into a unified curriculum that extends along the entire range of student differences and that becomes, in effect, the basis of a career-oriented education program.

The two-year community college is today the best equipped of postsecondary institutions to provide nontraditional approaches to education. The popularity and number of these institutions are increasing rapidly for many reasons, including ease of entry, low cost, small classes, teaching-oriented programs, and the proximity of campuses to home. These schools also offer students a second chance, an opportunity, to try out careers through internships, externships, practicums, and community-business consortiums, and the option, after two years of taking vocational and career-oriented programs, to terminate their education or transfer to a four-year college or a university.

The public community college is becoming the most versatile of all postsecondary education institutions. It is able to provide the flexibility and adaptability necessary to meet the ever-changing technological, academic, and societal requirements for life preparation. It is coming of age under the spiraling demands of a modern technological society for increased manpower and education needs. It offers hope that in this nation there shall not exist an educational gap that can be breached only by the economic, social, or intellectual elite. For most proponents who believe the community college epitomizes the multifaceted nature of American education, the following philosophy expresses their view: "The American way of life holds that all human beings are supreme, hence of equal moral worth and are, therefore, entitled to equal opportunities. . . . The basic function of public education then should be to provide educational opportunity by teaching whatever needs to be learned to whoever needs to learn it."[7]

6. Gail M. Inlow, *The Emergent in Curriculum* (New York: John Wiley, 1966), pp. 56–57.
7. "The Philosophy of Education of the Juliet Township High School and Junior College" (Joliet, Ill.: Board of Education, 1950).

Blocker writes that the primary problem that the community college faces is challenging students to grow to the limit of their abilities while avoiding policies that eliminate, discourage, or exclude those students unable to respond immediately to each challenge.[8] There is a fine balance between lowering the quality of education and encouraging students with low levels of motivation and previous unimpressive academic achievement to attempt post-high-school studies suited to their dispositions and talents.

Finding this balance is the point at which the nontraditional approach must reach its zenith, for nontraditional education should serve those students seeking a new educational articulation with the real world primarily through vocational and career-oriented programs. Some people might argue that collegiate training must not be watered down to allow for increased equality of opportunity. I agree, but there need not be a watering-down of standards simply because a nontraditional approach is offered as an alternative.

USING THE NONTRADITIONAL FOR LIFELONG LEARNING

The principle of the nontraditional approach to education emphasizes the best in the so-called lifelong learning mode to allow all people the optimum results in work, recreation, and welfare, which make up today's living pattern for most Americans. In Michigan, about 400,000 students are enrolled in public and private postsecondary institutions, which appears to be about optimum for what is offered. However, 700,000 adults in the state do not have a high school diploma, and 800,000 other adults are seeking some form of education beyond high school.

The wise college administrator will recognize the implications of such statistics and embark upon a nontraditional approach, utilizing vocational and career-oriented programs as the real life core for such programs.

However, to make the nontraditional philosophy operational, an ideal image of the community college must be constructed. The Michigan State Board for Public Community and Junior Colleges undertook such a task in 1967:

Public community colleges can and should provide additional educational opportunities leading not only to advanced academic study in our four-year institutions of higher education, but also to the best in continuing education programs, in vocational-technical, occupational and retraining programs, in general and in broad educational programs beneficial to the entire com-

8. Clyde E. Blocker et al., *The Two Year College: A Social Synthesis* (Englewood Cliffs, N.J.: Prentice-Hall, 1965), p. 131.

munity and to society, in diversified community enrichment activities and functions that will elicit maximum participation by both youths and adults.[9]

Michigan is committed to finding creative and successful methods to educate its residents and providing its students with the technological capabilities necessary to prepare for a career and for a fulfilling and secure life. The state's approach is to view the elementary, secondary, postsecondary, and university educational levels, each, as subsystems within the total "Career Education System." The approach involves a formal analytic process that is frequently described as a six-step accountability model to facilitate decision making for life-goal programming. The ultimate goal of each student is considered, together with the supporting objectives and the practical limitations and constraints. The resulting program is so designed that the education curriculum, supportive services, and organization remain flexible and open to each student's personal needs and career aspirations at all levels.

A career education system must allow for responsive administrative and staffing patterns and the interaction necessary for an environment of creativity and personal security. It must provide for the cooperative planning, mutual support in teaching, changing roles and degrees of responsibility, and interaction among staff levels that this instruction process demands. Thus, a state's education agencies must be able to assess continuously the complex factors necessary for success in providing career-oriented programs so as to remain sensitive to the educational needs of students and the manpower needs of the community.

Change is inevitable, but if it is to be successful, it must be easily implemented and any outcomes easily revised. Staff development, finances, and public relations have to be commensurate with a community's vocational and career-oriented educational commitment. During the change process, the college staff must view the shift from the traditional to the vocational and career-oriented program positively.

UNDERSTANDING SCHOOLS FROM THE INDIVIDUAL'S PERSPECTIVE

To understand schools and school systems for the future, one must relate them to the surrounding cultural, economic, historical, philosophical, and political circumstances. Education has been, and probably will continue to be, an expression of a civilization and of a political and economic system. A way to grasp the close relationship of the social environment to

9. "A Position Paper on the Role and Character of Michigan Community Colleges" (Lansing, Mich.: State Board for Community and Junior Colleges, 1967).

the development of an appropriate educational program is to view the social setting from the standpoint of the individual. Each person faces problems of self-fulfillment and self-development. Thus, for the individual learner, a rationally developed school program must meet vocational demands and requirements and the demands of citizenship and self-fulfillment.[10]

This rationale sets forth the assumptions, objectives, procedures, and outcomes for articulating vocational and career-oriented programs at different levels. Preassessment of students' skills is a vital part of each career-oriented program in order to provide realistic analyses of time and cost for outcomes. Using the students' past experiences as a base invites success and a positive self-image for the students to advance to the next level of competency.

I have described here the overall mission of Michigan's postsecondary vocational and career-oriented program as a catalyst for articulation between high school and college. It would, of course, be presumptuous to assume that one standard or format can be applied in all states. The future mission of the public two-year community college is based on the assumption that educational programs appropriate to changing societal needs and a heterogeneous student population can be formulated, but that these cannot be successful if the relationship of each institution to the system is provincial.

Every two-year college will succeed or fail in the same degree that it understands and provides for the educational needs of its clientele. The curricular design is determined by the needs of the community; it enlarges in scope as prudent investigation indicates. However, the two-year college can never assume that the curriculum task is "set." Communities change. Educational needs emerge or disappear, creating a need for continuous, uninterrupted, and intensive examination that will provide a basis for growth patterns to guide and affect educational service.[11]

These remarks in no way deny that a role in the nontraditional approach exists for baccalaureate institutions. On the contrary, the Union for Experimenting Colleges and Universities is conducting a high school–college, university-without-walls program in six states to admit high school juniors to college and to implement integrated programs leading simultaneously to both high school and college completion. This effort is not

---

10. Glenn Hass and Kimball Wiles, "Social Forces," *Readings in Curriculum*, p. 3.
11. James W. Thornton, Jr., *The Community Junior College* (New York: John Wiley, 1966), pp. 121–22.

simply an early admission program. Its aim is also to overcome the age barriers that impede educational progress. This program is only one of many significant attempts of colleges to ease students' passage from high school to college.

Declining enrollments will create strains within the higher education system, but enough adults desire to be served in different ways so that unique, nontraditional approaches to postsecondary education will flourish for years to come. The real issue now is whether or not tradition will permit the higher education community to respond.

A Degree by Any Other Name...
The Alverno Program

SISTER JOEL READ

VERY EARLY in its work, the Commission on Non-Traditional Study came to consensus that "non-traditional study is more an attitude than a system." The commission further noted with respect to learning that nontraditional study "deemphasizes time, space, and even course requirements in favor of competence."[1]

The commission members also asked, "Must non-traditionalists advocate the elimination of traditional institutions to make way for new ones?" The commission's "no" to that question was further elaborated by its chairperson, Samuel Gould:

> It would be better, especially in the short run, to help existing colleges and universities grant credits and degrees based on non-traditional approaches than to create new degree-granting institutions for this purpose. This course of action will match stability and experience with experimental forms and offer a combination which is both acceptable and reassuring.[2]

In the course of the extensive research carried out by and for the commission, a constantly recurring problem was noted. Many observers concerned with nontraditional study have examined this problem, which we at

1. Commission on Non-Traditional Study, *Diversity by Design* (San Francisco: Jossey-Bass, 1973), p. xv.
2. Ibid., p. xvii.

Alverno College also viewed as being central in developing our nontraditional degree program. Cross and Valley state:

> An immediate problem to face in expanding learning opportunities to non-traditional learners is the matter of academic credit. Not surprisingly, granting credit has become a central issue in the non-traditional movement. . . . But neither colleges nor the accrediting agencies have clearly defined just what is signified by *credit* and a *college degree*.[3]

Two researchers for the commission, Jonathan R. Warren and Ernest W. Kimmel, examined this point in great detail.[4] Warren notes:

> Even without the particular problems created by non-traditional programs, inadequacies in the credit system are apparent in conventional programs. For example, under the present system, satisfactory completion of a course results in the award of a fixed number of credits regardless of the student's level of performance. Grades vary with performance; credits do not. While proposals have occasionally been made to adjust the amount of credit received in a course to the student's level of performance in it . . . , they have not been widely considered. They raise serious doubt, nonetheless, about the desirability of a system in which students performing at a minimally acceptable level earn the maximum number of credits a course offers.[5]

And yet as Warren notes later:

> These existing problems in the evaluation of conventional classroom study have not seriously hampered conventional instruction, but similar problems in the measurement of performance and the award of credit may be major deterrents to creating programs of non-traditional study. Among the institutions surveyed for the Commission on Non-Traditional Study . . . 40 percent cited the assessment of non-classroom learning as an obstacle to the introduction of non-traditional programs, putting it in a virtual tie with lack of money as the most frequently cited deterrent.[6]

However,

> Whatever form learning experiences take—traditional or non-traditional—assessment of the *effectiveness* of the experiences and the award of credit must both be related to the purposes the learning experiences are to serve. The importance of educational goals in determining assessment practices is

3. K. Patricia Cross and John R. Valley, "Non-Traditional Study: An Overview," in *Planning Non-Traditional Programs,* ed. K. Patricia Cross et al. (San Francisco: Jossey-Bass, 1974), p. 6.

4. Warren, "Awarding Credit," in *Planning Non-Traditional Programs,* pp. 116–47; Kimmel, "Problems of Recognition," in *Explorations in Non-Traditional Study,* ed. Samuel B. Gould and K. Patricia Cross (San Francisco: Jossey-Bass, 1972), pp. 64–94.

5. "Awarding Credit," p. 126.

6. Ibid., p. 128.

already well recognized at the level of individual courses. In the future it should affect *the total degree systems as well* (emphasis added).[7]

The statement of goals or competences in determining assessment practices leads directly to the question of norm-referenced versus criterion-referenced testing.

> During the past decade, interest has been growing in the use of absolute rather than relative standards of performance for the assessment of educational accomplishment at all levels. . . . Performance relative to that of other students may be of interest for some purposes, such as comparing the effectiveness of different instructional procedures, but it has little value by itself as an indicator of the competence of individual students. If credit is to reflect student performance or capability, a student's absolute level of mastery of a specifiable learning objective is the attribute that should be assessed. . . .
>
> . . . Both traditional and non-traditional learning require criterion-referenced measurement to a substantial degree unless credit in both kinds of learning is to be awarded on the untested assumption that mere participation in the experiences themselves indicates that the desired learning has occurred.
>
> The necessary specificity of the criteria to be measured leads some instructors to fear that specific criteria will be trivial—that broad goals like understanding will be reduced to something like the recognition of minor facts without a grasp of their interrelatedness—and that the real goals of a course cannot be made as explicit as the requirements of criterion-referenced measurement demand. But specificity does not imply triviality. Criterion-referenced measurement need not be limited to trivial outcomes. In fact, it is one way to ensure that the assessment of performance [competence] is not limited with respect to desired course outcomes. If course objectives cannot be made explicit enough to be assessed directly, then no justification can be found for the presumption that any method of instruction, traditional or not, is effective.[8]

Among the preliminary reports made to the commission in 1971, Kimmel raised the same point:

> The development of such *criterion-referenced* or *absolute-standard* tests has many implications for the instructional process as well as for the process of evaluation. Such tests are built into most of the experiments with "individualized" or "individually prescribed" instruction. The test itself becomes the criterion against which an individual's performance is judged. Most of these experiments are being conducted at the elementary or secondary level. There have been only a few scattered attempts with isolated courses to

7. Ibid., p. 135.
8. Ibid., pp. 134–35.

apply these ideas at the college level. These attempts have usually been in the context of developing instructional strategies using contemporary technology. No one has attempted to develop an entire degree program based on these ideas. Such an attempt would involve a clearer and more detailed statement of the knowledge and skills represented by the awarding of a degree than any institution has made to date.[9]

Organizing learning toward stated objectives on a criterion-referenced basis is precisely what Alverno College has done. From 1971 to 1973, years paralleling the commission, Alverno defined outcomes of liberal learning that were finally stated as competences or skills to be achieved. A major effort to identify how to assess such competences on a criterion-referenced, rather than a norm-referenced, basis occupied all of the 1972–73 academic year, as did an effort to devise a system to make such assessment the basis for awarding degrees at Alverno.[10]

THE ALVERNO MISSION

The educational program at Alverno College at this time represents our decision to make explicit, in terms of demonstrably achieved competences, the definition of the degree we award. This decision proceeds from our philosophy of education and dictates all the components of our curriculum.[11]

At the heart of our education philosophy as a liberal arts college has always been the belief that our graduates should be individuals who have achieved freedom by developing a sense of responsibility for themselves and for society. In the past, we expressed that philosophy in a vision of ourselves as a college that, with others like us, preserved and transmitted the heritage that would inform the future.

Today, we believe we can be true to our philosophy only by expressing it in a new vision. That vision must be one of a college that aims to help people make sense out of our society so that they can contribute to a future that makes increased quality of life available to all persons. That vision must provide for the change that has become a major fact of contemporary life. It must assume that technology has made a reality of easy

9. "Problems of Recognition," p. 78.
10. Although the program for the 57th Annual Meeting of the American Council on Education separates nontraditional programs from the credentialing question, it is not possible to do so in describing the Alverno program because assessment—the basis of credentialing—is an integral part of the learning experience at Alverno.
11. This description of Alverno's program is based on the work of Georgine Loacker, one of the codesigners of the assessment process at Alverno College.

information storage and retrieval, and so must focus on the productive use of information. That vision must recognize that the development of sophisticated conceptual and technological tools to manage change places on educated persons a major responsibility—that of directing change in their individual and institutional lives.

Such a vision, we believe, can define us anew as a liberal arts college if it provides our students with tools to free them to live productively in today's complex society. What they will need is the ability to analyze, judge, and use the ever-accumulating information. They will also need to be able consciously to clarify a personal set of beliefs and values and develop commitment to them so that they responsibly affect their judgments and decisions.

We consider it our mission to provide such learning for our students so that they can be capable of managing change successfully in their own lives; become integrated, functioning humanists; acquire a transdisciplinary view of a complex and rapidly changing world; choose, plan, and design their own professional direction and career orientation; and do competently what they have learned.

GOALS OF LIBERAL LEARNING

To integrate into a developmental educational experience all of these elements—management of change (process), academic experience (content), and professional direction (motivation)—we identify as our core learning strategy competence-based learning (CBL). In effect, the student goals become those competences students must achieve to graduate. In that achievement process careful direction is provided for students in relating goals to values and career aspirations, in making maximum use of learning resources, in assessing stages of development, and ultimately in earning a degree. Competence-based learning at Alverno is a process whereby certain abilities required of a student and the criteria used in assessing satisfactory demonstration of those abilities are made explicit, and the student is held accountable for meeting those criteria.

We have identified the eight competences or abilities that are essential for a person today to function personally and professionally so as to be productive and to be true to her or his beliefs. This level of functioning requires that persons be able to make decisions, to develop initiative, and to acquire confidence and responsibility for implementing these abilities, in short, to manage one's life. Thus, the eight student goals that currently define Alverno College's concept of liberal education are:

1. Develop effective communication skill.
2. Sharpen analytical capabilities.
3. Develop workable problem-solving skill.
4. Develop a facility for making independent value judgments and independent decisions.
5. Develop facility for social interaction.
6. Achieve understanding of the relationship between the individual and the environment.
7. Develop an awareness and understanding of the world in which the individual lives.
8. Develop knowledge, understanding, and responsiveness to the arts and humanities.

Although the eight competences do not comprise an exhaustive list, we believe they sufficiently demand of our students the demonstration of those skills, behaviors, and attitudes that are integral to liberal education and responsible living in our society.

Because a student is accountable for attaining these competences, we define them functionally, each as a development of six levels (see Appendix below). The levels within each competence represent progressive complexity. However, a given level in one competence—especially at the initial levels—is not equivalent to another level in that competence or to the same level in another competence; the division into levels of each competence has its own rationale. Analysis (Competence 2), for example, which is an essentially cognitive competence, is sequenced in steps of increasing conceptual difficulty, beginning with the most apparent and therefore most easily discernible components and leading progressively to those that must be inferred from an increasingly complex combination of data.

Communications (Competence 1), on the other hand, combines cognitive, affective, and psychomotor skills and identifies a competence that has been an explicit goal of the students' previous education. Consequently, the first step in students' achievement is the ability to determine where they are in relation to where they want to be so they can develop a way to get there.

The identification of levels within each competence, therefore, is a means by which we at Alverno make the education process more viable. It enables us to help the students pace themselves and gain a sense of accomplishment as being progressive rather than absolute and as providing satisfaction in achievement along the way.

The functional definition of the competences in developmental levels provides enough specificity to allow demonstration, assessment, and credentialing of self-directed learning and attainment. Thus, Alverno can promise what each student must *do* to graduate and what available help will enable the student best to learn how to do it and to what degree the student is, at any point, able to do it. Then students can meaningfully decide how to use their time and combine learning experiences.

DEGREE REQUIREMENTS

Alverno students know that graduation means that, beyond achievement of Level 4 of all eight competences, they have achieved Level 6 in at least one area and six more Levels 5 or 6 from among the other competences. The students' knowledge of their actual possession of these skills is confirmed by their transcripts, which specify the competence levels attained, as well as the contexts in which they have been attained. The transcripts also record mastery of any data that represent an area of academic content for which a qualified person has credentialed the student.

The shorthand by which we refer to the competence level as a unit of measurement is CLU (Competence Level Unit). When a student has demonstrated attainment of the competence levels required for an Alverno degree, we say the student has 50 CLU's (32 for the first four levels of all eight competences and eight for selected Levels 5 and 6—including at least one of Level 6—among the competences). This graduation requirement replaces the more traditional total semester hour requirement and the required completion of a specified combination of general education courses.

LEARNING EXPERIENCES

Learning resources at Alverno are any clearly identified and carefully specified opportunities for gaining knowledge that can lead to the achievement and validation of one or more competence levels. At present, most of the learning resources available are courses that have been translated into modules that make explicit the learning experiences and performance specifications for the CLU's they lead to. Other resources are off-campus experiential learning arrangements and several individualized study packets. On the increase are alternative designs and ways of carrying them out that use teaching assistance to varying degrees. The aim of all the resources is to integrate competence and content in a way that makes learning both meaningful. The content—as the nature of the eight competences suggests—ranges from the concepts of individual disciplines to concrete contemporary events or professional experience.

As Alverno students identify their professional goals and set themselves to attain them, they are able to design a program that includes whatever content is necessary. Students develop all levels of the eight competences in the context of some content—whether it be the subject area of one of the disciplines or a concept like environment or an experience in a setting like a TV station or a law court. Therefore, planning students' programs requires inventorying the data they will need to master, as well as the competences they might most beneficially intensify.

Once a student has achieved Level 4 in all eight competences, she or he should have sufficiently broad experience and background in selected areas to maximize opportunities for learning at Levels 5 and 6. Then the area in which the student has chosen to concentrate can provide the integrating focus for higher learning experiences. For example, a student determined to become a communications expert might conceivably produce a one- or two-year learning design that combines Levels 5 and 6 of three competences: C1 (Communication Capability), C5 (Social Interaction), and C7 (Understanding the Contemporary World). Or the student might perceive C1, C2 (Analysis), C4 (Valuing), and C8 (Understanding Arts and Humanities) as a combination that would best help her or him achieve personal goals within the chosen profession.

Similarly, a future nurse's clinical experience might meaningfully integrate the development of C3 (Problem-Solving Skill), C5 (Social Interaction), and C4 (Valuing). A student specializing in biology might undertake a learning project that will enable her or him to reach Level 6 in C6 (Understanding Environment), C3 (Problem-Solving Skill), and C1 (Communication Capability). Indeed, as specialists in different areas identify more explicitly the competences essential to individual professions, the possible patterns for integrated learning on Levels 5 and 6 will multiply. These patterns will provide functional definitions for concentrations in new areas in which students can develop their educational programs at Alverno.

ASSESSMENT

When students enter Alverno, they have an immediate opportunity, through the Assessment Process, to identify and credential their achievement within many of the eight required competences, starting at Level 1 of each area and proceeding to whatever level they can. Inherent in this process is the possibility of demonstrating college attainment without spending time on campus—advanced placement, in effect. Students who do not qualify for advanced placement nonetheless are assessed so they can understand early what they must be able to do and can thus have direction in setting themselves to do it.

The complete assessment program is coordinated by the Assessment Center and features a variety of procedures and instruments. For some competence levels, assessment is included in class procedure, and the instruments are designed and administered and the results evaluated by the faculty members. In the future, after more alternatives to courses exist at Alverno, modules for student learning—whether connected to regular course structure or not—may still include provisions for assessment and validation of some competences by the person who facilitates the learning.

For other competence levels that require more complex assessment processes, however, an external assessment plan is in operation that has potential for many variations. This plan is based on a team evaluation concept. Teams of assessors for each competence level are identified, trained, and organized and are on call according to their availability. The typical evaluating team for assessing student achievement at Level 1 of the competences, for example, is comprised of a faculty member, a business or professional person from the Milwaukee community, an alumna, and an advanced student. Such teams are selected from the trained reserve group as the Assessment Center accumulates student requests for assessment appointments of Level 1 of C7, C5, and C1.

Team members are carefully trained to assess student progress. A manual enumerates the achievement criteria and explains their meaning with examples of verbal and nonverbal indicators. In addition, workshop training sessions give team members experience in careful recording of behavior as evidence for their judgment and in achieving consensus from the evidence.

Evaluating student performance for Levels 5 and 6 will frequently take more time than that required for evaluating performance for Levels 1–4. The assessment will consequently require specialists and use of such techniques as process recording. At the final stage, students' performance will in many cases be interdisciplinary and will combine competences. Thus, new variations in the composition of the assessment team will evolve. Level 5 teams may possibly include faculty members from different disciplines offering the same competence; Level 6 teams may possibly include faculty members representing a discipline and a competence area and two persons from outside the college—an established professional or business person and a younger professional.

The Level 6 assessment, therefore, will be an integrating one. In addition to the discrete assessment of students' performance at each competence level, Level 6 assessment will provide an evaluation of the total effectiveness of students as productive persons. Students will also have had one other integrating, essentially diagnostic assessment when they have achieved Level 4 of the eight competences, which will result in an evaluative statement regarding students' direction for their permanent records.

The design and the developing character of the competence-based learning (CBL) program at Alverno reorganizes the elements of all levels of the educational process, which, at present, are still primarily the semester hour, the disciplines, and the classroom teaching pattern. The new organizing principles of developmental achievement of competence levels, new integrating frameworks for ordering reality, and new teaching patterns based on careful analysis of the nature of learning are extending, supplementing, and gradually replacing the old.

The learning environment in which CBL is implemented at Alverno was created by the interaction of several change agents as represented by the college personnel and the nature of the design itself. We expect the continued interaction of these two agents to maintain an educational environment that is an integral part of the contemporary world, where the management of change has become a way of life.

APPENDIX

ALVERNO COLLEGE
Milwaukee, Wisconsin

COMPETENCE-BASED LEARNING PROGRAM
Competences and Developmental Levels

With demonstrated achievement in any one of these levels the student receives one competence level unit (CLU). An Associate of Arts degree is awarded when the first 4 levels of each of the eight competences have been demonstrated. For a bachelor's degree, in addition to these 32 CLU's the student must achieve another 8 CLU's, at least one of them to be at level 6. In general, higher levels of any given competence will require more time and effort to achieve than will the lower ones.

Competence 1: Develop effective communications skill
  Level 1—Identify own strengths and weaknesses as initiator and responder in communication situations of the following types, including a variety of audiences: written, oral, use of graphs
  Level 2—Analyze written and oral communication situations
  Level 3—Communicate with clarity of message-exchange in communication situations of the following types, including a variety of audiences: written, oral, use of graphs
  Level 4—Demonstrate sufficient understanding of basic concepts of at least 3 major areas of knowledge to communicate in terms of them
  Level 5—Demonstrate understanding of communication as historical process involving development of meaning and form in relation to technological and cultural forces
  Level 6—Communicate effectively through coordinated use of 3 different media that represent contemporary technological advancement in the communications field

Competence 2: Sharpen analytical capabilities
  Level 1—Identify explicit elements of a work (A work may be an article, artifact, or process)
  Level 2—Identify implicit elements of a work
  Level 3—Identify relationships in a work
  Level 4—Analyze the structure and organization of a work
  Level 5—In the interpretation and/or creation of one or more works, develop new hypotheses, new conclusions, or new relations of materials and means of production
  Level 6—Produce a single work that demonstrates facility in 3 types of analysis: elements, relationships, organizing principles

Competence 3: Develop workable problem-solving skill
  Level 1—Identify the process, assumptions, and limitations involved in the scientific method
  Level 2—Formulate questions which yield to the problem-solving approach
  Level 3—Apply the problem-solving process to a problem
  Level 4—Apply the problem-solving process to a new area of knowledge (area different from problem in Level 3)
  Level 5—Design and implement original research project of sufficient complexity to involve direction of or collaboration with others
  Level 6—Demonstrate that problem solving is an assumed approach in one's own search for knowledge and one's reflection upon experience

Competence 4: Develop a facility for making value judgments and independent decisions
  Level 1—Identify own values
  Level 2—Demonstrate understanding of philosophy, history, religion, arts, and/or literature as reflection of values
  Level 3—Demonstrate understanding of relationship of values to scientific and technological development
  Level 4—Make value judgments for which you (a) identify viable alternatives and (b) forecast and weigh consequences
  Level 5—Demonstrate understanding of the validity of value systems differing from culture to culture

Level 6—Communicate value judgments effectively, either to defend them or to persuade others to them, and demonstrate commitment to them

Competence 5: Develop facility for social interaction
Level 1—Identify and analyze own strengths and weaknesses in group situations
Level 2—Analyze behavior of others within a theoretical framework
Level 3—Evaluate behavior of self and others within a theoretical framework
Level 4—Demonstrate effective social behavior in variety of situations and circumstances—both private and public, within one's own culture
Level 5—Demonstrate effective social behavior in variety of situations and circumstances, beyond as well as on college campus, involving different cultures or subcultures and large as well as small groups
Level 6—Demonstrate effective organizational activity

Competence 6: Achieve understanding of the relationship of the individual and the environment
Level 1—Identify environmental components
Level 2—Identify relationships between individual attitudes, beliefs, values, behaviors, and environmental components
Level 3—Demonstrate an understanding of the interaction effects of cultural and physical setting upon individual and group behavior
Level 4—Analyze alternative courses of action regarding a particular environmental problem on the basis of their feasibility, cultural acceptability, and technical accuracy
Level 5—Assess the consequences of various courses of action in regard to a selected environmental problem and the likelihood that goals will be achieved
Level 6—Defend a choice among solutions to a particular environmental problem

Competence 7: Develop awareness and understanding of the world in which the individual lives
Level 1—Demonstrate awareness, perception and knowledge of observable events in the contemporary world
Level 2—Analyze contemporary events in their historical context
Level 3—Analyze interrelationships of contemporary events and conditions
Level 4—Demonstrate understanding of the world as a global unit by analyzing the impact of events of one society upon another
Level 5—Demonstrate understanding and acceptance of personal responsibility in contemporary events
Level 6—Take personal position regarding implications of contemporary events

Competence 8: Develop knowledge, understanding, and responsiveness to the arts and knowledge and understanding of the humanities (Levels 1 and 3 of this competence are to be achieved for a total of 3 arts and/or humanities including at least 1 of each)
Level 1—For each selected art, express response and demonstrate understanding of elements, and for each selected humanity, demonstrate understanding of the elements characteristic of its method
Level 2—Express response to and demonstrate understanding of one of the arts in relationship to other arts, and demonstrate understanding of an artistic work as an expression of philosophy, religion, or history
Level 3—Express response to and demonstrate understanding of the arts, and

demonstrate understanding of the humanities, in both cases as expressions of interrelationships between the individual and society

Level 4—Demonstrate understanding of works of other cultures and their impact upon modes of expression of one's own culture

Level 5—Formulate independent judgments regarding the relative intrinsic and extrinsic values of artistic or humanistic expressions and persuasively communicate the significance of their worth

Level 6—Demonstrate facility of self-expression in one or more artistic or humanistic modes and commitment to their importance

Three Questions about Statewide Planning

JOHN K. FOLGER

STATEWIDE PLANNING may not have come of age, but it is a healthy adolescent. Fifteen years ago the Eisenhower Committee was arguing the virtues of institutional autonomy and freedom[1] and the undesirability of state-level regulation. State planning and coordination were relegated to a minor role and, it was hoped by many college administrators, would soon disappear from the scene, leaving the colleges and universities to do their thing.

Instead, during the past fifteen years virtually all of the states have established some organization for state-level planning and coordination, many have strengthened the role of the coordinating board, and about half a dozen have created statewide governing boards to provide even more central control and direction.[2]

The need for some kind of coordination and rational planning is now widely accepted; but as the number and influence of state-level agencies have increased, so has criticism of their activities. This situation is typical of adolescence: The more state planning grows up, the more it is criticized, especially by the older, established part of education.

I would like to discuss these criticisms in relation to three questions and, at the same time, to propose some answers to them.

First, How much planning? or, To what extent should we utilize planning, and to what extent should we rely on competition and market forces, to determine the future development of postsecondary education?

1. Committee on Government and Higher Education, *The Efficiency of Freedom* (Baltimore: Johns Hopkins Press, 1959).
2. For a detailed discussion of the development of statewide coordination, see Robert O. Berdahl, *Statewide Coordination of Higher Education* (Washington: American Council on Education, 1971). See also Lyman Glenny et al., *Coordinating Higher Education for the 70's* (Berkeley: University of California, Center for Research and Development in Higher Education, 1971).

Second, Who should do it? or, What is the political context within which planning should occur?

Third, How should it be done? or, Do we have an adequate technology of planning?

Let us look at each of these questions.

RATIONALIZATION VERSUS COMPETITION

The Second Newman Report makes the clearest case for greater reliance on competition and market forces in higher education: "We believe the need for centralization and rationalization has been overestimated and its dangers underestimated. It is possible to encourage competition within the educational community to provide the maximum opportunity for the student and the vitality necessary in the institution for constant reevaluation and self-renewal."[3]

The main concern of the report, however, is with the centralization of power and decision making, and the effect that such centralization has in reducing competition among institutions, not with the effects of planning per se:

> Surely there is need for coordination in postsecondary education. State-wide planning is essential. . . . state agencies are the logical locus of such coordination. A number of these agencies . . . have also demonstrated that they can be a force for diversity among institutions. But this is only one kind of innovation—planned from the top to meet a widely perceived need. There is also a need to capitalize on the imagination of the many potential educational innovators who start from the bottom . . .[4]

The Second Newman Report identifies a number of other foes of educational innovation within higher education: for example, the barriers to competition and innovation erected by professional societies, the bureaucratic tendencies within big universities, and unionization and other guild-type organizations of faculties. In fact, of the many forces that limit the competition between new approaches to teaching and learning, on the one hand, and the established ways of doing things, on the other, the effort to rationalize higher education through state planning is one of the newest and probably one of the weakest.

Even while the virtues and evils of socialism versus capitalism have

---

3. *The Second Newman Report: National Policy and Higher Education,* Report of a Special Task Force to the Secretary of Health, Education, and Welfare (Cambridge, Mass.: MIT Press, 1973), p. 89.

4. Ibid., p. 86.

been hotly but pointlessly debated, our economy has evolved into a system that does not look much like the classical conceptions of either Karl Marx or Adam Smith. Similarly, while we in higher education get hung up in disputes between the planners and the new advocates of laissez faire, our higher education system evolves through a mixture of half-realized plans, political power struggles, and price competition for students that is not very closely related to the effectiveness of education. There are, to be sure, several important areas where competition between institutions, and between faculty within institutions, can have beneficial effects. But the optimal use of competitive relationships does not reduce very much the need for planning to identify our goals and to design ways of achieving them.

The question is, then: In which areas will competition work to help us achieve our goals? How can the planning process identify those areas and help to maintain a free market? For example, we have, on the whole, done a good job in preserving the free market in ideas within our institutions. Faculty members have been free to present the truth as they have seen it, even when their ideas were controversial. Most colleges and universities, alert to the necessity of safeguarding the free market in ideas, have adopted procedures such as tenure to help protect that freedom. But in a period of near-zero enrollment growth, tenure contributes to the hardening of academic arteries by limiting the number of new people who can enter the faculty ranks. In preserving one free market, are we cutting down on innovations? Or is tenure really essential to maintaining the free market in ideas? These are important policy questions, but they will not be answered by market competition.

We need to consider also whether the current federal emphasis on supporting higher education through direct financial aid to students will actually help promote institutional diversity. Is it not possible that, in their efforts to attract students, institutions will limit themselves to those procedures and educational models that seem to be most attractive to students and will thus tend to become more homogeneous, less diverse?

Some of our goals for higher education—such as equalizing educational opportunity—will not be achieved through the free market but only through providing subsidies to low-income students. There are very good reasons for nonmarket strategies in an overall state educational plan, even one which is developed on the premise that competition should be encouraged wherever it will contribute to the achievement of educational objectives.

These examples should suffice to show that it is not an either-or situation: either planning or a free market. Where the operation of a free market will help us to achieve our objectives, the market should be allowed to operate. This does not diminish the importance of planning; it just makes the requirements of good planning more complicated.

Planning must determine when competition will promote our goals and when it will be either irrelevant or actually contradictory to our goals. If we can make these distinctions, we can construct an overall planning system that effectively uses competition but does not rely on a market solution to achieve all educational goals.

The Political Context

The second important question—Who does the planning?—is essentially a political question relating to the power and authority of the planners and to the extent of formal and informal participation by the various groups affected by the planning.

Let us first consider the issue of the power and authority of the planners. A plan, like a budget, is a mechanism for control, and one of the principles of administration is that planning should be done at the level of management that has the responsibility for carrying out the plan. It is only a small step from this proposition to the idea that if an agency has been assigned responsibility for state planning, it should also have the power necessary to see that the plan is carried out.

This was a step that the Carnegie Commission was unwilling to take. Its view of the role of state planning and governance, as outlined in *The Capitol and the Campus,* was that state agencies should confine themselves to planning and coordination; they should not manage, administer, or govern institutions from the state level.[5] The key word in this context is *coordination.* What exactly does it involve? If it includes control of program development and, to some degree, of budget—as is the case with the stronger coordinating agencies across the country—then coordination borders on governance powers, since the state agency in these cases has effective veto power over the academic development of institutions. If it includes planning and advisory powers only—as is the case with some of the weaker coordinating agencies—then the Carnegie Commission's prescription has clearly been filled, but the medicine is likely to be too weak to combat any serious infection within the higher education system.

The history of the last decade indicates that the "advisory only" co-

5. Carnegie Commission on Higher Education, *The Capitol and the Campus: State Responsibility for Postsecondary Education* (New York: McGraw-Hill, April 1971).

ordinating agencies have usually been strengthened to give them more power. State legislatures and governors expect the state agency for higher education to come to grips with the major problems in higher education, and if "advice" does not get the job done, then the tendency has been to give the agency some controlling and directing powers as well.

The power of the state planning agency affects the kind of plan it develops. A state plan for higher education is an attempt to chart the path to the state's educational goals in a manner that is (*a*) objective and effective and (*b*) politically acceptable. The planning literature emphasizes the rational and objective aspects of the process, but it is usually the political aspects that state planners talk about informally among themselves. Unless there is a minimum consensus on a plan, it has no possibility of being implemented. The ability of the state agency to get consensus on and support for some of the unpopular ideas in the plan (such as the need to limit the further development of doctoral programs) depends in part on how much influence it has in general, and how much weight (in a political sense) institutions feel they must give to its planning proposals. Thus, the agency that has only advisory powers must develop a plan that is immediately acceptable to its educational constituency; it has no real leverage for making the higher education community accept unpopular proposals, however important they may be, in the view of the planners, to educational progress.

It follows from the above points that a state agency with strong enforcement powers is more likely than is a state agency with only advisory powers to produce a plan that concentrates more on the objective needs of the state and gives less attention to the political dimension.

Though the more powerful state agency has the opportunity to be more objective, there is no assurance that it will be. If the staff of the agency, or the board members themselves, are primarily attuned to the political dimension (both the politics within higher education and the politics of higher education as a part of state government), their plan will reflect that orientation. If a plan is to represent the public interest rather than simple political consensus, then the staff responsible for its development must be intelligent and technically competent to assess the complexities of the future in higher education.

The other central political issue in the planning process is the degree to which various interest groups participate in the development of the plan and the extent to which the state agency "listens to" each of these groups. As it formulates a plan to meet the objective needs of higher education in the state, the state agency must also balance competing political interests.

In this process, the established institutional interests have the advantage because they are well organized, articulate, and politically influential. Other important interest groups—such as students, minorities, and non-collegiate postsecondary institutions—may have a much harder time getting their views included in the state plan. The 1202 Commissions are one approach to better representation of all interests in the planning process; the increasing political strength of students, minority groups, and vocational interests is another, and probably more important, assurance that all relevant interest groups will have their views considered in the development of the state plan.

There is always a danger that making a plan politically acceptable will reduce it to banality. The state plan should not become a sort of lowest common denominator, a set of broad generalizations on which everyone can agree but which provides no clear guidance for action. It must address itself to the really tough questions.

For example, nearly everyone agrees that equal educational opportunity is a desirable goal. All state plans embrace this goal as something they favor. But when one goes beyond the broad generalization and tries to define just what is meant by "equal opportunity," some real difficulties and complexities emerge. Does equality of opportunity mean equality of outcomes? For example, if blacks have lower college-going rates than whites (as they do), does this mean they have less opportunity? Further, does it mean that minorities should be given preference in the allocation of student aid funds and in enrollment for special educational programs designed to overcome previous academic deficiencies in order to bring minority enrollment rates to a parity with total enrollment rates? Are these steps a required part of providing equal educational opportunity? At this point, substantial differences of opinion will develop as to how far higher education must go to provide equal opportunity. The way to maintain consensus on issues like this is to keep them general: We are all for equal opportunity in general; it is only when we get to the specifics that conflicts arise. But a plan made up only of broad generalizations provides little direction for action. However politically acceptable a plan may be, unless it addresses the important issues and makes clear recommendations about them, it will be ineffectual.

THE TECHNOLOGY OF PLANNING

The third question relates to the technical basis for planning: Are current methods of projecting the major influences on the development of higher education adequate? Do we have the techniques necessary for providing rational solutions to complex educational problems?

The answers to these questions are not very reassuring: Examples of poor techniques are more abundant than examples of effective techniques. Let us look, for instance, at enrollment projections, which are widely used as basic input to fiscal planning, academic program planning, and other areas of state planning. As I reported in a recent review, none of the major national projections of enrollment made in the early 1960s came very close to actual enrollment in 1970; they tended to fall far short.[6] State enrollment projections are even more subject to error in that they are more affected by migration. But even though most enrollment projections of the late 1950s and early 1960s were inaccurate, neither they nor the methodology by which they were developed received much criticism during the 1960s, primarily because, though in most cases substantial underestimates, they nonetheless projected considerable enrollment growth and thus generally supported institutional goals and ambitions. As long as these forecasts were consistent with the outlook of colleges and universities, weaknesses in the technical base of projection methodology[7] were not a matter of concern.

In another area of planning technology, analysis of manpower supply and demand, the projections have also been subject to rather large errors.[8] But unlike enrollment projections, manpower analyses have been heavily criticized, partly because they do not always support the goals and ambitions of higher education. Howard Bowen, for example, has pointed out some of the inaccuracies of manpower analyses, though he is more concerned with what he regards as the misconceptions underlying the manpower approach to planning.[9]

Thus, in at least two major areas of planning technology—the projection of enrollments and the projection of demand for and supply of graduates—our methods are crude and subject to considerable error. Other planning techniques, such as the use of economic models to simulate decision processes and to examine policy alternatives, are useful only insofar as their assumptions are appropriate to the actual processes of higher edu-

6. John Folger, "On Enrollment Projections: Clearing up the Crystal Ball," *Journal of Higher Education,* June 1974, pp. 405–14.

7. Ibid. The article identifies some of the methodological weaknesses.

8. A review of these errors is contained in John Folger, "The Job Market for College Graduates," *Journal of Higher Education,* March 1972, pp. 203–22.

9. "Manpower Management and Higher Education," *Educational Record,* Winter 1973, pp. 5–14.

cation. In many cases, their assumptions are inapposite and therefore their conclusions, upon which policy is based, may be erroneous. This is Howard Bowen's main point in his critique of manpower planning: that the assumptions about the relation between degrees received and jobs available are not realistic, and as a result the conclusions are not realistic either.

We must conclude, then, that planning technology is not very far advanced and that our data and methodology may be inadequate for planning the best way to achieve our educational objectives. If we can accept this rather critical assessment and approach planning as a process subject to continual revision and correction, then we will not oversell the capability of planning.

Clearly, the "state of the art" demands a flexible plan. But political pressures may operate to solidify certain policies once they are set out in the plan. For instance, the policy position which the state plan takes on the establishment of a new medical school will be supported by those interests that take the same position, regardless of the adequacy of the evidence. This process may lock the state planners into a particular position, even when the data on which it was based turn out to be incomplete or inaccurate. Perhaps the only solution to this problem is to involve decision-makers—at both the institutional and state levels—more completely in the planning process in order to make them more aware of methodological shortcomings and the consequent need to maintain flexibility.

In addition, politics places a time constraint on the planning process. Politicians are interested chiefly in what is going to happen during the remainder of their term of office; they are skeptical about long-range planning unless it contains projections of "progress" for the next year or two or three that will help the politicians when they face reelection. Thus, the plan must strike a balance between taking a long-range perspective and focusing on the more immediate time frame of administrations and political leaders. It must also strike a balance between making clear and specific recommendations and maintaining the flexibility necessary to qualify projections based on weak data.

Despite the importance of competition in making institutions responsive to student needs and in preserving a free market in ideas, planning is necessary too and will probably be even more important in the future, when resources become even scarcer. The advocates of more dependence on the market forces need to be clear about those areas where competition will promote desirable educational goals and those areas where it will not be helpful. For their part, planners need to focus state planning on the policy problems that are appropriate to the state's goals and to avoid turning the state plan into an instrument for managing and controlling institutions.

The question of who participates in the development of the plan is always crucial; any state plan has a political dimension. But a plan must be something more than a simple political consensus (which the legislature can achieve more easily and more democratically than educators can, in any event). State agencies that have strong coordinating authority are in a better position to deal with important and controversial planning and policy issues (such as maintaining institutional diversity) than are state agencies that have only advisory powers, since the former have more leverage in the implementation of their plans.

The technology of educational planning is not very sophisticated, and many of our analytic and projection models are inaccurate. In recognition of the weaknesses of our methodology, we must be alert to the need for frequent revision in our plans. Unfortunately, planning methodologies are judged more by the political acceptability of their results than by systematic analysis and critique. Those who approve of the conclusion in the plan support both the plan and the planners. Those who do not like the conclusion attack the methodology of the plan or the political motivations of the planners or both. Again, the best short-term solution is to involve policy-makers more thoroughly in the planning process so that they can better understand its strengths and weaknesses. The long-term solution is to improve our data and our analytic techniques.

The three steps that will move planning out of the adolescent stage most rapidly are (1) a clear delineation of those policy issues and goals that the state plan must deal with, (2) an understanding of the powers and responsibilities that must accompany the planning role if it is to be effective, and (3) improved data and methods of providing the information needed for effective planning. Answering the questions needed to take these steps will determine how rapidly the adolescent becomes an adult.

Regional Dimensions
of Planning and Coordination

WINFRED L. GODWIN

THE NOTION that a rational structure might characterize American higher education is a relatively new one. Historically our colleges and universities enjoyed independence of each other and of close scrutiny by political authority. Each operated under its own board, and each pursued its own destiny as it saw fit.

Logan Wilson once observed that, though it would be comforting to attribute this independence to a popular appreciation of the virtues of institutional autonomy, we may as well acknowledge that a good deal of public indifference to higher education is involved.

With the advent of mass higher education, and resultant large-scale expenditures of public revenues, pressure for a more systematic approach greatly increased. State governments, which assumed the heaviest burden of changing enrollment and support patterns, responded to these pressures by creating or strengthening state agencies intended to plan, coordinate, and, in some instances, govern higher education. These bodies have in a short time become an established part of the educational-governmental scene.

While differing widely in nature and effectiveness, the state bodies are, taken as a whole, the most visible expression yet of the strain toward coordination in higher education. But because state coordination is affected by so many other centers of influence and activity—at the institutional, state, interstate, federal, and national associational levels—we can only conclude that American higher education remains a highly diverse and decentralized enterprise.

This paper focuses on one center of activity related to state-level interests in higher education, namely, interstate—and, in particular, regional —planning and coordination. Initiated slightly before the intensified effort in the mid-1950s to expand state-level coordination, regional coordination has occurred largely through statutory agencies created under interstate compacts, enacted first in the South and later in the West and in New England. The establishment in 1966 of the Education Commission of the States provides the first nationwide interstate approach.

The concept of region is based on the association of a variety of factors in a geographic area, giving the area an identity and justifying its treatment as a unit for governmental planning and action.[1] Consistent with that concept, the experiences of the three regional compacts have varied, discouraging generalizations that apply equally to all three.

Nonetheless, the available evidence indicates that each has resulted in (1) better utilization of graduate and professional programs, (2) cooperative ventures to strengthen disciplines and professions, (3) a clearer picture of the needs in higher education in three major regions, (4) substantial research on the organization and operation of the higher education enterprise, and (5) expansion of institutional research and self-study and of efforts to develop more useful evaluative data.

On the other hand, the existence of these regional agreements has not altogether deterred unnecessary duplication of graduate and professional programs that states now find intolerable. Nor has it resulted in as extensive an interstate sharing of curricula and facilities as many would like to see. Of more significance, regional education has had only qualified success in moving from its initial attempts to satisfy specific needs through interstate sharing to more general efforts to strengthen higher education throughout the region. In the South, an emphasis on the regional agency's relationships with state governments and its consultative and advisory role to them has had a substantial influence on political attitudes and state decisions to expand, support, and coordinate higher education.

Born in a period of relative deprivation, regional education developed during the most affluent era of American higher education. The several compact agencies have engaged in a wide array of program activities: research on institutional organization and management, improvement of undergraduate teaching, use of educational technology, curriculum development in various disciplines, and extension of opportunities for minorities, to mention only a few. In addition, they have provided administrative and fiscal mechanisms for various operating programs, including new regional library networks.

All such activities reflect the central concern of regional compacts for the orderly development and effective use of institutions and programs. An important question now is, How can regional efforts contribute effectively to the planning, coordination, and general strengthening of higher educa-

1. For a discussion of the concept of region, see Lawrence L. Durisch, "The Region as a Unit for Governmental Planning and Action," *The Future South and Higher Education* (Atlanta, Ga.: Southern Regional Education Board, 1968).

tion in the period of uncertainty that confronts us? I suggest that they can be helpful in four areas: (1) resource sharing and planning, (2) improvement of the state planning process, (3) facilitation of the federal role in higher education, and (4) strengthening of relations between political and educational leaders.

SHARING AND PLANNING RESOURCES

While all states have moved to provide a fuller array of educational offerings, complete self-sufficiency remains neither desirable nor attainable. The collective impact of inflated costs, a funding plateau, and a slowdown in enrollments makes the practice of sharing resources—one of the original missions of regional education—increasingly advantageous. For example, many states will continue to be without, and indeed do not need, programs in certain professional fields. To assure interstate access to and support of such programs, traditional contractual arrangements should be utilized to the fullest.

In addition, now that the seemingly unlimited expansion of graduate institutions and programs has been arrested, and some retrenchment is under way, the possibilities of an even broader cooperative use of graduate programs are being explored. Educational common markets have been created or expanded. These arrangements permit states and institutions to participate in a joint allocation of functions, thus avoiding unnecessary duplication and assuring that all students in a multistate region have access to all necessary programs. Such efforts, even on a modest scale, may help to preserve some rare and low-demand—but nonetheless important—programs. The more general purpose to be stressed in such arrangements is the orderly development or curtailment of programs.

A third form of interstate sharing pertains to uncommon teaching and research facilities. Continuing, updated regional registers of such resources, with arrangements for their use by faculty and students, can benefit both graduate and undergraduate institutions, particularly if the arrangements include small travel grants for users. The Southern region has initiated such a program in the natural sciences and engineering, with the expectation that states will develop their own grant programs when privately funded regional grants are terminated.

In general, interstate planning of what is needed or desired has lagged behind interstate cooperation in using what we already have more effectively, which is understandable under circumstances of rapid growth and ever-swelling appropriations. Now, however, states acknowledge the need to be more cognizant of developments in neighboring states. Financial stringency aside, however, any state's needs are influenced by the interdependence of a highly mobile population. Planning under regional auspices has occurred in some fields—for example, nursing and graduate education in the agricultural sciences—with substantial results that have had an impact at both institutional and state levels as well as in professional circles, but obviously a field-by-field approach is a limiting one. A broader approach should also be addressed by regional groups and their member states. For example, more interstate planning would be helpful in education in the health professions, an area which has grown rapidly and somewhat haphazardly, sometimes with federal largesse that has had little concern for either state or interstate planning or long-term funding. An overall interstate assessment is needed to identify some of the more specialized fields in which multistate planning and action could meet anticipated needs, perhaps with federal subvention in the planning and development stages. Such an assessment should encourage further consideration of the role of private institutional resources in meeting state needs—something which state planning to date has generally lacked. It should also evolve a pattern of regularized joint consultation between state, interstate, and federal levels about the planning and support of education in the health professions.

The New England regional compact is now attempting to apply the interstate concept to the planning, construction, and operation of a regional school of veterinary medicine and of a regional school of optometry. Elsewhere, neighboring states are studying the possibility of creating satellite teaching and service hospitals linked to an existing college of veterinary medicine in another state. Previously regarded as unrealistic and unworkable, such arrangements may become realities in selected situations, and especially so if given federal encouragement.

Graduate education is another area in which interstate consultation and planning may help in determining policies for future support and development. Several recent reports by national groups on graduate education generally agree on the need for a strong system of graduate education in the United States, with the federal government playing a major role.

Graduate education is indeed a national resource to be cultivated, but if the interests of states, regions, and the entire nation are to be served, subnational dimensions must also be considered. The Carnegie Commission, for example, has recommended state and federal policies (1) to confine comprehensive doctoral programs to a relatively limited number of universities, perhaps sixty to one hundred, that have high-quality programs in many disciplines, and (2) to develop more limited graduate programs elsewhere. These recommendations have much to commend them, but in the interest of both quality education and public equity, full attention must be given to legitimate geographic requirements and to the necessity for some patterns of specialization along interinstitutional and interstate lines.

FACILITATING STATE PLANNING

The role of regional planning is not to diminish state planning but rather to strengthen it by expanding its context and by encouraging closer consideration of related developments elsewhere. Regional agencies can facilitate the state planning process through informational, research, and consultative activities. Every state uses internally developed information about institutional operations, appropriations, student mobility, and so forth, and access to comparative information generated at the regional level will improve the development and testing of alternative decisions.

The results from national data collection efforts are frequently disseminated too late to be helpful, and the unilateral exchange by state agencies entails both wasteful duplication of effort and the likelihood of poor compatibility once the data are collected. But regional information exchange can draw in advance upon national collection efforts; more important, it can add to that information such data as are relevant to the particular needs of its constituent agencies. Moreover, involving state agencies in the selection and design of data format lends local credibility to the data collected, since even the presentation of elementary data on full-time equivalent enrollment, appropriations, and faculty salaries varies greatly.

Once gathered, compiled, and disseminated according to the needs of the constituent state agencies, such information can be applied immediately in developing and justifying budgets. At longer range, such information can be fed back into state agency data banks serving the state coordinating and planning function. More comprehensive information exchange procedures, such as those developed under the auspices of the National Center for Higher Education Management Systems (NCHEMS), need to be adapted to state planning objectives and coordinated among state agencies. Cost information, in particular, must be amplified and appropriately qualified to be made meaningful.

Another regional contribution should be the analysis of information, once it is compiled. Given scarcer resources and unabated institutional aspirations, it becomes more apparent that norms transcending state lines are required, that programs must be evaluated continuously, and that states can benefit from research addressing itself to their particular definitions of the problems. Regional analyses go beyond a single state's efforts to solve its problems, but avoid entanglement in the national universe of state systems.

Such regional studies are selective, and they tend to be pragmatic. For example, degree productivity, or rather underproductivity, is a problem confronting all institutional and state planners. Productivity can be studied nationally, and should be studied locally. But much is to be gained by study from a regional perspective. For instance, a simple statistic like number of degrees produced by programs, when studied carefully enough to be kept in context, is valuable for decision making. Regional analyses of the proliferation of doctoral programs in a time of stabilizing or declining demand for Ph.D.'s can closely support the work of state agencies in gathering, analyzing, and summarizing information needed for the review of proposals for new programs and of the continuation of existing programs. A regional perspective can provide balance of emphasis, can help guard against the myopia of local aspirations, and can encourage growth where growth is indicated and caution where overextension threatens.

Another regional input to state planning should be manpower information. American academics are notable for a tradition of antivocationalism and a laissez faire attitude toward program development. Both have served to keep manpower information in a role of low priority as far as educational decision making is concerned, unless, of course, such information supports the case for a new or expanded commitment favored by institutional interests.

The blackout on manpower information in educational planning is also attributable to the paucity of practical information. Manpower information at the community level can be applied to limited parts of higher educational planning, especially in the areas of vocational-technical education, and manpower information at the national level also enjoys a measure of confidence. Manpower projections at the state level are subject to the vagaries of migration. Matching educational and occupational categories is a formidable task, and state higher educational planning has understandably avoided great dependence upon manpower projections.

As college attendance levels off and as educational requirements for given occupations stabilize, manpower projections may be given greater credence. In any event, there is a growing feeling that colleges and universities need to adjust more directly to the realities of the job market. This varies by field, but for most college programs, the most meaningful units of analysis extend across state lines. Developing and disseminating manpower information for application to state planning, then, is a third area in which regional agencies can assist state planning.

Consultation is a fourth appropriate way in which a regional agency can contribute to state planning efforts. The know-how acquired through experience in a variety of situations with regard to higher educational planning and coordination is a valuable asset. A regional agency is in a strategic position for identifying those persons who have dealt with problems similar to the ones faced by its constituents. The staff of a regional agency should, in the course of their ongoing operation, also develop competencies which are in demand. The consultation function is always subject to misuse in decision making, but the conditions under which it has tended to occur through regional auspices have served to enhance both state and regional interests. In some instances, the fact that the regional agency is able to provide continuing consultation over a period of time has been of special value in dealing with problems.

Facilitating the Federal Role

Through the Education Commission of the States and the State Higher Education Officers (a national organization), communication with federal officials about state-level concerns in higher education, including planning and coordination, has increased. This likely will have an increasing impact on the federal role in higher education, offsetting to some extent the influence traditionally exercised by the nationally organized institutional interests.

Also important are regional-federal relationships, which have been extensive, particularly in the execution of federally funded programs through regional agencies. To meet needs with regional dimensions, federal agencies must have input from regional bodies as they define broad policies and design guidelines. Without such information, they may unwittingly go counter to the intent of the legislation which they are seeking to implement.

The recent experience which my own organization has had with the Office for Civil Rights (OCR) of the Department of Health, Education, and Welfare illustrates how a regional body may help to serve both the federal agency and the states within the region. Soon after Judge John H. Pratt, in a District of Columbia federal court, ruled that OCR must act on ten state plans for racial compliance in higher education, communication between the director of OCR and SREB grew more extensive, a relationship that has continued. As a consequence, criteria for defining compliance in higher education were developed and modified from time to time as OCR has responded to the educational and administrative dimensions of state planning to achieve unitary systems in higher education.

In this instance, several steps facilitated effective planning. First, the regional board adopted a policy statement stressing the necessity for full compliance, but doing so in ways both legally and educationally sound and giving careful attention to differences among states in the structure and administration of public higher education and therefore in the nature of the problems likely to be encountered in efforts to achieve compliance.

Subsequently OCR encouraged the regional board to make suggestions for state planning which would be educationally and operationally sound. The regional board produced such a document through the work of a biracial group of staff and consultants and provided it to officials in institutions and in state and federal agencies.

At the request of the state higher education agencies in the region, the regional agency convened a meeting of the OCR director and his staff and the state agency directors for a thorough discussion and clarification of issues and procedures. This conference laid a basis for continuing communication by OCR both with the regional staff and with state personnel responsible for developing state plans. Since that meeting, the regional agency has maintained contact with federal agencies and with state agencies and will continue to do so during the monitoring period that follows the acceptance of the plans.

As this illustration indicates, the role of the regional agency in relation to federal and state agencies is not directive, nor is it that of a strictly intermediate body operating between federal and state agencies. The regional agency provides a means by which the federal government may be more responsive to states in relating federal policies to the wide range of differing local situations throughout the nation and by which states may make such conditions known and understood.

Regional compacts can assist the federal responsibilities in higher education in other ways as well. Earlier, I referred to the desirability of regional planning in the future development of educational resources. The federal government should encourage such planning through developmental grants or other financial incentives, particularly in those capital-intensive educational efforts whose impact transcends state lines and which serve the federal interest. The proposed regional schools of veterinary medicine and optometry are examples. A nationwide grid of regional library networks, as well as regional science information networks, are other examples, both already operational or in process but requiring federal support for effective development.

The Carnegie Commission has recommended a nationwide system of learning technology centers, organized and operated on a regional basis for the purpose of accelerating the development and use of instructional technology in higher education. The feasibility of cooperative development of quality materials for televised instruction has already been demonstrated. Significant economies of scale in such endeavors can be attained only on an interstate or regional basis, but their capitalization needs justify federal support.

STRENGTHENING POLITICAL-EDUCATIONAL RELATIONSHIPS

The Carnegie Commission, in a 1971 report, acknowledged that states generally have discharged their responsibility for higher education well, and particularly in the 1960s gave "spectacular support."[2] The Commission said: "The states should continue to carry the primary governmental responsibility for higher education they have borne historically. They have done well with it. Their guardianship has led to substantial diversity, to adaptation to regional needs, and to competitive efforts at improvement." The Commission concluded that, "As goes state support, as goes state understanding, as goes state acceptance of autonomy, so also goes, beyond any other external influence, the future of all higher education in the United States."

With over three-fourths of total enrollments in public institutions, and with state governments providing three times as much of the institutional income as the federal government, higher education leadership has no more important task than to foster relations with state governments based on mutual understanding and respect.

Interstate organizations have a special opportunity, in a period of increasing political skepticism about higher education, to facilitate the kind of dialogue and understanding between the educational and the political communities that can contribute to the continuing effective discharge of the states' responsibilities. Unencumbered by day-to-day affairs at state and institutional levels, these organizations provide a context free from localized pressures within which parties of differing views can examine and debate the constant responsibilities as well as the changing opportunities of each. One advantage of a regional compact, especially if it has balanced

2. *The Capitol and the Campus: State Responsibility for Postsecondary Education* (New York: McGraw-Hill, 1971), pp. 1–5.

representation of both political and educational leadership, is that it provides a manageable setting in which participants are generally familiar with neighboring state political structures and higher education conditions. This facilitates consideration of problems not only in terms of broad objectives but also of possible specific resolutions.

Involving legislators in the work of regional committees to examine special issues or program needs enlarges the legislators' frame of reference and also assures, to a degree, realistic and feasible recommendations. Regional legislative conferences and seminars elevate discussions of problems to a consideration of their origins and total dimensions. Meetings of regional boards in which legislators, governors, and educational representatives participate can serve to increase understanding of the perspectives of each on given issues.

The cumulative effect of such experiences in one region, where representation from executive and legislative branches of the state government and from higher education is mandated, has been, in the words of one university president, "a firmer basis for mutual confidence, respect and good will among educational and political leaders."

My own hope is that all interstate efforts in higher education would lay primary stress on this role. Their potential contributions in doing so are great at this stage in American higher education, particularly if the political-educational dialogue can be expanded on such issues as the future role of the comprehensive graduate university and support for it, state responsibility for the whole range of postsecondary education, and the nature of the state planning and coordinating process in a period of slow growth or retrenchment.

Interstate compacts represent a continuing quest for productive relationships between those governmental units in our federal system which have the greatest responsibilities for providing services, including education, to the public.

> The interstate compact comes into existence when unilateral state action is ineffective or, more significantly, when joint action promises to increase the effectiveness and the vision of the party states. The product of such arrangements has not resulted in sectionalism, but in a positive and often imaginative joint attack on common problems. As interstate compacts increase in number and in effectiveness—and they will if properly used—the regionalism resulting will continue to be an important feature of the federal system. The compact is making a contribution to sub-national and national unity.[3]

3. Durisch, "The Region as a Unit for Governmental Planning and Action," p. 138.

The oldest of the interstate education compacts became operational only twenty-five years ago. All have developed during a period when the total society was greatly expansive in its support and aspirations for higher education.

Despite widespread notions to the contrary, however, the rationale for the compacts was never rooted solely in financial adversity. Thus while they have demonstrated tangible benefits in terms of savings to the states, they also have contributed to the development of higher education in many ways, including the enhancement of state planning and coordination. Their futures are surely linked in measure to the fortunes of state-level planning, but in addition they have the obligation and opportunity to exercise leadership in their own right in addressing those issues affecting the well-being of both higher education and their member state governments.

To Keep from Being King

WARREN G. HILL

THIS PAPER represents the third part of a trilogy. In the position papers presented on statewide planning, John Folger has detailed current criticism of statewide planning and Winfred Godwin has analyzed interstate coordination and planning. Here, I shall examine the relationships among the players on the planning field and the uses of planning regions *within* states.

During this century, as the peoples of various countries have successfully sought a larger role in making the decisions that affect them, the number of kings in power has decreased steadily. This trend has not occasioned alarm among many of the governed (although it undoubtedly has brought some anxiety to those who stand in line for a given throne), and widespread movement is apparent to restore most of the defunct monarchies.

Nevertheless, I believe that in one segment of American society—specifically, higher education—the opportunity to create a new class of "kings" is very much with us and appears to be very attractive to many people who should know better. Higher education needs more kings about as much as door-to-door salesmen need the emergence of another Boston

Strangler. There are many of us in higher education who enjoy access to wide audiences, high salaries, and titles that suggest omnipotence but who may well find it difficult not to be king in the days ahead.

WHAT HIGHER EDUCATION HAS LOST

To oversimplify the situation, higher education finds itself, in 1974, in the following situations:

1. Higher education has lost much public understanding and support, primarily because of the life style exhibited on college campuses, the overt acts of students and faculty members, and, most recently, the inability of graduates to obtain employment.
2. Higher education institutions are viewed as being incompetent in the area of finance, unable to manage their affairs efficiently, and unwilling to be held accountable.
3. Colleges and universities are caught, in the case of public institutions, between executive and legislative competition for control of state enterprises so that higher education is being publicly identified as a priority area for centralized management for greater efficiency.
4. Colleges and universities are seen as being unaccepting of change and as unwilling to avoid unnecessary duplication and to cooperate.

None of these statements may be completely accurate about every college or university or applicable in every state, but they nevertheless reflect attitudes that exist in too many minds and are too often based on actual situations to be discounted or ignored.

Where does the opportunity to create kings exist? Let me, like Elizabeth Barrett Browning, "count the ways."

During the past several years, states have passed laws that create central agencies to govern or "coordinate" higher education. In most states, the statutes refer primarily to public institutions and only peripherally to private institutions. Governors and legislators have expected—and have received—recommendations regarding higher education from these central agencies that have run the gamut from how to define a resident student to complex master plans. What they have not received, in too many cases, are recommendations that are based on hard realities or that are intended to improve the return on the very considerable investment they are making in higher education. Central agencies and their staffs have found themselves torn between the conviction that they should be institutional proponents and the realization that their statutory obligations require objectivity and a close relationship to governors and legislative bodies. In how many instances do states have plans to adjust to stabilized or declining enrollment that minimize disruption and unreasonable "straight line" cuts in support? How many states have established priorities that cut across constituent unit lines, that is, whereby the needs of *all* the facilities in a state system are placed in rank order rather than on a campus or single-system basis? How many states have information systems that provide appropriate bases, at all levels, for decision making or for cost analyses that legislators and budget officers are prepared to accept?

If governors and legislators conclude that they are not obtaining the information they feel they need about higher education and that neither the institutions nor the central agencies they have created are able or willing to provide it, they may then arrive at one other conclusion: Let's do it ourselves, which is one source of unwanted kings for higher education. Another source would be when a central agency decides it can grab the brass ring by promising the governor and legislature that it can provide the needed information, asking only that the statutes authorizing its existence be beefed up and more clout be assigned. Still another source is the university president who suggests that the clock can be turned back, that all of the extraneous coordinating bodies can be eliminated, and that the university, with his nibs as its titular head, be authorized to operate the system.

Were governors and legislators to become kings, higher education would lose its unique function, format, and fragility, and would be left to be judged by the same criteria as all other public enterprises and subject to the discipline of an alien king. The result of control of higher education by a central agency would be decisions made for all operation levels by people whose involvement is peripheral, as with an "absentee landlord" king. A university president as king is wishful thinking. The clock is not apt to be turned back, the drive for centralization outside the institution probably will not abate, and those who nominate themselves or their institutions to govern the system will inevitably be seen by others who believe that higher education is essentially out of control as goats wanting to mind the cabbages.

HIGHER EDUCATION AND THE RELUCTANT CANARY

However we in higher education classify our kings, they do not appear to be the solution to our current dilemma. Faced with an insistent demand for accountability, improved performance, and greater concern for the students we were established to serve, however remotely, we must take the advice given the reluctant canary: "Peep or get off the perch!"

If we would not have higher education governed by unwanted kings, then we had best develop some alternatives. Several are viable.

1. To the extent that central agencies are developing recommendations in splendid isolation, they should change their ways and provide for the realistic involvement of campus representatives. The term *realistic* is deliberate here because the first reaction of many people will be that everyone from the campus (and the community that surrounds it) must be involved in every decision that is made. Harlan Cleveland has spoken of this phenomenon with a clarity that few can command:

> The very great benefits of openness and wide participation are flawed, then, by apathy and non-participation, by muscle-binding legalisms, by processes which polarize two adversary sides, by an excess of voting and parliamentary procedure, by the nay-saying power of procedural objections, by the encouragement of mediocrity—and one thing more. It seems clear now that very wide consultation tends to discourage innovation and favor standpattism.
>
> The mythology of the matter has it the other way around. More openness in decision-making is a radical litany; yet the multiplication of those consulted seems usually to sidetrack radical reform. An action proposal, especially if it is new and unfamiliar, will seem threatening or at least postponable to a large majority of previously uninvolved participants in the discussion.[1]

2. Institutions and their governing boards that militate against system-wide planning coordination should also change their ways and expend more time and effort in assessing legislative and public attitudes toward higher education.

Those of us who are engaged in higher education see state expenditures for higher education as an appropriate and necessary investment that will inevitably provide an excellent return. We find it difficult to understand why anyone would quarrel with that point of view. We may not have counted lately the numbers of people who do not see higher education as an unmixed blessing, who do not sympathize with our stated objectives, who do not appreciate our entreaties or our spokesmen, or who have listened too long to that harping message that you do not have to go to college to be a success. Institutional representatives appearing before state

---

1. "How Does the Planner Get Everybody in on the Act and Still Get Some Action?" (Address to the State Higher Education Executive Officers Association Annual Meeting, Kona, Hawaii, 1 August 1974), p. 10.

legislatures obviously enjoy varying degrees of success in what they are seeking to achieve, but some would do better if they denied themselves the luxury of lecturing the committee members, of being appalled at the general lack of insight of legislators, and of taking instant affront when tenure, salary, or teaching load is questioned. For public institutions, it is well to remember that legislators hold the purse strings and that they are asking —with greater specificity each year—the hard questions about these institutions' operations.

3. Additional effort could well be expended to find more productive ways to develop cooperation, as opposed to competition, among institutions. In a time of stabilized or declining enrollments, when public and private colleges are beset by financial problems and when the air rings incessantly with unrelated shouts for accountability, efficiency, new programs, compliance, more restrictive contracts, protection from out-of-state encroachments, unfair competition, et cetera, closer relationships among higher education institutions seem in order.

One cooperative activity in Connecticut that has provided excellent returns is the operation of six planning regions within the state; the presidents of all colleges and universities in each region meet monthly. The regions and meetings were initiated by the Connecticut Commission for Higher Education to accomplish two objectives: (*a*) receive a planning input that reflects needs of specific areas within the state (for example, no need may exist for more inhalation therapists in the state, but a critical need may exist in one of the six areas for such therapists), and (*b*) provide a forum and an opportunity for cooperation. Both of these objectives are being met, and the cooperative ventures that have been undertaken have not only been productive but also have elicited very favorable public response. Since the regions were established, their value has been displayed sufficiently to bring about new legislation authorizing the Commission for Higher Education to enter into contracts with independent colleges and universities to provide services, programs, and facilities to public higher education institutions where benefit could be obtained from such an arrangement. The vehicle to reimburse the independent colleges for the added cost they incur by cooperating with the public colleges is provided by state law.

Coordination of planning is neither simple nor easy. It becomes most difficult when the coordination is between public and private institutions. Very real problems exist with respect to tuition differentials, historical (and hysterical) antagonism, and "turf" ownership. Regional planning provides a useful means of obtaining objective evaluation of situations and of real or imagined problems.

Other sweeping recommendations could be made, but these three should illustrate that higher education's problems need an awareness and a willingness of members of the academic community to work together rather than under the ministrations of some self-selected or legislatively anointed "king."

THE PERILS OF BEING KING

Being a king is a hazardous undertaking and it might well be asked why the position is sought. A colleague of mine, Dr. Kent Fielding, upon delving into Sir James Frazer's *The Golden Bough,* has written a treatise concerning a practice used in ancient civilization that provides for me some reason why men agree to be kings or chancellors. After noting that both individuals and societies have a need for fulfillment as well as a means for expiating blame for failure, he made the following statement:

> To achieve this result for society, ancient men constructed the concept of sacrifice as an atonement for failure. Their concept in its crudest state took the form of a Corn King, appointed at seed time as a symbol of hope and sacrificed at harvest to free the public mind of blame. It seemed a better device than revolution which is a sacrifice of society itself. It conferred a kind of immortality on the society and made public an embodiment of the immortality wish of all men to be achieved by the seasonal sacrifice of one. In a symbolic sense the society lived by consuming its members and verified the symbolism with real blood sacrifice.
>
> Perhaps it is the subconscious wisdom of society's long agrarian tutelage that still cycles our democratic life into beginnings and endings of continuity. All of our public offices are constructed for aspiration and designed for sacrifice. Corn kings are chosen to embody our hope at its springtime and a season is appointed for measuring the harvest. The king may hold his scepter a season or two if the harvests are good, but to be such a king is to know that you must die. In the sacrifice as much as in the reward, there is a sense of social satisfaction that comes with the assurance that every ending brings the promise of a new beginning.[2]

Something in Fielding's statement brings chief administrators in higher education quickly to mind, as does another quotation that explains *why* a corn king allows himself to be selected:

Within that short span the living is intense with expectation and involve-

2. "The Democratic Corn King."

ment; death can be postponed for a time by energetic will and when . . . [death] comes at last it carries no finality.[3]

My plea is that the expenditure of "energetic will" be made not just to prolong the administrative lives of higher educators (and certainly not to clinch our hold on a kingdom), but rather to develop and sustain coordinated efforts that will provide maximum opportunity in higher education for the citizens of all of our states.

3. Ibid.

Alternative Functions and Structures in Credentialing

HAROLD L. HODGKINSON

AS ONE consequence of the recent decline in public interest in campus student activity, an increasing concern has arisen in many circles with respect to the legitimacy of the criteria used by higher and other postsecondary institutions in selecting the "meritorious," who then move into positions of leadership. This interest in demystifying the processes of credentialing is based on a number of factors:

1. As James O'Toole, Studs Terkel, and others have pointed out, numerous Americans are dissatisfied with their working life, feeling that it fails to provide them a sense of personal fulfillment.[1] Yet, the possibilities for changing jobs or occupations appear to be severely limited because employers tend to set formal education prerequisites before they will assess the candidate's actual strengths. Thus, many workers are blocked from opportunities to demonstrate their attainments.

2. Several recent court decisions suggest that, at least in certain areas, the conventional credentials do not relate directly to job performance and are, therefore, discriminatory. Steps must be taken to assure the courts that credentialing and certification systems perform with equity *and* functional efficiency.

3. Many American adults have educationally related needs that are not being met. For example, some persons want to pursue certain studies simply for the learning involved and have no interest in degrees or other credentials. Others are ready to be credentialed, and neither need nor desire further formal education. Still others wish help in clarifying personal and vocational goals, through the development of growth contracts and other structures.

---

1. O'Toole, *Work in America* (Cambridge, Mass.: MIT Press, 1973); Terkel, *Working* (New York: Pantheon, 1974).

4. Educational systems as now structured rely heavily on units of student-teacher exposure based on *time*—the credit hour and the Carnegie Unit. Even attempts to translate life and work experiences into collegiate terms (as in the project of the Commission on the Assessment of Experiential Learning) use credit hours, with little attention to what a credit hour measures or what other "credit" structures might be useful. Enough is known about retention of learning so that it is obvious that the knowledge for which the freshman gets credit hours has partially vanished by graduation time. The credit hour certifies only that certain exposures have taken place; it does not certify that at a given point (say, graduation) the student either knows certain things or can do certain things. The credit hour remains an indivisible particle or building block presumed to be integral to most educational activity, from awarding degrees to calculating faculty load and cost-effectiveness measures. Alternative forms of functional credit and credit calculation need to be developed.

5. According to David McClelland, the relationship between grades (our quality control indicator) and performance in adult life is rather limited.[2] It may have been a societal error to have assigned to higher education its dominance in selecting those to be favored by the meritocracy, when varied criteria applied by a variety of organizations might have fostered a more functional American pluralism and improved the quality of life. As colleges and universities move or are moved to more egalitarian practices in admissibility (most institutions are in actuality open door), access to the credentialing process must not be limited only to those who have degrees and diplomas from colleges and universities. Generally, all should be entitled to attempt credentialing, degree or not.

6. The B.A. degree is the most overused level for "upgrading" a vocation or profession. Frequently the degree has no functional relationship to the demands of the job. Often, too, those who establish B.A. programs in colleges and universities are confused about what occupational linkages, if any, the degree should provide.[3]

Higher and other postsecondary education need to make some response to the issues raised thus far. Responses should take into account both the concerns for equity and for ensuring competent performance by those credentialed.

2. McClelland, "Testing for Competence Rather than 'Intelligence,' " *American Psychologist,* January 1973.

3. Lewis Mayhew, *Higher Education for Occupations* (Atlanta, Ga.: Southern Regional Education Board, 1974).

SEPARATING DEGREES AND CREDENTIALS

To start, a strict separation between credentials (occupationally predictive) and degrees (general statements of intellectual interests but not intended to predict occupational success) needs to be made. The B.A. is clearly a degree and should not be used as a credential unless its job-predictive capacity can be demonstrated in special programs, for example, in competency-based teacher education programs. (Even here, degrees must be supplemented with teaching certificates.)

If the functional differences between degrees and credentials are drawn and adhered to, credentialing can become even more concerned with norm-referenced evaluations, and individuals will be asked to demonstrate that they can attain certain norms of performance which characterize successful workers in that field. At the same time, degree programs will become more concerned with criterion-referenced evaluation, providing students with essentially diagnostic information on what they are doing wrong so that performance can be improved. (For this reason, the University of Chicago many years ago split up the functions of teaching and evaluating.) Indeed, higher education institutions could provide many diagnostic and counseling functions to a variety of clienteles, whether or not they were enrolled for a degree. For example, Ottawa University will be offering such services in Kansas City, open to anyone who wishes help in writing a learning or growth contract or in finding out more about their abilities and interests. The services will be available on a cost-plus basis, with no assumption that any client will enroll at Ottawa.

Clarification and specification of credentialing and counseling functions, if implemented, might then allow people to think about occupational level and cultural activities and interests as being at least separable. A tendency now is to think that a policeman/woman who is interested in and reads philosophy or attends or performs in ballet is some sort of freak and that their occupational class makes them "ineligible" for those cultural pursuits that stereotypic thinking consider can be understood only by those with higher education. This cultural stereotype has been reinforced in the past by our social class system, which perpetuated the relationship of the highly educated with wealth and prestige as well. The system still works, and people who have a college degree still make more money than those who do not. However, the amount of benefit appears to be declining to the point where it may soon be said that a better predictor of lifetime earnings than years of education will be whether or not the person is a member of a unionized work group. This development would have important implications for blue-collar culture.

As many blue-collar workers begin to have higher incomes than most white-collar workers, the range of demands for personal and cultural recognition and esteem may become greater than the occupational system can confer. Therefore, the entire range of cultural and intellectual pursuit ought to be at least potentially available to citizens without regard for their occupational level. As James O'Toole has pointed out, there are three times as many laborers with IQ's over 130 as there are college professors with IQ's over 130, due to the relative size of the two working forces.[4] These persons, working below their mental capacity, are often responsible for vandalism and poor performance out of sheer frustration with their work and lack of alternative avenues to accomplishment and esteem. Even if they could not become candidates for degrees or credentials, increasing their access to a variety of intellectual and cultural pursuits might significantly improve their self-esteem. Of course, no such alternative can be a panacea, but given the difficulty of changing the world of work, what is proposed here may be more realistic than some of Mr. O'Toole's suggestions for changing the nature of work activities.

A New Structure for Credentialing and Counseling?

An important question is whether or not the alternative functions can be performed adequately within existing structures. My opinion is that they cannot, and that a new structure is needed which can bridge the gap between degree-granting and credentialing, normed and diagnostic assessment procedures, counseling and testing, the demands of employers and the needs of employees, making a living and making a life.[5]

The new credentialing and counseling structure, as I envision it, can be called a "Regional Examining Institute." Ideally, three to five of these institutes should be started with federal grants. Because state-level political forces might easily intrude into such an institute, it is preferable that they be organized by regions. Agencies like WICHE and SREB could oversee the start-up phase. The Regional Examining Institute (REI) would not offer courses as such but would: provide access to credentialing mechanisms for employers who felt this need; offer a sophisticated counseling

4. "Education, Work, and the Quality of Life," in *Lifelong Learners—A New Clientele for Higher Education,* ed. Dyckman W. Vermilye (San Francisco: Jossey-Bass, 1974), p. 16.
5. See Harold L. Hodgkinson, *How Much Change for a Dollar? A Look at Title III* (Washington: ERIC Clearinghouse on Higher Education, 1974).

and diagnosing center to be available to anyone who wished to use it; maintain a *student attainment bank* (a credit bank in which credits have been translated into actual measures of performance); carry on an advocacy system for clients whose performance indicates that they should be given jobs by employers or degrees by institutions of higher education; function as the degree-granting mechanism for those whose attainment level is demonstrably high but to whom there is no college or university able to grant a degree. A *new* institution is needed because the functions described are interdependent and overlapping, and almost impossible to coordinate through existing organizations (see figure 1).

The development of proficiency examinations for occupational and some professional credentialing clearly should involve not only assessment of relevant academic work but also the kind of skills known to employers who are representative of a given field and to bridging persons, who might be described as "distinguished practitioners"—people probably without degrees but with a sufficient skill in the practice of the vocation or profession to merit the term "master." The practitioners should be accorded equal rights with those who have *studied* the vocation. For example, in the field of dentistry, professors who teach theory and no longer work on patients are often referred to as "dry-finger dentists." For examinations in dentistry, both the expert practitioner and the professor should be included, as well as some voices representing other interested parties such as patients, administrators of dental services, and so on. Similarly, the professor of social work and the expert community organizer should meet on equal terms, with representation as well from various communities to be served—particularly employers and clients. Such credentialing assessment procedures should be as direct as possible, measuring proficiencies, not aptitudes. A variety of testing strategies should be used: videotape of the candidate's performance in a simulated situation, in-basket exercises, gaming and simulations, the use of jury panel raters where necessary, and so on.

There are three components to every evaluation problem: (1) *criteria* (What factors do we wish to measure?), (2) *standards* (How well must people perform on these criteria in order to "pass"?), and (3) *technique* (How can we measure the attainment of these criteria?). Given the three, the most difficult is usually standards: Should the level be set at that of the lowest performing person who holds that job, the mean or median performance level, or the level of the very best practitioners? When candidates are abundant, the employer will be tempted to set the level as high

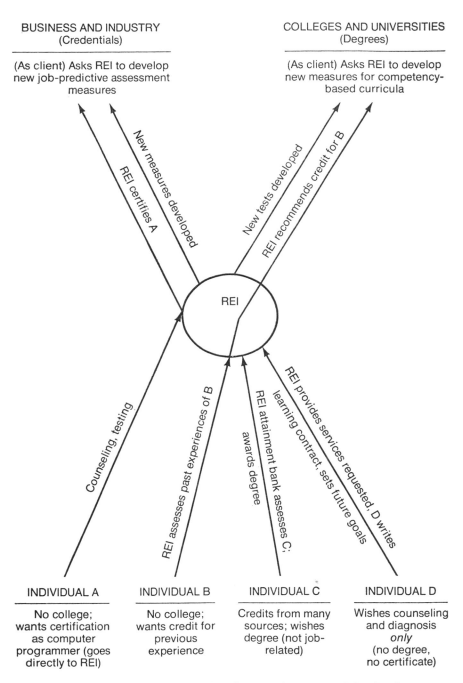

BUSINESS AND INDUSTRY
(Credentials)

(As client) Asks REI to develop new job-predictive assessment measures

COLLEGES AND UNIVERSITIES
(Degrees)

(As client) Asks REI to develop new measures for competency-based curricula

New measures developed

REI certifies A

New tests developed

REI recommends credit for B

REI

Counseling, testing

REI assesses past experiences of B

REI attainment bank assesses C; awards degree

REI provides services requested; D writes learning contract; sets future goals

INDIVIDUAL A

No college; wants certification as computer programmer (goes directly to REI)

INDIVIDUAL B

No college; wants credit for previous experience

INDIVIDUAL C

Credits from many sources; wishes degree (not job-related)

INDIVIDUAL D

Wishes counseling and diagnosis *only* (no degree, no certificate)

Fig. 1. Suggested kinds of services by a Regional Examining Institute

258

as possible, making the employee a pawn in the hands of a fluctuating supply-demand market. The REI should serve as a third force, maintaining equity for the candidate and reasonable efficiency for the employer while ensuring that criteria and standards are related to the proficiencies being measured.

The counseling functions of the REI are of crucial importance, for the adult American has little access to sophisticated and humane diagnostic services dealing with vocational, personal, and intellectual aspects of his life. Counseling activities might include development of personal and learning growth contracts, academic equivalency testing based on attainment levels rather than credit hour equivalents, development and review of portfolios, preparation for credentialing evaluations, and various client advocacy roles. The REI could also be responsible for the routine administration of the various credentialing procedures developed internally and for other procedures that were mutually agreed upon by the REI and representatives of the employee group. If costs could be kept low enough, a series of "How'm I doing?" evaluations could be established, providing diagnostic information on virtually any activity the client wished to be checked out on. The purpose here would be primarily to increase self-confidence by keeping a running record of an area in which the client was trying to improve.

In another important function, REI would establish a point of linkage between the higher and postsecondary "communities." Both groups could use the services of the REI, perhaps gaining some important contacts and shared techniques, ultimately working toward uniform standards for similar proficiencies. Such a "culture fair" liaison seems urgently needed.

Here, then, are a few alternative functions and one alternative structure dealing with assessing, validating, diagnosing, and improving individual attainments. They are not pat solutions to complex issues but, rather, a response to those who argue that current practice cannot be changed. These changes will involve higher and other forms of postsecondary education in new tasks as well as with new segments of the American population, and it may mean working with organizations that have strange sounding names, whose legitimacy has not been proved by the established legitimizers, even though their *competency* can be amply demonstrated. From these new encounters may come a clarification of mission and processes for institutions of higher and other postsecondary education, a result that may well be worth the pain. It also seems likely that higher education institutions will be able to serve their conventional constituencies more effectively if this demystification takes place.

Toward an Examining University: New York Regents External Degree

DONALD J. NOLAN

FOR NEARLY fifteen years, the Regents of the University of the State of New York (USNY) have played an active, special role in the assessment of experience, or the credentialing of learning that takes place on the job, in the public library, through travel—anywhere but in a college classroom. Here, I shall concentrate on the Regents' efforts in the evaluation of nontraditional learning, especially their credit-by-examination and external degree programs which, I believe, form the basis for their "examining university." First, however, the special meaning that the Regents apply to the term "university" suggests the need to describe the unique organization that is the University of the State of New York.

Created by the state legislature in 1784 as the Regents of the University of the State of New York, the "institution" was intended, in the short run, to provide trustees for King's College (later, Columbia University) and, in the long run, to establish a unified educational system for the people of New York, under the control of state government. Today, it is the oldest continuous educational agency in the nation. A "university" similar to the better known University of France (although Napoleon's creation occurred more than two decades later), the University of the State of New York encompasses and has responsibility for all things educational in the state, including the private and public higher institutions—New York has more than two hundred—as well as the elementary and secondary schools, museums, libraries, historical societies, and other agencies whose primary business is education.

Presiding over the university are fifteen lay men and women elected by the legislature for seven-year terms. The Regents appoint a commissioner who administers the State Education Department and who serves as president of USNY. The Regents and their commissioner determine the state's educational policies and establish standards for maintaining quality schools; charter colleges and universities; approve and supervise academic programs leading to college degrees; and license and discipline for most professions except law. The Regents are authorized to grant degrees but in the past have limited their activities to the conferral of honorary doctorates and the degrees earned by students at private colleges possessing temporary charters.

But to most people in New York the Regents are best known for the high school achievement tests that bear their name and for the University of the State of New York, which is often mistaken to mean SUNY (the State University of New York) or NYU (New York University), both of which are part of USNY. USNY is routinely referred to as the State Education Department, a bureaucracy of some dimension which serves as the executive and administrative arm of the Regents. But public awareness of education, brought about by higher taxes, busing to achieve racial balance, failing colleges, and other matters of societal concern, has led to a renewed interest in the Regents and their agency. Although some might prefer the anonymity or mistaken identity of the past, there are others, wishful thinkers perhaps, who see in all of this a potential for better understanding among an educated citizenry in the future.

Call it what you will, the Board of Regents, the University of the State of New York, or the State Education Department, this institution is one of a kind in education. Henceforth I shall use these various labels interchangeably, in the interest of maintaining the proper level of ambiguity for a scholarly presentation.

THE REGENTS EXTERNAL DEGREE PROGRAM

The Regents quietly burst upon the higher education scene with their external degree program in 1970 when Commissioner of Education Ewald B. Nyquist proposed that they award undergraduate degrees to anyone who could qualify, with or without the benefit of classroom attendance. What seemed to many to be a radical idea was to Mr. Nyquist and the Regents merely an extension of the belief that what a person knows is more important than how or where he acquired the knowledge, a principle embodied in New York's College Proficiency Examination Program, introduced by the Regents nearly a decade earlier. In the four years since Mr. Nyquist's announcement, the State Education Department has become the nation's first and only "examining university," offering academic recognition in the form of credit and degrees to students it has not taught.

Through their external degree and College Proficiency Examination (CPE) programs and other services which I shall describe, the Regents encourage, facilitate, and assess college-level learning among a large number of adults who, for whatever reason, do not attend conventional colleges or universities. Under "conventional" I include all higher educational institutions that teach, evaluate, and award degrees to their students, even though learning may take place on or off campus, through correspondence or extension courses, by television or tutors. New colleges like Empire State College, Minnesota Metropolitan State College, and the many universities without walls have at least one thing in common: they all provide instruction. The Regents do not. Instead they offer external degrees, equivalency examinations, a credit bank with transcript and evaluation services and, most recently, a systematic approach to the evaluation of courses offered by business, industry, government, and other sponsors whose primary purpose is not education. These Regents services and programs are available on a voluntary basis, in addition to the regulatory functions in accreditation in the state's conventional colleges and universities, noted above. These comprehensive higher education services are accessible to students and institutions alike.

Currently the Regents offer six external degrees, listed here in the order in which they were developed: associate in arts, bachelor of science in business administration, associate in applied science in nursing, associate in science, bachelor of arts, and bachelor of science. The requirements for each degree are established by distinguished faculty members drawn from USNY's private and public colleges, usually working in committees of ten or fifteen members, with assistance from higher education and testing specialists of the State Education Department. Although each degree program is different, there are some common elements: there are no admission requirements; students need not reside in New York State; there is no age limit; the method of preparation is not prescribed; all general education and most professional requirements may be satisfied by passing courses at accredited colleges; no classroom attendance is required.

The degrees are external in the tradition of the University of London which during the nineteenth century operated as a nonteaching university with a faculty but no students on campus. Degrees were earned by external students who passed examinations prepared at the London campus. The London external system continues today, alongside a conventional university for residential, or internal, students who attend formal classes. The Regents external degrees similarly are earned by external students, but there is no corresponding conventional university with internal students unless one considers the amorphous USNY for this role.

In both the London and New York programs, the faculty publishes its degree requirements and the ways in which these may be met. The rest, theoretically at least, is up to the student.

Much is being done, however, to assist the independent learner for whom the Regents external degree was designed. The faculty committees have prepared detailed examination descriptions, study guides, and bibliographies which have been made available without charge to librarians and conventional colleges, as well as to enrolled students. Hundreds of volunteers—primarily librarians, nurse educators, guidance counselors, and college faculty—advise external students across New York State. Some degree candidates are asking for opportunities to meet with their fellow students to share experiences and compare notes. In short, it appears that the conditions and services found on college campuses are gradually being added and that the "college" is being reinvented. No doubt an entrepreneur or two will emerge to fill the instructional void. Thus far this has not happened, probably because of the tremendous number of collegiate and noncollegiate courses of study already in place in the state and the nation and because of the nature of the examinations which must be passed.

As noted earlier, students participating in New York's examining university are independent of it as far as instruction is concerned. They are free to choose their own method of acquiring knowledge and, to a lesser extent, they are free to meet degree requirements or earn credit in the manner best suited to their needs. For instruction, they may choose any or all of the many ways available, including formal classroom studies. For validation of their academic achievements, either they or their program of studies must be evaluated.

CREDIT THROUGH TRANSCRIPT AND COURSE EVALUATIONS

Let us start with the evaluation of programs of studies. At present the system most heavily relied on is also the one most widely accepted in academic circles: the regional accrediting bodies. Courses reported on official transcripts from regionally accredited colleges and universities may be used to meet general education requirements for all external degrees. Faculty committees, working with the USNY registrar, determine the acceptability of courses to meet the professional requirements in business administration and in nursing and to satisfy major or concentration patterns in the arts and sciences. Only courses in which a passing grade was earned may be applied toward general requirements, and only those that the candidate desires to apply toward the degree are evaluated. For general education purposes, there is no time limit beyond which a course completion may not be considered for credit. However, for a course to be considered for waiver in the nursing and business components of the A.A.S. and B.S.B.A. degrees respectively, the academic work must have been completed within ten years of the date of enrollment in the Regents External Degree Program, it must cover all the topics included on the examination developed to measure achievement in that subject, and it must carry a grade of *C* or better.

In addition to the accrediting bodies, the American Council on Education's Office on Educational Credit (formerly, Commission on the Accreditation of Service Experience, or CASE) provides reliable guidance for assessing programs of studies. For nearly thirty years CASE and now OEC have been evaluating military service school courses and have made college-level credit recommendations where appropriate. By faculty vote, the Regents External Degree Program follows the credit recommendations established by CASE and OEC when evaluating military courses for credit. The policies governing the use of college courses—time limits, grades, and the like—also apply to military-sponsored educational programs.

Of the first 1,225 who received the associate in arts degree from the Regents, over 80 percent earned credit by submitting college transcripts for evaluation, and of the college-going group, over 20 percent had attended three or more colleges. Inasmuch as 772 of the associate in arts graduates were active-duty members of the armed services, their extensive use of military service schools is not surprising: 277 earned credit for 500 courses evaluated by CASE.

But colleges and the armed services are not the only sources of quality educational programs. For many years excellent instructional programs have been offered by business, government, industry, and labor unions to employees and apprentices, and often these courses have been assigned credit by neighboring colleges. Indeed, cooperative relationships have frequently resulted, with the college providing general education courses while business or industry offered instruction in technical or special areas. This relationship obtains especially in the case of labor unions providing apprenticeship programs. During 1973–74, the State Education Department conducted a pilot study in which it evaluated nearly one hundred courses sponsored by five New York-based organizations: General Electric Company, New York Telephone Company, New York City chapter of the American Institute of Banking, Eastman Kodak Company, and State Police Academy. Each course was assessed by faculty consultants drawn primarily from USNY institutions, and credit recommendations were made where appropriate. A publication containing the course descriptions, the procedures by which they were evaluated, the credit recommendations, and the names of the faculty consultants who made them, is made available to individuals, agencies, businesses, and colleges for their consideration.[1]

For the next two years the Regents and the American Council on Education will jointly conduct a more extensive evaluation of instructional programs sponsored by noncollegiate institutions.[2] The results of the USNY-ACE project will be made known to the Regents external degree faculty as well as to the academic senates of conventional colleges. It is hoped that the credit recommendations for instruction sponsored by civilian noncollegiate institutions will receive as wide use as those made for their military precursors.

These approaches to evaluating formal programs of collegiate-level instruction in noncollegiate settings will probably never cover all modes of learning, even within the categories already being examined. For example, only those industry and government-sponsored programs that have large numbers of students will make their way into the USNY-ACE project. Private business schools, which are excluded because their primary purpose is education, have another alternative in New York. They may ask the Regents to accredit programs that the school believes are of collegiate level and, as such, should lead to a degree. Thus, more than twenty private business schools have been empowered by the Regents to offer an associate degree in occupational studies, and many more are exploring the possibility.

Under the Regents program, correspondence courses sponsored by the extension divisions of major universities may be used for credit provided they meet the criteria applied to all other course work taken at accredited institutions. Not covered as transfer credit, however, are correspondence courses sponsored by noncollegiate agencies and schools such as the mem-

1. *A Guide to Educational Programs in Noncollegiate Organizations* (Albany, N.Y.: State Education Department, Office of Noncollegiate Sponsored Instruction, December 1974).

2. The project is financially supported by the Fund for the Improvement of Postsecondary Education and the Carnegie Corporation of New York. Not incidentally, grants from the Carnegie Corporation, the Ford Foundation, and the Kellogg Foundation gave the Regents External Degree and College Proficiency Examination Programs their start.

bers of the National Home Study Council. Students who complete these or similar courses which, by Regents criteria, do not enjoy appropriate accreditation must demonstrate their knowledge or competence by examination. It is this area of testing that presents the Regents' examining university with its greatest challenge and opportunity.

CREDIT BY EXAMINATION

The Regents initiated their own credit-by-examination program in 1960 through the College Proficiency Examinations. Currently, the more than thirty examinations in the arts and sciences, education, and nursing each can yield three to twelve credits, depending on the respective faculty committee's recommendation. Except in applied music, for which a live audition is required, the examinations use paper-and-pencil multiple-choice and essay questions to determine proficiency. Minimum passing scores are established by the faculty on the basis of the CPE performance of college students completing comparable college courses. Since the CPE's were first administered in 1963, more than 60,000 credits have been granted by colleges and universities in New York and elsewhere. By far the most useful CPE's have been those in the nursing sciences, which have permitted licensed practical nurses to accelerate their registered nurse programs and R.N.'s to earn their bachelor of science degree in nursing without repeating courses.

The external degree program brought about the need for more examinations in general areas as well as in special fields and for different types of tests.

The faculty committee for the associate in arts degree, responsible for general education policy within USNY, voted to use both the New York College Proficiency Examinations and the general and subject examinations of CLEP—the College-Level Examination Program of the College Entrance Examination Board. Appropriate scores on CPE and CLEP tests may be used to satisfy general education requirements for all Regents external degrees as these have subsequently been determined by the various faculty committees. It was also voted to accept passing scores on USAFI tests, in accordance with the recommendations of the American Council on Education, and also the College Board's Advanced Placement Examinations. Some of these examinations may also be used to meet portions of the professional components in business and nursing, but thus far the most significant use of CPE, CLEP, and USAFI has been made by students in the associate in arts program. The first 1,225 graduates earned nearly 10,000 credits through these standardized tests, over half of them through USAFI. And 163 of the graduates, or 13 percent, earned their degrees completely by examination.

The faculties in business and nursing, despite their confidence in the available standardized tests, felt a keen need for specially designed instruments in their respective fields of study. The test development process followed by these two groups of scholars was elaborate but may be described in brief. Each group began with the premise that they could agree on what was expected from a graduate of a nursing or a business program in terms of knowledge and areas of competence, and that they could develop examinations to determine whether or not an individual qualified for a degree in either of these fields. The faculties in nursing and business also accepted another important given: students must be able to earn the degree entirely by examination, in addition to more conventional alternatives.

The business examinations (numbering sixteen) are now being administered to the general public. Students elect a major in accounting, finance, management, or marketing, and may satisfy the business component requirement for the degree by passing as few as six or as many as nine separate examinations, depending upon the level of entry into the testing process. Patterned on the College Proficiency Examinations approach, each test was developed by a faculty committee of experts in that subject and was normed on college students. The tests combine multiple-choice with essay and problem questions. At present nearly fifteen hundred students are enrolled in the business external degree program, with the first graduates expected in the fall of 1974, about two and one-half years after the opening of the program.

The faculty in nursing decided to prepare seven examinations to measure an integrated curriculum, covering such topics as commonalities and differences in nursing care, health, and occupational strategy. This pattern was chosen instead of traditional subject areas such as fundamentals of nursing, and maternal-child, psychiatric-mental health, and medical-surgical nursing, for which College Proficiency Examinations are available but at the baccalaureate level. The Regents external degree in nursing is at the associate degree level.

A necessary component of a nursing degree at any level is the clinical performance examination. This critical test will be administered entirely in a hospital setting, although admission to it will be limited to candidates who have successfully passed all seven of the paper-and-pencil examinations. During a two-day period candidates will demonstrate their clinical abilities through a number of patient-care situations, each of which will require the students to plan, carry out, and evaluate the care required by the patient. The safety of the patient will be paramount at all times, and fully licensed registered nurses will be present throughout all parts of the clinical examination.

Students who take the clinical performance test will enjoy the same legal status as student nurses in instructional programs, inasmuch as the external degree program is registered by the State Board of Nursing. Most of the fifteen hundred persons currently enrolled in the nursing program have, in fact, had considerable experience in the health care field, as licensed practical nurses, registered nurses seeking a degree in addition to their R.N. license, medical corpsmen, or aides. The clinical performance examination in particular and the nursing external degree in general could constitute a considerable step up the career ladder in a field long plagued by educational dead ends.

SPECIAL ASSESSMENT

The final piece in the assessment system of the Regents examining university is one that many students are currently seeking. What do you do with a student who has acquired knowledge in subjects for which no standardized tests exist or for which the available tests are inappropriate? The faculty decided on a "special assessment" process, a flexible approach to measurement that would include oral, performance, or written examination, and the evaluation of a candidate's portfolio—artistic, literary, or musical. In every case, however, credit is *not* assigned simply for experience. The emphasis in special assessment would be on the knowledge acquired, by whatever means.

"Credit for life experience," the popular name for special assessment, has thus far had limited use in the Regents program, primarily for two reasons. First, its use is restricted to general education areas. To meet the professional component requirements of the business and the nursing degrees, students must pass the specific tests developed by the faculty for that purpose or must present appropriate college courses. Many of the early requests for special assessment have come from businessmen and nurses with considerable practical experience. The second reason for the limited use is economic. Special assessment is expensive. A student may pay $250 for the examination that usually requires two separate days scheduled several weeks apart, and it is conducted by two to three faculty members and testing specialists. The CLEP general examinations, in contrast, cost

$30 (for two or more) and may result in the student's earning twenty-seven credits for knowledge demonstrated.

Interest in special assessment is expected to increase with the establishment of the general baccalaureate degrees and the associate in science. In most of the B.A. and B.S. degree programs (except nursing, business, and a few others), students may choose a liberal studies option or a typical concentration, and special assessment may be used in any field to earn credit toward the degrees. Students in the new associate in science may earn up to thirty credits in free electives, and many will elect to do so through special assessment.

The bachelor's degree faculty extended the list of available standardized tests when it voted to award credit for Graduate Record Examinations (GRE) and Undergraduate Program (UP) Field Tests of the Educational Testing Service. However, most people whose knowledge of a subject has been acquired outside college will doubtless opt for a specially prepared, more individualized examination than a GRE. On the other hand, students who had nearly completed a major sequence in college may find the GRE or UP approach more suited to their needs. The phrase "their needs" leads to the critical question in the examining university scheme, What are the needs of the students?

THE STUDENTS AND THEIR NEEDS

In our experience the "students," young and old alike, want to get ahead. For some, this means college credit and degrees; for others, it means a teaching certificate or a license as a registered nurse or as a certified public accountant. For most persons, personal satisfaction ranks as high as a better job, career advancement, or acceleration in a formal program of studies on a campus.

Who are these students?

Briefly, students enrolled in one of the external degree programs range in age from nineteen to seventy-four; they come from all fifty states and several foreign countries; 60 percent are males; over 85 percent are employed full time as members of the armed services, practical and registered nurses, teachers, homemakers, peace officers, business men and women, and clerical workers; only 2 percent consider themselves full-time students.

From March 1972 through July 1974 nearly 6,000 individuals had enrolled in the first three programs: associate in arts, 3,000, of whom 1,225 have graduated; bachelor of science in business administration, 1,500; and associate in applied science in nursing, 1,500. The remaining degree programs were opened for enrollment in midsummer of 1974.

Thousands of additional students have used the examinations made available by USNY without working for an external degree. Since 1963 approximately 37,000 College Proficiency Examinations have been given in the arts and sciences (3,000), education (3,000), health education (4,000), nursing (23,000), and foreign languages (4,000). Many, if not most, students tested in education, health education, and foreign languages were attempting to obtain a certificate to teach in New York State. The majority of the nursing tests served to advance hospital school graduates toward the college degrees. Overall, New York colleges and universities have granted more than 60,000 credits for passing grades on these tests.

Since May 1973, when the Regents external degree examinations were first offered, nearly 5,000 tests have been taken (3,000 in nursing, 1,000 each in business and foreign languages), mostly to meet requirements for external degrees in nursing and business. In the field of accounting alone more than 800 tests, CPE's, and Regents external degree examinations have been administered.

ASSESSING ACCEPTANCE OF THE PROGRAM

While we do not have statistics on the extent to which colleges are recognizing the external degree tests, we do have some idea of how they accept the external degree itself: of the first 400 associate degree graduates surveyed, over half are now attending 88 colleges in 32 states, as juniors. The federal government, which employs 812 of the first 1,225 graduates, recognizes the degree for career advancement. Students report a favorable attitude among employers toward the business degree, which will be awarded soon.

Prospects are just as bright in the professions. Accounting majors will be admitted to the CPA examination under the same conditions as those for graduates of conventional programs. Similarly, nurse graduates of USNY may sit for the state licensing examination, inasmuch as the external degree program has provisional accreditation from the Regents, the State Board for Nursing, and from the Middle States Association of Colleges and Secondary Schools. Middle States approval was sought even though the Regents are themselves a recognized accrediting body, in order that the program could benefit from an outside review and avoid conflict-of-interest charges, apparent or real. The National League for Nursing will also be asked to approve the nursing degree for similar reasons. For the

Regents' examining university, voluntary accreditation by nationally recognized regional bodies is all the more important because many of its students reside outside New York State.

Accreditation or approval, whether national or regional, must also be obtained from practitioners of the profession in which competence is being certified as well as from the general-purpose agencies and the academic community as a whole. Many faculty members participating in USNY have been describing their involvement in scholarly publications which should be helpful in gaining acceptance within the profession. But it will be up to the external degree graduates themselves to earn appropriate recognition from their more conventionally prepared peers by performing successfully in businesses or health care agencies. While many will continue in positions they held before receiving their degrees, others will assume new positions of responsibility as a result of their additional certification. Without the corroborative evidence of successful on-the-job performance, however, articles in professional journals will have little effect.

If we are to reach a point where job performance can (and probably should) be distinguished from a degree, of utmost importance will be the development of instruments with which to measure that performance. As matters now stand, the Regents are offering examinations that may be used as part of or separate from degree programs, depending upon the needs of the student, the higher education community, or the employer. These academic, professional, technical, and vocational evaluation services would be beyond the capability of most conventional colleges to provide. And in most cases certainly, beyond their interests as well.

USNY also serves as a repository for student records, through the Regents Credit Bank. Designed for persons *not* pursuing a Regents degree, the credit bank assesses proficiency examination scores (CPEP, CLEP, USAFI, GRE, UP, etc.), transcripts from military schools and selected civilian agencies, as well as from accredited colleges, in accordance with the policies established by the external degree faculty. A single, composite transcript is maintained for each enrollee and forwarded wherever he may designate. The Regents believe that employers and higher educational institutions alike will readily recognize a comprehensive and academically consistent transcript from the University of the State of New York for job advancement and academic placement.

With nearly fifteen years of experience behind them, the Regents are moving toward the establishment of a comprehensive examining university, one that will expand upon the already considerable service it now provides to students and institutions. It is obvious, however, that much work lies ahead, especially in testing and counseling. If this university and others like it that will emerge are to meet their potential, there is a need to move toward greater coordination and cooperation among the national and state agencies that prepare examinations. This move is necessary not only to avoid costly duplication of effort, but also to develop and maintain the best possible testing instruments. The diversity of our institutions assures me that such cooperation will not lead to some stifling "national" norm or monolithic system of higher education.

I have chosen to present here a rather general outline of the Regents examining university, without dwelling on its inherent problems or arguing its merits. It has many of both. The concept of an examining university and in particular the Regents' model of it deserves careful consideration by the academic community in the years ahead.

The Fatuity of Credentialing Everyone and Everything

HAROLD ORLANS

IT IS just and right to employ people in accordance with their ability and experience, not the letters after their name or the certificates in their files. Yet the world is not an entirely just place and those credentials—Ph.D., M.D., B.Sc., A.B., and so forth—are indispensable for many jobs and, for many others, can tip the balance toward the lettered applicant. Napoleon observed that an army could be run with medals; men die for a trinket. Americans are not so different when it comes to their own symbols of worth. It generally helps and seldom hurts to have the right letters after your name. If that were not the case, degree credit enrollments would be much reduced (as was attendance at the American Museum of Natural History when public toilets opened nearby).

In our highly mobile, egalitarian society, where birthplace, class, and education are not immediately evident from a person's appearance and speech (as they are, or were, in Britain), academic credentials serve significant economic and social functions. Should they not, then, be more readily dispensed not only by academic institutions but by new examining bodies? If the credential that certifies graduation is indeed satisfactory evidence that the graduate is qualified to do certain kinds of work—to type or to teach, design a house, write a letter or prescription, or at least add and spell correctly—should it not be given, gratis or for a fee, to anyone else who demonstrates that he can do the same thing? And if a license to practice a profession or trade is issued to anyone who passes a state examination, should not anyone be eligible to take that examination, regardless of his formal educational preparation?

Government is supposed to treat all individuals alike and nondiscriminatorily. It should regulate entry to any business, trade, occupation, or profession only to protect the public health and safety. A society which prizes personal freedom and ostensibly prizes competitive enterprise should remove any licensing barriers to safe and competent practice, especially in lucrative professions providing expensive services in short supply. Should that be done by licensing the graduates of foreign medical schools and authorizing doctors licensed in one state and nation to practice in another? Should practical nurses be used to ease the shortage of registered nurses; marriage counselors, that of clinical psychologists; and psychologists, that of psychiatrists, by broadening through law and private regulation the scope of the work they are permitted to do and are reimbursed for by insurance companies and government programs? In principle, yes. In practice, we are ensnared by regulations designed to protect us.

SOCIAL AND TECHNICAL STANDARDS OF LICENSURE

The byzantine politics of the professions, their power over state licensing boards and examinations, and the difficulty of isolating the technical qualifications necessary for competent practice from those which serve to maintain the monopoly and income of established practitioners—any of these things makes modest reform more likely than transformation of the licensing system. We cannot leap out of history by an appeal to reason. Tests do not write themselves; they are prepared by members of the very profession whose performance we wish to define objectively and democratically, so that a qualified spaniel could practice medicine. Laymen are not competent to intrude, and it is difficult for professional men to distinguish standards which serve the public interest from those which serve their own. Hence, we are all subject to "the Tyranny of the Experts."[1]

Technical and social standards of performance cannot be cleanly sep-

1. See Jethro K. Lieberman, *The Tyranny of the Experts: How Professionals Are Closing the Open Society* (New York: Walker & Co., 1970).

arated. For example, knowledge of the language—and not merely a crude but a sensitive knowledge—is important to clinical practice in medicine, psychiatry, psychology, management consulting, or law. Client satisfaction and the quality of service are plainly dependent on the practitioner's perceptiveness, manner, and conduct. Are such matters relevant to initial licensure or subsequent relicensure? In principle, no, when they reflect "purely" social standards with discriminatory consequences—as distinct from those, like legal and ethical standards, which apply equally to all candidates. In practice, however, social and technical standards can be inseparably intertwined, and those which prevail inevitably represent the outlook of the men who set them. If Philippine doctors and black plumbers wrote the licensing examinations for doctors and plumbers, more Philippine and black applicants would presumably pass them.

The social and political dimension of performance requirements is evident in the double standard applied by licensing laws to new applicants, on the one hand, and, on the other, to established practitioners exempted under grandfather clauses. James Shannon, when director of the National Institutes of Health, once charged that many doctors were "licensed to kill" because, woefully out of touch with recent medical developments, they could misdiagnose and mistreat patients, with lethal results.[2] The requirement of continuing education for relicensure constitutes a recognition of the problem. It would be fully dealt with if all licensees were reexamined every five years and had to receive the same score on the same tests as new applicants.[3] If that happened, many older and influential men might lose their licenses, or the passing score might have to be lowered. Since either course would reduce the dominance of established practitioners, neither is likely to occur.

DEGREES: EARNED OR BOUGHT

The issuance of academic credentials for knowledge or ability acquired without the normal term of academic servitude is increasingly fashionable.

2. Address at the meeting of the Markle Scholars, Lake Placid, N.Y., September 1966.

3. A more modest recommendation confined to recertification rather than relicensure was made by the Carnegie Commission on Higher Education: "In view of the rapid rate of progress of medical and dental knowledge and the associated problem of educational obsolescence of practicing physicians and dentists, the Commission recommends the development of national requirements for periodic reexamination and recertification of physicians and dentists. These functions should be carried out by specialty boards and other appropriate [private] bodies" (*Higher Education and the Nation's Health* [New York: McGraw-Hill, 1970], p. 76).

It is stodgy and futile to flout fashion, the more so when it is just to many individuals and rewarding or indispensable to many institutions. Nonetheless, its dangers should be more fully discussed and more directly confronted. Among them are the threat to educational standards, the hazards and limitations of excessive reliance on examinations, and the debasement of the currency of credentials by overprinting.

A rising volume of college credit is being offered to enrollees for "knowledge" or "experience" attested or untested by examination and for "work experience" and "nontraditional" programs taken by registered students. External degree programs and "universities without walls" are expanding; regional "credit banks," educational "passports," "output measures," and the assessment of "experiential learning" are being explored. The approaches lean heavily on the frail reed of "scientific" measurement and share the social sciences' proclivity to cloak, romanticize, or sterilize and, thereby, distort humdrum reality. Colleges and universities are reaching far from their home state with makeshift quarters, correspondence methods, and ad hoc local staff to offer extension courses for credit and degrees to nonresident, part-time, and short-term students. The threat to educational standards is evident. It was ranked first by university respondents in a 1972 survey of obstacles to the introduction of nontraditional programs and new policies for the award of credit.[4]

Some of these activities and the methods used to promote them are embarrassingly like the practices of degree mills, correspondence schools, and proprietary schools, which Middle States Association of Colleges and Secondary Schools' witnesses testified in the Marjorie Webster case were not fit to associate with regionally accredited institutions. The regionals have been reexamining this policy and, if the standards of for-profit and nonprofit institutions seem closer now than in 1966, that can be for two reasons.

There can be no doubt that, overall, the massive thrust of "nontraditional" education has been sanctioned and promoted by leaders of the higher education establishment, by the Carnegie Corporation of New York and the American Council on Education, the National Commission on Accrediting and the regional accrediting commissions, the Carnegie Commission on Higher Education and the Commission on Non-Traditional

4. As reported in *Non-Traditional Programs and Opportunities in American Colleges and Universities 1972* (Berkeley: University of California, Center for Research and Development in Higher Education). Fewer respondents from colleges and still fewer from junior colleges considered the "Institution's concern about its academic standards" an obstacle.

Study, the U.S. Office of Education and state education authorities. Roger W. Heyns argues that "arbitrary bureaucratic requirements not inhibit movement from one learning experience to another. . . . Our means of credentialing, whether . . . by educational institutions, professional . . . associations, or state licensure agencies, must be prepared to provide recognition on an equitable and valid basis for all learning regardless of how and where it takes place. Social justice requires no less. Inequities in credentialing may be the last major area of discrimination in the United States."[5]

The responsible leaders of higher education are well aware of the dangers posed by too rapid, formless, and normless relaxation of the traditional requirements for entrance, credit, degrees, and accreditation, and by too heated competition for students. Stephen K. Bailey spoke out forcefully, two years ago, about the "Serpents in the Basket of Shiny Apples":

> unless very special precautions are taken, credit and degrees for off-campus students by examinations alone can lead to a parade of academic horribles: cram courses organized by fast-buck proprietary schools, a deadly standardization of subject-matter, tutoring to the test. . . .
>
> [Contrariwise, if] programs are allowed to cut away from traditional college-normed examinations, and embark upon highly experimental credit-giving for subjectively evaluated "experience" . . . , academic standards may be severed from any and all recognizable moorings . . . [and] the credit or degrees earned by the external student may have no acceptability for purposes of academic transfer, graduate studies, or employment.[6]

Nonetheless, the need and opportunity to corral more students has led those who are, and are not, concerned about educational quality to move in similar directions. A race is on to stake out property in the new territory, confusion abounds, and the honest citizen must look after himself. It will be some years before the farms are fenced, roads are laid, the mails are reliable, and law and order reigns. Until then, many citizens receiving credit and degrees for knowledge acquired off campus resemble the middle-aged crowd in the *New Yorker* cartoon listening to their benevolent, berobed king proclaim from his balcony: "It is my wish that this be the most educated country in the world, and toward that end I hereby ordain that each and every one of my people be given a diploma."[7]

5. Address to the Southern Association of Colleges and Schools, Houston, Texas, Dec. 9, 1973.

6. Bailey, "Flexible Space/Time Higher Education: Serpents in the Basket of Shiny Apples" (Address at meeting of the American Association for Higher Education, Chicago, March 1972).

7. The cartoon is reproduced in John R. Valley, *Increasing the Options* (Princeton, N.J.: Educational Testing Service, 1972), p. 4.

Honorary degrees are a quaint, harmless, and, when merited, rather endearing way to honor distinction in scholarship and the world of affairs. An honorary degree is *not* paid for (though it may, like an ambassadorship, be given for a benefaction; time should pass to mellow the exchange), and it is meretricious to pass one off as earned. When cited, it should be identified as honorary. The distinctive identification of external degrees should, likewise, be expected of honest institutions and individuals. Depending upon the caliber and reputation of a program and its graduates, such a designation may come to mean less or, as with the external degree of the University of London, more than a degree earned in residence. But it should be honestly labeled.

Similar to an honorary degree is the degree which, I understand, Oxford conferred on faculty members who were so unfortunate as not to have earned one there. In their splendid conceit, the dons would recognize no other degree, not that of the old Cambridge or the new; yet if they were to be a society of equals, they should have equal degrees: hence their magnanimity.

The unearned Oxford degree is amusing but, too often, the earned American degree is not. If a master's degree is required for kindergarten teaching, then a master's will be earned—and paid for; and it happens not infrequently that the very faculty who award the degree lobbied for the requirement. Likewise with the requirements for graduation from barbers school, secretarial school, law school, nursing school, college, and graduate school. The linking of degrees to jobs is unfair, wasteful, and not infrequently involves flagrant self-serving by supposedly disinterested scholars. But it is so entrenched and has enough plausibility and practical convenience that it will not soon be eradicated.

Who can condone—and who can eliminate—the compulsory instruction of young and adult students in subjects which may not interest them, which they may not retain, and which have no practical or intellectual relevance to their work or life? Nonetheless, the longer the time spent in attendance and the more stable the institution, curriculum, faculty, and student body, the better can an informed observer assess not only the graduate's knowledge but also his educational experience. In some institutions, that experience is still meaningful; a significant community remains; significant friendships form; social, political, and intellectual groups are defined; faculty still talk with their students, get to know them, and can assess their character as well as their knowledge. The years at college or professional school, in short, produce more than an earned degree, and that degree signifies more than a certain competence or incompetence in designated subjects. It signifies a formative life experience and, to any prospective employer (or spouse!), a point of departure for learning more about the applicant. Of course, the same earned degree can signify a hundred different things; that is a virtue as well as a weakness. A credential based solely upon an examination tells us nothing about the holder but his performance on one occasion, and that is a pitiful basis for any important decision.

The Battle between Tests and People

So much is being made of examinations as a means of rectifying the failings of education-based occupational and social placement, one would think they had no failings of their own—that the number generated by a computer-scored test was as reliable and valid a measure of competence as the distance between two lines on a platinum bar is a measure of length. Those who look to examinations to promote equality of opportunity should examine the debates on the discriminatory nature of IQ, college admission, law school, and educational assessment tests.[8] There are no culture-free (bias-free) tests because tests are written and taken by culture-bound men. Unlike surveying and aerial photography, which do not affect the terrain being mapped, educational testing not only measures knowledge: it generates it. The more important a test becomes, and the more widely it is employed, the more it, like a distorting mirror, shapes the knowledge it is supposed to reflect. Manuals and cram courses emerge on how to pass it. The arts of multiple choice are mastered while those of spelling and writing are lost. Many professional and trade schools have a merited reputation as "cram schools" designed to help students pass the licensing examination for law, medicine, or pharmacy, dental hygiene, cosmetology, or aircraft mechanics.[9]

8. See, for example, the report of a recent conference at Hampton Institute, Va.: "A major national effort was begun here . . . to curb abuses in the testing of blacks and other minorities and to find new methods of assessing intelligence. . . . The project takes its cue from the widely reported charges that standardized tests are inherently biased against minority groups. . . . Its emphasis, however, is not necessarily to eliminate existing tests, as some have urged, but to work toward 'positive' alternatives. . . .

"The conference was held against a background of mounting opposition to testing among educators. Some groups, including the National Education Association and the Association of Black Psychologists, have called for a moratorium on standardized testing" (Robert L. Jacobson, "Curbs on Bias in Testing Set as Goal," *Chronicle of Higher Education,* April 9, 1973, pp. 1, 4).

9. The situation in licensure exams for dental hygienists, cosmetologists, and air

What Stephen Bailey called "tutoring to the test" occurs in the New York high schools, which have long been geared to the sockets of the Regents examinations. "The trustees of the College Entrance Examination Board have noted with concern the increasing tendency of secondary school students to seek the assistance of special tutors or of special drill at school in the hope of improving thereby scores earned on College Board examinations."[10] The trustees contend that coaching has little effect on these scores; they are less certain of its effect on tests in specific school subjects.[11] It is hard, though not impossible, to believe that so widespread an activity can be so futile. Nonetheless, coaching has plainly changed the character of the educational process, which, the trustees affirm, is "corrupted in some schools to gain ends which we believe to be not only unworthy but, ironically, unattainable."[12] Their careful statement does not

---

craft mechanics has been described as follows:

"It is not uncommon to find a special course given during the last year of a dental hygiene program which is designed to prepare students specifically for the examination."

"The fail rate [in state licensing examinations] among students who have attended schools of cosmetology tends to be low. The reason for this is suggested by comments made by the head of one such school in New York . . . [who] was very proud of the fact that 99.9 percent of his students pass the written test on their first attempt. . . . He explained that throughout the year, students are drilled on questions from a review book published by Keystone Press . . . [which] contains about 90 percent of the questions that are likely to appear on the examination. 'On the day of the test, we have the students report to the school at 9 A.M. and we drill them on questions that are almost identical to those they will find on the examination when they take it at 3 o'clock.' "

"The F.A.A. [Federal Aviation Administration] licensing requirements exert a powerful influence on the curriculum in the schools which train [aircraft] mechanics. Educators interviewed acknowledged that they teach whatever the certification tests require, regardless of its relevance . . . schools place heavy emphasis on preparing students to pass the F.A.A. written examinations" (Benjamin Shimberg et al., *Occupational Licensing and Public Policy* [Princeton, N.J.: Educational Testing Service, October 1972], pp. 44, 240–41, 273–74; published as *Occupational Licensing: Practices and Policies* [Washington: Public Affairs Press, 1973]).

10. "Statement by College Board Trustees," in *Effects of Coaching on Scholastic Aptitude Test Scores* (New York: College Entrance Examination Board, 1968), p. 8.

11. In 1960, the trustees stated that "the Verbal part [of the SAT] seems totally insensitive to drill, while the Mathematical part for some groups may, with effort, be raised by . . . an average of 25 points on a 600-point scale" (*A Description of the College Board Scholastic Aptitude Test* [New York: College Entrance Examination Board, 1960], p. 8). In 1968, they stated that "intensive drill for the SAT, either on its verbal or its mathematical part, is at best likely to yield insignificant increases in scores"—i.e., "average increases of less than 10 points on a 600 point scale. . . . We have said nothing about the tests of achievement in specific school subjects. These have not been studied in the same way as has the aptitude test. . . . We suspect that the question of coaching for these tests is a matter of choosing a method of teaching the subject" (*Effects of Coaching*, pp. 8, 10).

12. *Effects of Coaching*, p. 11.

consider the contribution that testing itself has inadvertently made to the corruption of the educational process.[13]

That corruption is most directly manifested in the evidence of cheating which surfaces periodically and, indirectly, in the security measures taken against it.

Scandals involving cheating on final examinations have recently been reported at the Air Force and Naval Academies. At the former, thirty-nine cadets were found guilty of cheating; the superintendent of the latter indicates that, in most years, twelve to fifteen midshipmen are expelled for cheating.[14] In June 1974, nine of twenty-one Regents examinations were canceled following the theft of answer sheets or test booklets at three Brooklyn schools. An investigator posing as a high school student had no difficulty buying copies of two tests for $15.00.[15] In Japan, medical license exams reputedly sell for $10,000—a small price for relieving pressures that can lead to suicide. A special licensing examination prepared for the Puerto Rican Board of Medicine had to be abandoned after it was compromised: on one occasion, everyone got a perfect score. According to Cornell law professor Norman Penney, president of the Law School Admissions Council, the "going rate for a ringer . . . [for the Law School Admissions Test (LSAT) was] several hundred dollars." After "an increasing number of notices appeared on college bulletin boards on which ringers offered to take the exams for a fee and sometimes guaranteed a certain score," a thumbprint identification of examinees was imposed. While the problem of cheating "is obviously troubling," Penney believes that it is no greater in law than in other professions.[16]

Photographs are now required for admission to several examinations (including the Medical College Admissions Test and the Graduate Record Examination); handwriting samples are taken; driver's licenses and other

13. That unwelcome contribution was set forth by Banesh Hoffman: "The nation . . . is placing enormous reliance on machine-graded multiple-choice tests as a measure of ability. But, unhappily, it can be shown that they have grave defects. Our confidence in them can have dangerous consequences not only for education but for the strength and vitality of the nation" ("The Tyranny of Multiple-Choice Tests," *Harper's*, March 1961, pp. 37–44).
14. See Michael T. Rose and Donald A. Peppers, "Air Force Integrity," *New York Times*, June 20, 1974, p. 39, and "Naval Academy Expels 7 for Cheating," *New York Times*, July 10, 1974, pp. 1, 14.
15. See stories in the *New York Times*, June 18, 1974, pp. 1, 18; June 19, 1974, p. 30; and the editorial "Voluntary Regents'," June 29, 1974, p. 28.
16. Quoted in Andrew Barnes, "Thumb Print Now Required for Law Test," *Washington Post*, Oct. 14, 1973, p. A 2.

identification may be inspected, and personal questions are used for spot checking, as in a bank. The seating plan is commonly recorded so that, when the computer singles out too-identical papers, as it is programmed to do, they can be checked against the seating arrangement. The computer also compares scores of the same candidate on repeated examinations and notes remarkable gains.[17] However, in the battle between computers and people, people sometimes win. Blank tests are handled like state secrets and, like state secrets, are occasionally leaked. Storerooms are broken into. Where the timing of examinations in different cities permits an advantage to be gained, some individuals take an examination solely to reconstruct it.

Activity of this sort, sometimes organized by teachers, is, of course, perfectly proper when it deals solely with past examinations. (Information booklets distributed by testing agencies often make available sample questions.) In dental hygiene programs, "Students who will be taking the [licensing] test are frequently asked to cooperate with the instructional staff by bringing back questions remembered from the examination. One educator explained that when she had been a student the process had been quite elaborate. Certain students were given responsibility for specific sections of the examination and almost everyone reported back faithfully."[18] Instructors in Buffalo cram courses for the Law School Admission Test reportedly encourage examinees to return and discuss the exam; questions used in practice sessions have mysteriously appeared in subsequent examinations.[19] That kind of instruction may be miraculous, legal, or, at least, unimpeachable, but it is morally and educationally depressing.

In recognition of the limitations of standardized tests, such attention is being given to other means of assessing skill and knowledge. The CAEL (Cooperative Assessment of Experiential Learning) project supported by the Carnegie Corporation even avoids the word "examination," concentrating instead on such techniques as interviews, rating scales, oral and written reports, gaming and simulation exercises, certified performances

17. A circumspect description of test security measures is given in Robert E. Smith, chairman, Board of Review, *ETS Procedures for Dealing with Impersonation, Copying, and Related Candidate Misconduct in National Testing Programs,* mimeographed (Princeton, N.J.: Educational Testing Service, Jan. 15, 1973), 6 pp., and in *The ACT Supervisor's Manual: Instructions for the Administration of the ACT Assessment* (Iowa City: American College Testing Program, 1973).

18. Shimberg, *Occupational Licensing,* p. 44.

19. See Ian C. DeWaal, "Affidavits Contend Course Similarities," *Spectrum,* State University of New York at Buffalo student paper, Oct. 30, 1972, p. 1.

and products, and the evaluation of portfolios.[20] The evaluation of proficiency by the direct observation of performance is also receiving attention in carpentry, plumbing, welding, engine repair, allied health, and other occupations.[21] Such direct evaluation is, of course, traditional in the fine arts, creative writing, architecture, and all the crafts and professions involving a period of apprenticeship.

However, all forms of testing and evaluation are impaled on common dilemmas: of selecting samples of work or knowledge which are representative and yet brief; standardizable and yet fresh and nonrepetitive; natural and yet performable under pressure in an artificial setting. The cheap, readily standardizable, machine-graded multiple-choice test has not escaped the problem of social bias and intellectual simplification. Alternative approaches are more expensive, avowedly subjective, or less widely accepted. As a test comes to be accepted, it tends to subvert its own ends by conditioning training in its field. Each test yields one piece of information. Together with other information, that piece can be useful but, alone, it is inadequate for assessment or placement.

ONE HUNDRED MILLION DEGREE-HOLDERS?

To certify knowledge by direct examination can serve many purposes. It can strengthen the market for educational services and industries. It might expand employment opportunities—but 100 million degree-holders cannot enjoy the same opportunities as 10 million. It can contribute to maturation or to idleness. It might enhance the social and self-esteem of many people —but the merit of being rare is greater than that of being common and soon it will be rare to have no degree.

The well-intentioned purpose of rationalizing the worlds of work and education is at best naïve and at worst objectionable. It assumes that occupations can be blocked into unit, objectively measurable skills and knowledge; that the skills (or their surrogate measures, certified by ac-

20. See Morris Keeton, *Accrediting Off-Campus Learning: A New Form of Academic Accountability,* offset (March 1972), 14 pp., and *CAEL: Cooperative Assessment of Experiential Learning,* Condensed version of a proposal submitted to Carnegie Corporation of New York, Educational Testing Service, offset (December 1973), 9 pp.
21. See Joseph L. Boyd, Jr., and Benjamin Shimberg, *Developing Performance Tests for Classroom Evaluation,* ERIC Clearinghouse on Tests, Measurement, and Evaluation, offset (n.d.), 14 pp.; Roderick A. Ironside and Adele Richardson, *The Dimensions and Specific Indicators Used to Define Competence and Quality in Medical Care,* September 1973; and material on the National Occupational Competency Testing Institute, all issued by the Educational Testing Service, Princeton, N.J.

credited institutions and testing services) can then be assembled, no matter how acquired (in life or school), to qualify any person with the requisite units for any job compounded of the skills they certify. This view of education and work is that of a time-and-motion engineer, an economist, a computer programmer, or a zealous behaviorist. It is rational, lean, functional, mechanical, and utterly artificial since, omitting what cannot be measured, it omits most of the things that give education and work, society and the individual their distinctive character. It amputates competence from its individual and social context. Seeking to eliminate bias, it eliminates 99 percent of life.

Still, the view is increasingly influential, drawing strength from our practical outlook and democratic convictions. For it is eminently practicable and administrable. Laws and regulations can be written gearing the new credentials to the old, jobs and promotions can be tied to the regulations, and dutiful civil servants, social scientists, and policemen can enforce them.

Independent, rigorous, and versatile means of certifying knowledge can have much value as an adjunct to living educational institutions. A vast, integrated national system of examining and certifying bodies, credit banks, and educational passports—a comprehensive, rationalized "learning society"—would be monstrous. It would not reform education but degrade it. It would not cure the disease of credentialism but succumb to it.

There is nothing new about the "educational passport." Recording, year by year, the bearer's educational history, jobs, residences, certificates, permits, and restrictions, it must be carried by citizens and produced for inspection in Communist countries. I do not suggest that the same instrument would produce all of the same effects here. But there are visible connections between rationalization and bureaucracy, between excessive "objectivity," excessive regulation, and the reduction of individual freedom and judgment. Excessive rationality is just another kind of madness.

Instructional Delivery Systems and Open Learning

FRANKLIN G. BOUWSMA

THE Corporation for Public Broadcasting recently funded a study to define the role of CPB in the field of education. The study, being made by its Advisory Council of National Organizations, will conclude in March 1975 with a series of recommendations to the board of CPB.

CPB has long been successful in broadcasting public affairs, cultural, and children's programs in cooperation with the public broadcasting stations across the country. Recently, interest in educational programming as expressed at state and local levels indicated that the needs of education should be investigated to find out what services might be performed by CPB, the Public Broadcasting Service, the local public television stations, and National Public Radio. The study, under way since February 1974, is being carried out by four task forces: Early Childhood Education, Elementary-Secondary Education, Postsecondary Education, and Adult Education. I shall discuss the work of the Postsecondary—Formal Task Force.[1]

The CPB project provides for several patterns to elicit recommendations, including various consensus techniques to encourage local and state

---

1. The members of the Postsecondary—Formal Task Force are: Franklin G. Bouwsma, vice-president for instructional resources, Miami-Dade Community College, *chairperson;* Luis Alvarez, national executive director, Aspira of America, Inc.; Robert Filep, director, Learning Systems Center, University of Southern California; W. Todd Furniss, director, Office of Academic Affairs, American Council on Education; Peter Goldschmidt, special assistant to the president, University of California; Samuel B. Gould, president, Institute for Educational Development; Gladys Hardy, former under-secretary of higher education, Massachusetts; Jessie Hartline, director, Open University Program, University College, Rutgers University; Tim Higgins, student, University of Wisconsin; Armand Hunter, director, Continuing Education Service, Michigan State University; Blyden Jackson, associate dean, Graduate School, University of North Carolina; Calvin B. T. Lee, chancellor, University of Maryland, Baltimore; Jack McBride, executive director, State University of Nebraska.

input. The initial recommendations were developed in five regional planning conferences (in San Francisco, Dallas, Washington, D.C., St. Louis, and Atlanta). At each conference, thirty persons—representing colleges, universities, community colleges, consortia, television and radio stations, community agencies, and the public—attended general sessions and also worked in small groups to develop recommendations which addressed critical issues in four areas: interagency relationships, content, design and production, distribution and utilization. The five conferences produced nearly two hundred recommendations. The recommendations were forwarded to the task force for consolidation and priority ordering for a nationwide Delphi exercise. The Delphi iterations, now under way, are designed to achieve national consensus on priorities among, and redefinition of, the conference-developed recommendations. About one thousand faculty members, administrators, and media experts will participate in the process. Meantime, a national consultants group, under the direction of John Witherspoon, former vice-president of CPB, has been collecting operational and research information for the task forces to use as state-of-the-practice, base-line data. In December 1974, the four task forces will meet with the Education Committee of the Advisory Council of National Organizations in a three-day session to merge all recommendations for a final report. The recommendations will then be submitted to the Advisory Council of National Organizations representatives for their approval before going to the CPB board in the spring of 1975.

The task force, then, has received the benefit of the best thinking available on potential needs of postsecondary education and patterns of instructional delivery systems being devised on local, state, regional, and national levels. Most of the information concerns trends in instructional delivery systems and the models being considered for replication.

Certain trends in postsecondary education are influencing instructional delivery systems in a variety of ways. The recommendations of the Commission on Non-Traditional Study and ensuing publications have strongly influenced planning in many institutions. Colleges and universities are redefining their missions with respect to adults, career licensure programs for business and professional service, minority education, programs for the elderly, and occupational retraining. Institutions are clustering in various ways to share scarce faculty, production resources, and broadcast time and to develop and exchange media materials for use in classrooms and external study centers. Audience sophistication is requiring that, if materials are to become widely accepted and used, production design and techniques must be upgraded. Because local budgets are tight, most innovative projects will have to be supported partly or wholly from outside funds. And the present open learning models are being regarded by many institutions as design for change in their delivery system.

The Commission on Non-Traditional Study enlisted help from hundreds of experts in making its analyses and formulating its recommendations. One year later, many institutions have accepted its general recommendations in planning their use of the media in open learning. Samuel B. Gould, chairman of the commission, summarized the recommendations that would call for major decisions and action during the next decade:

(1) Lifetime learning—basic, continuing, and recurrent—has a new appropriateness today and requires a new pattern of support.

(2) Colleges and universities must shift emphasis from degree-granting to service to the learner, thus countering what has become a degree-granting obsession.

(3) Faculty understandings and commitments must be reoriented and redirected, particularly through in-service development, so that knowledge and use of non-traditional forms and materials will increase.

(4) An organized effort must be made to promote intelligent and widespread use of educational technology with special emphasis on programming for cable television, computers, videotape recorders, and possibilities of satellite broadcasting.

(5) New agencies must be created to make possible easy access to information and develop better ways to disseminate it, to perform guidance and counseling services, and to be assessors and repositories of credit for student achievement.

(6) New evaluative tools must be developed to match the non-traditional arrangements now evolving, so that accreditation and credentialing will have appropriate measures of quality.

(7) Cooperation and collaboration must be encouraged among collegiate, community, and alternate educational entities so that diverse educational programs and structures may come into being.[2]

The recommendation for further collaboration and cooperation has produced the most pervasive trend in media development. As a result, several types of consortia have emerged in the past few years. A few examples are: community colleges organize to use common production facilities in an area covered by a given broadcast station; similar institutions within a state organize to use the same materials; a multicampus public university serves all participating institutions in the state; and

2. Gould, ed., *Diversity by Design* (San Francisco: Jossey-Bass, 1973), p. xviii.

similar innovative institutions are linked nationally by their need for unique innovative services. Sometimes a special consortium may be organized for a particular purpose. For example, in order to meet a national curriculum need, a national community college consortium of twenty institutions planned the course "Man and Environment" with Miami-Dade Community College and then each used it as its own course. Of special interest is the University of Mid-America Consortium of major state universities in Missouri, Nebraska, Kansas, and Iowa being formed on the basis of detailed planning at the State University of Nebraska. This large unit represents the first regional consortium to link adjacent-state institutions.

The Commission on Non-Traditional Study suggested, "Joint planning and cooperative action, initiated by participating institutions themselves, escape the serious dangers of federal or regional domination and at the same time provide every co-operating institution with a greater range of opportunities and a richer vein of resources than even the largest could achieve on its own."[3] The commission also pointed out that consortium arrangements will tend to change the operational and administrative structure of institutions involved:

> New kinds of collaboration which develop among academic institutions themselves as the result of non-traditional patterns also affect their structures. As colleges and universities allow students to move more freely from campus to campus; as adults find it convenient to take their academic work in various places with the blessing of some single institution; as such non-traditional resources as computers, television programs, or off-campus laboratories in oceanography, ecology, and urban development are sponsored by several institutions; as the talents of selected faculty members are shared among institutions—as all such developments occur, colleges and universities become increasingly interdependent and coordinate their structures and administrative processes accordingly.[4]

PROJECT OUTREACH AS DESIGN

It is my belief that the planning design for the Project Outreach consortium in Orange and San Diego counties, California, will be the model for most local and regional developments during the next ten years. It illustrates the detailed educational planning required as institutions move to organize for a collaborative effort. Project Outreach was stimulated by a grant under title i of the Higher Education Act of 1965. It is designed around the outstanding talents and facilities of three different types of

3. Ibid., p. 112.
4. Ibid., p. 43.

public institutions in Southern California—the University of California at San Diego, San Diego State University, and the Coast Community College District, Costa Mesa—and includes all public higher education institutions in the two counties.

The first phase of planning the system placed emphasis on televised materials:

> Objectives met by Phase I activities of Project Outreach as a means to working toward achievement of its overall goal include the following:
> 1. The development of an operational procedure whereby the three segments of higher education in San Diego and Orange Counties may jointly design, produce and offer televised instruction to the public.
> 2. The involvement of all other institutions of public higher education in the two counties in all phases of Project Outreach activity.
> 3. The exploration of cooperative participation with community agencies toward identifying target populations and their educational needs.
> 4. The study of non-traditional approaches to higher education.
> 5. The joint preparation of two pilot television programs to test the feasibility of inter-institutional cooperation in television course production.[5]

A Project Outreach task force included faculty members and administrators from the three institutions, other institutions in the area, and community representatives.

> The Project Outreach Task Force formed nine study committees assigned to identify and explore the advantages and obstacles inherent in cooperative planning and production of educational materials for use among the three segments of higher education. Those committees include General Administration, Academic Administration, State of the Art, Target Population, Counseling, Curriculum, Delivery Systems, Evaluation and Research, and Future Directions. Their members were selected from within the Task Force and were augmented by their chairmen to provide additional representation from participating educational institutions.[6]

The Phase I activity produced recommendations from the various committees, of which the following are examples:

Curriculum
> The most reasonable approach to developing curriculum for use by members of a consortium is to recognize that there are varying patterns available for use of the end product. In fact the variety of instructional alternatives for each segment and course is unlimited.

5. Bernard Luskin, *Project Outreach,* A Report on the Cooperative Effort of Three Consortium Institutions (Costa Mesa, Calif.: Coast Community College District, 1973), pp. 1, 2.
6. Ibid., p. 2.

Committee recommendations include the following:
1. Needs of the target population should be carefully identified in the course of curriculum selection.
2. Faculty who are to share in a product's use must be allowed input into its development.
3. Multi-talented instructional teams including teachers, instructional product-developers, media technologists and learning specialists should participate in course development.
4. Curriculum planners should investigate the availability of existing materials that can be incorporated within instructional television systems.
5. The concept of modularization should be employed, as it helps facilitate arrangement and rearrangement of individual segments and eventual updating of entire courses.
6. Components of instructional systems must be arranged so as to satisfy verifiable learning objectives.
7. Because television instructional systems provide for only limited student and teacher interaction, supportive group experience and teacher accessibility must be integrated into course design.

Of crucial importance are the supportive services which complete the system. They include printed materials, making available libraries and resource centers, and providing for on-campus and telephone interaction with instructors and operating counseling services.[7]

New Courses Delivered in New Ways

The State University of Nebraska devised a process for course development which many institutions use as their model for designing materials for new instructional delivery systems. C. Edward Cavert, director of instructional design at the State University of Nebraska, has described it:

> The system embraces the functions of Content Development, Design, Production, Evaluation and Delivery in an overall Management context which result in validated instructional courseware.
>
> The development process is briefly described as follows: In order to meet the instructional needs of a specified target population, goals for the academic requirements of the course are established. A strategy that incorporates a step-by-step sequence leading toward the goals is developed. Precise levels of learning objectives are formulated. From these objectives, test items can be written to assess only what was attempted to be done in design and production. Also from these objectives, the content material is structured to function as stimuli in the media. Media are selected for instruction by the nature of each individual instructional task. After instruction has been displayed to the learner in a prototype form, responses are tested to show cognitive learning. At the same time, learner reactions are

7. Ibid., pp. 4, 5.

surveyed to indicate attitudinal acceptance. From a diagnosis of the results of this formative testing, decisions are made to revise or remake the instruction if it does not work or to distribute it through the S-U-N delivery system if it does. Data about enrolled students permit individual personal goals to be recognized. The cycle of procedures begins again to develop material which completes a relevant learning experience for the individual.

The S-U-N course development concept uses the expertise of a variety of specialists. These include content advisors, media experts, instructional designers, educational psychologists, psychometrists, writers and producers to work together as a team to design and develop courses.[8]

He then lists the twenty steps for course materials development: establish a frame of reference for course development, define broad course goals, arrange content material, outline sequence for instruction, write specific learning objectives, prepare criterion test item pool, decide on structure to achieve objectives, assign media priorities, create stimulus situation, write instructional material, produce instructional material, prototype testing, instructional diagnosis, revision or remake, compile lessons, field test, initial operational dissemination, establish profile of enrolled target population, conduct needs assessment, redefine personal course goals. Although many institutions lack the capacity and resources to pursue such a rigorous design for instructional systems, most planners accept this model and encourage similar planning with their faculty and media specialists.

Will materials designed with such care be widely accepted by colleges and communities?

W. Werner Prange, dean of instructional services, University of Wisconsin—Green Bay, recently organized an exchange system for course materials among twenty colleges. He describes the quality requirements and needed controls:

> Students expect quality instruction in return for their investments of time and tuition; they will not settle for a mediocre recording on a television screen, an economical expedient which isolates them from the professor. Too many faculty members are convinced that technology will do nothing but eliminate faculty positions and degrade the quality of instruction. We need to change this attitude.
>
> Recorded courseware can be successful as teaching and learning tools only to the extent (1) that the courseware originates in response to real instructional needs among the students, and (2) that it is planned and pro-

8. Cavert, ed., *Conference Proceedings of the First Annual National Conference on Open Learning in Higher Education* (Lincoln: State University of Nebraska, 1974), p. 147.

duced by qualified and academically respectable instructors in cooperation with media and evaluation specialists.[9]

What is the potential for course materials distributed regularly into the community, and is there a substantial pool of students interested in such materials?

The oldest continuing open learning project, which remains a design model for materials distribution, is the TV College of the City Colleges of Chicago. Its audience is described in a recently published Fifth Report:

> Over the past eighteen years more than 150,000 individuals have en-rolled in TV College courses either for credit or not for credit. Surveys indicate that every telecourse is also viewed by a total of about 250,000 "casual" viewers, people who happen upon a program of a course, and feeling their interest piqued, watch several programs—or an entire series—because they find the program entertaining and informative. The important fact is, however, that every year some 6,000 or so individuals account for about 9,000 course registrations. (Some viewers take more than one course.) This is impressive evidence that there exists in the Chicago area a large audience of at-home viewers willing and able to exert the effort needed to complete college courses for credit.[10]

Given the potential audience, the delivery systems, instructional design capability, and a consortium of users and producers, what are the subjects to be presented? Possible areas for national open learning materials to be developed were suggested by Lawrence E. Dennis, chairman of the Massachusetts Task Force on the Open University. Dennis suggests several curriculum efforts, "public affairs, the issues of our time . . . problems of the environment . . . the family: child care, human relationships and family finance . . . the arts . . . the media . . . science and technology . . . health care . . . the management of organizations . . . international and multi-cultural studies . . . and the future."[11]

The most studied open learning program is the British Open University (BOU). Its influence on planning in this country has been profound, not so much as a national institution, but rather for its examples of practices that have proved effective. Cyril O. Houle describes the multimedia development that has captured the imagination of most planners:

> The original intention was to rely on teaching by television; now this has

9. Ibid., p. 213.

10. James J. Zigerell, ed., *Chicago's TV College: A Fifth Report* (Chicago: City Colleges of Chicago, Learning Resources Laboratory, 1974), pp. 13, 14.

11. Cavert, *Conference on Open Learning,* pp. 60, 61.

been supplemented by other means of instruction, among them background reading, correspondence teaching (including written assignments graded by a tutor or a computer), self-assessment tests, radio broadcasts, special counseling, and class instruction at study centers and one-week residential summer schools. Many other resources required for particular courses are used; among these, the science kits have received much favorable attention. Efforts are made to engage the best available talent to write and produce the diverse materials required for the program.[12]

Another Open University design solution to individualization of mass-produced instruction has been the organized distribution of materials and resources to community study centers. Of the recent technological advances in educational equipment, the most widely accepted are the audio-cassette and videocassette recorder-playback units. Such equipment, as it becomes standard in the services provided by the BOU study center, will itself constitute a new distribution system for higher education institutions.

The BOU study centers serve as community learning resource centers for the institution:

> Programs of non-traditional study should be reinforced by preliminary and continuing experiences which help students learn how to learn and which assist them in building confidence in their capacity to do so. In the Open University in England, the study centers fulfill this vital function. Many adults who embark on higher learning do not know how to proceed; they feel insecure and inadequate about the process, and they need advice and assistance on aspects of it. Instruction in how to learn, guidance through the varied processes of study, and the availability of both personal and instructional advice are important for their success. These efforts should be made with the basic and ultimate purpose of building independence, not continuing dependence.[13]

The study centers, now a major component in the BOU instructional delivery system, are located in all areas where there is significant enrollment and are regarded as critical to the program's success. "About 280 study centers (backed up by 12 regional centers) provide places near enough each student for study, counseling, review of radio or television programs, attendance at occasional courses and meetings, and association with fellow learners."[14]

PROBABLE ORGANIZATION MODES

At this time the movement to develop and distribute open learning materials is being led by two types of institutions, the large urban multi-

12. Houle, *The External Degree* (San Francisco: Jossey-Bass, 1973), p. 36.
13. Gould, *Diversity by Design*, p. 35.
14. Ibid., p. 36.

campus community colleges and the land-grant universities. Both types of institutions have always had, as a philosophy, a strong commitment to community or state service. This trend was noted by the Commission on Non-Traditional Study:

> Both the land-grant college and the community college represented new recognition of the goal of education for the many. Both were originally specific in their efforts to meet a clearly delineated need, but as they matured they incorporated new attitudes toward higher education, focusing on whom it might benefit rather than on precise and inflexible definitions of institutional mission. This adaptability was to be expected of them, and the most successful are those which have enthusiastically fostered such attitudes. They have made great impact on the future of hundreds of thousands of people and therefore on the nation. It is likely that the present movement toward increasing non-traditional alternatives will do the same.[15]

What are the trends for the near future?

Community-oriented colleges, broadcasting stations, newspapers, libraries, and other community agencies will continue to form linkages. Materials will be produced and exchanged through consortia and other collaborative devices. National libraries of materials in a modular format will be developed, with their offerings available to be used with local materials for open learning purposes. These projects will launch as open learning but, in time, become adjunct independent study projects and work their way into classrooms and laboratories, probably through videocassette and audiocassette modes.

The state universities, with their land-grant tradition of service, will follow a year or so behind the urban institutions, delayed by distance and multicampus organizational problems. They will tend to produce materials similar to those for the community college mission: freshman- and sophomore-level course materials, career programs, minority training and instructional materials, and general adult awareness programs. And the land-grant institutions will probably organize new structures within the system to free them to move quickly in curriculum and materials design.

Existing public broadcasting stations will become local, state, and regional production and dubbing centers and, in some instances, will also serve as distribution and media service centers for area postsecondary institutions.

The community colleges are likely to be the first group to establish a national exchange and materials library, for they already lead in open learning with respect to use and quality of materials produced. They ap-

15. Ibid., pp. 3–4.

pear to experience few constraints, and they have the ability to organize to serve community curriculum needs.

Financing for open learning will go to institutions that join other institutions, production centers, and community organizations in forming production and operating consortia. It is my belief that existing organizations and accredited institutions will be the leaders.

In the next ten years, fewer audiovisual classroom materials will be developed, as financing goes to open learning materials. Sophisticated technological schemes such as satellite broadcasting, computer-managed education, and interactive cable will move into higher education slowly and erratically.

The trend, then, is to develop open learning materials and multiinstitution materials and curricula. The pass phrase for open learning during the next decade will be "cooperate or stagnate."

The Media Paradox

MARGARET E. CHISHOLM

MEDIA SUCH as cable television, cassette recorders, cameras, and a host of other devices are commonplace to most people in our nation. Yet in higher education, a paradox seems to prevail: the sporadic attempts made at mass distribution of educational information have used complex, expensive delivery systems when the greatest potential among the means lies in simple, inexpensive equipment.

Let me begin by defining terms. "Educational technology is not only 'hardware,' but often includes 'hardware.' Neither is educational technology the same as media. Media are the means by which information is made available to the learner. Educational technology incorporates media and usually involves hardware, materials and methods of teaching."[1] This definition indicates the scope and comprehensiveness of educational technology and its potential for use in colleges and universities.

1. Donald P. Ely and Margaret Chisholm, *A General Information System for Educational Technology* (Washington: National Center for the Study of Statistics, 1974), p. 6.

The use of mass media in higher education has failed largely because its advocates have failed to take into account individual differences among students. By contrast, less sophisticated technological devices have steadily grown in influence—audio cassettes and portable video tape recorders, small and inexpensive filmstrip and slide viewers, 8-mm. cartridge projectors, calculators, and published programmed instruction. All of these latter devices and methods are on a small scale when compared with the colossus of a television system or a computer-assisted instructional network. As one surveys the investment in the smaller, more portable, and more flexible equipment, two advantages are evident: first, the cost is much lower than that required for an extensive distribution system, and, second, this approach meets the criteria for individualization of instruction.

James Finn, an authority on both the theoretical and the practical foundations of instructional technology, early recognized aspects of this paradox:

> We need perhaps, a little less "high-flying rhetoric" concerning both the promises and accomplishments and the failures and dangers of technology in education. We can no longer afford these Ciceronian luxuries; unbounded and unquestioned enthusiasm for this or that bit of instructional technology on the one hand or a failure of nerve in the face of the problems of technological development in education on the other. . . . The medicine man promises of technological panacea for education will only . . . result in regression and retreat on the part of the educational community when the hopes that have been aroused meet the hard nosed reality of the confounding educational system.[2]

According to Finn's thesis, claims were made for a single aspect of technology without considering it as part of a totally designed system and without considering the total educational needs, the technological milieu, the complex attitudes, the training levels of the educators and of students, or the sociopolitical forces within and outside the educational system.

Some examples of these enthusiastic pronouncements and predictions will illustrate his point. The New York *Dramatic Mirror* of July, 9, 1913, reported Thomas Edison as stating: "Books will soon be obsolete in the schools. Scholars will soon be instructed through the eye. It is possible to teach every branch of human knowledge with the motion picture. Our school system will be completely changed in ten years."[3] With parallel

2. "What Is the Business of Educational Technology?" in *Planning for Effective Utilization of Technology in Education,* ed. Edgar L. Morphet and David L. Jesser (New York: Citation Press, 1969), p. 38.
3. Paul Saettler, *A History of Instructional Technology* (New York: McGraw-Hill, 1968), p. 98.

optimism, one Josiah F. Bumstead in 1841 devoted a book to the blackboard, holding that "The inventor or introducer of the blackboard system deserves to be ranked among the best contributors of learning and science, if not among the greatest benefactors of mankind."[4]

When E. B. Kurtz and his colleagues at the State University of Iowa began broadcasting a successful educational television program, he held a highly optimistic view: "this new instrumentality [television], which bids fair to become the most potent agency for universal education ever conceived. For in due time, every home will have its own classroom, with professor, blackboard, diagrams, pictures, and students."[5] Other educational leaders have made similar pronouncements. Of particular interest is one made in 1940 by George F. Zook, then president of the American Council on Education and former U.S. Commissioner of Education, when he described the motion picture as "the most revolutionary instrument introduced in education since the printing press."[6]

More recently, there have been claims that television, programmed learning, and the computer each will have a greater influence on education than did Gutenberg's invention of movable type.

EDUCATIONAL TECHNOLOGY: A SOLUTION IN SEARCH OF A PROBLEM

The most pessimistic skeptics may well react by saying, Look at these brilliant educators and their predictions and see how wrong they were, and look at the current failures of technology in higher education. Why, then, is technology still included in the "Search for Alternatives"—the conference theme?

To begin, these claims must be carefully assessed, both for their sources and the times and situations in which they were made. Also to be assessed are the conditions under which mass media have failed in higher education. While these visionary educators are to be applauded for their optimism and enthusiasm, their advocacies all suffered one fault in common, that of having a solution in search of a problem. Instructional development must work in just the opposite way.

Although the introduction of media in higher education as an ap-

4. Charnel Anderson, *History of Instructional Technology, I: Technology in American Education: 1650–1900* (Washington: National Education Association, Technology Development Project, 1961), p. 23.

5. *Pioneering in Educational Television: 1932–1939* (Iowa City: State University of Iowa, 1959), p. 71.

6. Charles F. Hoban, Jr., *Focus on Learning: Motion Pictures in the School* (Washington: American Council on Education, 1942), p. 40.

pendage or a superstructure has largely failed, in an unsensational but effective way instructional development (the real instructional technology of our era) has begun to emerge and make a difference. In the past, most of those associated with the field of educational technology have attempted to present technology as the answer without having adequately studied or understood the problems within education. The approach used by the instructional development specialist is, first, to seek out the problems and then to identify an array of alternative solutions from which one or more can be selected to resolve the problems. The beginnings of this movement are now becoming visible in many community colleges and at certain universities—Syracuse, Michigan State, McGill, Michigan, Brigham Young, Florida State, Illinois, and Pittsburgh. The leaders in the instructional development movement are applied learning psychologists—educational technologists who systematically look at teaching and learning. They analyze extensively the tasks to be accomplished in any course or curriculum, work as members of course development teams to restructure existing courses and design new ones, and they build evaluation into each step. Perhaps the best example of how instructional development personnel work is demonstrated in the Institute of Educational Technology of the British Open University.[7]

The immediate paradox is well illustrated in the May 28, 1974, issue of the *Chronicle of Higher Education*. A front-page article describes the mixed reactions to Open University courses offered at the University of Houston, the University of Maryland, and Rutgers University. The study being reported indicated that "the courses clearly appealed most to those who had already demonstrated academic competence, came disproportionately from high-status occupations, and reported relatively high incomes." Further, according to the acticle, "to make the course appropriate for academically weak students, institutions would have to add significant new services."[8] The same issue of the *Chronicle* featured a special report on television in higher education. The lead asked and announced: "Whatever happened to the 'video revolution' on campus? Such a revolution, with conventional colleges shifting to technologically innovative modes of instruction, was predicted more than two decades ago. It has been a long time coming, and it is still not here." The article goes on to document that the essential

7. Joan Silleck, "Britain's Bold New Electronic University," *World*, Dec. 5, 1972, pp. 28–32.
8. "British Open U. Courses Found Unsuitable for 'Disadvantaged,'" *Chronicle of Higher Education*, May 28, 1974, p. 1.

failure of television in higher education is a function of faculty resistance.[9] The one exception noted is Chicago TV College which, for the last eighteen years, has offered college-level instruction to off-campus students in the Greater Chicago area.

The same issue of the *Chronicle* reports the prospects for the State University of Nebraska—"S.U.N."—which begins its program in fall 1974. The article notes that the S.U.N. system plans to use television as a major means of delivering courses in four midwestern states and goes on to describe S.U.N. plans for the next five years.[10]

The paradox is reemphasized by a back-page article of the same issue where Stephen K. Bailey, vice-president of the American Council on Education, articulates some ways in which professors can revitalize themselves. Among his recommendations is this one: "Faculty lives can be freed if faculty members will face up to the desirability of new mixes of pedagogic arrangements and to the imaginatvie employment of new educational technologies. I commend to them the Carnegie Commission's report, *The Fourth Revolution,* which deals perceptively and creatively with the new technologies. Audio-visual and programmed-learning techniques can be used to stimulate individual student learning while reducing the burden of daily preparation on the teacher."[11]

And so the paradox continues. The technology is here and is a vital part of our everyday lives. Even though mass and other media have become part of our everyday lives, higher education continues to resist potentials that are heralded by leaders in higher education. What is wrong? What are the indicators of a breakthrough? Will the gap between advocacy and practice ever be bridged?

A NEW PERSPECTIVE ON EDUCATIONAL TECHNOLOGY

At this point the distinction between educational technology and media must be reemphasized. According to the Commission on Instructional Technology: "Instructional (educational) technology is a systematic way of designing, carrying out, and evaluating the total process of learning and teaching in terms of specific objectives, based on research in human learning and communication, and employing a combination of human and non-

9. Malcolm G. Scully, "Video on Campus: Where's the 'Revolution'?" *Chronicle of Higher Education,* May 28, 1974, pp. 9–11.

10. "To Reach Adults Bypassed by Colleges, Nebraska Tries TV," *Chronicle of Higher Education,* May 28, 1974, p. 12.

11. "Helping Professors (and Therefore Students) to Grow," *Chronicle of Higher Education,* May 28, 1974, p. 24.

human resources to bring about more effective instruction."[12] And, as noted at the beginning, Ely elaborated on the components of educational technology.

Several years ago the late James D. Finn proposed a model for considering the use of media in higher education. He felt that media use in colleges and universities can be thought of as serving at several different levels: (1) the tool level, (2) the data level, (3) the behavior control level, (4) the meaning level, (5) the research level, (6) the systems level.

At the *tool level,* the instructor is provided with certain devices and materials that enable him to do what he is accustomed to doing but do it better. A commonplace example of such a tool (and the material to go with it) is the overhead transparency projector. In its simplest form it is analogous to a chalkboard, but it is more sophisticated and uses prepared transparencies to afford the instructor a powerful resource. At the *data level,* information no longer need be stored exclusively in conventional print. Data may be recorded on or transferred to various forms of photographic, magnetic, or other storage materials. Among the examples of media used at this level are microfiche, computer tapes, video tapes, high-speed motion pictures, audio tapes, and color still pictures. The *behavior control level* is commonly known as "programmed instruction." In such programming, great effort is devoted to preparing the content in some form designed either to shape the behavior (mainly verbal) of the student on a control basis or to lead the student through carefully planned sequences of subject matter. The programmed material may appear in print, on slides, films, audio tape, and so forth. At the *meaning level* a wide range of educational media are applied to building meaning into abstractions: a motion picture may be used to convey a concrete background from which a student may build meaning into an abstraction. The *research level* complements the data level. Today many forms of implementation are used in research to record, observe, and measure. Much of this instrumentation is, in fact, communication technology applied to research instead of instruction. A phenomenon may be photographed at thousands of frames per minute, dialects may be recorded, documents X-rayed. Such recordings and measurements may ultimately result in library material at the data level. This generation, however, is a different function.

At the *systems level,* a complex of instructional materials—books,

12. Sidney Tickton, ed., *To Improve Learning: An Evaluation of Instructional Technology,* A Report of the Commission on Instructional Technology (New York: R. R. Bowker Co., 1970), p. 22.

manuals, recordings, films, programmed materials, tests—are designed and created to cover an area of subject matter systematically so as to achieve precise objectives.[13] When educational technology is considered at the systems level, it takes on a new perspective. It begins, not with a medium in search of a problem, but rather with an array of problems in search of solutions.

For those who are convinced that the most significant development that could occur in education would be the appropriate utilization of technology in all parts of the educational system, it is reassuring to note that the number of advocates is increasing. One example is the widely distributed report of the Panel on Alternative Approaches to Graduate Education entitled *Scholarship for Society*. The panel, sponsored by the Graduate Records Examination Board and the Council of Graduate Schools in the United States, spent eighteen months in investigation to present a discussion of crucial issues and offer recommendations for viable change within the graduate community. The portion germane to the discussion here is entitled "The Use of New and Neglected Media." The problem is stated as follows:

> As a result of continuing and often badly confused debate about its merits, the new educational technology has yet to be generally recognized for what it is: a pivotal resource for the democratization of learning. Those who argue that this technology increases passivity among students, or that it mechanizes or depersonalizes the learning process are often well intentioned and sincere. . . . But this resistance is misconceived and the delays it has caused in the refinement and use of existing technology approach the scandalous.
>
> . . . And, possibly more important than any of this, full exploitation of the technological promise could lead to the abolition of educational lock-step, in time and space, and bring on a whole new teaching era for the elite as well as the disadvantaged—a time in which vividly individualized instruction, geared to personal idiosyncrasy and learning patterns would become the norm.[14]

After such statements on the potential values of technology, the most frequently asked questions are: How can we find out what is being done in other places, and how can our institution make a start in this direction?

Over the past two decades, numerous reports on the use of various tech-

13. James D. Finn, "A Possible Model for Considering the Use of Media in Higher Education" in *Extending Education Through Technology*, ed., Ronald J. McBeath (Washington: Association for Educational Communication and Technology, 1972), p. 235.
14. Princeton, N.J.: Educational Testing Service, 1974. Pp. 44–45.

nologies in higher education have appeared. An excellent catalog of the many new developments is Thornton and Brown, *New Media and College Teaching.*[15] Recently the *Yellow Pages of Undergraduate Innovations* was published by the Cornell Center for Improvement of Undergraduate Education and *Change* magazine.[16] Its three thousand entries are filled with examples of media utilization *in context,* whereas in past decades most advocates of new media have erred in promoting media for the sake of media. The new dimension, which offers a possible resolution to the paradox, is to look at media in context: to ask what the problems are and what the alternative solutions might be. Such an examination will suggest a variety of media alternatives that can be used successfully.

NEXT STEPS

And where to begin? An institution need not start with massive television or computer systems. Rather, an atmosphere must prevail that encourages and supports innovation; some financial support must be given; and some personnel and equipment must be made available. A natural and commendable first step is to employ a director of instructional development. Administrators who recognize and encourage innovations in teaching and learning are most likely to foster increased use of media.

I suspect that the media are in much wider use in colleges and universities than is generally realized because their visibility is low. The number of audio tutorial laboratories established for the sciences, the continuing use of foreign language laboratories, the availability of films, video tapes, and other audiovisual media in libraries, the use of audio cassette tape recorders for a variety of learning activities, all reveal that many institutions are using the media in nondramatic yet individualized ways. Meanwhile, the big, spectacular innovations such as television and computer-assisted instruction continue to languish in the search of appropriate problems.

The opportunities that the use of educational technology offers higher education are summarized well by the Commission on Instructional Technology in its report to the President and Congress of the United States: "Freedom and self-direction have always been accepted as goals of American education. The use of technology in education can increase the

15. James W. Thornton, Jr., and James W. Brown, eds., *New Media and College Teaching* (Washington: American Association for Higher Education and Association for Educational Communications and Technology, 1968).
16. Ithaca, N.Y.: The Center, 1974.

alternatives and permit the student to find his own direction more easily. The pluralism of educational objectives can only be reached by using a plurality of means."[17] Media within educational technology systems provide options and pluralism that will serve to individualize instruction. The media afford one significant solution to our search for alternatives.

ADDITIONAL REFERENCES

Alexander, Laurence T., and Yelland, Stephen L. (eds.). *Instructional Development Agencies in Higher Education.* East Lansing: Michigan State University, 1974.

Armsey, James W., and Dahl, Norman C. *An Inquiry into the Uses of Instructional Technology.* New York: Ford Foundation, 1973.

Carnegie Commission on Higher Education. *The Fourth Revolution: Instructional Technology in Higher Education.* New York: McGraw-Hill, 1972.

Dupin, Robert, and Tavaggia, Thomas C. *The Teaching-Learning Paradox.* Eugene, Ore.: Center for the Advanced Study of Educational Administration, 1968.

Issues and Public Policies in Educational Technology. Lexington, Mass.: Lexington Books, 1974.

MacKenzie, Norman; Eraut, Michael; and Jones, Hywel C. *Teaching and Learning: An Introduction of New Methods and Resources in Higher Education.* Paris: UNESCO, 1970.

17. Tickton, *To Improve Learning,* p. 33.

The Perceptive Eye

JACQUELYN MATTFELD

BROWN UNIVERSITY is the seventh oldest institution of higher learning in America. It boasts six libraries, holding more than two million volumes; a large number of priceless manuscripts, particularly in Americana and early American literature; extensive athletic facilities, historically provided for gentlemen and scholars, but now, in light of title IX, equally for scholarly ladies; a sumptuously refurbished alumni house; and gracious homes for the faculty and administration.

However, Brown has no media center. There is an assortment of slide projectors, record players, and tape recorders—many of which, through long neglect, no longer function—scattered among departmental offices and student organizations and in the possession of individual faculty members. But there is no overall university program or central equipment repository which faculty members may draw on in their teaching to take advantage of the many possibilities the media offer. In fact, university committee studies made this past year indicate that Brown is at least twenty to twenty-five years behind other colleges and universities, particularly those in the public sector, in the development of media resources. Why have Brown and many similar institutions fallen so far short in development in an area that obviously has become such an integral part of the learning process? This is an important and puzzling question, and one I hope to answer in the latter part of this paper.

However, let me note first some Brown successes in other areas with unconventional means of learning before commenting on the problems that many universities which so pride themselves on long academic traditions are having in adjusting to the very different concepts of the twentieth century, and what we must now certainly begin to think of as the twenty-first century.

CURRICULAR INNOVATIONS AT WORK

Because Brown has a strong scientific orientation, the computer and other so-called rational, if not traditional, approaches to learning have fared somewhat better than those that are purely visual or experiential. With the help of outside funding, Brown has embarked on pioneering efforts in two important areas of concern—interdisciplinary study and environmental control.

The university's Department of Applied Mathematics, one of our strongest, has developed over the past several years a computer learning system called "Hypertext." The term "hyper" here is derived from the mathematical sense of "multidimensionality," and the system is an imaginative refinement of the well-established concept of computer-assisted instruction. Hypertext differs from usual CAI programs in that it avoids "chunking" material into discrete and inflexible units of information. Instead, it allows the student, using a light pen, to see already programmed material and to record new relationships between materials based on a given text, be they in the physical sciences, the social sciences, or the humanities. More important, it allows the student to assimilate knowledge, develop his own allusions and cross references, and make his own deductions, which he himself may program, instead of his being led through a predigested set of facts, exercises, texts, or experiments, all products of another's mental process, as is the case in more conventional CAI systems.

If the hoped-for potential of Brown's experiment is realized, Hypertext, in addition to providing a unique way of learning, could, when fully developed, give us a solid resource base for interdisciplinary study, comparable to that which our conventional libraries provide for traditional disciplines. This would be a revolutionary step. For example, such a learning system could answer the consistent criticism—which in many cases is valid—that interdisciplinary education is not a serious academic pursuit, that it is superficial; that it simply dabbles in a number of disciplines and thus provides no opportunity to develop depth of knowledge or professional expertise; that advocates of the interdisciplinary approach may be genial, well meaning, and often quite interesting, but are relatively useless in coming to grips with the critical problems of our specialized society.

If successful, Hypertext will prove that interdisciplinary studies indeed *do* demand "discipline" in a most profound sense. It asks the student not that he follow the ordered thinking of another's mind; rather it allows him to organize his own understanding around the ideas and data he confronts in dealing with the interaction between his accumulation of abstract knowledge and the creation of his own intellectual structure.

In yet another field, Brown's Department of Chemistry, concerned about the hazards of handling organic compounds which are routinely used in undergraduate laboratory instruction, has developed what it calls the "Zero Effluent Laboratory."

Organic chemistry, for generations, has been taught without any thought given to the fact that it exposes students to chemicals and reactions that are both immediately dangerous and may pose long-term dangers to health. Thus, ZEL has been designed with two purposes in mind. First, it has created in the laboratory an educational environment that is pedagogically rigorous but does not expose the student to harmful chemicals which can also become pollutants. Equally important, the student is made aware at an early point in his scientific education that modern chemistry carries potential ecological hazards. In the ZEL, safe chemicals, reagents, and procedures have been substituted for dangerous ones. Further, the waste products of one experiment are used as the ingredients for subsequent reactions so that throughout the course chemicals can continually be recycled. Both purification and recovery techniques are taught, and at the end of the semester students are expected to return the same amount and type of chemicals that they were issued at the beginning or to be able to account for their loss through some natural process.

Several other departments at Brown are venturing outside the usual classroom instruction. For instance, in English a Functional Writing Program is being developed which not only employs imaginative variations on the widely used personalized system of instruction (PSI) concept but, based on the belief that to teach is the most effective way to learn, also affords freshmen and sophomores the opportunity to act as tutors and teachers for area high school students.

IGNORED LESSONS IN ACADEME

All of these experiments at Brown are exciting departures from the usual lecture-laboratory-discussion-section approach of most university course work. And yet none involves the eye (other than the reading one) or the ear in the learning process. In fact, it is evident that distrust is pervasive among the faculty and administration at Brown, as it surely is at many other traditional institutions, with respect to anything visual other than the printed page or perhaps diagrammatic images on the console screen, or of anything audio other than the spoken word of the lecturer, either live or recorded.

Is this reluctance to use the media, and in particular the visual, as a substantial part of the overall curricular design a result of fear of exploitation of higher education by technology and its "hardware" advocates, or does it stem from a fundamental misunderstanding of how central the visual has become to the intellectual process? I have no doubt that there is some exploitation. Media equipment carries high price tags and thus brings monetary gain to many. Yet, it is simplistic to dismiss film, the plastic and performing arts, video tape, and other forms of visual expression as simply entertainment (they often are) and therefore beyond the serious curricular concerns of a college or university.

The ways of approaching the teaching-learning process which a university espouses reflect how it sees its educational mission. It has become evident that those approaches still based primarily on book learning and the traditional ideas of scholarship are now running counter to the growing realization that linear perceptions, which derive from the eighteenth- and nineteenth-century view on which American higher education was originally established, are rapidly being eclipsed by those of "simultaneity." I do not come to this conclusion because of the post-World War II "media explosion," as significant as that has been. Rather, over the past seventy years traditional thinking patterns have been seriously challenged not only by such revolutionary theories as quantum physics and relativity, but also—and more important—by the arts, to which we are daily exposed and which offer new ways of seeing and fresh insights into the modes by which the human mind organizes its experience of the world.

The spirit of change has always been reflected in the arts, and in them the shift from linearity to simultaneity has been quite evident from the beginning of this century—in painting in the works of Picasso, Paul Klee, Kandinsky, Jackson Pollock, and conceptualist artists such as Oldenburg and Christo; in Proust, Joyce, Eliot, Faulkner, Vonnegut, and John Hawkes in literature; in Schoenberg and such current experimental composers as Xenakis in the multimedia in music; and in the later Fellini and Jean Luc Godard in film.

The arts of the future appear to be even more disturbing to our comfortable, bookish life. Expansion of the arts beyond the studio and gallery into organic life patterns, the redesign of our environment, or integration with such "nonartistic" fields as those of the laser and computer sciences —in short, into the sensory and kinetic rather than the static—indicate that future patterns of education must deal with total involvement with our world rather than withdrawal from it.

All of these expressions, in addition to sculpture and architecture, which have always had a simultaneous impact, have forced all of us to adopt a syncretistic view that understandably proves psychologically shocking to our conventional sequential perceptions. We see in it a disorientation of time and space, a perspective quite alien to the ordered functioning of a universe assumed by Newton, David, Mozart, Nietsche, or Darwin—whose mental processes molded the particular ways of thinking on which our universities were originally established. It is understandable, then, that traditional faculties view with apprehension, often with horror, if not terror, the idea of making the arts or any other visual or technological approach to learning a central part of the university's business. It means a serious wrenching of their psyches.

FORCES FOR CHANGE

And yet it is clear that this direction is one that we in higher education must take. Considering the interaction between the intricate political and social forces that have emerged in the last thirty years on this rapidly shrinking planet, it is evident that we must now move from the departmentalized and fragmented education of the past to a holistic one, one which serves to synthesize human knowledge and experience. The visual, transmitted through the arts and various forms of the media, provides us with this kind of educational integrity, an integrity well understood, if not always well articulated, by today's generation of students, but unfortunately not generally accepted by the administrators and tenured faculty who control our curricula.

It is ironic that universities such as Brown, chartered at a time in this country's history when revolutionary concepts of government and expanding visions of the world were emerging, cannot now see anew. But innovation does not come easily to any segment of society, and it appears to be particularly difficult for those academicians who, principally because of our profession's system of awards, have become almost exclusively scholars rather than concerning themselves with educational innovation. And although it is true that we approach foundations and other funding sources with the claim to be institutions highly qualified to establish national educational models for innovation and new learning systems, and in some cases this is so, the fact remains that in our day-to-day operations the primary rewards of salary, promotion, and tenure are based almost solely on scholarly articles and scientific research.

Such fundamental academic conservatism has created departmental structures and faculty attitudes which rarely reach beyond single disciplines; however, new media processes and other recently developed learning systems cut straight across these established boundaries—"established" only because time-honored—so that in a department like English, for example, serious divisions occur between old-line humanists who look on film or video tape or Hypertext as fads and frivolity and those teachers who see them as new modes of presentation which in no way compete with or negate traditional content. On the contrary, because of them, old ways more often than not take on new life.

This kind of debate and fragmentation within the faculty, as divisive as it now seems, may well be the catalyst for bringing conservative universities into the contemporary world. It will most certainly force all of us to come to terms with technology—perhaps the most important problem of our century, and one that heretofore academicians, whose task today is to help students prepare to deal with a society dominated by technology, have left largely in the hands of others.

And certainly, in academe, our struggle for economic survival will force the issue. The need to teach more students per section or to provide ways for students to teach themselves to conserve precious faculty time will necessitate the eventual acceptance of technology by even the most reluctant. However, acceptance is only a first step. Sound and creative use of new learning systems must be our ultimate goal, and that can be achieved only by ridding ourselves of our old visual prejudices. By being reeducated to new ways of seeing, we become capable of making more than one visual or intellectual decision, of perceiving the vast range of possibilities of learning, of understanding what's in the air around us.

This transition may prove to be a long and painful process for Brown and like institutions, and it is evident that those changes now taking place are coming, so to say, from the bottom up and not from the administrative top. Our students, having come to us from a simultaneous world, are now educating the faculty to the ways they learn most effectively, and the faculty, in turn, are bringing new perceptions to the administration. This process is arduous, but it may well be that such an evolution will result in the most lasting way to turn our prejudiced eye into a perceptive one.

Part Four

ADDRESSING POLICY ISSUES IN EDUCATION

Public Policy for a Pluralistic System of Higher Education

ELLIOT L. RICHARDSON

OUR NATION has been fortunate in having a system of higher education that is rich in diversity: pluralistic, innovative, and with compounded sources of originality and imagination across its breadth. In the last ten months, I have visited many, though still a small fraction, of the campuses in that system. At two-year colleges, four-year colleges, and great state universities, indeed in each of them I have found a kind of ferment that is an enormous asset to the strength of the institutions.

The question, I think, that most profoundly confronts higher education and related national policy is how to preserve diversity, pluralism, and decentralization of responsibility for the institutions of higher education. It is an old question which has been addressed again and again in the councils of the Council itself. And it is fair to say that where public policy is concerned, the question has not yet been adequately thought through.

There are, of course, understandable political pressures on accommodation to diversity which take the form of an approach to public policy that flattens out and erases diversity. No public policy, certainly none of the federal government, is adequate if it simply contributes to the prospect that the flattening-out process will be accelerated rather than retarded or reversed. I think it also fair to say that when those who represent all these diverse elements in higher education are in convention, their deliberations inevitably tend to result in recommendations that increase the likelihood that ten years hence, compared with now, higher education will be less diverse, less pluralistic, less innovative, and more homogenized and flattened out. I suggest that it is important to face head on the question, What

311

are the public policies that can not only preserve but also encourage diversity and pluralism in higher education?

Clearly, so it seems to me, the answer cannot be some simplistic formula of federal aid which doles out so much money per student at each institution of higher education. That method can have no other effect than to accelerate the process of homogenization, for such a formula only worsens the problem of the gradual diminution in the role of higher education of the smaller independent, non-tax-supported institutions. I understand that an estimated thirty such institutions have closed in the last year or so. Given the immediate economic situation, I think it is likely that the demise rate among such institutions will increase.

No one, of course, would argue for the preservation of any given institution merely for the sake of its survival alone, without knowing more. Some institutions may have had overblown ideas of their own importance. Some may have been unrealistically budgeted in terms of the faculty-student ratio or have had overly ambitious building programs. If that is so, perhaps the forces of economics should be allowed to snuff them out.

Not so, however, with respect to those institutions which contribute to the diversity in the fabric of higher education, which weave a rich and varied tapestry of learning rather than a uniform GI khaki.

Of course, I am not suggesting that tax-supported institutions are, by that very fact, forced into a mold of uniformity. On the contrary, some tax-supported institutions, such as Washington's Evergreen College (which I visited recently) and many others, are demonstrating the capacity to innovate, to experiment, and to enhance the diversity of the higher education landscape. Nevertheless, there is concern about and risk inherent in a situation in which the whole system of higher education in the United States becomes increasingly a system dependent upon direct tax support.

We have emerged from a national experience from which I believe the most profound and important lesson to be drawn is that the pervasiveness and obtrusiveness of government invites the abuse of power. As never before, we are vulnerable to a big, remote, impersonal government that is capable of manipulation by a handful of people. All the lessons of Watergate point toward the decentralization and dispersion of power, and demand the reversal of a tendency of decades for more and more of our individual lives to become dependent on the decisions of remote and faceless bureaucrats.

Now, I, myself, am a fairly well-versed bureaucrat, and I am not against my fellow bureaucrats; I like and respect them. But they cannot, working from Washington, or from any state capital, fulfill the role of those of us who think in terms of the community to which we belong, be it an academic community, a governmental community, or any other association that draws us into a sense of sharing. They cannot provide this, and they can unwittingly create a situation in which the very internal momentum of the bureaucratic process produces the danger of homogenization.

We have been through a period of fifty years in which the major political issues of this country have involved the question of national responsibility for the general welfare. During that time conservatives fought a continual rear-guard action, insisting that the government should not do this or that, whatever it might be, that was designed to represent a significant response to the real problems of some genuinely needy or helpless group. Those battles are fundamentally over. The remaining issues on that front are those of method and approach, not of principle. The visible, the emerging, the real and primary issues for today and the foreseeable future involve the relationship of the individual to government and the urgent need for the preservation of a sense of dignity and self-esteem in the face of all the homogenizing forces of modern society.

In a fundamental sense, our educational institutions represent a first line of defense against these processes; and therefore, they themselves must be protected against the risk of homogenization. So, I submit we had better face up to the question, What are the government policies that can best contribute to this? I believe that government policies must recognize the importance of preserving pluralism and must be concerned with checking the exponential trend toward the submergence of the smaller and independent institutions in favor of larger and larger tax-supported institutions. No matter how innovative and how well led, and no matter how well motivated are the public institutions, we also need the independent centers because they are independent.

The question then is, What does maintenance of diversity imply for public policy? I could give a quite detailed description, but it might not be wholly correct. It is fair to say that it would spring from the recommendations contained in the so-called MEGA proposal that was left behind when I went from the Department of Health, Education, and Welfare to the Defense Department in January 1973. I believe that the work on the MEGA proposal was the best thought-through and most solid staff work in which I ever had a part. And I think it was on the right track. (The name

"MEGA proposal," I agree, is a handicap, but when I offered a prize for a better name, I received nothing but facetious responses. The prize was not awarded, and the name has stuck.)

MEGA deals with the issue of public policy. It says in substance that the role of federal support for higher education should aim at recognizing the market, and the way to give the market optimum impact is to allow choice to be made by the student. The way to allow such choice is for federal funds to be directed primarily to student assistance, with recognition given to the cost of education as influenced by the student's choice of institution.

Of course, a number of other questions remain with respect to the form of the student assistance and the degree to which the assistance should depend on grants or on loans. The MEGA proposal suggests that primary reliance be placed on loans because grants used largely for this purpose could skew the choice in the wrong way and cause institutions, public and private, to build up tuition charges. This effect, I think, would be contrary to public policy. MEGA suggests, instead, that, above a given level of family income, reliance be placed on loans and that a national system of loan insurance be created, to be financed by a premium charge. The insurance would cover defaults by students whose later situation does not enable them to pay off the loan. Whatever the merits of the MEGA proposal, it does focus on how to help assure that diversity shall survive. And it does so by recognizing that, in order to preserve diversity, there will have to be a substantial increase in tuitions, and that federal policy must, therefore, somehow be directed toward helping to meet the higher costs of the non-tax-supported institutions.

The more I think about it, and the more I see of this country, and the more I see of the inevitable complexity of society which thrusts more and more responsibility on government, the more it seems to me we must directly and actively pursue policies designed to offset trends toward steadily increasing reliance on government.

During a two-week visit to the Soviet Union in the summer of 1974, the most interesting conversations I had were with Soviet officials who deal with a total state planning system. I asked them, "How will you adapt a system of this kind to a far more complex set of demands as you strive for a capacity to meet the requirements of consumers when they are in a position to demand a wider range of choice than they now have?" The only answer given was, "We intend to adopt American management systems." I have seen, from the standpoint of the biggest departments of the United

States government—HEW and Defense—the limitations of American management methods. I said to them, in effect, "You can't get there from here, if that is the way you are going to do it." You can't get there from here for two reasons. First, planning capability cannot that effectively displace the role of the market in a vastly complex and diversified structure. Second, if you try, the result will create a situation in which the individual is ultimately submerged and in which the planning system itself comes to make demands that seem to exist for their own sake. That, of course, is the very reverse of what our society is about.

I don't submit with great confidence that the MEGA proposal suggests the right governmental policy for preserving diversity. But I do submit it in the belief that its substance deals with the central issue of policy for the national system of higher education. Further, I submit that the question of means cannot be addressed simply on the basis that, "Well, all of us need money, so let's get together behind some proposal that will produce the same amount of money for each student in each of our institutions." The latter course, in effect, creates a situation in which money is distributed over the rising costs of everything including salaries, and nobody is better off than they were before. The smaller independent institutions will then continue to drop by the wayside, and diversity and pluralism will be gradually diminished.

I have confidence that the leaders in American education will find better answers than any I can suggest. And I have confidence in their integrity and in their dedication to the enduring values of education itself.

A Congressman's Views
on Student Assistance
and on Civil Rights Obligations

JAMES G. O'HARA

IN FEBRUARY 1973, I assumed the chairmanship of the House Special Subcommittee on Education, thereupon beginning the higher education of Jim O'Hara. Only time will tell whether or not I have been a good student, but I can attest that I have had a highly competent and very large faculty.

The leaders and spokesmen of the American Council and its neighbors at One Dupont Circle; the presidents and chancellors and deans of our institutions of higher education; the financial aid administrators to whom I have spoken and written by the thousands; the college and university administrators; the trustees; the local and state and federal education officials; the experts on the history, the organization, the administration, and the economics of education; all of these have given freely and generously of their time and, more important, of their friendship to a new student on the policy-making campus.

STUDENT AID

I wish I could unveil for the higher education community now the final details of a new "O'Hara Plan" for student assistance. But more remains to be done before a legislative proposal can be presented. I must, therefore, preface my remarks about the "Student Assistance Act of 1975"—if that is what we finally call it—by admitting it is *all* tentative, *all* of it good only for this day, *all* of it subject to further change, further improvement, and changes of my own mind if the evidence suggests it, and subject to the hopes and perceptions of my fellow legislators. With all those qualifications, I offer this summary of some possible features of an amended title IV of the Higher Education Act.

First, I would like to see a new emphasis on work opportunities as a major component of the student assistance package, and I would like to see institutions get some federal help to carry out expanded job placement and job development activities in the communities where institutions are located. Student employment is already the major form of student self-help. I think the government should encourage it, and the institutions should be able to work with the community in developing new student job opportunities, whether eligible for Work-Study subsidy or not.

Second, I would like to see the present Basic Grants program retained, but changed in several significant details. I would support, for example, making grants available for 100 percent of cost—but subject to a lower ceiling than is provided in the Education Amendments of 1972. We should also modify and simplify the BEOG Family Contribution Schedule by eliminating the consideration of family assets.

I would like to see a Supplemental Grants program, based both on need and on exceptional academic promise, with which a young person from a poor family might have at least as good a chance of obtaining a fully subsidized education on the basis of his ability to complete a differential equation as on the basis of his ability to complete a forward pass. I would hope that we continue and strengthen the existing trio programs to make special efforts to locate, encourage, prepare, and support students from severely disadvantaged backgrounds.

I believe that the loan program should continue, but I oppose anything designed to encourage more borrowing. I cannot support proposals for larger loans, longer-term loans, or income contingent loans. Taking the worry out of being close to bankruptcy is not my idea of helping students.

And, above all, I would like to see the needs analyzers become more realistic in the moral judgments they make about how families ought to save and spend money—and there are signs that this process is beginning. But, there are some who, in the name of equity, feel compelled to make sure above all that no one gets a penny he doesn't "deserve." I would like to see needs analysis pay more attention to discovering actual need in real life circumstances than to trying to identify imaginary affluence.

Finally, I will seek to construct a student aid system that recognizes that low tuition has done more for improved popular access to postsecondary education than have all the student aid programs put together. I will certainly give no aid and comfort to a system which tacitly encourages the raising of tuitions as a means of maximizing an institution's piece of the federal pie.

These are the outlines of a possible new student assistance program. The details will have to come from the students, from the parents, from the higher education community, and from my colleagues in the Congress. I look forward to having a finished product ready early in the next Congress. We have taken something like fifty days of testimony and suggestions on student aid, and what I have said so far is some of the product of those fifty days.

CIVIL RIGHTS OBLIGATIONS IN POSTSECONDARY INSTITUTIONS

The Special Subcommittee on Education has also had ten days of testimony on the subject of the civil rights obligations of postsecondary institutions. Those ten days have given me almost as much to think about and worry about, and offered more tough questions to answer than did the first fifty. I gather, from the testimony, from my mail, and from the tenor of the comments on this issue that I have heard from higher education and from my colleagues that I am not the only one worrying about those ten days. It seemed to me that this might be an appropriate forum in which to try to explain in more detail what the subcommittee has been doing in this area and where I think it will want to go in the weeks ahead.

I understand that there are some in higher education circles who believe that my hearings are leading up to an exemption of higher education from the civil rights laws or, at the very least, to a provision for different enforcement mechanisms for the academy from those that prevail in the machine shop. I am familiar with the proposition that the academic world has a better record than the industrial world, that it has different kinds of problems, and therefore that it should have less demanded of it by the law. But, I do not accept the argument that what is good enough for the tool crib is not good enough for the faculty club, that a rule that is appropriate in the marketplace is inappropriate in the lecture hall, that the registrar of students may legitimately do what the registrar of voters may not.

It is beyond dispute that the academy has in the past discriminated against job applicants and prospective students on the grounds of sex, race, color, religion, and national origin, and that such discrimination still exists. To assert that this illegal and immoral practice has been completely eliminated in the university of the 1970s is just as wrong as to suggest that it was totally absent from the university of the 1940s and 1950s. The law expressly extends to the campus a ban against job discrimination and a ban against discrimination in the extension of the benefits of federal programs. That law is explicit enough. Let's look at precisely what titles VII and VI of the Civil Rights Act of 1969 and title IX of the Education Amendments of 1972 say to you all, and what Executive Order 11246 says to the federal contractors among you:

Title VII says:

> It shall be an unlawful employment practice for an employer—
> 1) To fail or refuse to hire or to discharge any individual or otherwise to discriminate against any individual with respect to his compensation, terms, conditions or privileges of employment because of such individual's race, color, religion, sex, or national origin; or
> 2) To limit, segregate or classify his employees or applicants for employment in any way which would deprive or tend to deprive any individual of employment opportunity or otherwise adversely affect his status as an employee, because of such individual's race, color, religion, sex, or national origin.

Title VI of the Civil Rights Act and title IX of the Education Amendments of 1972, taken together, say that

> no person in the United States shall on the ground of race, color, or national origin [that's title VI] or sex [that's title IX] be excluded from participation in, be denied the benefits of, or be subjected to discrimination under any program or activity receiving Federal financial assistance.

And Executive Order 11246 seems to faithfully reflect that language. The order says:

> The contractor will not discriminate against any employee or applicant for employment because of race, color, religion, sex, or national origin. The contractor will take affirmative action to ensure that applicants are employed, and that employees are treated during employment, without regard to their race, color, religion, sex, or national origin.

The law and the language of that executive order, to the extent that it is administered according to law, seem to me to rest squarely on the constitutional and, even beyond that, the moral proposition to which the American people have given their full consent: that the laws, and the institutions subject to the laws, must be blind to color, deaf to accent, ignorant to creed, indifferent to sex, and impartial to national origin. The laws and the institutions they sustain and nourish do not know white or black, male or female, Irish or Polish or African or Jew or Greek. They know, and if they are true to our constitutional tradition, they may only know humanity.

I support that law, as it now reads, and I would join enthusiastically with those witnesses before my subcommittee who expressed grave alarm at the thought that anyone would tamper with the wording of those laws. It seems to me that the statutory texts I have read would be hard to improve upon. I think that law ought to be enforced, and enforced vigorously.

I reject outright the propositions advanced before my subcommittee that the law itself is wrongly directed and that we should move in the direction suggested by one witness who said: "A fundamental change is taking place in American society. . . . A shift from the rights of individuals to the rights of groups. What this suggests for me," the witness continued, "is that the primacy of equality of opportunity must be replaced with the far more important primacy of the equality of results."

I have to reject, too, the proposition offered somewhat more tentatively by a witness who was asked if, when a group of Americans has been discriminated against, it then becomes legitimate for the law to look upon that group's distinctive characteristics as a proper point of preferential differentiation in job selection. That witness replied, with visible reluctance, that it would be proper, but only with regard to groups who have a history of past discrimination, and then only for a temporary period.

I think the university, not for itself alone, but for all of the society in which it lives, must gently but firmly reassert the proposition that sex, race, color, national origin, and creed are completely irrelevant to job qualifications, and that the way to end the practice of taking them into account is to end it—not simply to look for a new set of victims. Certainly, I agree with those who argue that it isn't enough to say, "You shall discriminate no more." But it is at the next step that I part company with those who, in the great pragmatic American tradition, ask for the proof of the antidiscrimination pudding. They say, "How do we measure whether or not a school is discriminating until we can count heads on its faculty and see whether or not the mixture is 'properly representative' of the pool from which it ought to be drawn?"

I don't have an easy answer to the question, How do we prove that the university is obeying the law? The law does not mandate that 51 percent of the faculty or administrative staff shall be women, or that 14 percent shall be black, or 5 percent of Spanish-speaking ancestry, any more than it mandates that 49 percent must be men or 86 percent shall not be black. The law does not, in short, mandate results. It mandates that discriminatory practices be avoided. It does not mandate "proportionate representation," but it does mandate an end to giving preference to one sex or to one race over another without regard for motives. And more than incidentally, the law does not specify which race or which sex may not be given preference, it says unequivocally that none can be. There may be no easy, uncomplicated way to prove that a wrong is being committed. But law enforcement has never been easy, and a free society has to pay that price if it is to remain free.

We have developed over the centuries a few principles related to law enforcement that may be of some value to us in this supposed dilemma over how we prove the law is not being violated. One of them is the proposition—constitutionally of equal importance with the principle of non-discrimination—that we do not expect a person suspected of crime to prove that he has not committed it. We may think he has, we may have a very strong hunch that he has, but we have to prove his guilt; he does not have to prove his innocence. The same requirement ought to apply to employers, including universities, suspected of violating the laws against discrimination. The law should be applied vigorously and without exception, but it should be applied in the same way the law against any other misdeed ought to be applied—subject to proof, subject to due process.

Another principle that we might usefully apply—and perhaps it is more a moral than a legal principle—is the concept that revenge is a poor basis for justice. I cling to the old-fashioned belief, which I have been told is merely a cloak for racism, that there are no such things as group rights. I believe that human rights can only be protected individual by individual, and that at the root of our belief in equality of opportunity is the assumption that sex, color, race, creed, and national origin are so utterly irrelevant to an individual's qualification for a job that they cannot be considered, even in the name of "overcoming the effects of past discrimination." The law says that very clearly in forbidding in several places the consideration of those qualities, under any circumstances, as a basis for employment or for any public benefit.

Incidentally, I think I have discovered the difference between "goals" and "quotas" in the course of my hearings. "Goals" are, as you are told, truly voluntary, and your government is not requiring you to meet them. But the quota (although forbidden by the law) is the only way in which you can be sure of satisfying your government that you are making a "good-faith effort" to reach those "voluntary" goals. I think this is the kind of subterfuge that you have a right to protest. Some years ago, when the Congress was first beginning to consider the concept of federal aid to education, some of our most determined opponents warned us that "federal aid" would lead to "federal control." They used the word "inevitably." I thought then and I think now that federal control of the internal workings of an educational system is not "inevitably" involved in any program of federal assistance. Nor do I think it is inextricably involved in the use of the federal police power to achieve the legitimate constitutional objectives of ending race and sex discrimination.

But I am concerned that the bureaucracy, in taking the position that it must be able to go beyond the law and the Constitution in order to enforce the law and the Constitution, is extending federal control and federal involvement in the workings of institutions far beyond where it must be allowed to go. We do not have to make the academy a tool of the state, but I am concerned that if we do, we may never be able to reverse that course.

I did not come away from the hearings on the civil rights obligations of postsecondary institutions with the feeling that all the problems had been clarified and the road ahead made straight and unencumbered. The history of even this free society shows that if injustice and discrimination can operate, they probably will. I do think that there is an enormous reservoir of good will available by which we can put an end to discrimination on the basis of race, or sex, or national origin. But, I doubt we can, except by the crudest form of discrimination, end up with a pattern of employment in each and every department of a university which will faithfully reflect anything except the workings of chance and the accidents of individual merit.

I believe with all my heart that some day, as we were told in an hour of national greatness, our children "will live in a world where they will not be judged by the color of their skin but by the content of their character." That was the dream evoked in us all and for us all by Martin Luther King, Jr., one August day, eleven years ago, as he stood on the steps of the Lincoln Memorial.

That dream was worthy of the place. It was worthy of the man. It was worthy of the Republic, and of the best that is in us all. Let us not, in pursuit of that dream, fall into the very discriminating practices that we seek to eliminate.

The Search for Alternatives

RICHARD W. LYMAN

LET US consider a few randomly selected indices of the cultural chaos and malaise of our time. They are in no way extraordinary; indeed, that will be part of my point: they are quite commonplace.

First, an advertisement for a moving picture quotes the critical reviews:

> A bruising blockbuster, both funny and vicious. It builds to a crashing climax. An avalanche of brutalizing fury. Director Aldrich has honed his brand of screen violence into razor-sharp perfection.[1]

One assumes that those who paid to spread this advertisement across a whole page of the *New York Times* considered this a flattering description of the film and a close approximation of what Americans look for in entertainment.

Another, far quieter and milder kind of advertisement, promotes a real estate development. An artist's conception illustrates several people gathered in and around a swimming pool. One man, resembling an Olympic champion in his prime, is depicted in midair, diving into the pool. In the foreground are slender women in bathing suits; they appear to be about thirty years old, except that they are wearing one-piece swimsuits. Why they are not in bikinis and why the picture is an artist's conception and not a photograph becomes clear when one reads the text of the ad:

> It's Sunday afternoon. Do you know where your parents are? If they lived here, at Strathmore Terrace, they'd be having the time of their lives. And you'd feel less guilty. Because they'd be with congenial friends . . . at the pool; playing shuffleboard or lawn bowling; or in the clubhouse lounging; or puttering in the community vegetable garden. One thing's certain; they wouldn't be lonely. Strathmore Terrace is the ideal private adult community.[2]

Note the code words, "private adult community," the playing upon family disintegration as a sales point, and the illustration designed to suggest that

1. *New York Times*, Aug. 23, 1974.
2. Ibid.

at Strathmore Terrace the swimming pool is fed by nothing less than the Fountain of Eternal Youth. One cannot even be sure what the promoters mean; they urge readers to "bring your parents (either one must be at least 55) to Strathmore Terrace." I assume that they mean "at least one," but they haven't figured out how to say it.

Finally, let me turn to a news account of a seminar offered to continuing education students at a leading private college. The instructor is speaking:

> One of the lessons of evolution is that every species will become extinct. Adaptation to his environment . . . has allowed man to survive where other species have become extinct. Man's direction of evolution now is the gradual development of cyborgs—cybernetic organisms, a combination of human and machine in functioning and intimate relationship . . . as with my mother, who is a severe diabetic. She needs insulin shots three times a day, and that makes my mother an organic extension of the pharmaceutical industry.[3]

I just hope Mom wasn't listening.

Why bring up these mundane but, I think, highly symptomatic vignettes? Certainly not to attack the advertising industry, nor to urge some form of censorship, direct or indirect.

A visitor from another planet or another century, confronted with three such examples of life in the United States today, would, I believe, learn quite a lot about us by studying them carefully. He or she (or it—I shall not speculate about the sexual condition on other planets) would see how far we are from having conquered the age-old propensity of the human race toward violence. Indeed, we might appear to relish mayhem so openly and unashamedly as to make the visitor wonder whether sadomasochism had not become for us a way of life.

Our visitor might make some unflattering deductions about our veracity, including the starting point for all forms of truth-telling, honesty with one-self. Perhaps I am being too harsh; perhaps it is to the credit of the promoters of Strathmore Terrace that they did not promise complete absolution from guilt for neglecting one's parents—only some degree of relief.

In the absence of contrary evidence, our visitor would also be led to believe that the mind plays a small and perhaps diminishing part in our culture. For instance, the avocational pursuits featured in the real estate ad require only the intellectual acuity to distinguish weeds from cabbages or to carry on poolside conversation. Understandably, the "ideal private

---

3. "Colloquium Gets Adults Back to College," *Los Angeles Times,* July 26, 1974.

adult community" does not include a library among its many attractions. But then a community dominated by over-55-year-olds will no doubt contain a higher-than-average proportion of cyborgs, many, if not most, of whom will be too preoccupied with their "functioning and intimate relationship" with machines to have time for books, paintings, concerts, or the legitimate theater.

DISTRACTIONS FROM EDUCATIONAL MISSION

Educators ought not to be able to confront such indices of our cultural condition with complacency. In our search for alternatives thus far we have tended to ignore what might be called the general state of the culture, our attention focusing instead on management questions, questions of institutional autonomy and responsibility, questions of accessibility of education's benefits.

We have neglected the general condition of our culture for another reason; having come to recognize the inherent shortcomings and the potential suppression of minority subcultures in the melting pot conception of our society, we have shied away from the general and emphasized the particular: we celebrate, sometimes recreate, ethnic traditions of all sorts.

I don't know how we could have avoided these preoccupations, nor do I suggest that we should have tried. A glance at discussion topics before national forums reveals our continuing—and justified—concern with problems that are essentially administrative or political. The programs quite accurately reflect the concerns of the higher education establishment in this country at this time. Given the size of our money problems alone, it is small wonder if most college presidents find it difficult to see an objective beyond sheer institutional survival. And given the often brutal encroachment of lay authorities upon academic terrain, as regents override presidents and faculties, legislatures override regents, and the federal government and the courts undertake to decide who shall have tenure and how the football team is to be fed, it is no wonder that, in their spare moments away from worrying about survival, most presidents are wholly preoccupied with preserving what they can of institutional autonomy in American higher education.

The question I would like to raise is whether, in our search for new things to do, new justifications for our existence, and new stories to tell the public about what we are and what we are for, we have not strayed dangerously far from a proper degree of concern for the overall state of the national mind and spirit. When the *Chronicle of Higher Education* carries as a front-page headline the following comment by the executive secretary of the Modern Language Association: "On a national level we have failed to meet the challenge of illiteracy among college-level students," we glimpse some of the reasons why brutalizing movies and stupefying retirement playgrounds sometimes seem to represent the limits of human aspiration in our culture.[4]

One of the reasons why the surrounding society seems so reluctant to provide adequate funding yet so eager to offer unasked-for guidance must be that we appear uncertain of our fundamental objectives, let alone how we are going to achieve them.

The answer is not a single, all-purpose definition of higher education, a Procrustean couch upon which none of us could really lie in comfort. Quite the contrary, what is needed is institutional self-definition. Each institution must decide as clearly and unambiguously as it can what it is and what it is trying to accomplish. We need this, I suggest, more than we need the search for alternatives. Indeed, were we actually to set about the task of self-definition seriously, we would find the Holy Grail without an explicit search. Like Pogo, we would be able to say, "We have met the Alternatives and they is us." We would have achieved the genuine pluralism that we love to talk about at conferences.

If this is so, why have we not long since done it? Why does everybody talk about institutional self-definition and so few do anything about it? The difficulty is an old one. Laurence Veysey, in *The Emergence of the American University,* opines that by 1910, "both intellectually and in terms of its structure, the American university was becoming too diverse easily to define. . . ."[5] (This is why one finds such entries in Veysey's index as "President, deviousness of, required by role.")

Somewhat paradoxically, institutions were becoming more like one another at the same time that they were becoming undefined and undefinable, at least in terms of any single, overriding purpose. Veysey notes this trend as existing around the turn of the century; recent research suggests that the trend may have been accelerated and has certainly not been reversed.

This diversity of objectives within a single institution, coupled with homogeneity of objectives on the part of higher education as a system, derives, I submit, from the fundamentally responsive character of education in the United States. In some ways, the current furor over "accounta-

4. "Crisis in English Writing," *Chronicle of Higher Education,* September 23, 1974, p. 1.
5. Chicago: University of Chicago Press, Phoenix Books, 1970. P. 311.

bility" is a bit ironic, since historically education in the United States has been more accountable (at least in the broad sense) and less isolated from popular tastes and aspirations than in any other major nation. This is not to say that we can ignore our technical shortcomings, such as our chronic inability to explain clearly and in consistent terms why we need more money.

Again ironically, the struggles of the late 1960s were often fought over the alleged *un*responsiveness of higher educational institutions to the outside world, when in fact it was our responsiveness to public demands that caused us to bureaucratize ourselves, outgrow our institutional clothing, and appear to be eager to help the government defoliate Southeast Asia or dehumanize subjects of behavioral research.

And we're still at it, nervously peering at the world around us in search—of alternatives? Yes, in fact we seek *anything* that might ingratiate us with the public, be it high school students or chairmen of legislative subcommittees. The more it changes, the more it is the same thing. Once we tried to appease students in hopes that they would stop trashing our windows or sitting in our offices. That didn't work, of course; student radicals, though often wrongheaded and more corruptible than they imagined themselves to be, were not to be bought off by sycophantic presidential phrase making. But are we not now trying to appeal to the not-yet-students by promising to fulfill all of their often conflicting or impossible expectations of college?

THE FORCE OF MISSION

I am not arguing that this country's institutions of higher education should cease to be responsive to public needs or even to public demands. (Need I point out that the two are not always synonymous or even compatible with each other?) I am arguing the futility—worse, the self-destructiveness—of *each* institution or type of institution attempting to be totally responsive. We need more presidents with the courage to say, as did the head of a liberal arts college responding to a survey recently conducted by Howard Bowen:

> High quality small private institutions . . . seem (1) fearful about asserting the validity of their basic purpose [because it really is elitist and narrow] and (2) overly eager to make themselves sound like mini-universities: lots of educational options, flexible requirements, open admissions, etc. . . . We should say directly that we do general education and pre-professional work for better-than-average students with a theoretically oriented but teaching

faculty, that we consider ourselves only part of the total needs of American higher education, but that we believe we can do this part better than any other kind of educational institution.[6]

Instead, we have too often attempted total responsiveness, tempered by bureaucracy and professional protectiveness—the worst of all worlds. For instance, it is proposed to teach auto mechanics for credit in a university in which the faculty is knowledgeable about such matters as "The Limits of Rhetorical Device in the Federalist Papers," or "Psychodynamics of Creativity." Instead of saying, "Nonsense, you must have misunderstood the nature and purposes of this institution," we set up the course in the Interdisciplinary Center for Innovative Extradepartmental Projects, which the faculty supports or at least tolerates as long as it remains safely underfunded and diverts students from raising awkward questions about what the departments are doing.

For this condition we have little excuse, because we have examples in our own history and experience as a people of where such an approach leads. I refer to the Life and Hard Times of the American High School Through the Ages. A dozen years ago, the late Richard Hofstadter, in his masterly study of *Anti-Intellectualism in American Life*, put it bluntly:

> The problem of numbers had hardly made its appearance before a movement began in professional education to exalt numbers over quality and the alleged demands of utility over intellectual development. Far from conceiving the mediocre, reluctant, or incapable student as an obstacle or a special problem in a school system devoted to educating the interested, the capable, and the gifted, American educators entered upon a crusade to exalt the academically uninterested or ungifted child into a kind of culture-hero. They were not content to say that the realities of American social life had made it necessary to compromise with the ideal of education as the development of formal learning and intellectual capacity. Instead, they militantly proclaimed that such education was archaic and futile and that the noblest end of a truly democratic system of education was to meet the child's immediate interests by offering him a series of immediate utilities.[7]

As Hofstadter went on to remark, "The history of this crusade . . . demands our attention."[8] He was right. It still does.

In the words, out of context, of Lenin, "What Is To Be Done?"[9] By way

6. Unpublished survey conducted in behalf of the Association of American Colleges.

7. Hofstadter, *Anti-Intellectualism in American Life* (New York: Random House, Vintage Books, 1962), p. 328.

8. Ibid., pp. 328–29.

9. *What Is To Be Done? The Burning Question of Our Movement* (London: Martin Lawrence, 1902).

of answer, I have no comprehensive formula—and only a few suggestions.

1. We should remind ourselves that there is still meaning in the old national motto, *e pluribus unum*. It need not be to the detriment of our many and valuable subcultures that we are concerned for the overall culture that we share. If there is corruption in high places, if there is a pervasive nastiness and antihuman quality in too many of our leisuretime pursuits, if there is a shrinking of public spirit and a dangerous degree of self-seeking sterility in private aspirations in America, educators do not bear the whole responsibility, but we cannot disclaim our share. If it makes us uncomfortable to admit this—as I believe it does—that discomfort is a sign of ill health in the educational enterprise. We are more at ease discussing tuition, management dilemmas (however agonizing), and the nongrowing pains of the steady state—important questions but problems of means rather than ends.

2. We should pledge ourselves to Truth in Educational Packaging. As anyone knows who has recently tried to help a son or daughter choose a college, our literature tends to be uniform and characterized by inflated claims and a studious avoidance of any reference to shortcomings or even to institutional limitations. We ought to be as skeptical of jargon and double-talk in our own pronouncements generally as we are of other people's. We should be especially concerned not to substitute changes of labels for needed changes in substance. It is more important that an institution genuinely practice equality between the sexes than convert titles from "Chairman" to "Chairperson." Surely when it comes to truth-telling, higher education occupies the position of Caesar's wife, but you would never guess it from much of our contemporary practice.

3. We should be willing to forgo an opportunity now and then. Not all of them are good for you. If an Institute of Aspidistra Artisanry exists just over the border in another state, have the nerve to tell your faculty, your students, your legislature, your chauvinistic graduates that you won't support the addition of a parallel institute on your campus, because you need to focus on doing well what you are doing already. If your institution is like most American colleges and universities, it is probably already doing too much.

4. We should dare to be disunited. The American Council on Education is a broad umbrella; its president is a generous-hearted man. Still it gets criticized in Washington for being unable to produce agreed positions on behalf of all higher education. We can hope that the demand for consensus will break of its own weight, now that "higher education" seems destined to yield to the still broader and more meaningless expression "post-

secondary education." We should not pretend to a commonality of interest that does not exist. But, by the same token, each segment of the huge and sprawling enterprise of postsecondary education has an honorable role to play and can take pride in playing it well. Furthermore, each will have its day as a minority, so tolerance and mutual forbearance among the segments is not only humane but also sensible. Among the saddest facts about our condition today is that each interest seems compelled to claim ultimate primacy lest it lose out in the general competition. In order to argue the claims of one set of students or potential students, it is not necessary to denigrate those of another. We are not educating nothing but "new students," in the sense intended by Patricia Cross's book.[10] But neither can we pretend that what was good enough for Dink Stover at Yale is relevant to the advantaging of the disadvantaged today.

5. We should tackle some of the real and obvious problems that cry out for action, instead of retreating into the far easier "search for innovation." One simple example—granted, of relevance only to a minority of American Council on Education institutions—is the notorious practice of awarding generous grants-in-aid to student athletes without requiring any showing whatsoever of financial need. The only serious argument that I have heard against terminating this practice is the disgraceful one that we cannot trust ourselves or our graduates to be honest. If this be so, how can we demand honesty of other segments of American life?

6. And last, we should not be demoralized just because somebody tells us that we are. Even the *New York Times* can err. For all our faults, admitted and unadmitted, and for all the stubborn and even ominous problems that we face, the higher education system in this country constitutes the most serious, the most open, and the most successful effort yet made in the history of mankind to provide for every citizen education to the limits of his or her ability. To the extent that we are demoralized, our anxiety is *not* demonstrated by our reluctance to speak out on every national and international issue, whether we know anything about it or not. Surely, a more telling sign of our demoralization is our willingness to accept all criticism from outside, no matter how ill-informed or wrongheaded, and to spend our energies flailing around for ways to become all things to all persons.

Higher education, like everyone and everything else, is facing tough times and some unprecedented problems—as well as a great many prece-

10. K. Patricia Cross, *Beyond the Open Door: New Students to Higher Education* (San Francisco: Jossey-Bass, 1971).

dented ones. Education, like government, is somewhat the victim of its own propaganda and hubris of the early sixties. We promised then far more than we could perform. We are now paying the consequences.

It is not dishonorable—much less a sign of demoralization—to admit shortcomings and to try to act accordingly.

On with the job.

Reporting from the White House

HELEN THOMAS

IT IS AN HONOR for me to be here and to address the elite of the academic world. If I were to relate to you at all, in some small way, it would perhaps be with the historians or the political scientists.

But then, I have been on campuses at times with Presidents, and during some years Presidents dared not venture on a campus. It was the acid test. The violent sixties must have been tough and dreadful in some ways for those on campuses, and, yet, there was a sense of solidarity—that protest was a legitimate way. Certainly the student candlelight marches around the White House during the Vietnam war were not welcome to the Presidents imprisoned inside, convinced of their own certitude. I was in the Oval Office during a picture-taking when President Nixon remarked in a very loud voice while a half-million protesters were marching on the ellipse after the Cambodian invasion, "I'm going to watch the football game on television this afternoon."

Tranquillity on campus is vastly more preferable from anyone's standpoint, especially a President's. And yet need that be synonymous with a lack of interest or caring about what happens in Washington—a temporary bowing-out of the world around? I hope not.

I also was with President Ford at Ohio State University when he happily told a graduating class that he had not noticed any protest signs. Let's hope the retreat is not total and that students will be participants as well in a country that needs their energy and caring.

I have always said that I was fortunate to have a ringside seat to history, covering the White House. It was never more so. The rush of events, mostly tragic, has absorbed us all. For the first time in the history of our country a Vice-President and a President have fallen from power, in disgrace.

It is still impossible to put Watergate behind us. But one thing we do realize is that it has diminished us all. It had a life of its own, the inexorable momentum of a Greek tragedy. We saw it played out before our very eyes, and there was nothing we could do. No one could have watched the White House during 1974 and not observed the slow disintegration at the seat of power, a severely crippled government, groping, a former President Nixon's struggle to survive the inevitable shipwreck. For two years, he stood before the mast, toughing it out, insisting that he wanted to get to the bottom of Watergate, protesting his innocence, declaring he was going to fight like hell, conducting "Operation Candor," promising to go down to the wire on impeachment, if, as his daughter Julie said, only one senator stood for him. In the end, he capitulated after days of agonizing and a strong push from his closest associates, his intimates who with strategy and psychology decided that it was time for him to throw in the towel.

To this day, the former president does not believe he committed an impeachable offense, according to his family and his former aides and all those who saw him during the dying days of the Nixon dynasty. He believed, and still does, that a combination of his political enemies and the press were the main instruments of his demise. Nixon's antipathy for the press goes back almost to the beginning of his political career. So it is no wonder that when he came into the White House, with all flags flying, an orchestrated campaign, with Spiro T. Agnew as spearhead, was conducted against the press, particularly TV commentators.

At the White House the news also was carefully managed, and Nixon announced that he would hold press conferences "when it is in the public interest." Of course, he was to determine when it was in the public interest, and so he held them on rare occasions, drastically fewer times than any of his recent predecessors. We seek news conferences because the press, under our present democratic setup is the only institution that has the possibility of questioning and therefore making a President personally accountable to the people for his policies and actions.

Perhaps Nixon's fears were correct, for in the end the press played its part in exposing the government abuses that led to Watergate. And there are still segments of society, perhaps understandably, who want to kill the messenger who brings the bad news—who prefer to go to the seashore.

President Truman, who understood what public life entails, used to say, "When the press stops abusing me, I'll know I'm in the wrong pew."

I remember on April 30, 1973, when Nixon delivered a televised address and announced the resignations of H. R. Haldeman and John D. Ehrlichman, he later came into the press center, a shaken man. With a break in his voice he told reporters, "When I'm wrong, keep giving me hell. I want to be worthy of your trust." And the press secretary, Ron Ziegler, came out to tell us that all of his statements on Watergate during the ten previous months were "inoperative." We were simply to wipe the slate clean of the thousands of words Ziegler had spoken on the subject. Apparently he never heard the story of the boy who cried wolf. The Nixon administration's credibility hit a new low and so did national confidence in the government.

But, in fairness, the credibility gap began in full sway under Johnson, and because of it he was forced to renounce another term in the presidency.

Cynical and skeptical as the press may seem, there is no joy in the fall from grace of any President. Ask not for whom the bell tolls; it tolls for us. We are all too aware that the White House, if nothing else, must be a place of moral leadership—a place that people can revere, where honor prevails. When it is less, the nation suffers, as we have seen. Often comes to mind the John Adams prayer engraved in the mantle in the State Dining Room, below the magnificent portrait of Lincoln, asking for "blessings on this house . . . may only good and wise men live here. . . ."

In the last six months before Nixon left the White House, I felt I was on a death watch. The dialogue between the press and the President was over. There was nothing left. He held no press conferences and he cut off all communication between us. So, on his last day in office, a few hours before he announced he was resigning, we were all locked in the press center for twenty minutes because the President wanted to walk from his hideaway office back to the White House without seeing anyone.

"Watch what we do, not what we say" was former Attorney General John Mitchell's apt caveat to this phase of our history.

So then the country heaved a gigantic sigh of relief. Gerald R. Ford took over the reins of the presidency. He swore on a Bible, aptly turned to the favorite passage, "There is a season to . . . every purpose; . . . a time to laugh; a time to mourn."

At the White House it seemed that we had opened the doors and let the sunshine in. Here was a man who spoke of truth and honesty in refreshingly simple expressions. Truth is the glue that holds government together. Honesty is the best policy. Homilies. The country loved it. What's more, he toasted his own English muffins in the morning and put his feet on his desk in the Oval Office. He was accepted, and even when his jokes were not so funny we all laughed. When he told Congress that he wanted "a good marriage" and not "a honeymoon," a TV reporter came up to him later and complimented him on the humor in his speech.

"I'm really not as dull as you think," said Ford, laughing.

No one cared whether he was dull or inspired, conservative or liberal. He was a fresh face, stepping in to restore confidence in a badly shaken country. He had the world on a string—for a month, that is. During that period he held a news conference and fielded the tough questions with ease, as if he enjoyed it. He told the American people that he probably would pardon Nixon but not until the judicial process was pursued. Less than ten days later, acting, he said, from his own conscience, after church on a Sunday morning, Ford said Nixon had suffered enough and gave him a total pardon.

He said that would close the book on Watergate. Instead, it engulfed him. His unpopular decision cost him the good will he had when he assumed office. It also cut heavily into the support a new President is always accorded. He admits he did not anticipate the strong reaction to the pardon —the White House received the second highest volume of protest mail in its history on the subject. But the President still is convinced he did the right thing.

The timing and the question of Ford's words, measured against his actions, were disturbing to an already skeptical people. But now, in a rare show of accountability on the part of a President, he agreed to appear before a House Judiciary Subcommittee to explain his reasons for the pardon and to say whether he knew the special prosecutor was building a criminal case against Nixon at the time.

Nixon has called the pardon the "most humiliating day of my life." So apparently no one fared well.

Presidents are entitled to make mistakes. But sometimes the road back is long. Kennedy had his Bay of Pigs, and when he assumed all responsibility, his stock rose. LBJ had Vietnam, and only when he renounced further political ambition did he rally the country behind his peace efforts.

But now, in his brief two months in office, Ford is beset by his wife Betty's cancer operation. She had already hit her stride as one of the most modern of the first ladies. She smokes and takes a drink in public; admits she takes tranquilizers; took a pro-abortion stand; said she would stump for the Equal Rights Amendment; and allowed as how her children probably experimented with marijuana.

On campus this may not be big stuff, but at the White House it is. First ladies have had more taboos and have had to be more circumspect than Caesar's wife. If they shared Mrs. Ford's avant garde views, they never said so—publicly. On a happy note, she appears in good spirits, and I predict she will resume her active life in the White House, which has had a dazzling beginning, with even more zest—knowing that life is to be lived.

As for the press, when Ford came in with a promise of "openness and candor," some of us felt, this is where we came in. Nevertheless, when Jerry ter Horst was named press secretary, a veteran reporter who had covered Washington for many years and understood that a President cannot govern without credibility, we felt we had "Camelot" for one brief shining hour. Ter Horst quit after the Nixon pardon because he said he had been misled by other White House advisers and because he did not agree with the policy. His resignation was a blow to the press corps, but a boon as well for integrity. One wonders if more such men had occupied the White House a few years ago and blown a whistle or two, had listened to their consciences instead of bragging about walking over their grandmothers in pursuit of political victory, there might never have been a Watergate. One man's courage is a majority.

The White House is heady stuff and it takes a mighty big person not to succumb to the power and privileges bestowed on those in such an ambiance. The twilight of the presidency—the palace guard—the jockeying for favor with the president—the competitiveness between people who should be working together—it is still there, true to the French quotation, The more it changes, the more it is the same.

But not completely. President Ford's press relations are good. He is not afraid of reporters. He says he likes the give-and-take; he holds news conferences with ease; and he doesn't mind being on the firing line, apparently. He does shoot from the hip on some of his answers. Presidents also must understand the consequences of their answers.

I never had any real sympathy for politicians per se in calling the White House the loneliest place on earth. We all know how desperately candidates covet the highest office in the land, with their friends bankrolling them to the tune of millions of dollars.

To know how young we are, almost two hundred years old, one has but to realize that we have had only thirty-eight Presidents in our history. Each has had his own style, and each, going back to George Washington, has had his problems with the press. FDR handed a correspondent the Iron Cross during World War II when provoked by a story; Truman called

Drew Pearson an SOB; Kennedy canceled the *Herald Tribune*. And Nixon had his "enemies list."

No one can look back on these days and not think of Martha Mitchell. She was on target and the first to dramatize the issue that, unfortunately, sometimes politics can be a "dirty business." In happier days, I remember Mitchell saying of his outspoken wife, "I love her; that's all I can say." And Nixon in the beginning said, "Right on, Martha."

Power and the exercise of it is what the presidency is much about—and that's when Henry Kissinger comes in. He calls power the "ultimate aphrodisiac." It's intoxicating, instant helicopters, worshipful people, and a protective clique around you, telling you what you want to hear. I think we reporters just about wiped out the so-called "backgrounder"—meaning stories without identifying the source when we kept writing, "A high White House official with a thick German accent said today." Our modern-day Metternich, Kissinger, now happily married, did enjoy his onetime swinger image, after the sequestered life of a Harvard professor. Once, when I wrote that Kissinger was seen walking along the beach hand in hand with a beautiful, dark-haired girl, he came up and said, "Auburn haired."

"We can't have a crisis this week, my calendar is full," quips Kissinger.

And there have been many memorable moments for me in the White House. There was the dinner party J.F.K. gave for the American Nobel prize winners and his toast, "Never have so many intellectuals gathered under one roof since Thomas Jefferson dined alone."

In more recent times, I shall not forget the White House dinner Nixon gave in honor of retiring Chief Justice Warren. The same Warren whose liberal decisions Nixon had denounced. White-haired Warren raised his glass and said, "I leave with malice in my heart toward none."

And when Nixon honored former West German Chancellor Brandt and they recalled their mutual political vicissitudes, Nixon said, "I'm an expert at coming back."

I remember Liz Carpenter who put P. T. Barnum to shame in the White House flak department. In exasperation with the press, Liz would say, "No kind deed goes unpunished."

In 1968, when Johnson's term was drawing to a close, his eyes by this time on the history books, he scooped up a group of newswomen covering a reception and led them to the family quarters where he held forth for about an hour. As he talked, we wrote furiously. Pretty soon I had run out of paper and was grabbing onto napkins and matchbooks. Lady Bird kept coming into the room, trying to break it up with a "Now, Lyndon." After an hour, Johnson handed out gold charm bracelets, and with a wide grin, he said, "Now, you know it's all off the record."

The greatest story I ever covered was the Nixon trip to Peking, a cultural shock for all of us. It seems like a dream that only a few years ago I was sitting around with my new Communist revolutionary friends, hoisting a Mao Tai or two—the Chinese version of white lightning—drinking to the health of Mao Tze-tung. The fact that it wasn't a secret cell meeting but in living color on your TV sets shows how far we have come in breaking the ice with an old enemy. And for that the nation owes a debt of gratitude to former President Nixon.

It was a thrill to go to the Great Wall, but I though Ziegler's stage managing of the scene reached its zenith when he told a small "pool" of reporters following Nixon, "If you ask the President how he likes the Great Wall, he will be prepared to answer."

Sure enough, when Nixon emerged, an intrepid reporter asked, "Mr. President, how do you like the Great Wall?"

"I must conclude," said Nixon, "that the Great Wall is a Great Wall."

Reporters, I believe, should remain always skeptical and untiring in their quest for answers to demanding questions, especially asked of those in public life who hold in their hands the public trust.

As for myself, I believe we make our greatest contribution by keeping an eye on Presidents and keeping the people informed, to keep democracy alive.

AMERICAN COUNCIL ON EDUCATION

ROGER W. HEYNS, *President*

The American Council on Education, founded in 1918 and composed of institutions of higher education and national and regional associations, is the nation's major coordinating body for postsecondary education. Through voluntary and cooperative action, the Council provides comprehensive leadership for improving educational standards, policies, and procedures.